W0036054

Philosophy as Saṃvāda and Svarāj

Thank you for choosing a SAGE product! If you have any comment, observation or feedback, I would like to personally hear from you. Please write to me at contactceo@sagepub.in

—Vivek Mehra, Managing Director and CEO,
SAGE Publications India Pvt Ltd, New Delhi

Bulk Sales

SAGE India offers special discounts for purchase of books in bulk. We also make available special imprints and excerpts from our books on demand.

For orders and enquiries, write to us at

Marketing Department
SAGE Publications India Pvt Ltd
B1/I-1, Mohan Cooperative Industrial Area
Mathura Road, Post Bag 7
New Delhi 110044, India
E-mail us at marketing@sagepub.in

Get to know more about SAGE, be invited to SAGE events, get on our mailing list. Write today to marketing@sagepub.in

This book is also available as an e-book.

Philosophy as Saṃvāda and Svarāj

Dialogical Meditations on Daya Krishna and Ramchandra Gandhi

Edited by
Shail Mayaram

SAGE www.sagepublications.com
Los Angeles • London • New Delhi • Singapore • Washington DC

Copyright © Indian Institute of Advanced Study, 2014

All rights reserved. No part of this book may be reproduced or utilized in any form or by any means, electronic or mechanical, including photocopying, recording or by any information storage or retrieval system, without permission in writing from the publisher.

First published in 2014 by

SAGE Publications India Pvt Ltd
B1/I-1 Mohan Cooperative Industrial Area
Mathura Road, New Delhi 110 044, India
www.sagepub.in

SAGE Publications Inc
2455 Teller Road
Thousand Oaks, California 91320, USA

SAGE Publications Ltd
1 Oliver's Yard, 55 City Road
London EC1Y 1SP, United Kingdom

SAGE Publications Asia-Pacific Pte Ltd
3 Church Street
#10-04 Samsung Hub
Singapore 049483

Published by Vivek Mehra for SAGE Publications India Pvt Ltd, typeset in 10/12 Times New Roman by RECTO Graphics, Delhi and printed at Saurabh Printers Pvt Ltd, New Delhi.

Library of Congress Cataloging-in-Publication Data

Philosophy as saṃvāda and svarāj : dialogical meditations on Daya Krishna and Ramchandra Gandhi / edited by Shail Mayaram.
pages cm
Includes several papers presented at a Seminar held at the Indian Institute of Advanced Study, Shimla from April 28–30, 2008.
Includes bibliographical references and index.
1. Krishna, Daya—Congresses. 2. Gandhi, Ramchandra, 1937–2007—Congresses. 3. Philosophy, Indic—Congresses. I. Mayaram, Shail, editor of compilation.
B5134.K734P55 181'.4—dc23 2013 2013042442

ISBN: 978-81-321-1121-4 (HB)

The SAGE Team: Sutapa Ghosh, Punita Kaur Mann, Rajib Chatterjee and Rajinder Kaur

Contents

PART III: Modes of Saṃvāda

PART IV: Language, Selfhood and Philosophy

PART V: Re-thinking Issues in the Arts/Ethics/ Science/Mathematics

PART VI: On Life and Death and Dying

Foreword

On a tombstone in a cemetery in Panjim is the epitaph: 'Don't cry for me because I have died but rejoice because I have lived.' These are words that aptly capture our memories of the philosophers, Daya Krishna and Ramchandra Gandhi. They were two of the most interesting minds of the last half century in India, thinkers who were equally proficient in both Western and Indian philosophical traditions and who, in their personal and professional communications, raised interesting and novel questions for us to consider today. When I first composed the previous sentence, I did not use the word 'philosophers', saying only Daya Krishna and Ramchandra Gandhi, but on rereading it I felt it to be too bald and incomplete. The salt seemed to be missing. The word 'philosopher' was needed, was in fact crucial to make the sentence both whole and wholesome. I had to tell myself that it was about remembering them as philosophers that was the inspiration for our seminar.

Ramchandra Gandhi and Daya Krishna had just passed away within a few months of each other. The Indian Institute of Advanced Study (IIAS), where both had spent some time in an earlier decade, and where both had been integral to its vibrant community of minds, felt that we must pay our tribute to them by celebrating their lives and thoughts. The IIAS felt duty-bound to honour two playful and probing minds by organizing a seminar relating to their philosophical persona, not just because of what they had contributed or who they were, but also because of what they had come to represent. This book is an outcome of that wonderful deliberation that took place over more than two days. The deliberations, in fact, could not be contained by the two days allotted to the seminar, and with hindsight, this seemed inevitable if we were to truly honour these two philosophers. Being conventional was not an option available to us.

Daya Krishna and Ramchandra Gandhi (the use of their names together should not be construed to suggest that they shared a common philosophical view) were two spirits who, in both their irreverence and reverence, opened up new vistas for those of us who read them and listened to their lectures. We could, in fact, not always tell when they were being irreverent, and that is what made them so interesting. Their perceptions on what was valuable and vacuous, profound and pedestrian, offered sometimes with acerbic comment, teasing wit, or appropriate solemnity, were simply delightful. Did you ever hear Ramchandra tell you about the book by the Indian existentialist titled *Beans and Nothing Less*?

They were, undoubtedly, two of the most perceptive minds of the last half century in India who showed us new ways of reading a text or interpreting a thinker. Because they straddled with equal felicity both the philosophies of the East and the West, and did so ever so playfully, probing their individual intellectual journeys in an intellectual biography would be of great value for the current Indian public sphere that wants, and is struggling, to navigate a path between a derivative discourse and a nationalist one. Decolonizing the mind is an activity that both would certainly endorse. It remains unfinished business in India.

I did not have the good fortune of knowing Ramchandra and Daya, having had the privilege of only a few occasional meetings, and hence my sense of their intellectual life—derived second-hand from the stories told by friends, foes and admirers—is very limited. When I put together the many things that I have heard, and try and construct an image of their intellectual quest, I am reminded of two essays that I feel can be read as offering insights into their life project, if they had one. Is it absurd to say that Daya and Ramchandra had a life project? Perhaps one talks about a life project in a more interesting way and hence, I believe, it is possible and legitimate to make such a suggestion. Given the quality and depth of their minds and their intellectual life, they were the best persons to debate issues raised in two essays, one by K. C. Bhattacharya, titled 'Swaraj in Ideas' and the other, A. K. Ramanujan's 'Is There an Indian Way of Thinking?'

Both Ramchandra Gandhi and Daya Krishna invested greatly in acquiring a certain competency in the Western canon; and hence the philosophical engagement of their later years, when they departed from this canon, needs explanation. Can this be seen as a contribution to a svarāj in ideas? Were they trying to understand what is meant by saying that there is an Indian way of thinking, one that works with a set of universals, different from the ones of the Western canon since these are determined by time and space considerations? Both Ramchandra and Daya can be seen to open the door, today, to a deep philosophical engagement with the Indian philosophical heritages. This is an engagement that recognizes the profundity, complexity and relevance of these philosophical texts and thinkers. Their engagement was thus very contemporary not in a sense of chronology but in a sense of speaking to the philosophical questions of today. K. C. Bhattacharya would have approved of this exercise in the light of his dismay that our minds had been enslaved. His lament bears quoting at some length.

> Springing as these ideas do from a rich and strong life—the life of the West—they induce in us a shadow mind that functions like a real mind except in the matter of genuine creativeness. One would have expected after a century of contact with the vivifying ideas of the West that there should be a vigorous output of Indian contribution in a distinctive style to the culture and thought of the modern world … (but) … barring the contribution of a few men of genius, … there is not much evidence of such creative work by our educated men.[1]

If we look at the intellectual journeys of both Ramchandra Gandhi and Daya Krishna, we see in their work an attempt to represent, in interesting new ways, the Indian philosophical tradition. Looking at their ideas, and getting a sense of how they chose between options at the different forks in the road that they would necessarily have encountered would be very revealing. Exploring why they did, if they did, ignore the many road signs that the Western canon had erected in their minds, as they negotiated issues of ethics and public morality, would tell us a great deal of what it is to evolve a balance between the Western and the Indian philosophical currents. Did they accept A. K. Ramanujan's observation that '[i]n cultures like India's, the context-sensitive kind of rule is the preferred formulation'?[2] The essays in this collection on svarāj and saṃvāda may throw some light on this question. It should be seen as a valuable contribution to our continuous attempt to decolonize the mind.

28 April 2012

Peter Ronald deSouza
Director
Indian Institute of Advanced Study, Shimla

Notes and References

1. K. C. Bhattacharya, 'Swaraj in Ideas', Reprinted in *Four Indian Critical Essays*, ed. Sisirkumar Ghose (Calcutta: Jijnasa, 1977), p. 31.
2. A. K. Ramanujan, 'Is There an Indian Way of Thinking? An Informal Essay', in *The Collected Essays of A. K. Ramanujan* (New Delhi: Oxford University Press, 2004), p. 41.

Acknowledgements

Any book is an accumulation of debt! The Introduction received a rich discussion when it was presented at the IIAS, Shimla in 2009 and at the Department of Philosophy, Tel Aviv University in 2010 and at CSDS when the concepts of Svarāj and Saṃvāda were discussed in 2012. The advice of Daniel Raveh and Rakesh Pandey to the shaping of the volume has been invaluable. I am grateful to the feedback on the Afterword following presentations at the Department of Philosophy, Delhi University in 2011 and to the Ramchandra Gandhi Seminar group in 2012 as also for the responses of UR Ananthamurthy, Arindam Chakrabarti, Mukund Lath, Mrinal Miri and several others. The imagined conversation between the philosophers in the Afterword owes itself to the persuasion of many persons. This exercise is about lines of philosophical difference, but also convergence as Daya Krishna and Ramchandra Gandhi have reflected on some of the most crucial issues in the history of thought.

A warm thank you to Arindam Chakrabarti for his sketch of Daya Krishna and Arpana Caur for her painting, Dharti. According to Arpana, with her upward raised arm Dharti yearns for a better tomorrow, unsullied by human greed and violence. Jasjit Mansingh and Punam Zutshi's work and thoughts on the cover and text have been particularly useful. The fellowship of the Ramchandra Gandhi Seminar and the contributors to this volume has been enormous.

CSDS has been a great place to do this work being highly supportive of an intellectual project involving philosophy.

Hema and Kaqa Hilal have always been forthcoming with their editing skills and Rajkaran, Vikas, Manoj and Harsh have provided many cups of tea.

A special thanks to Rekha Natarajan, Neelakshi Chakraborty and Gayeti Singh and to R. Chandra Sekhar, Sutapa Ghosh, Punita Kaur Mann, Shreya Lall and Alekha Chandra Jena at SAGE.

Finally, a warm acknowledgement of those who make up 'home' including Arvind, Abhinav, Siddhant and, of course, Shaitan, our beloved dog for providing all those excuses to run in Lodi Garden!

Note on Transliteration

The Library of Congress system has been followed for the romanization of Indian languages. The conventional italics have been dropped for saṃvāda and svarāj, emphasizing that our effort must be to mainstream words from different conceptual vocabularies into English.

Introduction

Shail Mayaram

This is a book that was conceived in the wake of the passing from the scene of two of India's most important philosophers, Daya Krishna and Ramchandra Gandhi. The idea was to collectively discuss their respective intellectual contributions and speculate on how one might take forward the work of two persons who are among the most brilliant minds of our times. I use the term 'brilliant' to also allude to that very special luminosity of self-consciousness that all those who came in contact with them experienced.

It was the first activity that Peter deSouza envisioned, much before he formally took over as director of the Indian Institute of Advanced Study (IIAS). He referred to it as a healing enterprise, symbolic of the will of the Institute's new administration to rise above older factional struggles and to revive and resuscitate its once vibrant intellectual life, put it on the global map, so to say. I happily accepted the responsibility of coordinating the seminar and wrote a proposal on philosophy as saṃvāda and svarāj, terms that are used in this volume in the sense of deep dialogue and genuine freedom, respectively.

A review of the striving for svarāj in ideas, effectively intellectual decolonization, is particularly important for India having completed 60 years of the republic and the centenary year of Gandhi's *Hind Swaraj* in 2009–2010. Saṃvāda was a category important to both thinkers, whose own work can be mapped as a terrain of many saṃvādas, and indeed of reimagining the idea of saṃvāda. Multifaceted saṃvādas and their complex webs of meaning are particularly important in our troubled times. Both thinkers interpreted saṃvāda in divergent ways and in doing so took it beyond the category 'dialogue'. This provides an illustration of the cognitive gain that might accrue in using non-Western categories.

At a personal level, I owe a huge debt to Daya Krishna and Ramchandra Gandhi—*pitr* and guru *riṇ*—to both of whom no homage can ever be adequate. The months I spent organizing the event and subsequently working with contributors to the volume have been for me painfully beautiful, as among everyone I contacted, there was a wellspring of emotion manifest in their stories and reminiscences. Many of the articles pay tribute to the two thinkers' intellectual vibrancy even as they adopt a critical distance so essential for creative thinking.

The seminar held in Shimla from 28 to 30 April 2008 brought together participants from across disciplines including philosophers, physicists, political scientists and sociologists. The two philosophers had practised their craft in the 'traditional' sense of philosophy as meta-discipline, which must leave no branch of knowledge uninvestigated. The presence of both thinkers at the seminar was experienced and commented upon by many participants. The idea of involving participants from abroad was eventually dropped, the Home Ministry's norms having made it prohibitive, which we realized while processing Daniel Raveh's participation. Illness did take considerable toll on group originally planned—G. C. Pande, Yashdeo Shalya, Prahladachar, Mukund Lath were unable to join us; age, frailty and temporary incapacity to undertake the journey prevented D. P. Chattopadhyaya, Vivek Dutta, Krishna Baldev Vaid, Ramesh Chandra Shah and Ashok Vajpeyi from joining us.

In my opening remarks at Shimla, I said that what was important, as Ramchandra Gandhi would have reminded us is that 'We are' (in the fashion of the 'I am' of Ramanine theology), under the vast canopy of the sky, surrounded by the non-anthropocentric reminder of mountains and monkeys, trees and birds inhabiting the estate of the former Viceregal Lodge (turned Rashtrapati Niwas) that represents profoundly svarāj and *kuraj*, freedom and unfreedom. Our *satsang* (being together) must capture the moment of collecting and 're'collecting, reviewing critically and creatively, and taking thought forward.

I feel truly extraordinarily privileged in having been close to both philosophers. In the case of Ramchandra Gandhi, one experienced a consciousness that was marvellous in its mysticality, mesmerizing in its magic and able to bring forth the miracle of life out of nothingness; a philosopher with the imagination of an epic poet, a painter and a playwright. I recall vividly his performed (in his case philosophy was always performed with the gestural *nṛitya* of a dancer) description of a story based on the *Bhāgavata Purāṇa*: Kṛṣṇa enters the womb of Uttarā as a butterfly, wounded humanity is stitched together by the proximity of the divine and Parikṣit, the Examined One, is born.

With Daya Krishna, one encountered a mind that was relentlessly rationalist and iconoclastic (no truth must be left unchallenged, unquestioned) but with a vision of knowledge that combined music and mysticism, politics and philosophy, and science and society. He was childlike in his capacity for fun, clapping hands when good friends or good food were in sight.

We gathered in Shimla to partake in the *līlā* of these two philosophers, using the term in its multiple senses. For Daya Krishna, it is manifest in the play of the *gopī*s with Kṛṣṇa, who are so in love with their own love that they do not want to apprehend the 'other' Kṛṣṇa, which is why, he maintains, the *gopī*s do not follow Kṛṣṇa when he leaves Vrindavan never to return. This is similar to the fear that Arjuna feels when Kṛṣṇa reveals his *viśvarūpa* (divine universal form) and so asks him to resume his familiar form. Is the *gopī*s' love for their own love, a metaphor for Daya Krishna's own love of philosophy?[1] For Daya Krishna, it is important to approach bhakti ratiocinatively—to see its cognitive dimension and to universalize it. Ramchandra Gandhi spells out, in contrast, the deep spirituality of the advaitin-bhakti path that could potentially transform world politics itself. He would sometimes recount a folktale of Rādhā and Rukmiṇī that he had heard from Vidya Niwas Mishra. The question was who would cross the deep gorge on a rope? A trembling Rukmiṇī tread carefully fearing for her life. Rādhā, thinking only of her love for Kṛṣṇa and not of herself, danced and pranced across to the other side.

Let us first reflect on the question, what is the svarāj of the svarāj in ideas? K. C. Bhattacharya had in a landmark lecture titled, 'Svarāj in Ideas', spelt out a lasting question for India's intellectual life concerning the colonization of the mind. It was delivered 10 years after the publication of Gandhi's *Hind Swaraj* and published much later.[2]

The debate seemed to have receded until 1984 when Ramchandra Gandhi, K. J. Shah, Probal Dasgupta and Sharad Deshpande put together and edited a debate in a special issue of the *Indian Philosophical Quarterly*.[3] Ramchandra Gandhi defines svarāj as the order where the self seeks to be ruler, centre and source of all things. He identifies this as *svāsthya* (*svā-asthya*) that is not sickness and *sarvodaya* (*sarva-udaya*) that is not selfishness. The self is intrinsically related to the other and this knowledge comes, he maintains, 'Only in and through the truth of advaita [the non-duality of being], *the truth that you and I are not other than one another.*'[4]

One can identify certain assumptions common to both philosophers although the presuppositions of dialogic communication are, of course, very different.

First, that svarāj is neither narrow nationalism nor nativism. Intellectual svarāj is clearly grounded in selfhood (on *sva*), on the idea of consciousness as intrinsically self-reflexive. It is individual-centric but not individualistic and has to do with the capacity of the self to relate to the other and hence, has implications for communal life. As Ramchandra Gandhi puts it, it has to do with 'the realisation that all knowledge is self-knowledge'.

There is also a regard for Indian civilization as distinctive, which is common to both thinkers. Daya Krishna refers to it as being like no other in terms of its plurality of intellectual traditions and relentlessly questioning spirit and Ramchandra Gandhi because it yields 'advaita, non-duality, which is the truth of all things but deserves to be called the truth of India because without advaita India cannot be the distinctive area of civilisation and realisation that it is'.[5] Daya Krishna, in contrast, was distinctly anti-advaitin, although his last work brings together Kant and Śaṃkara and he also suggests a fresh understanding of the Buddhist *śīla* or virtues.[6]

Both thinkers then represent divergent journeys into the different dimensions of saṃvāda and svarāj, which I attempt to map in the following section followed by an attempt to see the intellectual moves being made by contributors to the volume.

Ramchandra Gandhi

Reclaiming Religion

For Ramchandra Gandhi, saṃvāda means the human capacity to enter into dialogue with the divine. In modern India, the *svar* of *sva* (the notes of self) are enunciated, he asserts, by the *saptarṣīs*, the seven sages: Sri Ramakrishna, Swami Vivekananda, Rabindranath Tagore, Sri Aurobindo, Ramana Maharshi, J. Krishnamurti and Mohandas

Karamchand Gandhi; the list sometimes also included Narayana Murthy or Narayana Guru.

It is exemplified in the life of Ramkrishna Paramhans, who, Ramchandra Gandhi maintains, bears witness to the maternality of life.[7] An enormous reconciliation occurs in Ramakrishna's life, since she is regarded as an *avatāra* or reincarnation of Viṣṇu and then becomes a devotee of Kālī and dares all to discover the heart of the divine feminine. As a young boy he goes into *samādhī* as Viṣṇu and then as Śiva at the age of seven years. A crucial moment occurs when he is denied priesthood of a temple and instead becomes priest of a Kālī temple that has been built by an untouchable. He washes the toilets of untouchables with his long hair; then becomes a Muslim, putting away all images. He performs the namaz prayer with a Sufi, drinks with a tantrika.

The saṃvāda recurs in the life of Narendranath who becomes Swami Vivekananda after 1896 when he is initiated—the combination of *jñāna* and *bhakti*, knowledge and devotion.[8] At the Kshir Bhavani temple in Kashmir, his heart is heavy, he thinks of *icchā mṛtyu* (voluntary death) and performs a *pūja* with a *khīr* offering. It is then that the Divine Mother speaks—in Ramchandra Gandhi's reading for the first time in recorded history as a voice from the sky—admonishing him for his lament that she failed to protect herself from invaders and let her temples be looted. 'What is it to you? Do I protect you or do you protect me', she asks, the female voice from the sky bringing Hinduism into the traditions of Revealed Religions. The story of this Revelation is recorded by a brother monk. This is the ultimate message to a politics of righting historical wrong. It is *sādhanā* which yields this statement, not history.

And then there is Ramana Mahrishi who brings back the Father, as Arunachala (Śiva), whose *svānubhūti* takes place concurrently with Gandhi's political svarāj.[9]

Advaita versus Annihilationationism

The title of Ramchandra Gandhi's most important work, *I am Thou*, is a response to Martin Buber's well-known book, *I and Thou*, its foundational idea derived from Ramana who had suggested, 'Why not say, I am Thou.' Ramchandra Gandhi articulates a conception of philosophical advaita that is at best peripherally interested in debates on the advaitic commentarial tradition (although he shares Daya Krishna's critique of

Śaṃkara's restrictive interpretation as representing advaitic closure contrasted with the universality of the Upaniṣad).[10]

One can identify here a deeper notion of saṃvāda between self and other. For Ramchandra Gandhi, selfhood is non-dual, which is that each one of us might be all things and nothingness too. He spoke, time and again, of the need to give up exclusive identities. Each time we think of others, we must remind ourselves that apparent others are really variant images of ourselves. This is what is involved in ethical behaviour, which is really widening self-awareness. 'Ethics and ecology are insufficiently empowering without enlightenment', he states. Clearly this is a very different notion of enlightenment from the European.

Ramchandra Gandhi connects the seemingly contrary ideas of aboriginality and advaita. He also counterposes advaita and annihilationism; advaita and anthropocentrism; all thingness with nothingness (*pūrṇa* and *śūnya*). Annihilation is not only injury to the other, it wounds the self and as he put it, 'Annihilation of the other is one's own self-defeat as one loses the object of hate.' The secular humanist imagination, Ramchandra Gandhi points out, suffers from both Eurocentrism and anthropocentrism. It has been the ideology of those who plunder nature. Both religious politics and secular politics have annihilationist agendas.[11] Ramchandra Gandhi's version of advaita counters both annihilationist politics and anthropocentric ecologies. It intimates a vision of svarāj that takes on board some of the most challenging issues of global politics.

The 'Saṃvād-Svarāj' of Sindhutva

What undergirds Ramchandra Gandhi's work is a very distinctive idea of Sindhutva that he uses to confront Hindutva. This is foregrounded in his discussion of Mohandas Karamchand Gandhi who represents the conjunction of truth and non-violence. Ramchandra Gandhi articulates for us philosophically a vocabulary made familiar to us by Mohandas Karamchand Gandhi, including the notions of *sat* (reality), *satsang* (the sense of being with one's neighbours) and *sanmati* (the wisdom of inclusiveness).

Elsewhere I have argued that Ramchandra Gandhi is distinctively an ethical philosopher.[12] The idea of *sanmati* is one of his key concepts signifying wisdom and goodwill that covers a range of meanings such as *bhāīcārā*, atonement and fighting for the alleviation of the suffering of others. *Sanmati* as *mokṣa* and martyrdom is, in Ramchandra Gandhi's view, a greater ideal than *satyāgraha*, the urge to Truth or *sadāgraha*, eternal insistence.

At Shantiniketan, I disagreed with Makarand Paranjape's reading of Ramchandra Gandhi in which advaita becomes an aspect of sanatani Hinduism. He writes in a keynote address delivered at Shantiniketan,

> The political importance of *I am Thou* is this in upholding the civilisational heritage of India and in recognizing that the modern Indian nation state, flawed as it may be, is its custodian. It is for this that this nation must be reformed, strengthened, saved. Ramubhai does this by trying to make sanatani Hinduism, especially advaita, not just compatible, but central to India's religious plurality. He does so, on the one hand, by a far-reaching defense and reinterpretation of the diverse components of Hinduism, by invoking its major Gods and Goddesses, saints and philosophers, and methodologies of self-realisation. On the other hand, he also engages vigorously from such a position with what he considers distortions of svarāj and self-realisation, whether these are the excesses of Abrahamic religions, the perversions and violence of modern ideologies, modernity and its discontents-and the intolerances native to Hinduism, including caste and gender oppression and aggressive, fanatical religio-cultural nationalism....[13]

One might counterpose Paranjape's reading with a statement Ramchandra Gandhi makes in *Sita's Kitchen*:

> Indian spiritual self knowledge cannot become self-realization without encounter with other non Indian spiritual traditions and without sharing time and space with them. Held in topographical and historical embrace by the birth-place and kitchen zone of Ayodhya, the Bābarī mosque is evidence not of Hindu humiliation but of its venturesome sādhanā of self realization.[14]

Ramchandra Gandhi insists that we ask Hindutva leadership the question, 'Are we only Hindus? Are we not also trustees of all cultures and faiths? Is the slaughter of innocent men, women and children evidence of power? Is organised, murderous retaliation likely to be a resolution of Hindu-Muslim differences?'

Moreover, one needs to recognize the very different advaita that Ramchandra Gandhi articulates and its expansive, oceanic quality. Babu, the protagonist of his novel, *Muniya's Light*, identifies Christ as the first martyr of Advaita.[15] In *Availability of Religious Ideas*, he refers to the miraculous as coming from nothingness, which is the great contribution of Buddhism to thought.[16] Saṃvāda, then, for Ramchandra Gandhi, is about self-understanding, but also about truth.

Daya Krishna

The Life of Reason in the Non-West

Daya Krishna's philosophical project partly seems a response to the question: What is the trajectory of Reason in the non-west whether in India, in China, and in Buddhist, Hindu and Islamic philosophy?

This is explicitly articulated with respect to Indian thought in his second lecture delivered at IIAS, Shimla,

> if we want to understand it, we will have to dig deeply for the hidden conceptual structure of Indian thought; for the hidden problematic and the hidden rationality. Unless we bring out the rational, the argumentative, the *pramāṇa-śāstra*, i.e. logic, the conceptual structures by which they have tried to understand reality, the problems that they have attempted to deal with—we cannot understand Indian civilization.[17]

This was an attempt he made in his work, *The Problematic and Conceptual Structure of Classical Indian Thought about Man, Society and Polity*.[18]

Daya Krishna's point of departure is very different from that of Ramchandra Gandhi. He consistently maintains,

> The spiritual quest is merely one part of the Indian civilization; why do we tend to forget the other parts, such as the knowledge quest, the philosophical quest, the scientific quest, the aesthetic quest and hundreds of other quests; quests which have changed over time and periods.

Hence his critique of the *mokṣa*-centricity of Indian philosophy.

Philosophical 'Saṃvādas'

In Daya Krishna's work, one can identify also many conceptions of saṃvāda. One of his important initiatives was what he called 'creative encounters with texts' exemplified by what he called the Jaipur experiment, an effort at collectively engaging with the *śāstra*s on *dharma*, *artha* and *nāṭya*.[19] The other major experiment was the actual organization of dialogues in the hope of possible philosophical futures when scholars of traditional Sanskrit/Arabic/Persian learning would open themselves to new questions derived from western or other traditions of thought. One of these was known as the Rege experiment named after M. P. Rege and published as *Saṃvāda*.[20]

A dialogue on bhakti attempted to universalize the phenomenon of devotion and encourage thinking about it philosophically.[21] A dialogue on Śilpaśāstra was held in Amber, Jaipur and brought together traditional *sthapati*s and architects. I was in college then, but do recall some of the phenomenal energy of those dialogues and was fortunate to be present at the dialogue on Kāshmir Śaivism (with a special session in an open ground in Gulmarg). Rajni Bakshi wrote to me,

> Dayaji initiated and personally nurtured a process which brought together Islamic maulvis, Hindu pandits of various schools of orthodox philosophy, Jain and western scholars and Nyaya pandits engaged in intricate dialogues with logicians in the western tradition.
>
> It was through such meetings that students like me got a glimpse of the fact that there is an elaborate and indigenous tradition of Islamic theology-and how painfully neglected it is by the modern universities. I have vivid memories of an aging maulvi-saheb, almost in tears, saying: '*Dayājī ne hamaīṃ bulāyā, hamārī bāt sunī, varnā to hamaīṃ zindā kaun samajhtā hai* [Dayaji called us, heard us, otherwise we are not even regarded as being alive]' (personal communication, 10 April 2008).

Mustafa Khawaja salvaged for me the letter of invitation and the questions sent to scholars of Islamic philosophy about reflection in Arabic and Persian (appended to his article). Subsequently, two dialogues were held in Lucknow and Hyderabad.

Surely, not all that took place in the dialogue involved saṃvāda. In some cases, it actually broke down. I remember the meeting of the scholars' group including Daya Krishna, Ram Chandra Dwivedi, Arindam Chakrabarti and Mukund Lath with Laxman Joo, then celebrated as one of the greatest living exponents of the school of philosophy that is popularly known as Kashmir Saivism. Laxman Joo responded to their questions with complete silence; his emphasis on the *sādhanā pakṣa* of that school disappointed the scholars. After their departure, he asked Bettina Bäumer, '*Yeh nāstik kaun the* [Who were those non-believers?]' (personal communication, 14 January 2010). In some cases, there was actually argument and exchange and an effort to understand diverse epistemic positions. Daniel Raveh's article for this volume suggests some of the processes of mutual transformation that might be entailed by that space of intercultural encounter.

Svarājist Strains

Daya Krishna is clearly against nostalgia for the past and indigeneity. He criticizes the nativist position and elsewhere lambastes nostalgia. Nonetheless, the Introduction to *India's Intellectual Traditions* mentions K. C. Bhattacharya's article, 'Swaraj in Ideas'. One can identify an implicit svarājist aspiration in Daya Krishna's interlocutory voice, which recurs in several of his articles. He points out that these have been dubbed provocative but they stem not from an attempt to shock and provoke, but from his own sense of shock of philosophical failures.[22] I profile these in the following discussion:

Critique of Sociology/Indology of Varṇa

Daya Krishna engaged considerably with Indology and anthropology, specifically with the understanding of Indian society in terms of *varṇa*s, *aśrama*s and *puruṣārtha*s. This is part of a larger critique of classificatory models constitutive of a tradition–modernity syndrome, which Daya Krishna returns to again and again. *Varṇa* theory is said to be embedded in the *Puruṣa-sūkta* of the *Ṛgveda*. Its *pramāṇatva* (authority), however, sacralizes Śūdras by making them an integral part of *puruṣā* and they can hardly be seen as non-Aryans. As Daya Krishna puts it in one of the Shimla lectures,

> The common consent regarding the Vedic tradition is that its central concern is located in the *yajña*, the Vedic sacrifice. I do not agree with it, but well, it is the common consent. If the Vedic tradition is centered in the *yajña*, how can we claim to uphold universal values? And we do claim universality; unless you claim it, you cannot be a civilization. And this civilization raises the following question: are the Śūdra and women entitled to *yajña* or not? What a question! Anybody who can even raise such a question has ceased to be a human being. I am more than serious! If one excludes women, one has excluded half of humanity! Then how is it possible to speak of universality? And if a large class—and the Sūdras form the largest class in the society—is excluded, one has excluded the majority.

> If this is the case, let me ask you: where is the so-called Vedic consciousness? Why do we suppress this from our minds? We have to reflect on it. If this is not the original sin, it is the original guilt of Hinduism or the Indian civilization. The answer for this preposterous question is well known: the Sūdras were excluded; the women were included, but merely reluctantly. This reluctance itself is strange to my mind.

Daya Krishna urges a need to re-read the *Puruṣa-sūkta* of the *Ṛgveda* as also three *sūkta*s of the *Śukla Yajurveda*:

> [The *Puruṣa-sūkta*] It is not merely about the four *varṇa*s as people usually think, but rather it speaks of the whole cosmos; it talks of the sun and the moon, and the earth, the waters, the rivers. It talks of the cosmic *Puruṣa*, and the human *puruṣa* is depicted as a part of it. If the hymn distinguishes between the sun and the moon, it does not mean that the sun becomes higher and the moon becomes lower. Here let me draw your attention to the three *sūkta*s of the *Śukla Yajurveda*. It is a reply, within the Vedic period itself, to the *Puruṣa-sūkta* of the *Ṛgveda*. Here it is said—and attention must be paid to this [Vedic statement]—that '*ābrāhmaṇa aśūdra prajāpatya*'—'These are not *Brāhmana*s nor *Śūdra*s but the children of Prajāpati', the children of the person who has created this universe. This is the real answer to the *varṇa* problem: the *varṇa*s do not exhaust humanity! There is a large part of humanity outside the *varṇa* classification, which has as much right to be considered as human beings. 'Prajāpatya,' 'the children of Prajāpati'—What has happened to this voice of protest? Friends! It has been suppressed and this suppressed voice of protest, found in the text, is unimaginable, unbelievable; we have built an artificial picture of this country, according to which there are four *varṇa*s, four *āśrama*s and four *puruṣārtha*s. This triple fourfold scheme is just plainly, simply, literally wrong.[23]

Elsewhere, Daya Krishna points out that the Mīmāṃsā texts do not recognize the theory of four *varṇā*s, additionally there are groups who do not belong to one of the four *varṇa*s: the Rathakāra who installs fire during rains and the Nisada chief.[24] Clearly the *varṇa* scheme could not accommodate the complexity of groups of Indian society; this was a problem that several writers contended with. Hence Vijnanesvara's question of the *varṇa* of a *gaṇikā* (courtesan), which Manu explains away by his reference to mixed marriage. Further, the Satyakama Jabala story of the *Chāndogya Upaniṣad* and those of the *Mahābhārata*, describing the birth of *ṛṣīs,* create a picture of a society where legitimate sexual relations between persons from different *varṇās*/*jāti*s were widely prevalent.[25] The *varṇa* theory, he argues, has become an intellectual straitjacket:

> The impulse to see all the diverse *jātis* in India through the lenses of the *varṇā* theory has led scholars to force the intricate complexity of the situation at the ground level, varying from place to place and region to region, into a uniform perception dictated by the requirements of a particular reading of the theory based on certain selected texts, or even of only certain portions of them, ignoring the counter-evidence of the other texts or of other portions of the same text, or of the facts actually prevalent at a certain level or in a certain region, or even of a different interpretation of some or all of these together.[26]

Dumont and Marriott share common presuppositions and fail to look at the counter-evidence (Daya Krishna refers here to Marriott's writing prior to his article, 'Constructing an Indian Ethnosociology').[27] What are relations of different castes who are part of a single *varṇa*, he asks. There are tensions between different groups of brahmans, many of whom do not intermarry; some even refuse commensality. There is also the existence of various associations of men from different castes, mentioned by Panini and documented by Radha Kumud Mukherji.

Daya Krishna refers to the lack of historical perspective among social anthropologists who ignore the changing relations between castes, rise and fall of castes and the birth of new castes.

Critique of Indian Textual/Commentarial Tradition

For Daya Krishna no text, tradition or thinker is sacrosanct or above questioning. In particular, he stresses the importance of re-reading vaidika, upaniṣadic, *smṛti* and sūtra texts. This would reveal how *śruti* comes to be constructed in a unitary fashion erasing the hitherto highly plural tradition. In the pre-Mīmāṃsā period, he argues, there was no such thing as the *śruti*, as each *śākhā* had its own Samhitā, Brahmāṇa, Āraṇyaka and Upaniṣad, which was authoritative for its followers with much rivalry between them. The *Mīmāṃsāsūtra* and *Gṛhyasūtra* that claim to be 'true' interpretations of *śruti* 'reveal *not* its unity, but the deep internal fissures and conflict within it'. They came to present, however, an appearance of 'unity' and called themselves Pūrva Mīmāṃsā and Uttara Mīmāṃsā, the latter being called Vedānta.[28] The followers of both sūtra texts, to date, exclude the Śūdras unlike what the *pūrva pakṣa* of both texts argues, and so constituted an 'orthodox' tradition of thought.

Daya Krishna writes,

> Manu's silence about the vedic and the upaniṣadika counter-evidence casts grave doubts about his honesty as a thinker, but also on the *śruti-pramāṇya* of the *Smṛti-Śāstras*, just as Śaṃkara's deliberate mistranslation of the upaniṣadika [Satyakama Jabala] story casts doubts not only on his intellectual honesty but also on his genuine acceptance of the *prāmāṇya* of the upaniṣads, which alone were pre-eminently the *śruti* for him, or on his faith in the relevance of advaita for the *vyavahārika* realm.[29]

In another Shimla lecture, Daya Krishna exclaims,

> The *Brahmasūtra* raises the question whether everybody is entitled to Brahman-knowledge. We talk of the universal message of Indian spirituality, and yet, the *Brahmasūtra* raises such a question! What has happened to the seer? I could not believe it when I read. I asked myself how it is possible. I read it accidentally; it was a translation of the *Brahmasūtra* by a sannyāsi belonging to the Ramakrishna Mission. This person, who is supposed to belong to the tradition of Ramakrishna and Vivekananda, translated it, and says that Śūdras and women are not entitled to the knowledge of the Brahman. Imagine! Vivekananda talked about the universality of the Indian religion for the entire world. And the translator explains why the truth of the Upaniṣads, the truth of Brahman, should not to be available to Śūdras through the *Brahmasūtra* but merely through the Puranas; and he does not feel any incongruity.... If you read the commentary of Śaṃkara on the *Brahmasūtra*s in this connection, you will also be surprised. Where is the Advaitin? Where is the person who believes in All-identity and no-difference? He is making a distinction between the *Śūdra*s and the non-*Śūdra*s. Please tell me, where is the realization?[30]

Interrogating the Dominance of Advaita and Obliterating that of Buddhism

Daya Krishna roundly criticizes the proclamation of vedic/advaita dominance and the erasure of Buddhist dominance in the first millennium. On upholding the centrality of vedic stream from the sixth century BC to AD 1200, he holds Wilhelm Halbfass responsible for 'suppressio vari, suggestio falsi'. As a result of the ahistoricity of the history of philosophy, the rise and fall of schools, as also radical shifts and developments have gone unnoticed and there is no attempt to connect them with theoretical developments in other civilizations.

He acknowledges that the Upaniṣads do 'breathe a common philosophical atmosphere and are witnesses to a common enquiry and discourse which seems substantially different from the one that is found in the āgamic literature of the Buddhist and the Jains'.[31] But of the total works by different schools of Indian philosophy, they comprise much less than the prolific literature of Buddhists and Jains. Buddhist thinkers such as Nāgārjuna, Asanga, Vāsubandhu or Dharmakīrti are seen as thinkers and not identified with schools; and from Nāgārjuna (AD 150) there is a radical critique of all *pramāṇa*s regarding their capacity to grasp the nature of ultimate reality. Potter's Bibliography in his *Encyclopedia of Indian Philosophies* shows that there are more than 400 entries relating to Buddhist works and thinkers as against 83 others including Kashmir Śaivism and Śaiva Siddhānta and 39 Jain works, that is, a ratio of 1:4.[32]

Thus, the entire period of a millennium and a half is dominated by the intellectual and spiritual presence of Buddhism, which has either been ignored or presented as a minor motif. The 'history and philosophy of India from 500 BC to AD 1000 has to be rewritten placing Buddhism at the centre and viewing it as chief protagonist', Daya Krishna argues.[33]

Trans-civilizational linkages must be kept in mind, Daya Krishna argues, as the history of Buddhism in the first 750 years is a story of its spread in West and Central Asia and China and Tibet, a development which must have also influenced the development of Buddhist thought. Buddhism, it needs to be recognized, also has a marginal impact on Nyāya and Advaita Vedānta. It is only after AD 1200 that the radicalism of Buddhism was replaced by the radicalism of Advaita Vedānta. Vedānta is supposedly the most dominant and distinctive philosophy of India, but there is little evidence of its presence before Śaṃkara and for quite some time after him, Daya Krishna asserts. There are few Vedāntins in the period preceding, very few commentaries on the Vedas indicating the neglect of Vedas and Buddhists continue to be way ahead of Vedāntins of whom there are only 8 till AD 1000.[34] Clearly there is no Śaṃkara Digvijaya! And it is really only Śaṃkara who institutes the famous myth of *prasthāna trayi*, making the Upaniṣad, *Bhagavad Gītā* and *Brahma-sūtra*s central to the textual tradition. In addition, Daya Krishna also takes the politically incorrect position that Śaṃkara was not responsible for disappearance of Buddhism from India. Further, it was only in the nineteenth century again that there is a renewed interest in Vedic exegesis beginning with Dayanand and Sri Aurobindo. But these interpretations ignore the ritualistic *yajña*-centric interpretation and emphasize its non-ritualistic, mystical meaning.

The propounders of theory of *adhyāsa* or illusion, Daya Krishna contends, have imposed one on the history of philosophy.[35] Dazzled by the second millennium, they have retrospectively seen the first millennium in its light. The response of N. S. Dravid, J. N. Mohanty, K. J. Shah, Harsh Narain and Pratap Chandra to this article and the one titled 'Vedānta: Does It Really Mean Anything at All?' leads to his counter-response in 'Shock-proof', 'Evidence-proof', 'Argument-proof' world of *sāmpradāyika* scholarship in Indian philosophy.[36]

To G. Mishra's argument that 96 [advaitika] *bhāṣya*s are referred to by Ramānuja, he responds, Were they destroyed? By whom, non-advaitika vedantins?[37] To Balasubramaniam's point that the Upaniṣads and Brahma Sutras are integrally related, he responds that the Upaniṣads were not knowledge in the śāstric form and were read without reference to the Brahma Sūtras and by those interested in Vedānta. Suresh Chandra refers to common practitioners and Daya Krishna asks regarding them, whether empirical investigation can be established? Daya Krishna refers to himself as neither Vedāntin nor anti-Vedāntin. *Niḥsanga buddhi*, he asserts, is especially important for an advaitin who should not be attached to a specific *nāma* (name), *rūpa* (form) or doctrine.

This volume comprises three different kinds of articles: those that analyze Daya Krishna and Ramchandra Gandhi as philosophers and elucidate facets of their concerns and conceptual imagination, those that seek to take their work forward and those that use conversations with either of the two philosophers as their point of departure.

Of Love, Liberation and Līlā

Fred Dallmayr builds two contrasting portraits of Daya Krishna and Ramchandra Gandhi in their differing understandings of freedom. According to him, Daya Krishna, who stands mainly in the tradition of critical philosophizing, emphasizes intellectual or rational liberation, while Ramchandra Gandhi points towards 'ontological' freedom or liberation where freedom means not just the removal of external constraints but the transgression of the ego in favour of advaita. The two modes of philosophizing represent, Dallmayr argues, competing and oppositional positions in both traditions of Western and Eastern philosophizing.

Ramchandra Gandhi's integral pluralism opposes all dualisms such as transcendent/immanent, subject/object, self/other and friend/enemy as also theologies that array the human world against nature and existence with nothingness leading to annihilatory politics.

Anuradha Veeravalli profiles the 'Ram*līlā*', that is, conceptions of love and play in Ramchandra Gandhi's thought. This involves the oneness of ātman-brahman in its many-centredness and the play of world appearance. There is also the play of human life in everyday communication and cooperation and the centrality of both *sambodhan* (addressing) and saṃvāda. Anuradha sees Ramchandra Gandhi as also raising the question: Why not-self is encountered in contexts of terror and pain, defeat and loss?

Bettina Bäumer's contribution reflects on the possibility of continuance of dialogue even after one's earthly form passes and that arises from connectedness. She sees Daya Krishna as asking whether dialogue is possible and that its precondition is transcending one's position. It is possible, he says (Bettina quoting him), if we try to 'become the other, to be the other, to think from the viewpoint of the other, to identify with the other'. 'Let us try', is his challenge. He also gives a key: 'The heart of Indian civilization is the search for de-identification—de-identification with the body, with the mind, with the intellect, with thought...—and the challenge of all civilizations is to de-identify with the past, with their concepts...' Bettina maintains that this is a reference to the basic ideal of all Indian spiritual-philosophical systems of arriving at a state of thought-free awareness, of *nirvikalpa* (*samādhī*), in which reality is perceived in its own light. What he hinted at, she points out, was a state of inner freedom.

The Idea of Svarāj: Contesting Asymmetries of Power and Knowledge and Constituting Alternative and Ethical Politics

Richard Sorabji's article highlights the importance both Daya Krishna and Ramchandra Gandhi gave to Mohandas Karamchand Gandhi. He brings out how M. K. Gandhi shared, with the ancient Greek and Roman Stoics, values such as emotional detachment. Gandhi's belief in nonviolence conceived as an inner state of mind, was based on an attitude of love for all presaged by the Stoics from 300 BC onwards; they represented an intellectual position in which the world including foreigners and slaves would be treated as one's close family. Sorabji views each as deepening the other's position—the Stoics as providing logical structure while Gandhi put into practice the Stoic ideal of emotionally detached action—the goal being the activity of researching or archery not achieving it or hitting the target. He sees a parallel also with Christian values including chastity and with Augustine and the pagan Greek philosophers. M. K. Gandhi refers to Tolstoy as the second greatest influence in his life that led him to abandon belief in violence and regard non-violence as an inner state of mind, an ocean of compassion, rather than the outer practice of certain Indian groups that could be indifferent to actual suffering in animals. This stance derived from Christ's Sermon on the Mount and the idea of turning the other cheek as a response to violence. But the greatest influence on his life was that of ascetic Rajchandra whose reading of the *Gītā* had a profound impact on him. Sorabji raises the question of why Gandhi used the *Gītā*, which exemplifies destruction and counterposes Arjuna's attachment to one's family represented in his reluctance to kill his kin. Detachment instead involves chastity, truthfulness, fearlessness and poverty. Indeed, for Gandhi, *svadharma* may require that the interests of my relatives be sacrificed. Gandhi goes to the extent of writing that love, the active state of *ahiṃsā* requires—as in the context of his own son Harilal's alcoholism, debt and temporary conversion—that 'I may not help him to do so by continuing to support him; on the contrary, my love for him requires me to withdraw all support from him although it may mean even his death.'

Tridip Suhrud has picked up two themes that were very close to M. K. Gandhi's thinking: *brahmacarya* and the idea of the inner voice. Ramchandra Gandhi is not mentioned in this essay, but the article extends Tridip's own saṃvāda with him. If Ramchandra Gandhi's writing reminds us how svarāj can go horribly wrong, culminating, for instance, in genocidal violence, there is also a comprehension of the highest meaning of svarāj as self-rule and moral conduct, which is when the self, purified by Truth, emerges from inner-directed prayer. As Tridip Suhrud's fine piece puts it, 'Because Truth is not merely that we are expected to speak. It is That which alone is, it is That of which all things are made, it is That which subsists by its own power, which alone is eternal.' M. K. Gandhi deepens the meaning of svarāj and spiritualizes his politics by connecting the political with the inner voice. Svarāj happens when we learn to rule ourselves.

While modern Western civilization decivilizes, M. K. Gandhi suggests an alternative understanding of civilization in which the moral precedes, undergirds and pervades the political. He sees the inner voice as the voice of God, but it is not one beyond us. One can, however, only hear it when one reduces the ego to zero, surrenders to Satya Narayan and allows the emergence of conscience. This is what makes possible *satyāgraha* or soul force. Hence for M. K. Gandhi, the vital importance of prayer that enabled him to hear his inner voice and perform one's action in a detached manner. The practices of fasting and *brahmacarya* are also essential to *satyāgraha* and the quest for svarāj make it possible to see the interrelatedness of truth, *ahiṃsā* and *brahmacarya*, which is an attempt to bring all senses into harmony with each other.

In an account of his own journey of 'learning to converse', Michael McGhee addresses the predicament of decolonizing knowledge. He recounts his realization of the stark asymmetry of intellectual power relations that the encounter of the West with the philosophical other meant: a re-description/domestication of native intellectual traditions as 'spiritual' while on the other side the hegemon reoriented thought, practices and institutions. The fallout of the fascination with the West is described by Roy Mottahedeh as *gharbzadegī* or West-strickenness, referred to by J. L. Mehta as 'the trojan horse'. He describes how the collection of articles titled 'Swaraj in ideas' (a special issue of the *Indian Philosophical Quarterly*), edited by Ramchandra Gandhi and others, germinated an East/West philosophers' get-together called Convivium that he and Prabodh Parikh co-organized. Michael points out that K. J. Shah and Daya Krishna 'make the idea of conduct and demeanour, as criteria of an inner condition, a central feature of the philosophy of religion rather than the usual, accepted notion of "belief", a notion which purports to be universal but which in fact betrays an unacknowledged, specifically Christian bias'.

Modes of 'Saṃvāda'

Fr Devasia sees Ramchandra Gandhi as exemplifying divine madness. He analyzes Ramchandra Gandhi's exploration of the dark cave, *nihitam guhayam* of the *yakṣa praśna* wherein the truth about dharma is elaborated. The idea of the Self has dominated Indian philosophical traditions as in Upaniṣadic thought, realization is postulated on the understanding that the non-Self is the Self and in Ramana Maharshi's contention that self-enquiry must follow the I-thought. Fr Devasia identifies parallels in Kant's questions: What can I know? What ought I to do? What may

I hope? What is the human person? He sees Ramchandra Gandhi's central problematic, Who am I and his *mahāvākya* as 'the Self is' [I am]. Fr Devasia suggests that for Ramchandra Gandhi, the sacrament of communication through address is celebratory of self-awareness. In addressing the other, the addressee is moved to self-consciousness.

For Daya Krishna, as Daniel Raveh emphasizes, philosophy is all about saṃvāda—an open dialogue, an encounter between self and other. After his passing away, he finds the saṃvāda taking place within himself. Raveh uses a dialogue between Alexander of Macedonia and an Indian sadhu mentioned in Vikram Chandra's novel *Red Earth and Pouring Rain*. The dialogue arose from Aristotle's request to Alexander to bring a wise man from the subcontinent. It highlights the asymmetry of power in the emperor's threat to kill him, in calling himself the king of kings, in his insistence that the sadhu stop asking questions and his demand to know the mystic path the sadhu follows. The sadhu retaliates by calling him maha-idiot, rather than maha-raja and refuses to succumb to the fear of death. But in the course of the saṃvāda a relationship is established between the sadhu and the translator (who protects him by filtering the questions). A further saṃvāda can take place between reader and a text creating a 'realm of between'. There is also the saṃvāda between the arts, Raveh argues, referring to one of Daya Krishna's recent articles titled, 'Art and the Mystic Consciousness'. This disagrees with traditional conceptions of disengagement as freedom, such as Patanjali's *kaivalya*. Daya Krishna points out that freedom comes from engagement rather than disengagement and lies in the capacity to withdraw from all 'externality' but also to return to the world at the level of the mind, intellect, imagination, body and so on, demonstrating an affinity with the karma-yoga position of the *Gītā*, Sri Aurobindo and Mohandas Karamchand Gandhi.

Khawaja M. Zaffar (Meem Hai Zaffar) describes his saṃvāda with his teacher, Daya Krishna, suggesting how saṃvāda can create the grounds for svarāj. In Shimla he had stated, 'I feel orphaned. He was my spiritual father-responsible for my rebirth.' He points out that Daya Krishna did not value *śabda pramāṇa* (word as testimony) and instead challenged the weight of Indology/Spirituality/Orientalism that undermined the life of reason in India. The trajectory of reason is distinct from western logos and Daya Krishna referred to it as *nihsanga buddhī*, an intellect without preference or attachment. The appendices to Khawaja's article highlight the questions Daya Krishna posed in his dialogues with ulema and scholars of Islamic learning at Lucknow and Hyderabad.

Language, Selfhood and Philosophy

Bijoy Boruah offers a theory of what he calls virtue metaphysics (as distinct from virtue ethics) building on Ramchandra Gandhi's *The Availability of Religious Ideas.*[38] He argues that being a self is at heart a matter of becoming a self, which is a process of attaining virtue or comprehensive virtue, that is, it has both descriptive and normative/valuational content (is about fact, but also value). Ramchandra Gandhi postulates human communication on the addressive relation between I and You, which in turn is grounded on the imaginative viewing of the other as a soul in which the you is cast non-attributively and non-predicatively as yourself. In doing this, he does not adopt the controversial substantivist view of the self as the soul. 'I see you as a person, a unique being, not as a substance—a thing', writes Gandhi and emphasizes, 'the mode of non-substantival seeing of one another which is the seeing of one another as souls'. This idea of a human soul brings forth the pure subject of consciousness, bracketing out all predicates that fix identity. I can also adopt the non-predicative stance towards myself.

The you-stance in the context of address indicates the universality and ontological primacy of pronominal (pre-substantive) identity vis-à-vis predicative identity and the person's potentiality (even if the actuality is a betrayal of this personal essence). The act of addressing alludes to an ethics of minimal care. The spiritual or S-dimensionality of the self explores the interior enabling conditions for the possibility of a virtuous self. The virtue of the self is cultivated by unburdening oneself of 'thick' individuality and coming to terms with the universal consciousness. Forgiveness, Bijoy argues, involved in the judgement of mercy is grounded on the pristine innocence of pre-substantive human subjectivity, while guilt is postulated on substantive subjectivity.

Prasenjit Biswas' contribution is based on Daya Krishna's forthcoming book, *Toward a Theory of Structural and Transcendental Illusions*. It suggests how Daya Krishna's thought entails a shift of focus from reason and sensibility (and its *a priori* forms) that have dominated philosophical thought to self-consciousness, which makes consciousness its object. As Biswas highlights, Daya Krishna privileges acting and feeling over knowing and the imaginative over the sensible. Consciousness creates worlds—aesthetic and moral. Being is characterized not only by the will to power or desire that is associated with bondage but by a 'freedom' that entails the possibility of 'creating' worlds intersubjectively. Biswas points out that Daya Krishna sees the self-other as a 'feeling-relationship' that is simultaneously inter-subjective. 'Language gives almost infinite freedom to imagination to build whatever it likes', writes Daya Krishna.

Ramesh Pradhan argues that while the moral question dominates the spiritual quest of Daya Krishna, the spiritual question dominates the moral quest of Ramchandra Gandhi. Morality for Daya Krishna involves the pursuit of what he called active and contemplative values, the former relating to the welfare of others and the latter centred around one's own consciousness and which, being concerned with inner freedom, enlightenment and peace, are self-oriented. In both philosophers, Pradhan sees a denial of the transcendence/immanence binary. Since for both the timeless and mystical is of paramount importance, he describes both philosophers as non-dualists, an imputation that Daya Krishna might certainly have resisted.

For Ramchandra Gandhi, the thought, 'This world', which constitutes the logical heart of the immanentist 'world-view', is an illegitimate thought. Prayer, however, he states, 'non-cognitively make[s] available to me the category of transcendence'.[39] For Daya Krishna, one can only rise to a higher world through the world below; hence there is no discordance between the two. He cites Daya Krishna that the axiological 'ought', on the other hand, is not socio-anthropo-centric as much as it reveals the transcendent nature of the value claim and orientates humanity to a trans-human dimension. Daya Krishna concedes full reality to the world of time and history the way Sri Aurobindo does without adopting the latter's metaphysical categories. However, like the advaitin he concedes that we cannot finally be confined to the world of time and history. There is already in us the urge for the Infinite which compels us to transcend the empirical world.

Arindam Chakrabarti refers to Daya Krishna as the archetypal argumentative Indian. He responds, in this paper, to a question Daya Krishna had raised at a Convivium session in Liverpool in 1995 with respect to Locke's distinction between primary and secondary qualities. Daya Krishna had asked: What are the secondary qualities of the self, for example? We start with the distinction between objective and subjective qualities, between what the material apple really is and how it tastes to a fever-afflicted tongue. The material substance, or its insensible parts, thus, are supposed to have both objective and subjective attributes. What about a non-material substance such as a self or a conscious person? Well, does it have primary and secondary qualities? What would be the secondary qualities of my Self? Does it make any sense to distinguish between what I really feel and what I only seem to feel? How can you apprehend mental qualities in yourself which are not objectively there in you but appear to be there in yourself? How could you yourself be mistaken about what you are currently feeling? If I seem to feel it, then do I really feel it. Doesn't the objective-subjective distinction break down with qualities given to the inner sense? Could you ever distinguish between what you objectively are and what you think you are, when what you think is part of what you objectively are?

Arindam's response involves a negotiation of these questions through the tradition of Analytic philosophy. He concludes, 'With all due humility of a realist about mental states and a fallibilist about first person ascriptions of such states, though, I would still like to confess that I really do miss Daya Krishna. I don't think it is a mere appearance of missing. Even sometimes when I do not seem or appear to miss him, I think I do.'

Probal Dasgupta maintains that the PLA (Private Language Argument) 'affirms the social nature of language' and the 'role of caring in the socialness of language'. The informal context is a sanctuary that includes a relaxed mode and a tense mode that harbours energies of passive resistance/struggle against power and public and formal systems like the state, which is also the site of hegemony. Probal uses Wittgenstein's insight into the socialness of language with the milieu notion of contextuality, the milieu as the locus of the private and finding one's milieu as enabling one to relax.

Shankar Ramaswami's powerful essay refers to the death of the mother of an adivasi migrant worker called Madodari as matricide caused by deliberate neglect of her sons and doctors. He weaves into this Ramchandra Gandhi's interpretive framework of *prāyaścitt* building on M. K. Gandhi's response to the Bihar earthquake as a karmic consequence for Hindus who bear responsibility for the sin of untouchability. 'In the carnage of the Noakhali riots, we—society as a whole—and not only the direct perpetrators, in not protecting the lives of the murdered, established that those persons did not belong to us', suggests Ramchandra Gandhi.

> The Gita-sar is correct: "What of yours has been taken that you cry?" God bestows all, not to us as possessors and manipulators, but as trustees, of all things, beings, nature as a whole. If we fail to recognize this, if we do not see all things as "ours" (*apnā*) to honor, protect, and nurture, then we effectively forfeit these things, and compel God to take them back.

Shankar generalizes from this the cancerous *karm* of *kalyug*, in which society has not been trustees for its civilizens (*vasīs*, dwellers), hence the violence, the many Noakhalis and matricides of the present. Using Ramchandra Gandhi's philosophical framework, he points out that regenerativity itself has been murdered.

Madodari's own death became a *prāyaścitt* and a martyrdom, 'witness to the truths of non-attention, deprivation and suffering', and a dying for the *adharma* of her sons, doctors and society as a whole. Ramaswami has been making the case that Ramchandra Gandhi's own death is a martyrdom since he was an anguished witness to numerous existential and ecological crises.

C. K. Raju poses the problem of philosophers having become irrelevant on ethical issues. He sees ethical autonomy as the core of svarāj, ethical models being anchored in beliefs about time. Time suggests the interface between science and religion. The de-theologization of physics leads to a new notion of time that goes beyond Christian and Islamic conceptions. Raju suggests bringing physics and philosophy together in a new ethical principle arising from a new notion of time involving a tilt. He valorizes 'order', which both Daya Krishna and Don Miller were critical of and suggests that the term harmony be used as combinatory of both order and spontaneity.

S. Lokanathan's article continues his discussion with Daya Krishna who was interested in the question of measurement, its two facets being time and space. Here he responds to a series of questions Daya Krishna raised in a letter to him about the relation between different branches of mathematics including algebra, geometry, topology and logic. They also concern the axiomatization of geometry, arithmetic and logic and the relation between them and what it has contributed to the 'knowledge enterprise'. The result is a masterly essay.

Lokanathan explains axiomatization in mathematics as deriving from Euclidean geometry. While Euclid provided a visual geometry, Hilbert's work rendered points, lines and planes into abstract entities, axioms being the relations between these abstract entities. Paradoxically, the severing of mathematics from reality bestowed it with a new certainty. It made mathematics a theory of relations of entities rather than of entities themselves which were left undefined.

Neelima Vashishtha's chapter—titled 'The Applicability of Indian Aesthetic Theory of Rasa to the Visual Arts: A Rejoinder to Daya Krishna's Article, "*Rasa*—The Bane of Indian Aesthetics"'—responds to Daya Krishna's well-known critique of rasa theory, elaborated in his article,

'*Rasa*—The Bane of Indian Aesthetics'. In this chapter, he points out that Bharata's rasa theory understands the human situation only in terms of the 'emotional meaning' and not the ideals or values one pursues to make it meaningful, which include human relations, nature, transcendence and so on. Vashistha's essay raises the question of how new rasas might be devised such as *avasāda*, to contend with states of emotion such as despair, absurdity, disorder and banality that might mirror better modern life forms occasioned by poverty, violence, pain and alienation.

Notes and References

1. Daya Krishna expressed a lifetime's devotion to Indian philosophy in an Urdu *sher* (couplet)

   falsafe mein umar guzrī par milā kuch bhī nahīn
   phir bhī nā jāne bāt kyā tabīyat abhī haṭatī nahīn

   A life spent in philosophy, my gain is still a cipher
   one cannot fathom why the mind refuses to withdraw.
2. K. C. Bhattacharya, 'Swaraj in Ideas', *Visvabharati Quarterly* 35 (3–4) (1960 [1919]): 382–393. See for a discussion Shail Mayaram, 'Facets of Intellectual Decolonisation: Revisting the Svarāj in Ideas Debate', in Untitled Hind Swaraj Centenary Conference volume, ed. Rajeev Bhargava (Delhi: Routledge, in press).
3. K. J. Shah, Ramchandra Gandhi, Probal Dasgupta and S. S. Deshpande, eds, Editorial, *Indian Philosophical Quarterly*, special issue, Svarāj in Ideas, 11 (1) (1984): 379–381.
4. Ramchandra Gandhi, 'Svarāj of India', *Indian Philosophical Quarterly*, special issue, Svarāj in Ideas, eds K. J. Shah, Ramchandra Gandhi, Probal Dasgupta and S. S. Deshpande, 11 (1) (1984): 461–471.
5. Ibid., p. 17.
6. Daya Krishna, *Towards a Theory of Structural and Transcendental Illusions* (Project on the History of Indian Science, Philosophy and Civilization, 2012).
7. Ramchandra Gandhi, Sages of India, Ramakrishna, Workshop, Academy of Fine Arts and Literature, Delhi, 2006.
8. Ramchandra Gandhi, Sages of India, Vivekananda, Workshop, Academy of Fine Arts and Literature, Delhi, 2006.
9. Ramchandra Gandhi, *Muniya's Light: A Narrative of Truth and Myth* (Delhi: India Ink, Roli Books, 2005).

10. Ramchandra Gandhi, *I am Thou: Meditations on the Truth of India* (Pune: Indian Philosophical Quarterly Publications no. 8, University of Poona, 1984).
11. Ramchandra Gandhi, 'Ethics, Ecology and Enlightenment', interview with Chandan Gowda. *The Hindu*, 18 November 2007.
12. Shail Mayaram, 'Ramchandra Gandhi: The Personal Is the Political Is the Philosophical', in *Ramchandra Gandhi: The Man and His Philosophy* (Delhi: Routledge, 2013).
13. Makarand Paranjape, 'Ramchandra Gandhi's 'truth': Non-dual Mediations and Meditations', Keynote address, National Seminar on Ramchandra Gandhi: Faith and Enquiry, Department of Philosophy and Religion, Viswabharati, Santiniketan, 15–17 March 2008.
14. Ramchandra Gandhi, *Sita's Kitchen: A Testimony of Faith and Inquiry* (Delhi: Wiley Eastern, 1994), p. 17.
15. Ramchandra Gandhi, *I am Thou*, p. 17.
16. Ramchandra Gandhi, *The Availability of Religious Ideas* (London: Macmillan, 1976).
17. Daya Krishna, 'Civilizations: Past and Future I', *Civilizations: Nostalgia and Utopia* (New Delhi: SAGE Publications, 2012).
18. Daya Krishna, *The Problematic and Conceptual Structure of Classical Indian Thought about Man, Society and Polity* (New Delhi: Oxford University Press, 1966).
19. Daya Krishna, ed., *India's Intellectual Traditions: Attempts at Conceptual Reconstruction* (Delhi: Motilal Banarsidass, 1987).
20. Daya Krishna, M. P. Rege, R. C. Dwivedi and Mukund Lath, eds, *Samvāda: A Dialogue between Two Philosophical Traditions* (Delhi: Indian Council of Philosophical Research in association with Motilal Banarsidass, 1991).
21. Daya Krishna, Mukund Lath and Francine E. Krishna, eds, *Bhakti: A Contemporary Discussion* (Delhi: Indian Council of Philosophical Research, 2000).
22. Daya Krishna, *New Perspectives in Indian Philosophy* (henceforth *NPIP*) (Jaipur and Delhi: Rawat, 2000), p. 5.
23. Daya Krishna, *Civilizations: Nostalgia and Utopia* (New Delhi: SAGE Publications, 2012), pp. 98–99.
24. Krishna, *NPIP*, pp. 195–196.
25. Ibid., p. 199.
26. Ibid., pp. 201–202.
27. Daya Krishna points out with regard to Dumont's response to the articles published in *Contributions to Indian Sociology* that his reply did not respond to the interlocutory articles and chose to respond primarily to Marriott who had not even contributed to the journal. *NPIP*, p. 204.
28. Daya Krishna, 'The *Vedic* Corpus and the Two Sūtra-texts Concerned with It: The *Mīmāṃsāsūtra* and the *Brahmasūtra*', in *Contrary Thinking:*

Selected Essays of Daya Krishna, eds Jay Garfield, Nalini Bhushan and Daniel Raveh (New York: Oxford University Press, 2011), pp. 257–271.

29. *NPIP*, p. 200. In the story recounted in the Chāndyoga Upaniṣad, Satyakama, the son of Jabala asks his mother about his gotra or lineage (*kim-gotro`smi*). She responds that she worked as a servant so she slept with many men (*bahu caranti*) and that she has no idea who his father was. Gautama muni did not accept low-caste disciples but because Satyakama told the truth, he told him that he was a brahmana. This 'great *ācarya*' (i.e., Śaṃkara), Daya Krishna comments, thus makes '*śruti acceptable* to the social prejudices of his time....' *NPIP*, p. 97.
30. Krishna, *Civilizations: Nostalgia and Utopia*, Lecture 2, Civilizations: Past and Future.
31. Krishna, *NPIP*, p. 25.
32. Krishna, 'Indian Philosophy in the First Millennium AD: Fact or Fiction', *NPIP*, ch. 3.
33. Krishna, *NPIP*, p. 42.
34. See Krishna, 'Where are the Vedas in the First Millennium AD?', *NPIP*, ch. 4.
35. Krishna, 'Vedānta in the First Millennium AD: The Case Study of a Retrospective Illusion Imposed by the Historiography of Indian Philosophy', *NPIP*, ch. 5.
36. Ibid., ch. 4.
37. Krishna, *NPIP,* p. 96.
38. Gandhi, *The Availability of Religious Ideas.*
39. Gandhi, *Sita's Kitchen,* pp. 1–25.

Prologue

Shail Mayaram succeeded in persuading me to write a Prologue to this impressive volume. I told her that I was no philosopher nor was I a participant in the seminars held in Jaipur and understandably not present in any one-to-one dialogues between them. It reminded me of my long association with both of them, particularly Dayabhai. Yes, I did know both of them at a purely personal level and was aware that they dialogued with each other openly and freely with depth and incisive argumentation. It is difficult, very difficult indeed, to write, comment or evaluate the contribution of those you have known at a personal level, more so, when they have risen to the status of gurus and teachers of another generation.

Shail Mayaram's own proximity to Dayabhai and her communication with Ramu in the *satsanga*s he held must have been an advantage though not without some intrinsic or certainly tacit challenges. Reading through her introduction, so beautifully and sensitively textured, it occurred to me that I would restrict myself to making some observations in regard to a few issues of great importance and value.

As I perused the introduction and some articles and the imagined dialogue between Daya Krishna and Ramchandra Gandhi that Shail Mayaram has constructed with such finesse and sophistication, my thoughts went back to many, many decades. These are the memories of Hindu College around 1942. It was Professor S. K. Saxena who first identified the genius of Daya, and he was sure that irrespective of his making any grade in the examination, he would certainly travel a long way and ascend many peaks in the realm of philosophy. And the other teacher, Dr Indrasen, who later relinquished teaching to join Sri Aurobindo Ashram in Pondicherry, instilled in Daya the desire for exploring uncharted paths. The presence of these two intellectuals for me was not just a matter of nostalgia but instead a renewed awareness on the method of transmission of knowledge and inculcating attitudes of exploring the realm through innovative methods.

Professor Saxena was not only an unconventional teacher but was also very caring of those he nurtured. Daya was very special for him. As far as I know he succeeded in taking Daya as a Fellow at the East-West Centre in Hawaii. The seeds of 'interrogating' any proposition, to my mind, were laid by Professor Saxena. Daya travelled a long way with him but also beyond his mentor in this intellectual journey of investigating and interrogating with ease. Daya was not alone because he had three other lifetime friends. I refer to Vivek Dutta, Sita Ram Goyal and Ram Swarup. Gosh, how heatedly they could debate over any issue on those wooden benches of Hindu College then at Kashmiri Gate. Professor Saxena always encouraged the very few girl students, just about a score to a thousand boys, to participate in these discussions. Of course, I heard Daya and Vivek converse, argue and differ in college and yet stay close. This volume brought back very many memories of these dialogues.

As far as I am concerned, my communication with Dayabhai continued intermittently—at times frequently and at times after long gaps. Invariably, I was a silent listener to the dialogue between Daya and other philosophers, particularly Professors D. P. Chattopadhyay, Balasubramanian and D. Prahlada Char, never having the courage to intervene.

During the last decades of his life, on his visits to Delhi he would stay at the India International Centre. Whenever he found time or had the inclination, he would walk up to my office, enter with a smile and then pop the question as to what subject we both would have a conversation on. I teased him, 'Dayabhai, you should be with the Buddhist monks where debating is done with wooden plank and physical movements'. He would respond with a laugh and say, 'You mean that I do "fencing"'. I said, 'Well Dayabhai, you do "fencing", for you know the art of "fencing". Attack and defence is the sophisticated art of training the physical movements in philosophic arguments. You are a master in this art of "fencing" in the realm of thought and intellect (*buddhi*)'.

I had heard Daya speak at the seminar on the *Nāṭyaśāstra* and also read his article, 'The Search for a Conceptual Structure of the *Nāṭyaśāstra*', in the volume, *India's Intellectual Traditions*. I told him that while I appreciated the views of the participants, especially those of K. J. Shah and V. Y. Kantak, and particularly his introduction, I had some questions as a humble reader of the *Nāṭyaśāstra* for decades. We had a very engaging discussion on whether a *Rasa* theory propounded by Bharata in the *Nāṭyaśāstra* should be held responsible for all the ills of the trajectory of Indian aesthetics, whether at the level of theory or practice? I said to Dayabhai, 'Don't you think that you should then also question what is it within the Indian tradition which allows for dialogue, divergences and even counter questions without invading the very earth of fundamentals of the worldview'.

We argued for long. On my part, I thought it was imperative to place before Daya my own journey of investigation of the many, many texts not only on aesthetics, but also the Indian arts, where this premise is both followed and interrogated within the textual tradition.I also said to him, 'You have not addressed the question of its transmission and how it travelled across. Why didn't you ask the question where was the *Nāṭyaśāstra* composed, why did one find the earliest manuscripts in a place like Nepal and how did centuries later the commentaries of Abhinavagupta reached Kerala? All these questions also need to be addressed'. He laughed and replied, 'OK Kapila, why don't you publish a rejoinder? I think you have a point'. Our affectionate bond didn't allow me to publish a rejoinder, although Dayabhai egged me on. Reading Neelima Vashishtha's article for this volume, which is a rejoinder to Daya Krishna's article, '*Rasa*—The Bane of Indian Aesthetics', revived memories of those conversations.

The most exhilarating moment was when Dayabhai wrote me a long letter after reading my book on the *Mewari Gita-Govinda* and said, 'Kapila, *ānand ā gayā, ānand ā gayā*' [Ed. High praise of the book].

And in the very last meeting with him, at the outset he said, 'Today, we are going to talk about dance as "thought"'. I said, 'Dayabhai, am I going to talk about dance or dance of thought?' He laughed and said, 'You know, I have been thinking whether there can be thought without word, and therefore, whether dance or movement is pure thought?' Shail Mayaram's volume reminded me of these and many other dialogues with him.

The chapters in the volume are based on a stimulating seminar, *Philosophy as Saṃvāda and Svarāj*, that took place in Shimla at the Indian Institute of Advanced Study and which I participated in. My mind instantly went back to the first decade of the Institute. I remembered Dr Niharranjan Ray, the first Director of the IIAS, as also the many engaging and path-breaking interdisciplinary seminars. It was in one of those seminars that I heard Ramchandra Gandhi at his dramatic best.

As for Ramu, this association goes back to the bonding between our mothers, as we were almost neighbours in Connaught Circus. Only a few Indian families were residing in this part of the city. So, my mother would often say that she was going to meet Lakshmi, Ramu's mother. I would also visit their house and also get to meet Ramu and his siblings,

Gopu and Tara. Later, Tara was my student in Miranda House and she has continued to be a close friend. Ramu was a constant in the premises of India International Centre and I watched him in his role as a guru. He leaves behind many an admirer.

Let me now share some responses to Shail Mayaram's Introduction, and the Imagined Dialogue between Daya Krishna and Ramchandra Gandhi. With great care and industry, she has structured her volume in a manner that there are some explicit threads which run through both the Introduction and the Imaginary Dialogue. This is an awesome task that she has accomplished with great sensitivity as also analytical skill.

Shail Mayaram says that Dayabhai was an iconoclast. I would modify that by saying, no, not an iconoclast, he was an interrogator, whether it was eastern or western philosophy. She refers to his reading of the *Puruṣa-sūkta* of the *Ṛgveda* and how Daya points at the solidification of a verse to validate societal hierarchy, normally understood as the *varṇa*. Here I am taking the liberty of quoting Raimundo Panikkar: '*Puruṣa* is not only the cosmic Man; it is also the personal aspect of the whole of reality.... Everything that is, is a member of the one and unique.'[1] As for me, I would humbly like to ask, tell me of another civilization where feet are venerated. So, here is an ontological and epistemological problem, for if a culture venerates feet, then by the same analogy the 'Śūdras' must be part of an inclusive vision. The distortions and the disjunctions that have taken place reflect a very complex dynamic of thought and social structure.

Daya pertinently refers to the exclusion of the 'Śūdras' and the reluctant inclusion of the women in the Vedic *yajña*. As someone who has been involved in the organization of these *yajña* especially when the *agni chayna* was held in Panjal in the 1970s and the subsequent *yajña*s held in Kerala under the direction of the late Dr T. I. Radhakrishnan, it was clear that the *yajña* was the concretization of the vision of the primordial man, step by step, brick by brick, person by person, certainly in defined roles in specific time. It would be a partial statement to speak of either hierarchy or total exclusion and inclusion at the level of societal structure. I can go on and on to give instances of reversal of roles, reversal of hierarchy in specific space and time. This is evident to anyone who has witnessed performances of ritual dance-drama in all parts of India.

To turn now to Daya's views on Indian philosophers writing in English. I happened to introduce Professor Jay L. Garfield to Daya, when Garfield and Nalini Bhushan (a cousin) were engaged in editing a volume *Indian Philosophy in English.* As quoted by the editors in their Introduction to this book, Daya Krishna said,

> We have been fed on the Western presentation of Indian philosophy, which hardly captures the spirit and history of Indian philosophy.... If I were not to know Indian philosophy myself, I would say that (their presentation) is wonderful, that it presents it clearly, with great insight and understanding. Now that I know a little Indian philosophy, I say that they did not.... They are not concerned with the problems that Indian philosophers were concerned with.

As one knows, Daya travelled a long way himself. He acknowledges his debt to Badrinath Shukla in this journey. It will be remembered that it was Daya who initiated a meaningful, active and on-going dialogue between traditional pandits and contemporary Indian philosophers. In his remarkable introduction to the volume entitled *Developments in Indian Philosophy from Eighteenth Century Onwards: Classical and Western*, brilliantly written by him, Daya interrogates the very cognitive enterprise of history and then develops his argument in regard to the nature of both continuity and discontinuity in the intellectual journey of Indians.

> History, as a cognitive enterprise, seems to be amongst the strangest of endeavours undertaken by man for it claims to know the past, that is, something which does not presently exist. But, how can that which is 'not', be understood? For to understand that, it would be to endow it with some sort of 'being'. The anomaly and paradox inherent in this attempt to know and understand the past has generally been ignored, as it raises questions about the very foundations of the enterprise in which historians are engaged....

Shail Mayaram draws pointed attention to the need for 'intellectual decolonization' and for adopting 'non-western categories' to comprehend the trajectory of not only Indian philosophy, but our social structure and contemporary disjunctions. The relevance of *sva,* i.e. selfhood, svarāj in the deepest sense of intellectual freedom, and saṃvāda not to be equated with dialogue, is her concern. Quite deftly, she recreates the saṃvāda between these two unusual minds of our times.

She highlights the difference between Daya and Ramu's perspective on Indian civilization. For Daya, it is the plurality of intellectual traditions and a relentless questioning spirit, while for Ramu it is *Advaita*, the non-duality, which defines the truth of India. For Daya, it is not only the spiritual quest but he lays due stress on the knowledge quest, the philosophic quest, the scientific and aesthetic quest in equal measure. As for Ramu, saṃvāda is all about self-understanding and arriving at the truth.

The dialogue between Daya and Ramu continues whether it is in the understanding of the philosophic principle of *Advaita* or its ramifications in the life of thought, intellection, not to speak of experience.

Understandably, there is an interesting reference to Martin Buber and his much discussed book, *I and Thou*. It reminded me of a major seminar, *Intercultural Dialogue and the Human Image*, held at the Indira Gandhi National Centre for the Arts in 1994, which revolved around Buber's formulation *I and Thou.* Ramu's perspective is not *I and Thou*, it is instead *I am Thou,* the title of his own book. Although an ardent admirer of Ramana Maharshi, Ramu's own musings, alas, cannot quite reflect the experiential depth of the Master. Also, there was some difference between Daya and Ramu in respect to *Advaita*. Daya had critiqued *Advaita* and Śaṃkara. Oh, there is more one could say, but no more.

Let me now refer briefly to the imaginary dialogue so poignantly and meaningfully created by Shail Mayaram. Reading through these pages, some images come to my mind. It was like two boatmen on the same boat, sometimes oaring in consonance and sometimes in great dissonance. The boat, however, remained afloat on the tides and waves of a vast ocean with fathomless depths and unbound horizons. The two boatmen not only sought to measure those depths but also navigate those waters and yet look up to the skies, to identify, if not reach, the *saptarṣī*s. Had they? Finally, the boat, the boatmen, the dancers of thought were perhaps beyond the realm of razor sharp intellect. The dialogue between the *saptarṣī*s of the sky and the *saptarṣī*s of experience may have led to silence.

18 November 2013 **Kapila Vatsyayan**

Note

1. Raimundo Pannikar, *The Vedic Experience: Mantramañjari (An Anthology of the Vedas for Modern Man and Contemporary Celebration)* (Delhi: Motilal Banarsidas, 1977), p. 73.

PART I

Of Love, Liberation and *Līlā*

1

Figure and Ground: Reflections on Two Exemplary Indian Thinkers

Fred Dallmayr

It was with great sadness that I learned of the passing away of two leading Indian philosophers: Daya Krishna and Ramchandra Gandhi.[1] What renders the loss particularly grievous is the fact that the two were not just ordinary academicians but exemplary and even iconic Indian thinkers. In a way, the two, during much of their lives, represented two different possibilities of Indian thought, two alternative conceptions of the meaning of philosophy. On the whole, Daya Krishna identified philosophy with critical analysis and the striving for exact knowledge, whereas Ramchandra Gandhi placed himself in the tradition of the great Indian 'seers', the teachings of the Upaniṣads and the *Bhagavad Gītā*. While the former aimed at rigorous rational truth (*episteme*), the other preferred to cultivate liberating insight and wisdom (*sophia*). There can hardly be a deeper gulf than this among practitioners of philosophy. Yet, when everything is said and done, the two thinkers in the end were not hostile to each other and came to appreciate their respective contributions. Thus, on a limited scale, something like a 'saṃvāda' or dialogical understanding came to prevail between them.

I was fortunate enough to be acquainted with both thinkers—though not in equal measure. With Daya Krishna I was linked through a loose bond of friendship, a bond established through periodic meetings and discussions. Repeatedly I met with him at conferences organized by the

East-West Center in Hawaii; on other occasions we would meet and share a meal at conferences in Delhi, Pune and other places in India. One particularly joyful occasion happened in Hawaii some 12 years ago when we went to dinner together in a Hawaiian village restaurant with a folkloric ambience (Bhuvan Chandel joined us there). I was greatly impressed by the immense range of Daya's erudition, his familiarity with all kinds of Indian and Western texts, and also by his sociability and lively wit. In my view, Daya was a world-open, cosmopolitan thinker, easily at home in many different places. It was, no doubt, this quality which enabled him to absorb so quickly and thoroughly some Western philosophical trends, especially the outlook and style of analytical philosophy. My acquaintance with Ramchandra Gandhi was more limited. I met with him several times in Delhi, especially in the International House where he frequently stayed. I was struck by his pensive attitude and by the intensity of his search for 'truth' in both the philosophical and the religious sense (*satya* and *sat-chit-ānanda*). Although he was familiar with modern and contemporary Western thought, especially the Whiteheadian strand, his intellectual roots were clearly in the older Indian tradition, particularly in the 'non-dualist' philosophy (Advaita Vedānta) inaugurated by Śaṃkara and continued by a long line of religious-philosophical thinkers.

Daya Krishna's Defence of Reason

Daya Krishna is known chiefly for his book titled *Indian Philosophy: A Counter Perspective* (of 1991), a somewhat iconoclastic text aiming to correct a number of misconstruals of Indian thought. The chief misconception the text seeks to correct or deconstruct is the notion that Indian philosophy is essentially 'spiritual' and even 'mystical', in contrast to the rigorous, rational character of Western philosophical inquiry. 'Who does not know', Krishna writes in a somewhat mocking vein, 'that Indian philosophy is spiritual? Who has not been told that this is what specifically distinguishes it from Western philosophy, and what makes it something unique and apart from all the other philosophical traditions of the world?' In Krishna's view, this conception is entirely untenable and at odds with major strands of traditional Indian thought (including Nyāya, Vaiśeṣika and Cārvāka), hence his verdict that this 'spiritual' characterization is 'completely erroneous'. Another misconception closely related to this characterization is the claim that Indian thought is basically marked by a practical objective: the orientation toward spiritual liberation or *mokṣa*. Krishna calls this the 'Bhattacharya model'. According to this model, he writes,

> Indian philosophy is the essential theoretic counterpart to that which, when practically realized or verified, is called *sādhanā* (practice) or *yoga*. . . . In the language of Bhattacharya, it is philosophic reflection alone which makes us aware of certain possibilities which demand to be actualized, even though the process of actualization itself is not philosophical in nature.

What this means is that the cognitive propositions of philosophy have no independent status and can only be verified in practical application.[2]

Among other misconceptions challenged in the text are the alleged authoritative status of the Vedas and Upaniṣads in traditional Indian thought and the claim that Indian philosophy comes packaged in distinct 'schools' attached to specific doctrines or dogmas and hence impervious to further questionings. Against all these erroneous construals Krishna upholds a view of philosophy basically congruent with its Socratic and Western analytical self-understanding. This outlook, we read, 'thinks of Indian philosophy as philosophy proper and not as something radically different from what goes under that name in the Western tradition'. Above all, this view denies 'that Indian philosophy has anything to do with *mokṣa* and asserts that the alleged association is due to a complete misunderstanding of the actual situation'. This denial has important corollaries, corollaries summed up by Krishna in the statement that Indian philosophy, properly conceived, 'is neither exclusively spiritual nor bound by unquestionable, infallible authority, nor constricted and congealed in the frozen moulds of the so-called "schools" which are supposed to constitute the essence of Indian philosophy by those who have written on the subject'. The basic aim of Krishna's text is to liberate Indian philosophy from prevailing prejudices and 'mummified' straitjackets in order to render it a viable partner in worldwide intellectual inquiries: 'Indian philosophy will become contemporarily relevant only when it is conceived as philosophy proper.'[3]

In the ensuing chapters of the book, the iconoclastic or deconstructive implications of Krishna's approach become palpably evident and have led to no small amount of controversy. Here it must suffice to lift up a few main points. One prominent theme—previously mentioned—concerns the role of spiritual liberation (*mokṣa*) in traditional Indian thought. Relying on a number of texts, Krishna has no difficulty in showing that such liberation 'is not the exclusive concern of Indian philosophy; nor is it its predominant concern either'. It is time, he insists, that the 'myth' of *mokṣa*'s central role be dispelled and Indian philosophy be 'treated seriously as philosophy proper'. Another major theme involves the authoritative or privileged status of the Vedas and Upaniṣads. Although frequently asserted and even presented as distinctive of Indian philosophy, Krishna finds the claim mired in confusion and dogmatic double-talk. For, as soon as one asks the question, he states, 'as to what it is whose authority is being invoked or denied, one does not find from the texts or the tradition any clear or definite answer'. According to the book, similar questions can be asked, and similar obscurity prevails, regarding the status and meaning of the Nyāya-Sūtras and of the Sāṃkhya-Kārikā reputed to be the oldest known text of the Sāṃkhya School of Philosophy. Two chapters (easily the most contentious) are devoted to the status and meaning of Advaita Vedānta as inaugurated by Śaṃkara. The first chapter charges Śaṃkara with building his theory of 'non-dualism' (Advaita) on dualist premises (deriving from the Sāṃkhya School). The second takes aim at the idea of 'Vedānta' itself, asking, 'Does it really mean anything?'—a question resolutely answered in the negative. Although acknowledging that Vedānta is 'the most dominant, alive and continuous tradition of Indian philosophizing', Krishna concludes that it is 'only a word full of emotional significance, good for propagandistic purposes but, basically, signifying nothing'. Hence, the term 'needs to be banished from the realms of thought, if we are to be serious about thinking'.[4]

Although best known and most widely cited, the preceding book was not Krishna's only 'counter perspective' or effort at critical reconstruction. A few years later, he published a book titled *New Perspectives in Indian Philosophy* (2001) which offered a critical re-examination of the entire tradition of Indian thought from the Vedas and Vedānta to Mīmāṃsā, Nyāya and Navya Nyāya. There is no point here in reviewing the entire course of critical analyses; it must suffice rather to distil the central animus or motivations inspiring the work. Foremost among these motivations is the desire to rejuvenate Indian philosophy by liberating it from ingrained habits of rote learning and sterile repetition. In Krishna's words, the chief aim of his book—and especially of its discussion of Vedānta—is 'to outline a strategy for creative thinking in general and philosophizing in particular'. What he finds distressing in Indian thought is a certain backward-looking tendency, a proclivity to view philosophy in the 'rear-view mirror' without a corresponding effort to renew thinking by bringing it to bear on ongoing issues and discussions. From the angle of many traditional pandits, philosophizing means simply 'an articulation of that which has already been thought as if there were no imperfections or incompleteness in it, or as if it was finished picture or product of thought'. Deliberately invoking Kantian language, Krishna stresses the need to strengthen the critical impulses in philosophy. His book, he notes hopefully, will contribute to 'making us free from our "dogmatic slumbers" and making us aware of the need for a fresh look at the philosophical traditions of India, so that they may become alive once again and be pursued with renewed vigor once more'.[5]

Another animus permeating the book is a certain anti-parochialism or incipient universalism opposed to the erection of intellectual or geographical boundaries. This opposition applies to domestic or intra-civilizational developments where—with regard to the traditional 'schools' of thought (*darśana*s)—Krishna emphasizes their dialogical interaction rather than their doctrinal separation. His anti-parochial élan, however, is most clearly evident with respect to cross-cultural or inter-cultural relations. Complaining about the 'monadic self-sufficiency' of traditional Indian philosophy, Krishna finds it 'unbelievable' that 'hardly any attempt has been made to see its inner connections with developments of thought in other civilizations'. Lack of connection carries over from philosophy into the realms of social, political or legal thought as well as the domains of the natural sciences and the arts. In all these fields, the 'insulated' character of Indian tradition has been underscored by 'the almost total absence of any awareness of the way it has been influenced by thought current in sister civilizations, or the way it might have influenced them'. For example, the Persian, the Greek, the Central Asian and Chinese civilizations were 'in active interaction for long periods of time' with the Indian civilization, and 'it is extremely unlikely that they were not influenced by one another'. Significantly, Krishna lists among the civilizations influencing and being influenced by Indian thought also the world of Arabic and Islamic learning. 'From at least 1200 A.D. onwards', he writes, 'Islam may be said to have a definitive presence in North India'—a presence, however, which is largely sidelined or ignored: 'The histories of thought in the second millennium A.D. in this country show hardly any awareness of it or of the possible influence it might have had on the varied fields of intellectual life in India.'[6]

The broad civilizational and inter-civilizational issues raised in *New Perspectives* were for Krishna not just a passing concern. At the time when he wrote that book he was involved in an ambitious project of cross-cultural and even transcultural reflection whose result appeared under the title *Prolegomena to Any Future Historiography of Cultures and Civilizations* (second edition in 2005). Published by the Centre for Studies in Civilizations under the general editorship of D. P. Chattopadhyaya, the book reveals Krishna as a self-reflective thinker oriented toward global and world-historical horizons. Drawing some inspiration from the historical reflections of Kant and the later Husserl, Krishna finds the clue of civilizational development in the growth and maturation of reflective consciousness—although this accent is modified in several ways (to which I shall return later). In his words: 'Thinking about civilizations is thinking about "man" [human being] itself; it sees "man" as the "creator-builder" of civilizations through a vast collective effort lasting over millennia. . . . In this process, man "creates" and "builds" itself also.' In the course of history, he adds, nature steadily gives way to culture and natural inclinations to reflective, civilized dispositions: 'The "naturally" built institutions of society and culture undergo a radical transformation through the development of self-consciousness and increasing intervention on its part in the way they function before its intervention.' For Krishna, the progressive advancement of civilization through creative intervention reflects in the end 'the transcendental seeking of man' (in Husserl's terms: the maturation of transcendental consciousness). 'The successive embodiments in which the living consciousness articulates itself', we read, 'provide a clue not only to the meaning or purpose which is evidenced in them but also . . . to the seeking which is expressed through the successive evidences. There is, thus, a visible and invisible history to be captured.' Switching into a more linguistic or narrative idiom, Krishna adds that the maintenance and transmission of culture is 'symbolic in character and concerned with the understanding and interpretation of the symbols in which it is embodied'.[7]

As one should note at this point, civilizational narratives cannot be viewed in complete isolation from a world-historical angle. Actually, on this level one can notice both centrifugal and centripetal tendencies. Thus, alongside a search for 'relative autonomy and independence', one can also find

> a desire to relate oneself to a larger whole of which one would like to be a member as this would not only give one an added importance, but also

> the feeling of belonging to an unending quest of 'man' to which one might significantly contribute by his/her independent effort.

As Krishna's study makes abundantly clear, cultural identity—when seen from an inter-civilizational and world-historical perspective—is highly fluid and tenuous. In his words: 'The idea of the new frontier has become proverbial since the American experience'; yet, although not sufficiently recognized, 'there has always been a shifting frontier in the history of civilizations'. Underscoring his strong anti-parochial (and incipiently universalist) stance, Krishna adds:

> The point is that a civilization is not bound to the place of its origin nor even to the peoples amongst whom it may have arisen. . . . It is almost like the invisible spirit which moves from one place to another and is confined to no particular place, though there may be temporary illusions that it belongs only to a particular people or place or time.

Reinforcing this point still further so that it emerges almost like the motto of a world historical teleology, the study continues: 'Civilizations thus have to be disengaged from their entanglement and identification not only with geographical regions and particular peoples but also with some unchanging foundation lying at their beginning without which they will cease to be what they are.'[8]

To be sure, the absence of cultural or civilizational 'essences' does not involve the denial of historical experiences in which particular geographical regions and particular people played a recognizable role. Can one still speak—Krishna asks pointedly—of 'an Indian, Chinese or West Asian or European civilization'? The answer to this question resides in two considerations. The first relates to the fact that 'civilizations are not just a matter of the past but of the future as well' and that the historical development of many civilizations gives evidence of 'significant turns' and even 'radical breaks' which later merged with their past and became an integral part of their history. The second, still more crucial consideration has to do with the fact that 'all civilizations are basically human achievements' which have to be seen in 'a unitary manner as part of a common human enterprise' endowed with 'a claim to universality relevant for all humankind'. Viewed from this angle, civilizations can be seen as variations on a common enterprise—or better still: as participants in a shared and competitive endeavour. Civilizations, Krishna writes, must be regarded as shareholders in a common endeavour, a striving 'which has been carried on by successive generations over long periods of time, and which, though sometimes interrupted, has never been given up for long by human beings who have been even vaguely aware of what they have inherited from their past'. What is crucial for Krishna, in this context, is the fact of inter-civilizational contacts and the evidence of inter-civilizational learning over time. 'The significant factor', he writes, 'is not that civilizations have developed an identifiable personality of their own over millennia but that they have continually borrowed from each other's achievements and deficiencies.' Properly told, the story of civilizations hence has been 'both a cooperative and competitive enterprise' in which there has been 'an element of rivalry along with a deeper awareness that they are all engaged in the common enterprise of "man" on this planet which is as unending as time itself'.[9]

No doubt, the account of civilizational maturation presented in the book is captivating and uplifting. As it happens, however, the story of humankind's growing self-consciousness and self-constitution is intersected in the book by a number of comments which put pressure on the story's linearity. One comment concerns the very notion of self-constitution itself. One of the important insights to emerge from his study, Krishna remarks in his Preface, is that of 'the empirical *a priori* which normally is supposed to be a contradiction in terms in the analytic philosophical tradition dominant in Western philosophy'. Somewhat further along, he returns to the notion of concrete or 'immanent *a priori* conditions' of historiography, observing that 'unless we become aware of them, we would not see the constraints that the historical enterprise itself involves'. This idea of 'immanent' conditions clearly is hard to reconcile not only with assumptions of the 'analytic philosophical tradition' but also with the transcendental trajectory of a universal historiography of civilizations. The problem resurfaces more clearly towards the end of the book. There, reflecting again on human identity, Krishna writes: 'The simple truth is that the essential unchangeability of consciousness [which] has been accepted as an unquestioned and unquestionable axiom by all [is yet] strangely and paradoxically refuted every moment by the experiences of each and everyone, including the thinker himself.' This happens 'because of the "illusion" generated by self-consciousness which cannot see consciousness as an "object" even if it tries to do so'. The refutation becomes particularly clear if one turns from philosophy to the domains of 'polity, economy, and society'—as Krishna does in the concluding section. In his words, there are indeed 'internal' factors in the story of civilization which include 'the life of the imagination and what is called “spirit”’. Yet, there is another dimension. The ‘unasked question’ here is what happens to ‘man’ who is the centre of all this drama and whether history with all the changes in polity, economy and society will leave his ‘essence’ untouched, or transform and transmute him in a sense that is difficult to grasp as the very activity of thinking and understanding seems to be structured in such a way as to determine and give form to itself by conceiving of everything, including itself, as constituted by the differences that distinguish and define them as ‘this’ rather than ‘that’.[10]

Ramchandra Gandhi and ‘Assemblage’

The preceding comments show Krishna as a circumspect and multifaceted thinker—though without jeopardizing or erasing his emancipatory posture.[11] As it seems to me, Daya Krishna’s work stands basically in the tradition of ‘critical’ philosophy intimated by Socrates and deepened later by a string of thinkers from Descartes to Kant (and, in part, Husserl). Wedded to the project of human intellectual as well as social liberation, the tradition forms the linchpin of Western modernity—and probably of worldwide modernity today. The merits of this ‘modern project’ (so-called) in terms of human advancement are manifest—but its premises are no longer unquestioned. During the twentieth century, a number of thinkers have inquired precisely into the ‘immanent’ conditions of possibility of cognition and consciousness, that is, the conditions undergirding the Cartesian cogito and transcendental subjectivity. Some thinkers, following Ludwig Wittgenstein, have explored the embeddedness of thought in language, that is, its dependence on semantic, syntactical and performative criteria. Other thinkers, especially American pragmatists, have underscored the practical and context-bound parameters of human cognition. Still others—especially Martin Heidegger and Alfred North Whitehead—have delved into the ontological and quasi-metaphysical premises of human reasoning and ‘being-in-the-world’. What all these thinkers have in common is the turn from rational knowledge (*episteme*) to the precognitive reservoir of experience and understanding—a reservoir which, without being irrational or simply mystical, constantly eludes and transgresses the limits of cognitive grasp and control. In many respects, Ramchandra Gandhi has always placed himself in this philosophical genre.

Ramchandra's philosophical leanings are clearly outlined in one of his early works titled *Two Essays on Whitehead's Philosophic Approach* (of 1973). In his study, Ramchandra takes his point of departure chiefly from Whitehead's *Modes of Thought* (1938) which, together with *Adventures of Ideas* (1933), belongs to that philosopher's later writings. In *Modes of Thought*, Whitehead distinguished between two types of philosophizing which he called, respectively, 'philosophic assemblage' and 'speculative philosophy'. In his Preface, Gandhi expresses his conviction that Whitehead's own pursuit of speculative or systematic philosophy is likely to be 'seriously misunderstood' if it is not seen in relation to his discussion of philosophic assemblage 'which is an activity in many ways diametrically opposed to the agenda of speculative philosophy, yet complementary to it'. The distinction is explained more clearly in subsequent contexts. For Whitehead, doing speculative or systematic philosophy was 'an attempt to construct a coherent system of ideas which would be adequately explanatory of the nature of ultimate reality and therefore of the totality of existence'. To an extent, Whitehead himself pursued such an agenda. However, in *Modes of Thought* and other late writings, he acknowledged an 'inherent deficiency' in system-building and recommended 'assemblage' as a corrective device. Basically, the deficiency of system-building resides in the fact that it unavoidably limits the scope of inquiry 'by trying to force every kind of experience into a particular systematic pattern'. What is necessary hence is to find a way of 'widening our philosophical horizons', based on the recognition that our experience is broader than our systematic grasp. In Whitehead's own words, there is in all systematic thought a profound tendency of exclusion, of the 'putting aside of notions, of experiences, and of suggestions, with the prime excuse that, of course, we are not thinking of such things'. In *Modes of Thought* he calls this the 'pedantry' of systematic philosophy.[12]

In a way, Whitehead's notion of assemblage constitutes a kind of immanent *a priori* (as invoked by Daya Krishna)—but not in the sense of a Kantian condition of possibility. According to *Modes of Thought*, assemblage constitutes the 'first chapter in philosophic approach', but only in an inchoate, experiential manner; it allows (he says) for 'a free examination of some ultimate notions as they occur naturally in daily life'. In Ramchandra's reading, what Whitehead is suggesting is 'not a Kantian inquiry' designed to uncover 'the *a priori* system of presuppositions of experience'—for the simple reason that assemblage is 'not a systematic inquiry'. From a certain angle, assemblage is akin to a 'commonsense' mode of reasoning because commonsense shuns apodictic convictions and is full of 'shifts of interest and standpoint'. What Ramchandra finds particularly appealing in the commonsense approach is its tolerance of diversity and its taste for overflowing abundance. 'Commonsense is open-minded', he states; 'it has freer access to a variety of philosophical ideas'. In the ordinary course of experience and thinking, we are not tempted 'to downgrade the importance of an experience or idea for the sake of vested metaphysical interests'. Where commonsense is somewhat deficient in comparison with assemblage is in its inability to bring diverse experiences together in a loose web of significance; in fact, interrelatedness of meanings 'takes commonsense by surprise', especially when familiar notions resurface in unfamiliar contexts without sharp rupture. 'The aphoristic profundity of mystics and poets and some philosophers', Gandhi writes pointedly, 'consists in just this ability of theirs to reveal unsuspected relationships between familiar notions of large and adequate metaphysical generality'.[13]

As these comments indicate, assemblage for Gandhi is a source of inspiration, a resource of innovative discovery and disclosure which can never be exhaustively mapped by cognitive reason. In Whitehead's own words, the achievement of assemblage is 'novelty and disclosure', not 'coherence and systematization'; when approached in a tentative, experimental way, aspects 'hitherto dismissed as casual irrelevancies' are lifted into 'coordinated experience' or a web of significance. In contrast to the orderly overview provided by cognitive rationality, assemblage in its best moments yields 'chance flashes of insight' in areas which are 'large, ill-defined, and not controlled by any explicit boundary'. Ramchandra speaks in this context of 'the anarchic poetic approach of assemblage' which on occasion overcomes us with the 'surprise of a revelation'. At another point, he refers to assemblage as 'the natural response of our reflective consciousness to a world that exceeds us on all sides', a response cultivated especially (though not exclusively) by poets and mystics. Being attentive to ongoing experience is a lifelong endeavour and task; in a similar manner, the work of philosophical assemblage is unending and cannot reach final completion. As Gandhi emphasizes, following Whitehead, completeness and finality are the ideals of systematic philosophy—which ultimately is a subject for specialists. Philosophic assemblage, on the other hand, is an ordinary, non-academic practice; more than that: it is 'a habit of mind—the habit of striving after adequate generality of understanding which should receive the attention of every educated mind in its "escape from its own specialization"'. As Gandhi adds (picking up a theme dear to Daya Krishna),

'It is the essence of civilization to cultivate this habit of escaping from the narrowness of understanding.' Indeed, quoting Whitehead: 'It is civilization. . . . Civilized beings are those who survey the world with some large generality of understanding.'[14]

Apart from relying on Whiteheadean philosophy, Gandhi's *Two Essays* also invoked the testimony of Wittgenstein, William James and some (unspecified) phenomenologists and existentialists as pointing in the same direction.[15] Given this philosophical background, it is hardly surprising that Gandhi's thinking was led to a consideration of religion or religiosity—the latter seen not as a dogmatic belief system nor as an academic specialty but as a mode of experience. Just as, in Whitehead's account, assemblage was not the antithesis but the corollary and presupposition of philosophical inquiry, religious experience for Ramchandra constituted a recessed matrix and penumbra of philosophical thought—and hence a legitimate topic of reflection. The main results of his reflections in this area were a series of essays published together under the title *The Availability of Religious Ideas* (1976). Although acknowledging that religion or religious experience can be approached in different ways—for instance, as a set of shared beliefs in a community or as an academic subject matter—the Introduction to the book insists that the same experience is not antithetical to, but rather a legitimate partner of philosophy, more specifically the philosophy of religion. As Ramchandra points out, in light of these considerations, one might define the philosophy of religion, or an essential aspect of it, as follows: 'We might say that one is doing philosophy of religion when one seeks to understand the character of philosophical problems in relation to dominant, fundamental, religious ideas, and vice versa.' Understanding religious experience in this manner rests on the assumption or else belief 'that philosophical reflection and religious ideas are [not mutually exclusive but] available to one another in a mutually illuminating way' quite outside the range of communally shared doctrines or specialized academic research programmes.[16]

Among the 'available' religious ideas discussed in the book are such notions as the soul, immortality, God, prayer, the mystical, the miraculous and others—an array of themes whose subtle exploration far exceeds the scope of these pages. What I want to highlight here are some basic guideposts orienting the study. A crucial guidepost is the idea of a certain 'givenness' of experience, the idea that dimensions of experience are 'given' to and not constituted by consciousness; and that this givenness can further be qualified as relational and non-atomistic.

'The central philosophical conviction which sustains practically the whole of this book', Ramchandra writes, 'is that in the most fundamental sense of the word "given", what is given for philosophical reflection is the communicative form of human life'. Self-consciousness itself emerges from this primary communicative relationality; likewise, ethics or morality is wholly derived from the 'principles of caring' (echoes of Heidegger?) inherent in this communicative situation. Significantly, for Gandhi, relational communication extends to the realm of the divine—which implies 'the possibility of calling upon God without being under an obligation to first establish his reality', that is, 'the possibility and legitimacy of agnostic prayer'. Another, closely connected guidepost of the study is the primacy of being and doing over knowing and reasoning. In Gandhi's words, contrary to popular misconceptions, '*being a human being* or *being myself* is not an experience of mine to which I have an inward [cognitive] access' or which I can understand by introspection. Following Wittgenstein and others one must rather say 'that consciousness is a mode of being, not a mode of knowing, and that the character of concepts like "I", "You", "He", etc., can only be grasped by appropriate [semantic] analysis'. This argument carries over to the idea of the soul, which Gandhi describes as 'the idea of that as which we imaginatively see one another in acts of addressing one another'.[17]

A further important guidepost—perhaps overshadowing all the rest—is the notion of an inexhaustible assemblage, of an elusive 'wholeness' resisting cognitive grasp. Commenting on a possible meaning of the 'mystical', Ramchandra writes: 'There is the notion of the totality of all actual and possible states of affairs which is implicated in the notion of any particular set of actual and possible states of affairs.' The decisive consideration here is that 'nothing at all—nothing descriptive—can be said about the totality or system of all actual and possible states of affairs, for such a totality must be inclusive of all objects of description'. What follows from this is that the notion of totality or a totalizing system is (what one may call) 'a notion of the mystical—an essentially incomprehensible and yet ineliminable notion'. Closely akin to totality or totalizing system is the notion of 'absolute nothingness' which—Gandhi says—is 'implicated in every affirmative existential judgment to the effect that something, *as opposed to nothing*, exists'. This idea of absolute nothingness is a corollary of comprehensive being and, as such, again 'incomprehensible and yet ineliminable'. Based on the inevitable excess of assemblage over cognition—evident in the totality of being and radical nothingness—Gandhi rejects a positivist (or 'ontic') immanentism neglectful of this excess. 'Underlying all the essays of this book', he writes, 'is a rejection of what might be called "the immanentist view of the world and human life"'. This view expresses itself in statements like these: 'This world is all that there is', or 'This life of mine, terminated by my death, is all there is of "me"'. In opposing this view, Gandhi minces no words: 'I argue that the immanentist view of the world and human life is unacceptable not because it is a demonstrably false philosophical view, but because it is essentially unintelligible' (both religiously and philosophically).[18]

As one should note, Ramchandra's critique of positivist immanentism does not amount to an endorsement of rigid transcendentalism—an alternative which would split asunder heaven and earth, the divine and the human, the sacred and the secular. Together with these polarities, his thinking also is opposed to all other dualisms, like those between subject and object, self and other, friend and enemy. For this reason, his thought finds its proper place in the tradition of Advaita Vedānta—where advaita can be translated as 'non-dualism' (without complete synthesis), as differentiated unity or holistic difference (or what I have called 'integral pluralism'). In Gandhi's own words: 'Dualism is the conviction that self and not-self are everywhere pitted against one another'—that is, 'individual human beings against one another and against human collectivities; human collectivities against one another and against individual human beings'. But the range of dualism reaches even further into all areas of reality, pitting 'living species against one another; the human species against all other living species; all life against matter; all existence against nothingness'. Relentlessly pursued, the upshot of dualism is the 'temptation of annihilation' and 'despairing destructiveness'—a temptation 'now unfurling in all societies on an unprecedented scale' prompting a readiness 'to destroy all life and civilization on earth'.[19]

In the Indian context, dualistic destructiveness in recent times reached a pinnacle of frenzy in the town of Ayodhya, the reputed birthplace of Lord Rāma and also the site of an old mosque, the so-called 'Babri' or 'Bābarī masjid' (named after the Muslim conqueror Babar). At the height of the Hindu–Muslim conflict, Ramchandra visited Ayodhya to gain some first-hand experience; the result was a series of reflections which were published under the title *Sita's Kitchen: A Testimony of Faith and Inquiry* (1992; the preceding citations are from this text). What he discovered on his visit was evidence—generally acknowledged—that materials of an older Hindu temple had been used in the construction of the Babri mosque. But he discovered also something not generally known: namely, that the precinct of the temple-mosque also contained remnants of a still older shrine designated as '*Sīta kī rasoī*' and reputed to have been the kitchen of Rāma's wife and consort Sītā. The discovery triggered in him a deeper insight into the meaning of non-dualism or advaita: a meaning where heaven and earth, sacred and mundane are conjoined or entwined. The name 'Sita's Kitchen' (or rather its Hindi original), he writes, suggests 'an ambience of domesticity and divinity which happily includes the notion of an actual kitchen where Godhead-incarnate Sītā cooked delicious and nutritious food for the Raghava household' [of her husband], but which also 'stretches all the way beyond that architectural idea to the archetypal notion of the earth as the Divine Mother's laboratory of manifestation and field of nourishment for all self-images of self'. For Ramchandra, the status of Sītā in fact far exceeds her role as Rāma's wife and consort. As he states, in the spirit of Vaishnava religiosity, she is 'only in manifestation' his consort; in actuality, she is 'Mahalakshmi, Godhead', and her kitchen is 'the entire field of her self-imaging *Shakti* [divine energy], powerfully represented on earth. [For] it is on earth, in the embrace of the Divine Mother, that all are born, all creatures great and small, all forms manifest, noble or evil; and all are nourished'.[20]

Transgressing the bounds of Hindu religiosity, Ramchandra's reflections on Ayodhya have a genuinely ecumenical cast. During his stay there he remembered, perchance, his student days in Oxford and his visits to the university's oldest church, St Mary's. As it happens, that church more recently had installed a mural painting showing Mahatma Gandhi in a cross-legged posture with upraised arms. In Ramchandra's interpretation, the raised hands can be seen as highlighting Gandhi's non-dualism and rejection of exclusive identities: for, 'he was a Hindu, but insisted that he was simultaneously also a Muslim, Christian, Jew, Buddhist, Jaina, etc.—a believer in the truth of all faiths'. He also 'loved fellow human beings as himself, and had no difficulty in honoring their deepest concerns as his own'. Viewed against this background, the mural in St Mary's carries a strong interfaith significance: it 'draws attention to the neglected dimension of Christ's teaching that man does not live by bread alone, but by every word that proceeds from the mouth of God'. At this point, the old church in Oxford is subtly transfigured into 'a non-dualist church of Atman-Brahman-Mary', a church whose generous 'kitchen' is able, without exclusivist denial, to offer 'the full range of truth's cuisine to spiritually starved humanity'. In addition to Christian resonances, the Ayodhya experience also reminded Ramchandra of crucial Buddhist insights, especially the notion of the interconnection and non-separateness of all beings:

> The Buddha's teaching of the inter-relatedness of all evanescent items and their situatedness within non-initiative emptiness (*sūnyata*) or nirvana is also wholly consonant with [the site's] vision of the vibrant interdependence of all forms of life and their location within the nourishing embrace of Mother Earth.[21]

The greatest significance of Ayodhya for Gandhi, however, resides in its status as testimonial of Hindu–Muslim non-dualism/advaita. In his words: 'Ayodhya today presents an aspect of otherness to Muslims which is as stark as the aspect of otherness under which Hindus see the Bābarī mosque towering over the city of Rāma.' Otherness—one should note well, however—does not mean here separateness or polarity, but rather difference or differential entwinement, a holistic or 'integral' kind of pluralism. To be sure, this entwinement has been strained and wounded by recent excesses of violence when thoughtful Hindus and Muslims were 'marginalized as bombs of hatred erupted in the sky'. Yet, the long history of Indian spirituality also carries within it a healing balm which now needs to be revived and cultivated. 'Indian spiritual self-knowledge', Gandhi writes, 'cannot become self-realization without encounter with non-Indian spiritual traditions, and without sharing space and time with them'. This consideration is particularly relevant to the site of the temple-mosque. There, 'held in topographical and historical embrace by the birthplace and kitchen zone of Ayodhya', the Babari mosque can be seen as evidence 'not of Hindu humiliation but of its venturesome sādhanā (spiritual quest) of self-realization'. At this point, Ramchandra's *Sita's Kitchen* adds a passage which can be read as a paean to religious and cultural pluralism and non-dualism:

> The Bābarī edifice is a testifying tree which bears the flowers of nearly five hundred years of Islamic piety, and of nearly fifty years of Hindu bhakti. It could have grown only in the sacred soil of Sita's Kitchen, and cannot be transplanted anywhere else. Certainly the tree bears thorns too, thorns of medieval and modern vandalism. But it can give shade to pilgrims weary of hatred in the name of the sacred for at least another half a millennium. . . . Hindus and Muslims must forgive each other's trespasses in Ayodhya, if they wish their trespasses against each other all over India to be forgiven.[22]

Figure and Ground

The preceding discussion, I assume, has brought out some of the similarities as well as some significant differences between the two Indian thinkers. Both thinkers, one might initially say, link philosophy with a form of liberation and emancipation (svarāj); but they do so with very distinct emphases. As I have indicated, Daya Krishna stands mainly in the tradition of critical philosophizing; hence, his accent tends to be on intellectual or rational liberation, on the refinement of self-consciousness through critical analysis and the demolition of unexamined prejudices. On the other hand, Ramchandra Gandhi's main concern is with the deepening and maturation of experience rather than rational cognition; hence, his philosophical trajectory points more in the direction of what one may call 'ontological' freedom or liberation—where freedom means not just the removal of external constraints but the transgression of the ego in favour of advaita (or the non-duality of being). The two modes of philosophizing cannot easily be reconciled. In the traditions of both Western and Eastern philosophizing the two modes have often stood in stark opposition and intense rivalry. However, it may perhaps be possible to detect in this case also a kind of non-dualism and intellectual mutuality (saṃvāda).

On another occasion, reflecting on the relation between Western and Indian philosophizing, I invoked some arguments on the topic advanced by the Indian poet and philosopher A. K. Ramanujan. In an essay titled 'Is There an Indian Way of Thinking?' Ramanujan had distinguished between text and context and, more specifically, between 'context-free' and 'context-sensitive' modes of philosophizing. As a trained linguist, he traced the distinction back to the difference between two kinds of grammatical rules: namely, rules that are context-free in the sense of being universally applicable, and rules that are context-sensitive in being closely tied to their concrete application. Moving boldly from grammar to culture, Ramanujan found an analogous distinction on the plane of cross-cultural comparison. 'I think cultures (may be said to) have overall tendencies', he wrote, 'tendencies to *idealize*, and think in terms of, either the context-free or the context-sensitive kind of rules. . . . In cultures like India's, the context-sensitive kind of rule is the preferred formulation.' In an effort to buttress this view, his essay gave a number of historical examples: ranging from Manu's legislation (where rules were typically made contingent on caste and status) to the great Indian epics *Ramāyaṇa* and *Mahābhārata* (where each individual story or narrative is embedded in a larger metanarrative which contextualizes and gives meaning to each tale). Proceeding to the modern and contemporary period, Ramanujan offered some striking comments on modernization (or Westernization) and comparative development theory. In contrast to the context-sensitivity of Indian culture, his essay portrayed modernity as wedded to decontextualization: 'One might see "modernization" in India as a movement from the context-sensitive to the context-free in all realms: an erosion of contexts, at least in principle. Gandhi's watch (with its uniform autonomous time) replaced the almanac.'[23]

Another key for grasping the cultural difference resided for Ramanujan in literary theory and especially in the vocabulary of literary tropes. In the case of Indian literature and thought, he found a tendency to privilege 'metonymy' (where a part 'stands in' for a larger whole) over other expressions. For example, the term 'man' or 'human being' there does not designate a creature which is separated from nature, but one which 'stands in' for nature and the cosmos. Seen as 'man in nature' or 'man in context', he observed, the human being is conceived as being 'continuous with the context s/he is in'. The same point can be made with the help of Peircean semiotics. In semiotic terms, he argued, Indian thought accords primacy to indexical signs over symbolic expressions, with 'indexes' taken to be signs where signifiers and signified 'belong to the same context', that is, where the signifier is not externally related to the signified (in a subject–object dualism) but is itself the intrinsic carrier of signification. (Thus, one might say that a figure of Śiva or Rāma or Sītā does not so much symbolize something else, but rather 'indicates' its own meaning.) Turning to the fields of logic and sociology, Ramanujan explicated context-sensitivity by pointing to the pervasive Hindu concern with *jati*, that is, with 'the logic of classes, of genera and species, of which human *jati*s are only an instance'. Each *jati* or class here 'defines a context, a structure of relevance, a rule of permissible combinations, a frame of reference'. By contrast, contextual relevance and any reference to particular circumstances are sidelined in context-free or universalizing social arrangements.[24]

In my earlier discussion of Ramanujan's text, I expressed my admiration, but also voiced some reservations (which I shall not rehearse here in detail). My qualms are basically of two kinds. First of all, the distinction elaborated by Ramanujan applies not only to the relation between India and the West, but can also be found in the Indian context itself—the incipient 'dialogue' between Daya Krishna and Ramchandra Gandhi being a prominent example. Second, the opposition between text and context, or between context-freedom and contextual sensitivity, still seems to suggest a kind of dualism where the two frameworks can be neatly separated from each other, neglecting their intimate entwinement and mutual implication. For this reason, I prefer to turn to the image of 'figure' and 'ground'—an image introduced by *Gestalt* psychology but radically reformulated by Maurice Merleau-Ponty. In his *Phenomenology of Perception*, Merleau-Ponty criticized traditional rationalist philosophy —what he calls 'intellectualism'—for trying to articulate a universal and apodictic type of knowledge severed from perceptual experience. Practised in this manner, he noted, philosophy no longer seeks to account for concrete perception, but aims 'to coincide with and understand the perceptual process' epistemologically. The basic yardstick for this kind of undertaking is modern science and its cognitive achievements. In Merleau-Ponty's words: 'The real sin of intellectualism lies in having taken as its datum the determinate universe of science', that is, a universe of objects governed by external cause–effect relations. Against this epistemological stance, his text pits the experience of precognitive perception, an experience thematized by phenomenology in the wake of Husserl's work. From the phenomenological angle, there is 'a significance of perception which is not equivalent to the universe of [rational] cognition, a perceptual domain which is not yet the "objective" world, a perceptual being which is not yet determinate being'.[25]

As Merleau-Ponty acknowledged, it was *Gestalt* theory which has pointed a way beyond intellectualism. For, as that theory has shown, 'the alleged signs of [physical] distance'—such as the apparent size of the object or the number of objects interposed between it and us—are expressly known only in 'analytic cognition' which turns away from phenomena in favour of their objective presentation. In challenging this approach, *Gestalt* theory has brought to the fore 'the tensions which run like force lines across the visual field' and 'which breathe into it a secret and magic life by exerting here and there forces of distortion, contraction, and expansion'. Yet, despite these achievements, *Gestalt* psychology has not lived up to its promise. By retreating into sense-data empiricism, the theory construed bodily stimuli as external 'causes' rather than seeing them as 'signs or reasons'. With this construal, Merleau-Ponty notes, we are back in 'explanatory psychology' whose ideal was never abandoned by *Gestalt* theory 'because, as psychology, it has never broken with naturalism'. At this point, a bolder step is needed, a 'complete reform of understanding' which would allow us 'to translate phenomena accurately'. *Phenomenology of Perception* is uncompromising in staking out the different path to be followed. If we wish to grasp phenomena properly, we read, 'the objective thinking of classical logic and philosophy will have to be questioned, the categories of the [empirical] world laid aside . . . and a true "phenomenological reduction" undertaken'. Once such steps are undertaken, what comes into view is the role of a '*non-positing* consciousness', a consciousness 'not in possession of fully determinate objects'. At the same time, what emerges is a new figure–ground relation which cannot be reduced to a cause–effect nexus. Figure/ground here means 'a *logic lived through* which cannot account for itself', an '*immanent meaning* which is not clear to itself and becomes fully aware of itself only through experiencing certain natural signs'.[26]

The path sketched in *Phenomenology of Perception* was pursued and further elaborated in Merleau-Ponty's subsequent writings, especially in a series of essays published under the title *Sense and Non-Sense*. As the translators of the book point out in their Preface, Merleau-Ponty at that point drew inspiration from recent developments in philosophy and the human sciences—including Husserl's phenomenology, Heidegger's existential ontology, and the insights of *Gestalt* psychology—in order to articulate his own complex account of 'order in the perceptual world'. From the later Husserl he learned that rationality and meaning are not 'given beforehand' but emergent qualities of perception. Likewise, with *Gestalt* theorists he assumed that 'we *discover* meanings by responding to solicitations already in our experience'. The main insight he adopted from them was that 'whenever I perceive, I perceive a figure on a ground'. Thus, a spot on a page 'appears to be *on* the page' in the sense that the paper is perceived as present behind the spot. However, a more subtle relation is involved: 'Whatever appears suggests in its very appearance something more which does not appear, which is concealed.' For this reason, 'the figure can be said to have a meaning since . . . it refers beyond what is immediately given'. Reformulated in a more philosophical vein, this insight resonates with Heidegger's notion of the relation between revealment and concealment, between presence and absence (what Merleau-Ponty later will call the 'visible' and the 'invisible'). Without pursuing these ontological implications, the Preface leaves no doubt about Merleau-Ponty's affinity with Heidegger's work. 'Following Heidegger', it states, he 'calls the activity of organizing the world by responding to it from within "being-in-the-world" or "ek-sistence"'.[27]

Heideggerian affinities are particularly evident in *Sense and Non-Sense* in an essay dealing with the recessed ontological status of human beings (labelled, or perhaps mislabelled, there 'the metaphysical in man'). What Heidegger portrayed as the constitutive openness of human *Dasein* to 'being' (in its many forms), Merleau-Ponty describes as the basic human responsiveness to a broad range of experiences exceeding the grasp of rational-scientific cognition. As in *Phenomenology of Perception*, scientific knowledge is presented here as a limited mode of reasoning embedded—as in the figure–ground relationship—in a broad welter of uncharted and precognitive experience. In its ideal aspiration, Merleau-Ponty observes, science always 'takes for granted an absolute observer in whom all points of view are summed up', thus offering 'a true projection of all perspectives'. This projection, however, is not possible in the properly human world, and especially in the context of human interactions. Far from being an emblem of pure rationality, inter-human relations involve an ambivalent mutual exploration: namely, 'the taking up by each, *as best one can*, of the acts of others, reactivating from ambiguous signs an experience which is not strictly one's own'. At this point, we are no longer confronting external objects, but enter into 'communication with ways of being'. Seen from this angle, the lived world is not just a string of data amenable to 'systemic' cognition; rather, it 'recovers its texture', that is, its density as well as its depth. In Merleau-Ponty's words, existential phenomenology is not merely an inquiry seeking to 'complete the edifice of [scientific] knowledges', but rather offers a 'lucid familiarity' with the limits of these knowledges while remaining 'acutely aware' of their worth. This familiarity is not 'a little truth' for which we have to 'make room in some nook or cranny of the "system"'; it is the condition of our being-in-the-world.[28]

The preceding excursions into the writings of Ramanujan and Merleau-Ponty were undertaken for a point: the endeavour to find a bridge correlating the different philosophical agendas of Daya Krishna and Ramchandra Gandhi. Clearly, these agendas cannot neatly be synchronized or synthesized (especially not in an overarching 'system'). At the same time, however, their philosophical orientations are not simply antithetical or mutually exclusive. In my view, and as I have tried to show, the two agendas may be said to reflect a differentiated non-dualism (or else an 'integral pluralism') allowing for at least a limited form of dialogue (saṃvāda). My own preference is to see the non-dualism in terms of the figure–ground relationship as articulated by Merleau-Ponty. While, in the majority of his writings, Daya Krishna aimed at the progressive refinement of consciousness and critical rationality (largely in the tradition of Kant and Husserl), Ramchandra Gandhi sought pathways to the exploration of precognitive experience (enlisting for this purpose the testimony of Whitehead and William James as well as older Indian wisdom traditions). As it seems to me, both agendas aim at human freedom or liberation (svarāj), but they do so on different levels: the levels respectively of human reason (freedom from prejudices) and of ontological being (freedom from self-centredness). The two levels surely are in tension with each other, but do not ultimately contradict each other (as both Whitehead and Ramchandra agreed). Most importantly, the two perspectives are linked in their opposition to the reigning 'realist' creed of dualism, the Hobbesian war of all against all. In Ramchandra's words (echoing the teachings of his grandfather): this creed reflects ultimately the temptation of 'annihilation and despairing destructiveness', a temptation 'now unfurling in all societies on an unprecedented scale' prompting a readiness 'to destroy all life and civilization on earth'.

Notes and References

1. This is a revised version of a chapter that appeared in my book, *Integral Pluralism: Beyond Culture Wars* (Kentucky: The University Press of Kentucky, 2010).
2. Daya Krishna, *Indian Philosophy: A Counter Perspective* (New Delhi: Oxford University Press, 1991), pp. 3, 6, 23–24.
3. Ibid., pp. 14–15, 29.
4. Ibid., pp. 32, 63, 164, 170. On the topic of Vedānta, Krishna's comments are most stern and uncompromising (p. 170): 'The search for the meaning of Vedānta leads nowhere. . . . The most haloed term of Indian philosophical thought connotes nothing. It is an empty shell, mere verbiage, an absolute nothing. . . . Let us be serious. Let us banish it.' In the concluding chapter Krishna likewise deconstructs the traditional notion of the '*puruṣārthas*' or goals of life, stating (p. 205) that the notion 'has no place for the independent life of reason as a separate value. . . . This is a grave deficiency.'
5. Daya Krishna, *New Perspectives in Indian Philosophy* (Jaipur and New Delhi: Rawat Publications, 2001), pp. 3, 5.
6. Ibid., pp. 8–11.
7. Daya Krishna, *Prolegomena to Any Future Historiography of Cultures and Civilizations*, 2nd edition (New Delhi: Centre for Studies in Civilizations, 2005), pp. xii–xiv, 2. As he adds (pp. 2–3): 'The deepest understanding of any culture or civilization relates to the role of consciousness in the

maintenance, reproduction, and transmission of the symbols generated by it for conveying to other consciousnesses what it considers worthwhile and important.' (In the above I have put 'man' in apostrophes to indicate the intended gender neutrality.) Regarding precedents of this outlook, see Immanuel Kant, 'Idea for a Universal History with Cosmopolitan Purpose' (1784), in *Kant's Political Writings*, ed. Hans Reiss (Cambridge, UK: Cambridge University Press, 1970), pp. 41–53; and Edmund Husserl, 'Vienna Lecture: Philosophy and the Crisis of European Humanity' (1935), in *The Crisis of European Sciences and Transcendental Philosophy*, trans. David Carr (Evanston, IL: Northwestern University Press, 1970), pp. 269–299, where Husserl elaborated the idea of Europe 'as the historical teleology of the infinite goals of reason' (p. 299).

8. Krishna, *Prolegomena*, pp. 64, 80, 83. Applying these observations to the relations between 'West' and 'non-West', the study remarks (p. 216):

> The encounter of all past civilizations with the modern Western one is bound to result in the unfoldment of new potentialties in the valuational projects and visions of those civilizations and radically modify them, just as a new metaphor unfolds hidden meanings that were unsuspected before the creative writer used it for the first time.

9. Krishna, *Prolegomena*, pp. 84–85. At a later point (p. 262), Krishna defines civilizational history explicitly as a history of consciousness:

> The history of consciousness as it has evolved and changed and developed in 'human beings' has to be brought to self-consciousness and accepted by it, however reluctant such acceptance may be. This is, or should be, the real task of history and historiography as 'man' has to see himself as an 'essentially changing being' whose central fulcrum lies in his own consciousness as it can try to change itself self-consciously if it wishes to do so.

10. Krishna, *Prolegomena*, pp. xi, 16, 262, 279. Compare also this comment (p. 260):

> If the 'reality' of either the 'outer' or the 'inner' cannot be denied, nor the inter-relationship between them or the transformations and changes that these undergo all the time bringing radical changes in both the 'outer' and 'inner', then how can one meaningfully talk of 'man's' identity or the truth about him? The truth, if any, is in the 'situation' itself which, however, is ever changing.

11. Admittedly, the above presentation concentrates on a central strand in Krishna's work, while sidelining other dimensions or intellectual concerns.

One such concern was the Indian tradition of *bhakti* religiosity whose discussion was the topic of a learned gathering organized by him—and whose essence he located in a subjective 'inner' feeling of possibly universal significance. See Daya Krishna, Mukund Lath and Francine E. Krishna, eds, *Bhakti: A Contemporary Discussion* (New Delhi: Indian Council of Philosophical Research, 2000), especially pp. 65–70. A related concern which came to the fore mainly in his later life was aesthetics, with an emphasis on music (where, as far as I can see, Kant's *Critique of Judgment* remained canonical).

12. Ramchandra Gandhi, *Two Essays on Whitehead's Philosophic Approach* (Shimla: Indian Institute of Advanced Study, 1973), pp. v, 2–3. The citation is from Whitehead, *Modes of Thought* (Cambridge, UK: Cambridge University Press, 1938), p. 2.
13. Ibid., pp. 4, 6–7.
14. Ibid., *Two Essays*, pp. 8, 18, 24. The citation is from Whitehead, *Modes of Thought*, p. 5.
15. In his *Philosophical Investigations*, the later Wittgenstein famously defined the work of philosophy as consisting in 'assembling reminders'. See *Philosophical Investigations* (Oxford: Blackwell, 1953), p. 50. Regarding William James, Gandhi (p. 20) cites Whitehead's comments to the effect that 'he systematized; but above all he assembled. His intellectual life was one protest against *the dismissal of experience in the interest of system*'.
16. Ramchandra Gandhi, *The Availability of Religious Ideas* (New York: Harper & Row, 1976), p. 3.
17. Ibid., pp. 4, 9. Regarding ethics as a mode of communicative relationship, Gandhi adds (pp. 5–6):

> Now an act of addressing has significant moral, and not merely metaphysical, features. In addressing you, I seek, solicit a communicative response from you, I do not merely causally interact with you. And I cannot solicit a communicative response from you . . . without exhibiting minimal care for you [echoes of Heidegger again?]. Thus, insofar as I think the communicative thought 'you', I minimally value you. . . . And I cannot think the thought 'I' without casting myself as the object of another's caring communicative attention.

18. Ibid., pp. 8–9. Regarding 'nothingness' as 'inhilation' see Martin Heidegger, 'What Is Metaphysics?', in *Martin Heidegger: Basic Writings*, ed. David F. Krell (New York: Harper and Row, 1977), pp. 95–112. The idea of an 'incomprehensible and yet ineliminable' notion finds a parallel in the work Nicolaus of Cusa. See in this regard my 'Wise Ignorance: Nicolaus of Cusa's Search for Truth', in *In Search of the Good Life: A Pedagogy for Troubled Times* (Lexington, KY: University of Kentucky Press, 2007), pp. 58–79.

19. Ramchandra Gandhi, *Sita's Kitchen: A Testimony of Faith and Inquiry* (Albany, NY: State University of New York Press, 1992), pp. 18–19.
20. *Sita's Kitchen*, pp. 15–16.
21. Ibid., pp. 9–10, 22.
22. Ibid., pp. 13, 17–18. With specific reference to *bhakti*, the text comments (p. 17):

    The Bābarī mosque's medieval trespass into the kitchen area dramatizes the entry of Sufism into the corpus of Indian mysticism. Indeed, the cognateness of Abrahamic mysticism in general, and not only Sufism, with Hindu, aboriginal, and Buddhist mysticism is powerfully suggested by the continuity of the mosque's inner space of objectlessness with the void of the kitchen zone, which is continuous with the sphericality of the earth and with surrounding emptiness. And this continuity . . . is deeply evocative of ahiṃsā or non-violence, the virtue emphasized centrally by Jainism and savingly by Gandhi in our annihilationist age.

23. A. K. Ramanujan, 'Is There an Indian Way of Thinking? An Informal Essay', in *India Through Hindu Categories*, ed. McKim Marriott (New Delhi: SAGE Publications, 1990), pp. 46–49, 54–55. For my discussion see 'Western Thought and Indian Thought: Some Comparative Steps' in my book *Beyond Orientalism: Essays on Cross-Cultural Encounter* (Albany, NY: State University of New York Press, 1996), pp. 135–147.
24. Ramanujan, 'Is There an Indian Way of Thinking?' pp. 50, 52–53. On *jati* compare Harold A. Gould's essay 'Toward a "Jati Model" for Indian Politics' in his book *Caste Adaptation in Modernizing Indian Society* (Delhi: Chanakya Publishers, 1988), pp. 171–185.
25. Maurice Merleau-Ponty, *Phenomenology of Perception*, trans. Colin Smith (London: Routledge & Kegan Paul, 1962), pp. 46–47.
26. Ibid., pp. 47–49.
27. Hubert L. Dreyfus and Patricia A. Dreyfus, 'Translators' Introduction', in Maurice Merleau-Ponty, *Sense and Non-Sense* (Evanston, IL: Northwestern University Press, 1964), pp. x–xi.
28. Merleau-Ponty, 'The Metaphysical in Man', in *Sense and Non-Sense*, pp. 93, 95–96. To underscore the difference between such inquiry and rationalist 'system'-building, he adds (p. 94): 'If system is an arrangement of concepts which makes all the aspects of experience immediately compatible and compossible, then it suppresses metaphysical [ontological] awareness and, moreover, does away with ethics at the same time.' As it appears, the meaning of 'metaphysics' here was borrowed from Henri Bergson, *An Introduction to Metaphysics*, trans. T. E. Hulme (Indianapolis: Bobbs-Merrill, 1912).

2

Ram*līlā*: A Metaphysics of the Everyday

Anuradha Veeravalli

It could be no whim or accident that Ramchandra Gandhi named his daughter Leela. *Līlā* or 'play' is central to his understanding of the advaitic point of view as it presents itself in this world. The term 'Ram*līlā*' is therefore very close to Ramchandra Gandhi, the person and philosopher, too close to be just a clever pun.

A master punster himself, his puns too are of a cosmic, cosmological dimension. *I am Thou* begins with a dedication to Bose saheb and a reminiscence of the 'sunshine winter hours' of cricket-watching at the St Stephen's college cricket ground. Meditating on the quintessential play of non-dualism and dialogue that undegenerate cricket presupposes, democratic in structure and principle, with its inclusion of the audience as participant in the role of witnessing fielder and batsmen that enjoy second innings like souls reincarnate, he in one sweep, transfigures a lazy cricket ground to a self-consciousness of its metaphysical and civilizational implications, the macrocosmic in the microcosmic. In contrast is the egoistic and vindictive play of dualism in the lap of the perpetual possibility of non-dualistic play or *līlā*. 'All I for an I.'

Recounting an actual/(possible?) story of his friend, U. R. Ananthmurthy, introducing himself to a fellow delegate at an international conference, Ramchandra Gandhi pictured him shaking hands while he is supposed to have said, 'U. R. Ananthmurty'. His fellow delegate responded, insisting, '(U) You (R) are Ananthmurthy!' While few will disagree that Ramchandra Gandhi was one of the most creative philosophers that India has produced in the twentieth century, most choose to clearly distinguish his earlier work, associated more clearly with the academic philosophy of the University, from what they see as the 'ramblings' of the later years. I see him rather as someone who systematically, and persistently, looked at the world and therefore all philosophical issues, from an advaitic point of view, unfettered by a given 'authentic' traditional system of thought, or mere spiritualism. If there is one economical way of describing Ramchandra Gandhi's philosophical calling it would be his engagement with a metaphysics of the everyday. Thus it is the experiments with the method of Advaita that make it natural, and logically inevitable that the duality of the everyday must be confronted again and again, and again. For, the first question that must arise for one who believes that there is only one, and no second, no other, is the duality of and in the everyday. It is a challenge that cannot be ignored, and without meeting which, he cannot proceed. He would have to be relentless in meeting the challenge of dualism, everyday, again and again.

His response to this challenge is in terms of a theory of communication variously called love and play, which alone can display and overcome the apparent dualism of the everyday. This is what engages him right through his so-called 'analytic' as also his so-called 'rambling phase'. I suggest the focus and method of the engagement underwent no fundamental change through these phases except for becoming more persistent, thoroughgoing, and systematic, even feverish perhaps, as he proceeded to explore newer territories and issues in the metaphysics of religion, politics, literature and art. The theory of communication he proposes enables the daily practice of Advaita on the basis of two presuppositions:

1. The logical assumption of difference or the multi-centeredness of the self, or one may like to call it, a principle of unity in plurality.
2. The logical assumption that the perceived existence of others or otherness was an illusion.

> What appears in the world as human communication is the marvellous many-centred overcoming of the illusion that there are others, and the marvellous discovery that the place where 'others' appear to be is where we are ourselves, in addition to the place we take ourselves bodily to be. History and contemporaneity are a realization of advaita in combat and communication.[1]

This is what makes his point of view at once distinct from the orthodox *maṭha*, and from the insipid advaitic abstractions taught at the University. His discomfort, sometimes antagonism with the University was due to its inability to accept non-dualism as a point of view and method, but above all, I suspect, due to the dry unimaginative humourlessness of the everyday routine that made one numb and oblivious to the possibilities of its *līlā* and magic. Yet perhaps, he was his sharpest best at the university—the home of the dualists, where he honed and practiced his non-dualist skill in arguments with them.

The *ashram* or the *maṭha* on the other hand, presented a 'self'-obsession that excluded the other rather than 'addressed' it, the *līlā* of the world thus escaping it, as well. The orthodox *advaitin* would willingly join the dualist orientalist academic in arguing that if we accept the existence of *ātman-Brahman* then the existence of the world would be a contradiction. At any rate, to expect *Brahman* to mess around with the world—would it not be an act of impurity, inauspicious? He hears the dualist voice in both the orthodox *advaitin* and the scholar *pandit* saying,

> But should not that which is not Ātman-Brahman be formally an impossibility, a flat contradiction, unencounterable? Would not Parabrahma be spared the pain of saving the world and the labour of making jñanīs of unpromising jīvas were this the case, were it impossible for not-self to be encountered?

And his response is uncompromising, 'But this would be monstrously presumptuous to try to pity Parabrahmā, we must think again as to why not-self is encountered and encountered in all imaginable dimensions of pain and terror and defeat and loss.'[2]

It is that relentless struggle and tension between the oneness of *Ātman-Brahman* in its many centeredness and the tumultuous *māyā* of the everyday that he sought to witness and understand, often himself overwhelmed, and not unbroken, by the cosmic enormity of it all.

> Oneness is not exclusive of play, the play of world appearance, or the play of human life in intricate communication and co-operation. The intensity of the play, its darker and more traumatic acts and scenes, often camouflage the underlying oneness of which the world and human life are a play or a display; but without the oneness the display would be unintelligible and not only unbearable, rather it would be unbearable because essentially unintelligible. Two cannot play, they can only fight and destroy one another in gross or subtle ways. One alone can in play appear to

be two and play the great games and unfold the drama of recovery of self-knowledge.[3]

Intelligibility is the key here so that a twosome signals a breakdown of communication, a path of self-destruction, unless witnessed by their oneness. This forms the basis of Ramchandra Gandhi's fundamental thesis that the essential nature of language is communicative; it presupposes and signals the overcoming of the dualism of consciousness and the world—a resuming of the disrupted play, the deadlock reached between the hermeneutic and the analytic traditions in Western thought. Thus neither language and ostensive reference, nor language and self consciousness, are the focus of his analysis. His theory of language is formulated as an invitation to both to reassume play at Tiruvannamalai under the witnessing eye of Ramana whose provocative thesis that the heart is on the right side of the human body, defies the referential tangibility of the biological heart, as well as its vulnerability. This explains Ramchandra Gandhi's wish that Wittgenstein, and Camus and Simone Weil, had met Ramana. The essential nature of language is thus neither referential nor self-referential, but one of 'addressing' the other, presupposing the identification and invoking of oneself and other selves, as none other than a third, witness of oneself, and the other—

> The foundation of all human communication is addressing, the vocative identification of one another by human beings, that is the identification of one another not as beings of this or that kind, possessing this or that characteristic, but as themselves, nirguna centres of self-consciousness.[4]

If there is but one doubt about the systematic nature of this experiment and method of analysis, it is in the uneasiness one feels about the exclusively human-centric nature of Ramchandra Gandhi's understanding of 'communication'. One brief chapter, 'The world speaks to us' in *I am Thou* attempts to confront this problem. The world speaks to us and is in constant play with us 'quite simply because the only conceivable alternative to play would be our instant destruction'. Invoking Kant's dictum that 'all knowledge arises from experience but is not derived from it', he impresses upon it a communicative interpretation. The world disavows causal efficacy because it only occasions experience and does not coerce it. The transformation of world-experience to insight and knowledge is proof of this fundamental disavowal of causal efficacy, and confirms the truth that the world communicates with us. The growth of insight and knowledge into this communication lies in our progressive realization that the world is one with us, 'The world speaks to us; and as a speaker is Brahman, is real, not neither-real-nor-unreal-Maya. And advaita is its secret teaching in mauna (silence).'

But Ramchandra Gandhi sees the inherent problem of this position since the truth of Advaita seems to succeed only within the bounds of communication as speech and silence. What do we make of the instrumentalities of communication? Are writing, letter inscriptions, making, the visual arts, architecture, 'for all their magnificence and ingenuity, an apparent metaphysical failure?' Beginning with the question of the non-representational nature of representational forms, he, in response, lays the foundations for a metaphysical, advaitic theory of art criticism, the possibilities of which he explores in incisive, insightful and exhilarating critiques of the works of painters ranging from Nasreen Muhammadi's line drawings to Ram Kumar, Rabindranath Tagore and, of course, Tyeb Mehta.

But this is to turn the question around and discuss perhaps, non-representational form rather than the nature of representational form, that is, the nature of name and form itself, which is so crucial to our understanding of the physical sciences, a question he promises Advaita can address in the early chapters of *I am Thou*. It is a theme he never really seems to come back to, though one may say that he saw and articulated the possibility of its cosmological foundations. Is the silence on science, as he himself asks and answers in the case of representational forms of communication, a defeat or retreat that is inevitable? I ask this question at the risk of sounding like the proverbial Oliver Twist asking for more, after partaking of a veritable advaitic feast, if only to extend an invitation to have Ramchandra Gandhi back in the University, and for us to join in saṃvāda and *sambodhana*, to resume play.

Perhaps, one may suggest, it is not enough to see that it is that beyond name and form that we address, but also that it is only through and by name and form that we can address and invoke, and therefore that they are signs of the covenant of God, man and nature, of the unity in plurality, and plurality in unity. The offices of the trinity in Hindu theology thus can be seen to address the possibility of plurality in unity so that we may be able to invoke one another by name—Brahmā as conceiver of names and forms, Viṣṇu as the spirit that pervades all names and forms, and Maheṣa, the destroyer of the 'dualism' of unity and plurality, the unmanifest and the manifest, and thus witness to the potency of the name. If the trinity make possible the articulation of the plurality in unity, the three modes of knowing, or we may say, of *līlā* , that is, *jñāna*, *karma* and bhakti, enable man, or make intelligible to him the unity in plurality through a dialectic of naming and calling, vocation and invocation, extending these notions beyond the 'play' of speech and silence that Ramchandra Gandhi talks of, to one of the foundations of labour and office—work, and play, then.

Jñāna in this scheme of things involves the knowledge of name and form as the sign/witness of the relation between subject and object, self and other. Name signifies conscience, or *samjna* (which is incidentally the other Sanskrit term for 'name'), as mediator of *jñāna* (self-knowledge) and *vijñāna* (science/'discriminative' knowledge of objects). *Karma*, usually translated as action or duty, in the dialectic of naming and calling, would signify vocation, the work to which one is called, and through which one may, through the very vocabulary or names that constitute one's vocation, know and invoke the unity of self and other whether it be of man, nature or God. Finally, Bhakti etymologically signifies part/division, and partaking. The potency of name and form are realized in the overcoming of the dualism of self and other through vocation and invocation. Thus one participates in, and partakes of Creation, by pairing, sharing and making, in the labour of production and reproduction through naming and calling, vocation and invocation.

Notes and References

1. Ramchandra Gandhi, *I am Thou: Meditations on the Truth of India* (IPQ publications no. 8, University of Poona, 1984), p. 233.
2. Ibid., p. 115.
3. Ibid., p. 246.
4. Ibid., p. 150.

3

'Falling in Love with a Civilization': A Tribute to Daya Krishna, the Thinker

Bettina Bäumer

Dialogue, one of the great themes of Daya Krishna's life and thought, is an ongoing process, as life itself. It does not end with some conclusion arrived at, whether by consensus or by dissent. So also my—unfortunately limited—dialogue with Daya Krishna, which was refreshed and ongoing by correspondence (traditional letters), when it suddenly ended by his death. But that itself is a sign of the dynamics of his way of dialoguing. It saddened me that his last letter to me was not redirected when I was in Austria, and when I read it on my return to Varanasi, he was no more, and I could not respond in the ways we are used to in this physical world. And yet I am convinced that he knows my response, and my feelings of indebtedness and connectedness. This volume is a sign for the continued dialogue which does not believe in full stops.

I may be allowed to give my personal memories, apart from a more general appreciation of what Daya Krishna meant for the intellectual life of India in the twentieth and the beginning of the twenty-first century.

I am also fulfilling a task that he himself gave me in a letter dated 23 November 2005: 'You have met so many interesting people in India; you must write something about them.' He, Daya Krishna, is certainly one of them!

My memories go back to the early 1970s, when I met him in Jaipur. I forget other occasions, in Delhi in the company of common friends, and in Varanasi. I was basically shy to develop a relationship at that time, though I was always impressed by the freshness of his ideas and the challenge of his approach. It was perhaps more through common friends that I came close to Daya Krishna. Let me mention especially Vivek Datta, with whom an old friendship was renewed when Daya Krishna was in Shimla in 2005, and a truly memorable meeting occurred. Other connections were Kapila Vatsyayan, Mukund Lath and Sita Ram Goel.

I was attracted and impressed when he initiated his series of Saṃvāda dialogues between traditional Sanskrit pandits and modern (Indian) philosophers. His approach was important for me, for having studied philosophy and Indology in Europe and living in a traditional pandit environment in Varanasi, I had to go through this dialogue within myself, often without partners—with the great exceptions of Raimon Panikkar and K. Sivaraman. I attended some of these Saṃvāda seminars as a passive (and, as so often, the only woman and the only European!) participant. It was due to the kindness of Dayaji that he invited me (again, the only woman and the only westerner in the seminar) to such a seminar, conducted under the auspices of the Indian Council of Philosophical Research (ICPR), on Kashmir Śaivism, and that too in Srinagar. This was an incredible privilege and occasion, in so many ways. I was happy to be invited to stay in a house boat in Nagin Lake, not far from the University, in the company of Daya Krishna, Francine, M. P. Rege and Arindam Chakravarty, besides Ila Dalmia who was there as a friend.

The seminar was an exploration of Kashmir Śaivism, a relatively new discovery for Indian philosophers. Dayaji discovered it for himself, and was also viewing it critically. It was more the fact of meeting and discussing the issues involved, than a real contribution to the research on Kashmir Śaivism. In a sense historic, the meeting with the last and powerful representative of the living tradition, Swami Lakshman Joo, at the Guptaganga Hall in Ishbar, near his Ishvar Ashram, did not result in a satisfying dialogue, because the levels were too different: the merely intellectual approach of the scholars and the lived experience of the master. However, for me personally, this was the definitive meeting with a master who was both a great scholar and a living embodiment of the spirituality of the tradition. So, in a way, I owe to Daya Krishna my meeting with my master.

There was again a gap of some years before we met again. This time, more than any time before, it was even clearer that meeting him was never a casual affair, as it happens in so many seminars with academics.

It was a real meeting of minds and hearts. The occasion was my being a fellow at the Indian Institute of Advanced Study, Shimla, when he was invited as a visiting professor, to give some inspiring and challenging lectures on civilization. It was September 2005, and Bhuvan Chandel, the philosopher, was at that time the director of the Institute. Apart from Dayaji's lectures we met for discussions in his room. He knew my involvement with Kashmir Śaivism and asked me many questions. I don't know if I was able to answer but I admired his openness to new and, for him, unusual ideas. Both his critical attitude and his openness were challenging, because they came from a genuine spirit of enquiry.

The great and unexpected occasion was the book release of my Festschrift (Felicitation Volume) at the Institute, where he not only took part, but spontaneously gave a speech, of which I may mention the most important points. In a lovingly critical way he spoke about 'falling in love with a civilization'—meaning my love for the Indian civilization. And for him 'falling in love' meant a dangerous thing, because 'love makes one blind'. By implication he meant that I was blind to the critical, negative sides of the Indian civilization. But it did not remain a one-sided criticism; he immediately added a self-criticism of the Indian philosophers who have 'fallen in love' with Western civilization, Western ideas, and who often ape the West, ignoring their own cultural and philosophical riches. His description was sharp and accurate. He was pleading for an approach which does not remain one-sided. This has to be achieved by dialogue. Then he asked, 'Where is the dialogue? How is it possible?' Knowing my involvement with intercultural and inter-religious dialogue he also hinted at a dialogue between mystical experiences, not only ideas.

He was aware that dialogue is not a facile undertaking, because each side is so much identified with their own ideas and positions. Therefore he repeatedly said: 'but we should try'. Dialogue is only possible if we try to 'become the other, to be the other, to think from the viewpoint of the other, to identify with the other. Is it possible?' he asked. 'Let us try', was his challenge. He also gave a key, 'The heart of Indian civilization is the search for de-identification—de-identification with the body, with the mind, with the intellect, with thought ... and the challenge of all civilizations is to de-identify with the past, with their concepts. . . .' This was a clear reference to the basic ideal of all Indian spiritual-philosophical systems of arriving at a state of thought-free awareness, of *nirvikalpa*, where alone reality is perceived in its own light. What he hinted at was a state of inner freedom. His speech was a wonderful combination of the personal and the universal, so characteristic of him.

It was only later, when he had the book in his hands[1] and read portions of it, at least the introduction, that he responded very warmly. I may quote his letters:

> Jaipur, 5 November 2005
> Dear Bettina,
> It was a pleasure meeting you after a long time, and that too on an occasion which said so much about you. The tribute to you, both oral, metaphorical and written was so well deserved for the dedication, commitment and sincerity that you have embodied in your own self and symbolized for others. . . . Hope you are well. And, though winter comes, can spring be far behind?

How symbolic is this last sentence. Again he wrote on 23 November,

> Your letter and the photographs recreate the atmosphere that was there at the Institute when your book was released.
>
> I discovered the book you had given me. . . . Your 'yatra' is both fascinating and stunning as when one recalls or remembers one's life one does not know how it all could have happened as one does not 'feel' or see that way when one goes through it all. How can it all have happened and how could one have 'lived' through it all.
>
> In any case it was something to discover what you have been doing. It adds another dimension to our knowledge of the other's self. . . .

Dayaji's openness for dialogue was evident in two ways which I can only mention without elaborating on its implications. One, as already mentioned, was the dialogue which he initiated between traditional scholars and modern philosophers—Saṃvāda, a historical event in the field of Indian philosophy. Others may have written more in detail about these events and their outcome. Saṃvāda showed that Daya Krishna took both sides seriously, and he had to teach them to take each other seriously. His concern about the stagnation of Indian systems and his search for a continuous development of original thinking in the various Indian systems in the last centuries is related to this endeavour.

The second, and for me more surprising, interest of Dayaji concerned interreligious dialogue. On his own he discovered the figure of Swami Abhishiktananda, a French monk and *sannyasi* (1910–1973), who, being a Christian mystic, went deep into Upaniṣadic spirituality. Only later did

Dayaji discover that I was the president of the Abhishiktananda Society looking after his intellectual and spiritual heritage. What gave me special joy was that Daya Krishna discovered in the writings of Abhishiktananda the potential of a transformation of both Hinduism and Christianity, by an inner dialogue, and that he intuitively sensed his importance and the philosophical implications of his experience and thought. While reminding me of my (unfortunately unfulfilled) promise to write an article about him, he wrote to me:

> I hope you remember your promise to write on Abhishiktananda (Father Le Saux) for the JICPR. The work of these persons should be known more and appreciated for what they were attempting to do in their attempt to transform both Hinduism and Christianity into something else. The heart of Hinduism lies, perhaps, in the fact that it has no 'founding fathers' and that everyone is free to pursue his own path independent of any authority, spiritual or temporal. The power and authority of the spiritual personality is not derived from any institution in which one occupies a position. There are, of course, *maṭha*s and *sampradāya*s but they are always treated as secondary in this context. Also, they are more bound by tradition to which they belong and the quest they symbolize.
>
> The realm of the spirit seeks 'freedom' from all . . . 'externality' to which it is essentially bound as it is what it [is and] wants to know in order to be 'freed' from it.[2] (Jaipur, 5 November 2005)

Another aspect of his openness was Dayaji's engagement with the Veda. I would have loved to discuss with him his project of a rearrangement of the Hymns of the Rig Veda. In this context he also discovered that I collaborated with Raimon Panikkar in his anthology of the Vedas: *Mantramanjari, The Vedic Experience*. On 17 August 2007, he wrote:

> Dear Bettina,
> Someone from Shimla brought *you* and your message a few days ago.
>
> It was nice to remember and be remembered.
>
> I was just looking into Raimondo Panikkar's *The Vedic experience: Mantramanjari* and found your name there, as you had helped him with it.
>
> It is an extraordinary achievement and I would like to know a little about the way you all collaborated and the way it developed over almost a decade.
>
> It appears that it is an earlier draft of what he later came to formulate as Cosmotheandric where the Cosmos, the *Theos* [god, deity] and the *Anthropos* [human beings] are brought together in such a manner that each substantially affected and modified the other. . . .[3]

On receiving my reply he wrote back on 12 September:

Dear Bettina,
The fragrance of the Veda 'floats' through the air as one reads your letter.
The translation has been wonderful, but has not caught the attention....

His critical remarks about the anthology concerned 'too much introduction, and too much selection from the large Vedic corpus. Perhaps the editor did not want to leave anything.' He suggested to me to re-edit the book leaving aside the introductions, 'so that one can enjoy the flavour of the original directly and not be led by someone else'. This is another task he gave me which I have not (yet) fulfilled.

Dayaji's most encouraging remark concerned my involvement with Kashmir Śaivism.[4] In the same letter of 17 August he writes: 'I heard from Dr. M. A. Khawaja about your workshop on Kashmir Śaivism in Banaras. It is good to learn that you are trying to keep the tradition alive.'

There is no doubt that we are missing Daya Krishna, his lively way of philosophizing, his challenging and yet encouraging concern about India's living thought and its message for the world.

Notes and References

1. Sadananda Das and Ernst Fürlinger, ed., *Samarasya, Studies in Indian Arts, Philosophy, and Interreligious Dialogue, in Honour of Bettina Bäumer* (New Delhi: D. K. Printworld, 2005).
2. The style reveals that he dictated his letters, because of his poor eyesight.
3. Panikkar's concept of 'cosmotheandric' (experience, view of reality) is derived also, but not only, from his work on the Vedas which speak of three levels of reality: *adhibhautika*, *adhidaivika*, *adhyātmika*, but he has enlarged it to include other religious traditions. He sees in it an encompassing view of Reality, comprising the cosmic, the human and the divine dimensions, which has found different expressions in other traditions, with varying emphasis.
4. It should be mentioned here that the term 'Kashmir Śaivism' which has become common, designates a school of philosophy and spirituality traditionally called *Pratyabhijñā* (the School of Recognition), Trika (the Triadic School), apart from other Tantric traditions which have been absorbed in a great synthesis by Abhinavagupta in the tenth to eleventh centuries. It is distinct from Śaiva Siddhanta, which also flourished in Kashmir in

the Middle Ages but is now more prevalent in the South, and which is dualistic/pluralistic in its philosophical position. *Pratyabhijñā* is non-dualistic (also called *samvidadvayavāda*, the teaching of the non-dualism of Consciousness), which has not only philosophical-spiritual but also social implications, because the tradition is opposed to caste and gender discrimination.

PART II

The Idea of Svarāj: Asymmetries of Power, Knowledge and Alternative, Ethical Politics

4

Gandhi and the Stoics: Squaring Emotional Detachment with Universal Love and Political Action[1]

Richard Sorabji

The ancient Greek and Roman Stoics did not influence Gandhi, but some of their values were very similar, and I think that Gandhi and the Stoics throw light on each other. The Stoics acknowledged that their ideals had never been put into practice. Gandhi put into practice all his ideals and discussed the results, publishing criticisms of the results and his own replies. So he helps us to see to what extent similar Stoic ideals would have been practical and the extent to which their outcome would have been good or bad. Conversely, Gandhi has been seen as inconsistent, more politician than philosopher. The logically structured philosophy of the Stoics could have provided Gandhi with a consistent rationale for some of his attitudes. We can see how close he came to agreeing with such a rationale, and where he deviated from it.

This paper is on emotional detachment and the subject connects with a number of others. Most relevantly, it connects with Gandhi's belief in non-violence. Gandhi thought of non-violence as an inner state of mind, an attitude of love for all, which required a certain emotional detachment as a prerequisite. Love for all humans was also celebrated by the Stoics.

I want to raise two main questions about emotional detachment. How can Gandhi or the Stoics square emotional detachment with universal love? Is not love an emotion? Further, how can either party square emotional detachment with political action. Can political activity be emotionally detached?

The Stoics and Family Love for All Humans

To start with the Greek Stoics, their school was founded in Athens in 300 BC. They said something unprecedented in Western philosophy, that a certain kind of love, like that found among the closest family members, should be extended to all human beings, even to foreigners who spoke no Greek and to slaves. Such an extension would be natural. That is not to say that it would be easy, but it would be in accordance with nature.[2] This novel view was to have a benign effect at intervals in European history. Over 1800 years later in the sixteenth century AD a version of it was used to oppose the conquest of the American Indians in Latin America.

The Stoics and Emotional Detachment

Family love is a strong emotion. So how could the Stoics square setting up family love as a model with another recommendation of theirs? They thought (and this is an aspect of Stoicism with which I do not agree) that we should get rid of many, I think most, of our emotions. Their objection to most emotions was that they involve mistaken evaluations. To follow an account of Stoic emotion that I have sought to substantiate elsewhere,[3] the Stoics thought that one of the very few things that matters in and of itself was good or bad character. But we get emotional about a host of other things like wealth, pleasure, health and life itself. These things have a certain limited value. They are, or are connected with, objectives that we are naturally constituted to pursue. Moreover, they acquire a derivative value from the fact that good character, the objective that really matters, consists in a readiness to pursue such things for ourselves and others. So it is our duty to pursue these objectives energetically. But what if, through no fault of our own we fail to secure them for ourselves or others? Then what matters is whether we exercised good character by pursuing them in the right way, and whether the intended recipients exercise good character in face of their failure to get them. The objectives do not in themselves matter in the same way as good character. In Stoic terminology these objectives are *indifferent*, although they are indifferents which it is natural and right to pursue.[4]

Some emotions are exceptions. The Stoic is free, for example, to feel joy at God's good governance of the universe, because that involves no mistaken evaluations. The Stoics also allow temporary exceptions for pedagogic purposes, to help people to progress in the direction of good character. The Stoic Epictetus in the first century AD says that it is the mark of a good lecture on morality that the students should feel 'agony' at their lack of good character.[5] But agony is not what the perfected Stoic should feel.

The Stoics help us to get rid of unwanted emotions, and this is where I believe they are really helpful, because we all have emotions we would rather be rid of, even if we do not agree that most emotions are such. To get rid of emotions, we must understand the three different phases in the development of an emotion. First, by a daring generalization which I think is nearly true, they claim that every emotion is preceded by an appearance that benefit or harm is at hand and that it is appropriate to react accordingly. This appearance is not yet the emotion, but it is enough to cause what they call a 'first movement' or 'pre-passion'. By this they mean a shock which may be a physical one in the body, like crying, or a psychological sensation. That too is not yet the emotion. According to the fullest Stoic account,[6] the emotion occurs when we give the assent of our reason to the appearance that harm or benefit is at hand and that it is appropriate to react accordingly. Most people do not even realise that this is a distinct phase, because no sooner do they have the appearance than they give their assent to it. But Stoicism teaches you to stand back and say to yourself, 'that is the appearance, but should reason assent to it'? The Stoics have much advice on how to withhold assent. Is it really harm at hand, or merely the shock of something unexpected, which, however, is no harder to cope with than what you were expecting? Is the apparent harm any different from what everyone experiences? And is it really appropriate to react, or did you not yourself treat someone only the other day the way you have been treated? It is useful that the Stoics distinguish the first movement, the shock, from the question of harm. That helps to prevent the William James effect. William James once said: 'We do not cry because we are sad. We are sad because we cry.' That is an exaggeration, but there is some truth in it. People often think, 'Look, I am crying. I *must* have been maltreated.' But of course that does not follow. The crying is merely the shock, but it leaves the important question unanswered: Have you really suffered harm? What the Stoics invented was cognitive therapy—a therapy which calms the emotions by altering one's 'thoughts' about the situation.

The Stoics on How True Family Love Is Detached Love

I now come back to my question: How can the Stoics offer family love as a model of how you should approach all your fellow humans, if family love is emotional, and they want you to rid yourself of most emotions? The answer emerges again, I think, from the Stoic Epictetus. He suggests that the true Stoic will transcend 'ordinary' family love. Notoriously, he recommends that when you kiss your wife or child, you should say to yourself, 'I am kissing a mortal.'[7] That will prepare you for the possibility of bereavement, although it will surely also make you a little detached. Epictetus goes further. Ordinary family love can turn into hate in an instant.[8] A husband and wife have loved each other for twenty years. Suddenly a woman comes between them and love turns into hate. Two brothers look so charming. They love each other so much. But their father's inheritance comes between them and suddenly hate replaces love. Only the Stoic's love is true family love, because only the Stoic's love could never turn into hate. Why not? Because the true Stoic never attaches the same value to an inheritance or to sexual satisfaction as to his or her character, and control over one's own character has not been taken away. Epictetus admires the school of philosophers called Cynics who were even more individualistic than the Stoics. The true Cynic, unlike the Stoic, does not have a family at all. For the Cynic a family would tyrannize him: he would not be free, if he was worried about whether their lives were secure.[9] Epictetus reveals how one might defend the idea of the founder of Stoicism when he said 350 years earlier that only good people are family.[10] Epictetus is saying that it is people with the right values, people who value character above an inheritance and are therefore good, who are true family. For Epictetus, then, the family love that one should extend to all humans is presumably this rather detached family love. It is a love which values the family's life more than a Cynic would, but which does not value their life as highly as their character.

Emotional Detachment in Some Early Christians

The Stoic theory of how to avoid emotion was turned by a Christian of the third century AD into a theory of how to avoid sin. This was not a Stoic perspective. The Christian, Origen, took the idea of a Stoic first movement or pre-passion, and instead of regarding it as a mere shock, devoid of thought, described it as a 'bad thought', very nearly the phrase used also by Gandhi.[11] A bad thought for Origen is only a first movement; it is a temptation, but not yet a sin, because you have not yet given your assent or consent to anything. But it would be a sin if you consented to prolonging the bad thought or enjoying it, much more so if you consented to acting on it. This was made clear in the next century, the fourth century AD, by the Christian monk Evagrius, a semi-hermit in the Egyptian desert, who developed the idea of bad thoughts.

Evagrius distinguished eight bad thoughts which assailed him in the six days of solitude he accepted each week in the heat of the Egyptian desert, before joining his fellow monks on Sundays. These eight bad thoughts were turned in a later century by a process of expansion and contraction into the seven deadly sins. One of Evagrius' bad thoughts was a kind of bored depression (*akêdia*), which struck particularly at the hour of the noonday heat. The solitary monk had set himself to read so much scripture. But in the heat he stopped reading and started counting how many pages were left. Who has not done that? Finally he puts the book under his head as a pillow and has a little sleep. Another bad thought was the thought of avarice. How quickly thoughts of compassion can turn into thoughts of avarice: How much suffering there is in the world? The monk imagines visiting the nearest town to raise funds to help the poor. If he succeeded, how much suffering could be alleviated. And, come to think of it, there will soon be a vacancy in that town, because the present bishop is bound to retire, and if the monk had raised the funds, he would be the obvious candidate for the lucrative bishopric.

Evagrius describes how to forestall bad thoughts by noticing at what time of day different ones attack, or in what sequence. The beginner can get rid of one bad thought by stirring up an opposite one, although he should learn how to pass beyond that imperfect remedy. If he is assailed by thoughts of lust, he can get rid of them by stirring up thoughts of vanity: What would the head of the monastery think of him? Conversely, if he is assailed by thoughts of vanity, he can expel them in an instant by stirring up thoughts of lust.

It is again Christians, not Stoics, who provide parallels for Gandhi's concern with chastity. The Christian bishop Saint Augustine at the end of the century around 400 AD, like Gandhi, favoured celibacy in marriage after producing children, although he insisted that it should be only by mutual agreement of husband and wife. He was also worried by sexual dreams as a sign of failure in chastity,[12] as were many Christian males by sexual discharges after they had become desert ascetics. The similarities to Gandhi, however, were not, I think, in this case the result of any Christian influence. Similar difficulties and anxieties seem to afflict males who attempt chastity just because of biological human nature. Gandhi's interest in testing his moral progress would have been familiar not only to the Christian Augustine, but also to the pagan Greek philosophers. The Platonist, Plutarch, wrote a treatise on how to test moral progress. And Gandhi, who tested his chastity by sleeping beside some of his closest women supporters, could have drawn support from Plato's *Symposium*, if he had known it, where Socrates is presented as paying not the slightest attention all night when the young Alcibiades crept under his cloak and made sexual advances.[13]

Gandhi and Tolstoy's Non-violent Love for All Humans

Let us now turn to Gandhi. Gandhi described Tolstoy as the second greatest influence on his life and as having abolished his belief in violence. He learnt from Tolstoy that true non-violence is an inner state of mind, an ocean of compassion free from any trace of ill will for anyone. It is not an outward practice of refraining from killing animals. That practice of certain Indian groups seemed to Gandhi to be indifferent to actual suffering in the animals.[14] Tolstoy derived his idea ultimately from Christ's Sermon on the Mount, in which Christ, speaking of humans, not animals, taught that if you are struck on the cheek, you should turn the other cheek to your assailant.[15] In the work which most influenced Gandhi,[16] Tolstoy argued that this attitude would soon prevail everywhere, although it had taken 1800 years since Christ's sermon for humans to get beyond the idea of love for one's country and hatred of other nations. Gandhi followed Tolstoy in speaking of the 'law of love' and in saying that the law will work, just as the law of gravitation will work.[17]

But was this love extended to all humans? Gandhi was often felt as warm by his foes and as harsh by those closest to him, whether friends or relatives. A book and a film have been produced about Gandhi's apparent harshness to one of his sons, Harilal.[18] His love for all alike seems to have been a somewhat detached love. As to how love can be detached, I have offered as a model the attitude recommended by the Stoic Epictetus. Gandhi's love for all may have been in its effect not unlike that recommended by Epictetus, although his sources of inspiration were quite different. If Gandhi tells us that he learnt about non-violence as love from Tolstoy, he learnt about detachment from a quite different source, neither Tolstoy nor the Stoics.

Gandhi and Emotional Detachment: The *Bhagavad Gītā*

Gandhi learnt about emotional detachment from the *Bhagavad Gītā*, although his reading of the *Gītā* was no doubt influenced by the man he names as the foremost influence on his life ahead of Tolstoy, the ascetic Rajchandra. Gandhi translated the *Gītā* into Gujarati, using the Victorian English translation of Arnold and the translation from the Sanskrit of Tilak. Gandhi's lieutenant Mahadev Desai in turn translated Gandhi's Gujarati into English in such a way as to bring out Gandhi's interpretation. I shall use Mahadev Desai's rendering.

The Gītā *repeatedly tells us to avoid attachment especially to the fruit of action.*

2.47 Action alone is thy province, never the fruits thereof; let not thy motive be the fruit of action, nor shouldst thou desire to avoid action.

2.48 Act thou, O Dhananjaya, without attachment, steadfast in *Yoga*, even-minded in success and failure. Even-mindedness is *Yoga*.

3.25 Just as, with attachment, the unenlightened perform all actions, O Bharata, even so, but unattached, should the enlightened man act, with a desire for the welfare of humanity.

4.20 He who has renounced attachment to the fruit of action, who is ever content, and free from all dependence, he, though immersed in action, acts not.

18.6 But even these actions should be performed abandoning all attachment and fruit; such, O Partha, is my best and considered opinion.

18.26 That doer is called sattvika who has shed all attachment, all thought of 'I', who is filled with firmness and zeal, and who seeks neither success nor failure.

The Gītā *further advocates avoidance of emotion.*

2.40 Here no effort undertaken is lost, no disaster befalls. Even a little of this righteous course delivers one from great fear.
2.56 Whose mind is troubled in sorrows and longeth not for joys, who is free from passion, fear and wrath—he is called the ascetic of secure understanding.
2.57 Who owns attachment nowhere, who feels neither joy nor resentment whether good or bad comes his way—that man's understanding is secure.
12.17 Who rejoices not, neither frets nor grieves, who covets not, who abandons both good and ill—that devotee of Mine is dear to Me.

The Gītā *urges impartiality towards whatever one encounters.*

5.18 The men of Self-realisation look with an equal eye on a brahmana possessed of learning and humility, a cow, a dog and even a dog-eater.
14.24 He who holds pleasure and pain alike, who is sedate, who regards as same earth, stone and gold, who is wise and weighs in equal scale things pleasant and unpleasant, who is even-minded in praise and blame.

The Gītā *applies the need for impartiality to friend and foe, to children, wife, home and family. Indeed, it finds dear the one who (like the Greek Cynics) has no home.*

14.25 Who holds alike respect and disrespect, who is the same to friend and foe, who indulges in no undertakings—that man is called *gunatita*.
12.18 Who is same to foe and friend, who regards alike respect and disrespect, cold and heat, pleasure and pain, who is free from attachment.
12.19 Who weighs in equal scale blame and praise, who is silent, content with whatever his lot, who owns no home, who is of steady mind, that devotee of Mine is dear to Me.

13.9 Absence of attachment, refusal to be wrapped up in one's children, wife, home and family, even-mindedness whether good or ill befall.

Mahadev Desai supplies comments and he notes comparisons with the Christian Gospel. Christ demanded that disciples abandon their families (Luke 14.26). 'If any man come to me and hate not his father, mother, wife and children and brethren and sisters, yea and his own life also, he cannot be my disciple.' He taught (Matthew 5.44): 'Love your enemies, bless them that curse you.' Regarding the fruit of action, Mahadev Desai compares Tolstoy's *What I Believe*: 'The belief in a remuneration of work . . . rests on the assumption that we have a claim to something; but man has no rights and can have none. He is ever in debt for the welfare given him.' Elsewhere when the *Gītā* talks of one's own personal duty (compare Stoic *prosôpon*, *persona*) at 3.35 and 18.27, the learned Desai cites two Stoics, Epictetus and Marcus Aurelius. But he does not do so for the passages just cited. That comparison was left to Edwyn Bevan in a passage within a set of Oxford lectures published in 1913,[19] but Bevan's insight was not taken up.

Gandhi not only translated the *Gītā*; he also gave a set of discourses on it in his ashram at Ahmedabad in 1926. It may seem very strange that a man who so believed in non-violence should base himself on the *Gītā*, in which the Lord Krishna tells the warrior Arjuna that it is his duty to fight in a long and destructive war that left almost all the participants dead. In his *Discourses on the Gita*, Gandhi interprets the point as being that Arjuna's reluctance to fight was not based on any inkling of the idea of non-violence, but on a squeamishness about killing his relatives. He was perfectly prepared to kill others. It is that attachment to relatives, on Gandhi's interpretation, that the *Gītā* is attacking.[20]

Gandhi on the Detachment Needed for a Non-violent Mind

Gandhi wrote in *Hind Swaraj* (*Indian Home Rule*) in 1909 that four things are needed to become a passive, or non-violent, resister: chastity, truthfulness, fearlessness and poverty.[21] Chastity is needed because it is the greatest discipline. Many of the early male Christian ascetics in the desert agreed that it was the hardest discipline to keep, but Gandhi had the added belief, shared by some ancient Greek and Roman thinkers and by some of Gandhi's European contemporaries whom he cites,[22] that sexual activity emasculates. Fearlessness is not only about possessions, false honour, the government, bodily injury and death, but also about relatives. With poverty, you do not have to throw money away, but you must be indifferent about losing it. Gandhi uses the word 'indifferent' to describe an attitude of mind, rather than in the way the Stoics used it to characterize an objective.

Gandhi does not add, but he could have, that the very idea of private property involves readiness to defend it with violence from unwanted trespassers, if it is to be private. If a spouse is considered private property, the same would apply there. He could also have added that those who have given up private property and sex have less to lose, and so are freer to act without hatred towards an oppressor.

In his autobiography, first published in 1927–1929, Gandhi describes the 'process' of detachment, especially in connexion with his vow of chastity. He speaks like the early Christians of having 'undesirable thoughts'.[23] He says in the same breath, like Evagrius and Augustine, that without surrender to God's 'grace', one cannot master one's thoughts. He even says that he accepts the theory, which Augustine made prominent in Christianity, of 'original sin' inherited from the sin of the first human.[24] The part he accepts, presumably, is that no human can avoid sinning. When Bajaj asked him how to keep the mind free from lustful thoughts, he not only repeated the need for God's grace, but said that we must not allow thought to rule action, but need not fret about evil thoughts themselves.[25] This may remind us of Evagrius' idea that a bad thought is not itself a sin, although Evagrius would add that even before action, prolonging the thought can be a sin. Gandhi's omission of this point connects with his not having worked out, as Evagrius did, a technology for combating bad thoughts, apart from the one remedy on which Evagrius would have agreed, that diet is vital. Diet is what Gandhi recommends to Bajaj and repeatedly, for example, in his autobiography.[26] In Evagrius' view, lustful thoughts are not too difficult a temptation, provided thoughts of gluttony have been brought under control.

A Further Problem: The Stoics on Squaring Emotional Detachment with Goals of Action

I have so far spoken about how love, in particular love of all humans, could be emotionally detached. I have offered Epictetus' Stoicism as an example, even though it was not Stoicism that influenced Gandhi. But there is a further problem that the Stoics tackle and that Gandhi needed to tackle. How could the Stoics remain emotionally detached, if they were to engage in action, including political action, as they did? For does not action involve commitment to achieving goals, and is that compatible with detachment?

The Stoics held that normally a Stoic should engage in public life (*politeuesthai*). This would be expected of citizens in a small democratic city like ancient Athens, and in Republican Rome. But it remained an ideal even when Rome became an empire and the aristocrats lost power. Epictetus describes Roman aristocrats who still defied the emperor's wishes, and even made the emperor back down.[27] Admittedly, they did not plan like Gandhi to get rid of imperial rule. Rather, it would have been an achievement for a Stoic to be executed in defiance of a wrong dictate from the emperor.

A very brilliant answer was worked out by the Stoics as to how one can pursue the goals of action in an emotionally detached way, although their recommendation is not one that I myself could live up to. They take the model of archery practice. One needs a 'target' (*skopos*, *propositum*), or there will be no archery practice at all. But the important thing, the 'goal' (*telos*, *ultimum*) is not hitting the target. What if a bad aim hits the target because of an unpredictable gust of wind? Equally it does not matter if a perfect aim misses the target because of an unpredictable gust. What matters, the real goal, is 'aiming' right.[28] At the same time, the Stoic who introduced this idea, Antipater, head of the school from 152 to 129 BC, insisted that you should do everything in your power (*par' hauton*) to hit the target. The same used to be taught to English schoolboys about cricket. You play very hard to win, but what if you lose? Then 'the game's the thing'. It matters how you played, and how you lost, with grace and recognition of the other side. Playing the game was the real goal, winning merely the target. This value spread to American football too. In the immortal words of Grantland Rice, 'And when the last Great Scorer comes to mark against your name, He asks not if you won or lost, but how you played the game.'

This attitude makes a tremendous demand of us. We are working to gain our degree, or complete our dissertation, or publish our next book. But that is only a target to make the activity of researching possible. What matters is the goal, the activity of researching. The great advantage of this idea is that it gives no hostages to fortune. Even if death strikes you down the next moment, you have achieved the goal of researching. What is lost is only the target of completing the task. The Stoic, then, does not pin hopes on the future, but is content with the present. How many readers are capable of this recipe for serenity in action? Not myself, I have to confess, but I can appreciate its point. It combines doing everything in your power to attain a target with detachment from whether you attain it.

The Stoic's detachment is not an elimination of desires. What is eliminated is 'emotional' desire. The desire that remains in a perfect Stoic is unemotional because it sees the objectives for what they are: things 'indifferent', although natural and right to pursue as far as lies in your power. The Stoics even coined a word to designate this detached kind of desire. It selects (*eklegesthai*), rather than 'choosing' (*haireisthai*) naturally preferred objectives.[29]

Gandhi on Detachment and Goals of Action

In discussing commitment to goals of action, Gandhi sometimes speaks in ways like the Stoics. He quotes the Christian hymn, 'One step enough for me', and adds, 'to think of some remote future is building castles in the air. . . . The present means our duty at this moment. If we put all our strength into doing our duty, as we know it at this moment, we shall have made the highest human effort.'[30] He also says, referring to the *Gītā*'s detachment from the fruits of action, 'To be detached is never to abandon action because the contemplated result may not follow.'[31] But Gandhi also appeals to non-Stoic ideas. He continues the last quotation by saying, 'On the contrary, it is proof of the immovable faith in the certainty of the contemplated result following in due course.' The Stoics would never have sought assurance from the future, but viewed the future, like Gandhi in the earlier quotation, as offering so many castles in the air. Again the Stoics did not believe in the soul's immortality, whereas Gandhi is able to say that achieving a truly non-violent mind may take several incarnations.[32]

Gandhi's ways of detaching himself from goals of action seem to work well enough for the goal of achieving a truly non-violent mind. But what about political goals, which tend to involve a strict timetable, such as removing British rule from India? Sometimes Gandhi spoke as if achieving true non-violence was a prerequisite for that. But at one time he suggested that political goal might be achieved in a year, and in 1942 it has been suggested that he was worried that it might not be achieved in his lifetime. The Stoics were committed to engaging in politics, but under Roman imperial rule, they did not take on projects with a timetable. Gandhi did, and I am not sure that either the Stoic detachment from goals, or his own recommendations show how to remain detached in the right way from the achievement of such goals.

Gandhi's Non-attachment to Relatives

The *Gītā* provided Gandhi with a scriptural basis for maintaining a certain equidistance from friend and foe, kin and non-kin. Let us see how Gandhi applied the idea of non-attachment to relatives. The film, *Gandhi, My Father,* focuses on Gandhi's decision in 1909 not to give to any of his sons a scholarship offered for any one of the sons old enough to train as a barrister. Instead Gandhi freed himself to give it to someone else who proved a failure and then to someone else again. In 1903, the eldest son Harilal had gone to jail in the service of one of Gandhi's South African campaigns, and Gandhi wrote, 'I want every Indian to do what Harilal has done.'[33] But by May 1906, Gandhi had already written to his brother about Harilal's marriage, of which he disapproved, 'For the present at any rate I have ceased to think of him as a son.'[34] Harilal wrote bitterly to his father about the denial of educational funding in 1915. '. . . For a year I cried. I was bewildered. You did not lend me your ears. . . . I am married . . . with four children. I cannot . . . become a recluse. Therefore I have separated from you with your permission.'[35] In 1920, in the course of explaining 'love, the active state of *ahimsā*', Gandhi wrote, 'if my son lives a life of shame, I may not help him to do so by continuing to support him; on the contrary, my love for him requires me to withdraw all support from him although it may mean even his death'.[36] As the film presents it, Harilal's alcoholism, debt and temporary conversion to Islam were partly caused by his father's non-attachment. That is what one could have expected, and it constitutes a warning also to the Stoics, to the extent that their family love also involves a certain detachment.

With his wife Kasturbai, Gandhi spoke to her of his vow of chastity only on the day he took the vow.[37] Augustine would not have considered this consultation. Gandhi had a habit of rebuking her in public; in one case because she was slower to notice an ashramite's illness than she would have been with her son.[38] Once when Gandhi rebuked Mahadev

Desai's wife and Kasturbai at the same time, because they had both entered a temple during Gandhi's campaign for Dalits to be admitted to all temples, Desai, who was very upset, had the good humour to write in *Harijan*, 'To live with the saints in heaven is a bliss and a glory. But to live with a saint on earth is a different story'.[39]

Gandhi thought that a votary of self-reliance (*svadeshī*) would be his family's truest friend, if he caused his family to die of plague by enlisting their help with plague victims in their own village.[40] He discussed circumstances in which he would put to death a daughter, if he had one.[41] He particularly admired Harischandra as a 'beacon of truth', when, in the story, he reluctantly beheaded his wife and child, in order to be true to a vow to God. Westerners may compare the Judaic story of Abraham being ready to sacrifice his son Isaac simply because God had commanded it. Gandhi's interpretation is that since violence is an 'inner' state of ill will, the beheading by Harischandra was not an act of violence.[42]

Among the many demands made on those closest to Gandhi another that has worried people is his testing of his progress in chastity by having his closest women attendants sleep beside him.

Gandhi's mentor, Gokhale put to him that he had a strain of cruelty and put far too heavy burdens on people.[43] He had the grace to acknowledge that he had produced alienation and scars in those he loved.[44]

Gandhi's Deviation from the *Gītā*? Impartiality versus Disfavour towards Relatives

But did Gandhi always rest content with the *Gītā*'s impartiality towards relatives? There are signs that he went further and positively disfavoured relatives.[45] Commenting on the *Gītā*'s insistence on Arjuna's not sparing his own people (relatives), Gandhi added the word 'first': 'if one must kill, one should kill one's people first'.[46] He wrote, when his much loved son, Devadas, urged him not to fast, 'You are of course a friend and a friend of a very high order at that. But you cannot get over the son in you. . . . Your affection is rooted in attachment.'[47] He refused to accept a visit in prison from two sons at the end of a fast, saying, 'As the Government know, I make no distinction between sons born to me and numerous others who are as dear to me even as they are.' He also refused the attendance of relatives at his wife's death ceremonies in prison, if that was not allowed also to friends.[48] Rajchandra persuaded Gandhi that

Mrs Gladstone's devotion to Gladstone was 'perfectly natural', and that a servant's devotion would have been 'a thousand times more praiseworthy'.[49] In a conversation of 1909 with Mrs Polak in South Africa, Gandhi insisted rather peremptorily that a wife, and in general one's nearest, do not need to be always thought about or specially attended to, because they are part of oneself, like one's arm. This is 'identification, as all true love should be'. Mrs Polak put her point by saying,

> I think I sometimes prefer to be thought of, then, as someone a little further away. I don't want to be put on one side as an unconscious bit of the body by those I love. . . . I think it wrong to omit the acts of thoughtful courtesy and self-control to those who have the first claim upon our consideration, and to reserve our smiling best for the stranger. I see it happen and it vexes me, for I cannot justify it.

Gandhi replied, 'Then do not worry yourself by thinking about it!

This does not seem to be endorsed by the *Gītā*, or by the Stoics. It might be different if *she* identified herself as Gandhi's arm, or had taken a vow to serve as Gandhi's arm. But it would not be possible for each spouse to view the other as their arm. The Stoic view about parts is not that one person is part of another, but that each individual is part of the wider community of rational beings like a stone in an arch.[50]

Gandhi's Deviation from Stoicism: *Svadharma, Persona* and the Individual's Duty to Wife and Children

Although the Stoics' universal love is in a certain way detached, the Stoics do insist on our carrying out our duty as father, brother, husband. These roles are part of our identity (*persona* or *prosôpon*), and so help to reveal where our duty lies.[51] Epictetus is very scornful of a father who left home, because he could not bear to see his little daughter dangerously ill. As a father he should, like the mother, have stayed with the child. Epictetus' Stoic teacher, Musonius Rufus, called for equality between men and women.[52] The Stoics are able to combine a certain distance towards relatives with attachment to all because of their idea that hitting the target—saving the sick child or securing the other conventional objectives for it—must be energetically pursued, but in the end it is the pursuit that most matters.

Gandhi did help nurse his children when he was at home, and the Roman Stoics would have had no objection to Gandhi sometimes being abroad, as Cato was on his campaigns. If Gandhi differed from the Stoics, part of the reason may lie in his interpretation of his individual duty (*svadharma*). Like some of the Stoic *personae* or *prosôpa* he may have thought it to be given him by God. But he differed from the Stoics if he saw it as calling for the 'sacrifice' of relatives and of some of those closest to him, as did the dharma of Arjuna.

Gandhi and the Stoics: Mutual Illumination

I think Gandhi and the Stoics each shed light on the other. Gandhi had a 'scriptural' basis in the *Gītā* for belief in maintaining a certain equidistance from friend and foe, kin and non-kin, and in non-attachment to the fruit of action. Stoicism could supply a 'philosophical' basis for these attitudes, through its distinction between the duty of energetically pursuing natural objectives for oneself and others, and the ultimate importance of pursuing rather than securing them. Stoicism shows that there need be nothing anomalous or inconsistent in such an attitude, however unusual. It was only if Gandhi went further and actually disfavoured or sacrificed close friends or kin that Stoicism would lack a rationale.

In his turn Gandhi throws light on the Stoics. They both believed that few things matter in the end. The Stoics focused on character. Gandhi thought character and a small range of other things important. Since I believe that hundreds of things are important, I used to think that the belief in few was simply part of the unacceptable face of Stoicism. A good mother or father thinks it important whether their son would win at football tomorrow. Even if winning can appear trivial from one perspective, the support is not. But reflection on Gandhi has shown me that, if one wants a liberator of one's country, it may be necessary to have one or two people who think that few things matter. It is best if they are not in one's family. But to Gandhi his freedom did not matter, nor even his life. This meant that it was the Viceroy, not Gandhi, who was afraid when he was sent to prison and I hope to write about his freedom in prison on another occasion.

Gandhi also provides a picture of what the Stoic sage might be like at least in certain respects if he had ever existed. He further shows how far certain Stoic aspirations might be possible in spite of their impractical appearance. Stoic love for all humans, which was detached in the ways described, might seem an impossibility, especially as the Stoics admitted that it had not been realized. But Gandhi did achieve a similarly detached love for all. Gandhi was an experimenter and this was not the only respect in which he put to test ideals of a Stoic type. Some Stoics show an attraction for a past or future without private property, and for a future without law courts or armies. Gandhi's experiments and thought experiments reveal something about how far this might be practical or impractical.

Notes and References

1. This paper, written in the memory of Daya Krishna, was first delivered in January 2009 for publication by Dr Suparna Gooptu at the Gandhian Studies Centre, Department of History, University of Calcutta, and then delivered at the invitation of Vijay Tankha in February 2009 as the Bose Memorial lecture at St Stephens College, Delhi. I am grateful to all the participants who took part in discussion, and to Vinit Haksar, who first pointed out to me the interest of Gandhi's philosophy. Dayaji once organized a conference on one of my visits to Jaipur bringing together Greek, Sanskrit and Arabic traditions of philosophical commentary. He also treated Indian philosophy as a continuous tradition reaching up to the present. As a supporter of dialogue across the ages and cultural divides, I think he would have endorsed the idea of comparing ancient Greek and Roman Stoics with an Indian moral giant of the twentieth century.
2. The view is described by Cicero, *On Ends* 3. 62–68 and by Hierocles, *Elements of Ethics*, as reported by Stobaeus, vol. 4, ed. Hense, pp. 671–673. It is sketched in my *Animal Minds and Human Morals* (London: Duckworth, 1993), ch. 10.
3. Richard Sorabji, *Emotion and Peace of Mind* (Oxford: Oxford University Press, 2000), ch. 2, pp. 11, 13, 15–16.
4. Diogenes Laertius, *Lives of Eminent Philosophers* Book 7, 104–106.
5. See Epictetus, *Discourses* 3.23.30 and 37; 3.19.1; 4.9.10; 4.10.3.
6. Seneca, *On Anger* 2.4.1-4.
7. Epictetus, *Handbook* 3; *Discourses* 3.24.84-8; cf. 4.111.
8. Epictetus, *Discourses* 2.22.
9. Epictetus, *Discourses* 4.1.67 and 87.
10. So the founder, Zeno of Citium, is reported by Diogenes Laertius, *Lives of Eminent Philosophers* 7.32.
11. Origen, *On First Principles* 3.2.2; 3.2.4.

12. Sorabji, *Emotion and Peace of Mind*, ch. 26.
13. Plato, *Symposium* 218E-219B. The parallel was mentioned to me by Tarik Warel and K. P. Shankaran.
14. Gandhi, Speech on Tolstoy's anniversary, 10 Sep 1928, reprinted in Raghavan Iyer, *Moral and Political Writings of Mahatma Gandhi*, vol. 1, no. 59 (Oxford: Oxford University Press, 1986–1987).
15. Gospel of Matthew 5.38-40; Luke 6.29.
16. Tolstoy, *The Kingdom of God is Within You*, trans. (into English) Aylmer Maude (Garnett, pp. 97–102), pp. 131–136.
17. Gandhi, Discourse during evening prayer aboard S. S. Rajputana en route to London, published in *Young India* 1 October 1931, reprinted Raghavan Iyer, *Essential Writings of Mahatma Gandhi* (New Delhi: Oxford University Press, 1993), no. 151.
18. Candulal Bhagubhai Dalal, *Harilal Gandhi*, trans. (into English) Tridip Suhrud (New Delhi: Orient Longman, 2007); *Gandhi, My Father*, written and directed by Feroz Abbas Khan (2007).
19. Edwyn Bevan, *Stoics and Sceptics* (Oxford: Oxford University Press, 1913).
20. Mohandas Karamchand Gandhi, *Discourses on the Gita*, *Collected Works*, vol. 32, pp. 103–104. Similarly, Gandhi, Introduction to his Gujarati translation of the Gita, translated in R. Iyer, *The Essential Writings of Mahatma Gandhi*, no. 25 (Delhi: Clarendon Press, Oxford, 1991) and 'Meaning of the Gita', 11 October 1925, and Letter to Santosh Maharaj, 2 July 1927, reprinted respectively in R. Iyer, *Moral and Political Writings of Mahatma Gandhi*, vol I, no. 38 and 39 (Oxford, 1986).
21. Pp. 131–133 of the Ahmedabad 1924 edition.
22. R. B. Onians, *The Origins of European Thought* (Cambridge, 1954), pp. 109–110 note 4; 118; 149–150; Bikhu Parekh, 'Sex, energy and politics', *Colonialism, Tradition and Reform* (New Delhi: SAGE Publications, 1999, revised edition), ch. 6, p. 193, citing Gandhi, *Self-Restraint versus Self-Indulgence* (Ahmedabad, 1933).
23. Mohandas Karamchand Gandhi, *An Autobiography*, or *The Story of my Experiments with Truth* (Harmondsworth: Penguin, 1982), p. 291.
24. Ibid., p. 220.
25. Rajmohan Gandhi, *Mohandas, A True Story of a Man, His People and an Empire* (New Delhi: Penguin, 2006), pp. 278–279, cites this from Gandhi's *Collected Works*, vol. 23, pp. 139–141.
26. Gandhi, *Autobiography*, pp. 198–199.
27. Epictetus, *Discourses* 1.2.
28. Cicero, *On Ends* 3.22; Plutarch, *On Common Conceptions* 1070F-1071E.
29. Diogenes Laertius, 7. 104-5.
30. Gandhi, Letter of 1927 in Mahadev Desai's diary, reprinted in R. Iyer, *The Moral and Political Writings of Mahatma Gandhi*, vol. 2, no. 33, p. 70.

31. Gandhi, 'Still at it', *Young India*,15 March 1928, reprinted in R. Iyer, *The Essential Writings of Mahatma Gandhi*, no. 171.
32. Gandhi, *Harijan*, March 1936, cited by R. Iyer, *The Moral and Political Thought of Mahatma Gandhi* (New Delhi: Oxford University Press, 1973, Oxford paperbacks edition 2000), p. 101; Young India, vol. 3, *Ganesan*, reprinted in Tendulkar, ed., *Mahatma*, vol. 5, pp. 392–393.
33. Gandhi in *Indian Opinion*, 20 August 1903, quoted by Gopalkrishna Gandhi, *Gandhi*, *Essential Writings*, p. 103.
34. Gandhi, *Collected Works*, vol. 5, pp. 334–335, quoted by Gopalkrishna Gandhi, *Gandhi*, *Essential Writings* (New Delhi: Oxford University Press, 2008), p. 108.
35. Quoted from an earlier source by Rajmohan Gandhi, *Mohandas*, p. 197.
36. Gandhi, *Young India*, 25 August 1920, reprinted in *Mahatma Gandhi* (New York: Schocken Books, 1961), p. 161.
37. Gandhi, *Autobiography*, p. 197.
38. Quoted from an earlier source by Rajmohan Gandhi, *Mohandas*, p. 262.
39. Quoted by Rajmohan Gandhi, *Mohandas*, p. 415, from *Harijan*, 9 April 1938, in Gandhi *Collected Works*, vol. 73, p. 457.
40. Gandhi, 'The Law of Swadeshi', 31 May 1931, *Collected Works*, vol. 46, p. 255.
41. Gandhi, 'Jain Ahimsā', *Young India*, 25 October 1928.
42. Gandhi, *Discourses on the Gita*, *Collected Works*, vol. 32, p. 370.
43. Gandhi, 22 April 1914, *Collected Works*, vol. 12, pp. 410–411, cited by Gopalkrishna Gandhi, *Gandhi*, *Essential Writings*, p. 170.
44. Gandhi, Bombay theatre meeting 31 August 1924; *Young India*, 4 September 1924, *Collected Works*, vol. 29, pp. 65, 75, cited by Rajmohan Gandhi, *Mohandas*, pp. 283, 293.
45. I am grateful to Faisal Devji who first alerted me to this.
46. Gandhi, *Discourses on the Gita*, *Collected Works*, vol. 32, p. 103.
47. Cited by Gopalkrishna Gandhi, *Gandhi*, *Essential Writings*, p. 676 from Pyarelal ed., *Mahatma Gandhi*, *Last Phase* (Ahmedabad, 1956), vol. 2, pp. 703– 705.
48. Gandhi, *Collected Works*, vol. 77, pp. 70 and 236, cited in Gopalkrishna Gandhi, *Gandhi*, *Essential Writings*, pp. 515 and 520.
49. Gandhi, *Autobiography*, pp. 194–195.
50. Seneca, *Letter* 95, 53.
51. Epictetus, *Discourses* 1.11; 2.10.
52. Musonius Rufus, *Fragments*, Hense ed., 3; 4; 12; 13A.

5

A Still, Small Voice

Tridip Suhrud

I believe that the inner voice is the perfect knowledge or realization of the Truth. (Emphasis added)[1]

Mohandas Karamchand Gandhi (1869–1948) in his autobiography clarified the nature of his pursuit. He wrote, 'What I want to achieve-what I have been striving and pining to achieve these thirty years-is self-realization, to see God face to face, to attain *Mokṣa*. I live and move and have my being in pursuit of this goal.'[2] He worshipped *Satya Narayan*, God as Truth. He did not ever claim that he had indeed found Him, or seen Him face-to-face. But, Gandhi was seeking this Absolute Truth and was 'prepared to sacrifice the things dearest to me in pursuit of this quest'.[3] Although Gandhi never claimed to have seen God face-to-face, he could imagine that state; 'One who has realized God is freed from sin forever. He has no desire to be fulfilled. Not even in his thoughts will he suffer from faults, imperfections or impurities. Whatever he does will be perfect because he does nothing himself but the God within him does everything. He is completely merged in Him.'[4]

This state was for Gandhi the state of perfect self-realization, of perfect self-knowledge. It was a moment of revelation, a moment when the self was revealed to him. Although he believed that such perfect knowledge may elude him so long as he was imprisoned in the mortal body, he did make an extraordinary claim. This was his claim to hear what he described as a 'small, still voice', or the 'inner voice'. He used various terms such as the voice of God, of conscience, the inner voice, the voice of Truth or the small, still voice.[5] He made this claim often and also declared that he was powerless before the irresistible voice, that his conduct was guided by his voice. The nature of this inner voice and Gandhi's need and ability to listen to the voice becomes apparent when we examine his invocation of it.

The first time he invoked the authority of this inner voice in India was at a public meeting in Ahmedabad, where he suddenly declared his resolve to fast. This day was 15 February 1918. Twenty-two days prior to this date Gandhi had been leading the strike of the workers of the textiles mills of Ahmedabad. The mill workers had taken a pledge to strike work till their demands were met. They appeared to be going back upon their pledge. Gandhi was groping, not being able to clearly see the way forward. He described his sudden resolve thus:

> One morning-it was at a mill-hands' meeting-while I was groping and unable to see my way clearly, the light came to me. Unbidden and all by themselves the words came to my lips: "unless the strikers rally" I declared to the meeting, 'and continue to strike till a settlement is reached, or till they leave the mills altogether, I will not touch any food.'[6]

He was to repeatedly speak of the inner voice in similar metaphors; of darkness that enveloped him, his groping, churning, wanting to find a way forward and the moment of light, of knowledge when the voice spoke to him. Gandhi sought the guidance of his inner voice not only in the spiritual realm, a realm that was incommunicable and known only to him and his Maker, but also in the political realm. He called off the non-cooperation movement against the British in February 1922 in response to the prompting of his inner voice. His famous Dandi March also came to him through the voice speaking from within. Gandhi's search for a moral and spiritual basis for political action was anchored in his claim that one could and ought to be guided by the Voice of Truth speaking from within. This made his politics deeply spiritual. Gandhi's ideas of civilization and svarāj[7] were rooted in this possibility of knowing oneself. In 1909 Gandhi wrote his most important philosophical work, the *Hind Swaraj*.[8] Gandhi argued in the *Hind Swaraj*, that modern Western civilization in fact de-civilizes[9] and characterized it as black age or Satanic civilization. Gandhi argued that civilization in the modern sense had no place for either religion or morality. He wrote, 'Its true test lies in the fact that people living under it make bodily welfare the object of life.'[10] By making bodily welfare the object of life, modern civilization had shifted the locus of judgement outside the human being. It had made not right conduct but objects the measure of human worth. In so doing, it had closed the possibility of knowing oneself. True civilization on the other hand was rooted in this very possibility. He wrote; 'Civilization is that mode of conduct which points out to man the path of duty. Performance of duty and observance of morality are convertible terms. To observe morality is to attain mastery over our mind and passions. So doing, we know ourselves.'[11] This act of knowing oneself is not only the basis of spiritual life but also of political life. He defined svarāj thus: 'It is Swaraj when we learn to rule ourselves.'[12] This act of ruling oneself meant the control of mind and passions, of observance, of morality and of knowing the right and the true path. Gandhi's idea and practice of *satyāgraha* with its invocation of the soul-force is based on this. *Satyāgraha* requires not only the purity of means and ends but also the purity of the practitioner. *Satyāgraha* in the final instance is based on the recognition of one's own conscience, on one's ability to listen to one's inner voice and submit to it.

Perhaps the most contentious invocation of the inner voice occurred in 1933. In 1932 Gandhi had undergone a fast from 20 September to 25 September as a prisoner of the Yerwada Central Prison. This fast was undertaken in opposition to the decision of the British Government to conduct elections in India on the basis of communal representation. This fast had proved dangerous for his already frail body and brought him precariously close to death.

Even before he had fully regained his strength he shocked the nation by announcing his irrevocable decision to undergo a 21-day fast in May 1933. On 30 April 1933 he made a public announcement to go on an unconditional and irrevocable fast for self-purification. The fast was to commence on Monday noon of 8 May and end on Monday noon of 29 May.[13] He declared that this resolution was made in submission to his inner voice. He stated that he had tried in vain to resist the call. This announcement caught even his closest associates and fellow prisoners unaware; they did not know that a tempest had been raging within him. He described this act of listening to his fellow prisoner Vallabhbhai Patel. Gandhi said to Patel:

> As if for the last three days I were preparing myself for the great deluge! On many occasions, however, the thought of a fast would come repeatedly to my mind and I would drive it away . . . but the same thought would persistently come to my mind: "If you have grown so restless, why don't

> you undertake the fast? Do it." The inner dialogue went on for quite sometime. At half past twelve came the clear, unmistakable voice, "You must undertake the fast." That was all.[14]

Gandhi knew that his invocation of the inner voice was beyond comprehension and also beyond his capacity to explain. He asked, 'After all, does one express, can one express, all one's thoughts to others?'[15] Many tried to dissuade him from the fast, which they feared would result in his death. Not all were convinced of his claim to hear the inner voice. It was argued that what he heard was not the voice of God, but it was hallucination, that Gandhi was deluding himself and that his imagination had become over-heated by the cramped prison walls.

Gandhi remained steadfast and refuted the charge of self-delusion or hallucination. He said, 'not the unanimous verdict of the whole world against me could shake me from the belief that what I heard was the true Voice of God'.[16] Gandhi undertook the fast and of course survived it. Subsequently he explained the nature of divine inspiration.

> The night I got the inspiration, I had a terrible inner struggle. My mind was restless. I could see no way. The burden of my responsibility was crushing me. But what I did hear was like a Voice from afar and yet quite near. It was as unmistakable as some human voice definitely speaking to me, and irresistible. I was not dreaming at the time when I heard the Voice. The hearing of the Voice was preceded by a terrific struggle within me. Suddenly the Voice came upon me. I listened, made certain that it was the Voice, and the struggle ceased. I was calm.[17]

He argued that his claim was beyond both proof and reason. The only proof he could probably provide was the fact that he had survived the fiery ordeal. It was a moment that he had been preparing himself for. He felt that his submission to God as Truth was so complete, at least in that particular instance of fasting, that he had no autonomy left. All his acts were prompted by the inner voice. It was a moment of perfect surrender. Such a moment of total submission transcends reason. He wrote in a letter, 'Of course, for me personally it transcends reason, because I feel it to be a clear will from God. My position is that there is nothing just now that I am doing of my own accord. He guides me from moment to moment.'[18]

This extraordinary confession of perfect surrender perturbed many. The source of this discomfort is clear. Gandhi's claim to hear the inner voice was neither unique nor exclusive. The validity and legitimacy of such claim was recognized in the spiritual realm. The idea of perfect surrender was integral to and consistent with ideals of religious life. Although Gandhi never made the claim of having seen God face-to-face, having attained self-realization, the inner voice was for him the voice of God. He said, 'The inner voice is the voice of the Lord.'[19] But it was not a voice that came from a force outside of him. Gandhi made a distinction between an outer force and a power beyond us. A power beyond us has its locus within us. It is superior to us, not subject to our command or wilful action but it is still located within us. He explained the nature of this power. 'Beyond us' means a 'power which is beyond our ego'.[20] According to Gandhi one acquires the capacity to hear this voice when the 'ego is reduced to zero'.[21] Reducing the ego to zero for Gandhi meant an act of total surrender to *Satya Nārāyan.* This surrender required subjugation of human will, of individual autonomy. It is when a person loses autonomy that conscience emerges. Conscience is an act of obedience not wilfulness. He said, 'Wilfulness is not conscience. . . . Conscience is the ripe fruit of strictest discipline. . . . Conscience can reside only in a delicately tuned breast'.[22] He knew what a person with conscience could be like. 'A conscientious man hesitates to assert himself, he is always humble, never boisterous, always compromising, always ready to listen, ever willing, even anxious to admit mistakes.'[23] A person without this tender breast delicately tuned to the working of the conscience cannot hear the inner voice or more dangerously may in fact hear the voice of ego. This capacity did not belong to everyone as a natural gift or a right available in equal measure. What one required was a cultivated capacity to discern the inner voice as distinct from the voice of the ego. As, 'one cannot always recognise whether it is the voice of Rama or Ravana'.[24]

What was this ever-wakefulness that allowed him to hear the call of truth as distinct from the voice of untruth? How does one acquire the fitness to wait upon God? He had likened this preparation to an attempt to empty the sea with a drainer small as a point of a blade of grass. And yet, it had to be as natural as life itself. He created a regime of spiritual discipline that enabled him to search himself through and through. As part of his spiritual training he formulated what he called the *Ekādash Vṛata.*[25] The ashram or a community of co-religionists was constituted by their abiding faith in these *vṛata* and by their act of prayer. Prayer was the very core of his life. Medieval devotional poetry sung by Pandit Narayan Moreshwar Khare moved him. He drew sustenance from Mira and Charlie Andrews' rendition of 'When I survey the wondrous cross', while young Olive Doke healed him with 'Lead Kindly Light'. He recited the *Gītā* everyday. What was this intense need for prayer? What allowed him to claim that he was not a man of learning but a man of prayer? He knew that mere repetition of the *Rāmānāma* was futile if it did not stir his soul. A prayer for him had to be a clear response to the hunger of the soul. What was this hunger that moved his being?

Gandhi's was a passionate cry of the soul hungering for union with the divine. He saw his communion with God as that of a master and a slave in perpetual bondage, prayer was the expression of the intense yearning to merge in the Master. Prayer was the expression of the definitive and conscious longing of the soul; it was his act of waiting upon Him for guidance. His want was to feel the utterly pure presence of the divine within. Only a heart purified and cleansed by prayer could be filled with the presence of God, where life became one long continuous prayer, an act of worship. Prayer was for him the final reliance upon God to the exclusion of all else. He knew that only when a person lives constantly in the sight of God, when he or she regards each thought with God as witness and its Master, could one feel Rama dwelling in the heart every moment. Such a prayer could only be offered in the spirit of non-attachment, *anasakti*. Moreover, when the God that he sought to realize is Truth, prayer though externalized was in essence directed inwards. Because Truth is not merely that we are expected to speak. It is That which alone is, it is That of which all things are made, it is That which subsists by its own power, which alone is eternal. Gandhi's intense yearning was that such Truth should illuminate his heart. Prayer was a plea, a preparation, a cleansing that enabled him to hear his inner voice. The *Ekādash Vṛata* allowed for this waiting upon God. The act of waiting meant to perform one's actions in a desireless or detached manner. The *Gītā* describes this state as a state of *sthitpragñya*. The state of *sthitpragñya* was for Gandhi not only a philosophical ideal but a personal aspiration. The *Gītā* describes this state as a condition of *sthitpragñya*. A *sthitpragñya* is one who puts away 'all the cravings that arise in the mind and finds comfort for himself only from the *atman*',[26] and one 'whose senses are reined in on all sides from their objects',[27] so that the mind is 'untroubled in sorrows and longeth not for joys, who is free from passion, fear and wrath'[28] who knows attachment no where; only such a brahmachari can be in the world 'moving among sense objects with the sense weaned from likes and dislikes and brought under the control of the atman'.[29] This detachment or self-effacement allowed Gandhi to dwell closer to Him. It made possible an act of surrender and allowed him to claim;

> I have been a willing slave to this most exacting master for more than half a century. His voice has been increasingly audible as years have rolled by. He has never forsaken me even in my darkest hour. He has saved me often against myself and left me not a vestige of independence. The greater the surrender to Him, the greater has been my joy.[30]

What he craved was this absence of independence, lack of autonomy; because that would finally allow him to see God face-to-face. He knew that he had not attained this state and perhaps would never attain it so long as his body remained, as 'no one can be called a *mukta* while he is alive'.[31]

In this we have an understanding of Gandhiji's experiment and his quest. His quest is to know himself, to attain *mokṣa*, that is, to see God (Truth) face-to-face. In order to fulfil his quest, he must be an ashramite, a satyagrahi and a seeker after svarāj. He added two other practices to this search. One was fasting, the other *brahmacarya*. Fasting in its original sense is not mortification of flesh, but it is *upvās*, to dwell closer to Him. In this sense there could be no fast without a prayer and indeed no prayer without a fast. Such a fast was both penance and self-purification.

The ultimate practice of self-purification is the practice of *brahmacarya*. For Gandhi realization of Truth and self-gratification appears a contradiction in terms. From this emanate not only *brahmacarya* but also three other observances: control of the palate, *aparīgraha* and *asteya*.

Brahmacarya, described as a *mahāvrata*, came to Gandhi as a necessary observance at a time when he had organized an ambulance corps during the Zulu rebellion in South Africa. He realized that service of the community was not possible without observance of *brahmacarya*. At the age of 37, in 1906 Gandhi took the vow of *brahmacarya*. He had begun experimenting with food and diet as a student in England. It was much later that he was to comprehend the relationship between *brahmacarya* and control of the palate. These observances and strivings of self-purification were not without a purpose. He was later to feel that they were secretly preparing him for *satyāgraha*.[32] It would take him several decades, but through his observances, his experiments, Gandhi developed insights into the interrelatedness of Truth, Ahiṃsā and *brahmacarya*. He came to regard practice of *brahmacarya* in thought, word and deed as essential for the search for Truth and the practice of *ahimsā*. Gandhi, by making observance of *brahmacarya* essential for truth and *ahimsā*, made it central to the practice of *satyāgraha* and quest for svarāj. *Satyāgraha* involves recognition of truth and steadfast adherence to it, it requires self-sacrifice or self-suffering and use of pure, that is, non-violent means by a person who is cleansed through self-purification. *Satyāgraha* and svarāj are both modes of self-recognition. This understanding allowed Gandhi to expand the conception of *brahmacarya* itself. He began with a popular and restricted notion in the sense of chastity and celibacy, including celibacy in marriage. He expanded this notion to mean observance in thought, word and deed. But it is only when he began to recognize the deeper and fundamental relationship that *brahmacarya* shared with *satyāgraha*, *ahiṃsā* and svarāj that Gandhi could go to the root of the term *brahmacarya*. *Carya* or conduct adopted in search of Brahma, that is, Truth, is *brahmacarya*. In this sense *brahmacarya* is not denial or control over one sense, but it is an attempt to bring all senses in harmony with each other. *Brahmacarya* so conceived and practised becomes that mode of conduct that leads to Truth, knowledge and hence *mokṣa*. Thus, the ability to hear the inner voice, a voice that is 'perfect knowledge or realization of Truth'[33] is an experiment in *brahmacarya*.

Notes and References

1. *Collected Works of Mahatma Gandhi,* vol. 56 (New Delhi: Publications Division, Ministry of Information and Broadcasting, Government of India), 82. Henceforth, *CWMG,* this hundred volume set was published between 1958 and 1994.
2. M. K. Gandhi, *An Autobiography or The Story of My Experiments with Truth*, trans. (from the original Gujarati) Mahadev Desai (Ahmedabad: Navajivan, 1927/1999), p. x.
3. Ibid., p. xi.
4. *CWMG*, vol. 55, p. 255.
5. Ibid.
6. M. K. Gandhi, *An Autobiography or The Story of My Experiments with Truth*, p. 359.
7. There is no English substitute that captures the full range of meanings that the word svarāj. invokes. It has been loosely translated as freedom (which presupposes slavery) and self or home-rule (which presupposes political subjugation). Gandhi himself preferred to use the term svarāj.
8. M. K. Gandhi, *Hind Swaraj*, 1909. He translated it in English, which was published in 1911. All the references are from the thirteenth reprint

published in 2000 by the Navajivan Press, Ahmedabad. Hereafter, *Hind Swaraj*.
9. The Gujarati term that he used was *kudhar*, literally the wrong way.
10. *Hind Swaraj,* p. 31.
11. *Hind Swaraj,* p. 53.
12. *Hind Swaraj,* p. 56.
13. For the statement on the fast see, *CWMG*, vol. 55, pp. 74–75.
14. *CWMG*, vol. 55, p. 76.
15. Ibid.
16. *CWMG*, vol. 55, p. 256.
17. *CWMG*, vol. 55, p. 255.
18. *CWMG*, vol. 52, p. 244.
19. Ibid., vol. 53, p. 483.
20. Ibid.
21. Ibid.
22. Ibid., vol. 25, pp. 23–24.
23. Ibid.
24. Ibid., vol. 52, p. 130.
25. These 11 vows are: Truth, *ahiṃsā* or love (also called non-violence), brahmacharya or chastity, control of the palate, non-stealing, non-possession or poverty, fearlessness, removal of untouchability, tolerance or equality of all religions and swadeshi or promotion of native goods.
26. Discourse II: verse 55.
27. Discourse II: verse 68.
28. Discourse II: verse 56.
29. Discourse II: verse 64.
30. *CWMG*, vol. 55, p. 121
31. Ibid., vol. 37, p. 116.
32. M. K. Gandhi, *An Autobiography or The Story of My Experiments with Truth*, p. 266.
33. *CWMG,* vol. 56, p. 182.

6

Learning to Converse

Michael McGhee

I

The three of us sweated in the heat and swayed with the rhythms of the crowded suburban train as we talked or shouted rather, to make ourselves heard, hanging by straps in the crush, two Indians, Probal Dasgupta and Prabodh Parikh, and one Britisher, myself—all roughly of an age, in our late thirties. It was 1985 and Probal and I had travelled down from Pune on the Deccan Express to meet Prabodh in Bombay—and it had also been a chance for me to meet the incomparable M. P. Rege. The polymath and inexhaustible Probal had been a kind (but challenging) friend, and had gently but firmly introduced me to—opened my eyes to—the real life of India, including the nature, diversity and 'situation' of its intellectual life.

Things have changed dramatically since those days, a quarter of a century ago, but the urgent agenda then in the face of what was perceived as a monolithic and engulfing westernization was humorously summed up in an aside by the distinguished philosopher J. P. S. Uberoi, who talked wryly of wielding his lone Indian fountain pen against the massed typewriters of the West. The typewriters may have had their day but the 'issue' of cultural hegemony and its baleful effect on dialogue has not faded with the emergence of what we now call globalization.

The situation of Indian 'philosophy' at that time could be seen as an instance of a more general kind: How should the non-Western, postcolonial world respond to a nevertheless increasingly encroaching, not to say dominant Western culture? How, in particular, should Indians respond in the light of their own culture, in the light of their own philosophical traditions? Ideally we are talking here about a 'meeting' of cultures and a reciprocal self–re-examination in the light of the encounter with the other, which is surely the essence of philosophical dialogue. In the case of a hegemonic relationship, however, there is no such meeting, at least for the 'hegemon', but rather an incurious estimate of the indigenous ('native') culture in the terms of their own ideas. For the other, 'subaltern', party, however, there is still a question about the reception of an alien or foreign culture at all—how to receive or respond to its institutions, practices and ideas. One has to assess and reassess one's own culture and the foreign one, distinguish between truth and error, and between both of these and simple difference of perspective on a shared reality, discerning similarity and difference beneath surface difference and surface similarity of idiom and expression. These are indeed pressing questions, especially when it seems that the foreign ideas 'distort' reality, including one's own, and that the foreign practices and institutions are at best inappropriate to the conditions and at worst morally pernicious—though one has to add that all of these things are a matter of judgement and discernment and the categories themselves can be used as alibis to justify and protect indigenous forms of injustice.

There is particular critical work to be done by philosophers, at least at the level of ideas. But engagement with the western philosophical 'tradition' is one thing, mutual engagement with western 'philosophers' is another. The incuriousness of the old hegemonic culture lingers on, partly these days in the form of a resentfully tolerated 'multiculturalism', but manifests itself also in the entrenched attitudes of philosophers who do not expect to learn anything from other traditions—though they are perfectly happy to recruit others to their own cause. Little has changed in Western philosophical attitudes since J. N. Mohanty[1] and Daya Krishna[2] complained more than a decade ago about the ignorance, and hence the facile terms and false dichotomies, that had characterized comparisons made by Western philosophers between Indian and Western philosophy; it is an obvious truth that one needs to be interior to both traditions before one makes (invidious) comparisons. Genuine engagement, however, on the part of pioneering individuals, is liable to be shunted into a siding called 'comparative philosophy'.

II

Despite Uberoi's perception of the massed typewriters, 'western culture' is by no means monolithic but is constituted by many strands, tensions and contradictions, as is the receiving, in this case, Indian culture. So there is also resistance 'within' the Western tradition to ideas that seem to distort reality and to practices that seem morally pernicious. To put it in one way, ideology (of the mystificatory kind) is not usually either 'entirely' engulfing or 'entirely' overwhelming and some common ground is available between cultures. Perhaps unfortunately there is more than one kind of common ground, and common reactive mentalities can lead to violent opposition between those who feel threatened and alienated, as well as to alliances between them against a common enemy. The mobilization of threatened fundamentalisms against each other, the 'expressive' bombings of night clubs, the briskly repented collateral damage to wedding parties, have been only one kind of manifestation of alienation and unease in the face of the comprehensive westernization that has surged in the last decades.

The issue, of course, is hardly restricted to India. Thus, in his *The Mantle of the Prophet*,[3] Roy Mottahedeh discusses the Iranian writer Al-e Ahmad's sense of the cultural illness that he felt had stricken the towns and cities of Iran. Mottahedeh comments:

> For this illness Al-e Ahmad seized on a newly coined word, and he made this word a rallying cry for Iranians from the sixties to the present. The word translated literally, piece by piece, is 'West-stricken-ness', but even this clumsy translation fails to convey the sense of the Persian original, *gharbzadegi*. 'I say that *gharbzadegi* . . . is like cholera (or) frost-bite. But no. it's at least as bad as saw-flies in the wheat fields. Have you ever seen how they infest wheat? From within. There's a healthy skin in places, but it's only a skin, just like the shell of a cicada on a tree.'

The late J. L. Mehta[4] once talked of the disruptive forces unleashed by the Western 'marriage of science with technology': We are one world now through participation in Heidegger's 'world-civilisation'. Mehta was well known as a commentator on Heidegger—he is not making a naïve complaint about the dominance of a culturally neutral western science and technology, but associating himself, rather, with Heidegger's critique of the reality-obscuring 'stance' of 'commanding forth', the *Gestell* or 'enframing' that has determined the form of that dominance, and the form, therefore, of what remains to be resisted by those who are precisely becoming Heidegger's 'standing-reserve'.

Mehta asks whether it isn't true that 'Western thought . . . enters . . . like a Trojan horse . . . into the thinking of the Non-Western world' or 'like a virus . . . invisibly altering our perceptions of reality'. These images, of the Trojan horse or of a virus or an infestation, all carry the sense of an experience of being undermined in one's identity. The Trojan horse was the great image of stealth, treachery and occupation within the citadel of ideas. The idea of a virus is of something invisible to perception that nevertheless harms, undermines, debilitates, and it is the stealth and the invisibility that finally dismays us in the original sense of loss of power. The idea of an infestation that leaves the exterior skin intact but destroys the centre speaks powerfully of the felt loss of identity as one loses touch with one's roots by absorbing someone else's narrative, one in which one's character has already been assigned, and this by others.

I had already read, by the time Probal and I met Prabodh, a notable special issue of *Indian Philosophical Quarterly* published in 1984 and dedicated to the theme of 'Svarāj *in Ideas*'. Self-rule or self-determination in the political sphere was one thing, precarious as that might have been in geopolitical terms, but there was more to be done in dealing with the broken roots of the old colonialism still active in Indian soil. The collection was a set of responses by contemporary Indian thinkers to a percipient discourse to Indian students by Krishna Chandra Bhattacharya delivered in 1929 during British rule. I had found the collection compelling, not least because it further made real to me something of the self-understanding and inherited situation of the philosophers who had contributed to it and in whose midst I now found myself. But it also expressed a set of concerns that echoed my own concerns, which really gave birth to the idea of the Convivium[5] as Prabodh, Probal and I had our loud conversation on the suburban train. What my friends and other philosophers I was now reading were concerned about was the oppressive reality of westernization and its specific consequences for the work of Indian philosophers and their relationship to their own traditions. I saw and felt some of the same oppressive reality, though I called it by other names, materialism, perhaps, or secularism, or even just a loss of vision in philosophy, an absence of the imagination, of connection with 'life'—and 'that' connection was palpable in the case of Dayaji, Ramubhai and Rege. I wanted to insist that there was nothing monolithic about this 'westernisation', but rather that there were counter-currents in the West that mirrored Indian philosophical resources that could be mobilized for resistance; that one had to distinguish between the (super-)imposition of a foreign culture and the specific content of what was aggressively dominant in that culture; and that there was plenty of room for dialogue and a meeting of minds if the right conditions could be found.

The guest editors of *Svarāj* (K. J. Shah, Ramchandra Gandhi, Sharad Deshpande and Probal Dasgupta) referred in their introduction to the loss of svarāj in ideas as a form of Indian bondage, and, in so doing, echoed Mehta's metaphor of invisibility: 'a bondage more enslaving than political subjugation because of its invisibility and silent, creeping paralysing power, unforgivably persistent even after political independence'.[6] They here followed Bhattacharya himself in his 1929 lecture, who went on to claim that cultural subjection occurs 'when one's traditional cast of ideas and sentiments is superseded "*without comparison or competition*" by a new cast representing an alien culture which possesses one like a ghost' (my italics). He thought that the Indian cast of mind, an indigenous culture of a high degree of development, had 'subsided below the conscious level of culture'. If an entire system of ideas and sentiments—those of Western culture—have indeed been imposed or superimposed in this way, the consequence is that 'we either accept or repeat the judgements passed on us by Western culture, or we impotently resent them but have hardly any estimates of our own, wrung from an inward perception of the realities of our position'. 'Hardly any estimates of our own' but in their place, someone else's narrative, the received and incurious estimate of the imperial power whose ideology is absorbed in such a way that the colonised receive their identity and trajectory from the colonisers, long after they have gone.

I had visited the Philosophy Department at Poona University when I first arrived in the city and had been warmly received there, particularly by K. J. Shah and Sharad Deshpande. As it happened, I turned up in time to hear the first in a series of lectures by Ramchandra Gandhi on the philosophy of religion. Although it was clear to me at once that he had a brilliant mind, I was also shocked by what he was saying. When I look back at the scene I realize now that I was ignorant 'in fact' of the cultural context and fully self-conscious stance of his philosophizing, as well as of the dialectical and epistemological significance of what philosophers call the 'subject position'. I had myself fallen into the trap of the incurious colonist, failing to understand the relativity[7] of my own position which—and this is the point—I was hardly aware of 'as' one position among others: the irony of the subject position is its manifest visibility to all but the subject. I was able to pay lip-service to the 'idea' but I had never really been confronted by the reality, and it is confrontation with reality, I think, that reveals real rather than official attitudes. But I need to explain my sense of shock, and it might be best to start by recording a conversation I had with K. J. Shah, and by citing a passage from one of Daya Krishna's papers.

Shah had been discussing[8] with me the significance for Indians of people like Ramana Maharshi, and had observed that,

> It was the presence in India of men of such great spirituality, even in the twentieth century, that made the difference between western and Indian attitudes to religion; the presence of such spirituality was something that Indians were confronted with and had to take some account of.

Now, in an insightful 1961 paper published in his book *The Art of the Conceptual*, Daya Krishna had remarked, 'The capacity for inner freedom, abiding joy, and relevant response to external situations is so pre-eminent and abundant in spiritual persons that compared to them, ordinary, normal persons appear as deficient human beings' (p. 120).

It seems clear enough that Dayaji was saying something similar to Shah. Part of the point is that both philosophers effectively set out criteria by which we can distinguish the genuine from the bogus in the case of 'spiritual persons'. Much to my own liking and much more important, they make the idea of conduct and demeanour 'as criteria of an inner condition'—a central feature of the philosophy of religion—rather than the usual, accepted notion of 'belief', a notion which purports to be universal but which in fact betrays an unacknowledged, specifically Christian bias. Of course the notion of 'belief' is anyway a difficult and contested concept even within the traditions of Christian theology and philosophy, but here it is its assumed centrality for the philosophy of religion as such that is the issue. In terms of our unself-conscious westernization, it is an assumed universality: all philosophy of religion is really a philosophy of Christian religion, and what appears to diverge from that model is tied down to a Procrustean bed and hacked into shape. In the same paper Dayaji precisely remarks on the skewing of philosophy of religion that occurs because of an unconscious concentration on Christianity, an unconscious bias that has hardly changed since he made these remarks:

> The other great limitation of the discussion, to my mind, was its confinement, perhaps naturally, to Christianity alone. It was as if one were to reflect on aesthetic experience and confine one's discussion to Greek art

> or the Renaissance masters only. . . . That no one challenged this implicit limitation shows once again the difficulty of getting beyond the perspective of the culture one happens to be born in. (p. 114)

Ramchandra Gandhi himself was deeply affected by the life of Ramana Maharshi and the title of his 1985 book, *I am Thou*,[9] is taken from a remark of Ramana. In the lectures I attended Ramubhai sought to develop a philosophical argument in support of the non-dualist Advaita claim that he took to be poetically expressed in that remark. But, my sense of shock . . . I had introduced a new undergraduate course in the philosophy of religion at my own university in the UK several years earlier and had done so despite the scepticism and misgivings of colleagues who were, on the whole, of a materialist and 'anti-religious' persuasion. They thought that 'religion' (by which they certainly meant the Christian religion), theology and metaphysics had been decisively discredited long ago, and that it was a retrograde step to teach such things, though they probably also thought that at least it would provide an opportunity to discuss certain logical issues associated with philosophical theology. But I wasn't in fact concerned to teach a course on the philosophy of the Christian religion at all, partly because I had moved away from it—or from a certain model of it that had alienated me from approaches to other models—and become a practising Buddhist. Part of my motivation for inaugurating a course in the philosophy of religion lay in the felt need to articulate and give philosophical expression to the nature and implications of meditational experience, and this was giving me reason to reappraise my understanding of how to approach Christianity from a philosophical point of view as well. It also forced me to the view that conduct and demeanour as criteria of spirituality should replace 'belief' as the central topic. But I felt that the dialectical situation in British philosophy was a delicate one. I had to try to write about 'experience' in an environment in which the assumed paradigm was a degraded concept of 'belief'. It was refreshing and reassuring, then, several years later, to read Dayaji's comment on the symposium at which he gave his paper:

> The hours devoted to discussion in this symposium seemed characterised by a singular unconcern with religious experience, which is the *raison d'être* of any inquiry undertaken in this field at all. . . . There was, for example, much discussion of language in religious discourse, but little, if any, attention was paid to the way in which religious concepts arise from, and find their meaning in, religious experience itself. The 'operationalism' so obvious in the field of science did not seem quite so necessary in the field of religion to most philosophers assembled there. (p. 112)

However, I simply took it for granted that my own delicate dialectical situation was a general one, and that this was what one had to do if one was doing philosophy of religion. And here was Professor Gandhi talking about the ultimate unitive reality of *Brahmanātman* without, as it seemed, all that epistemological vigilance that seemed to me absolutely necessary, and had cost me so much intellectual effort—except that the epistemological vigilance that seemed to me absolutely necessary was in fact precisely 'situated' and directed towards a particular set of historical and conceptual concerns that did not affect Ramu's enterprise: the whole Death of God scenario, the relationship between an apparently discredited philosophical theology that sought to prove that there was a God, and the rationality of belief—whereas Ramubhai was concerned with such categories as *mokṣa* or liberation and the ultimate nature of Selfhood, to which the discourse of 'belief' was irrelevant.

It was not that we would not have had philosophical disagreements independently of our different points of departure, about the role of argument in philosophical reflection on claims about the Self by men and women who met the criteria mentioned by Shah and Dayaji, for instance. I think my shock was caused by a failure to realize that there were different points of departure and then to be confronted by one.

III

In the book mentioned earlier, Mohanty remarks that there now exists the possibility, for Indian intellectuals, 'not merely of studying Indian thought from the point of view of the Western philosophies, but also, by reversing that strategy, *of critically studying the Western philosophies from the vantage-points of the typically Indian modes of thinking*' (p. 22, my italics). Whether this can be done at all depends on the vitality and intelligence of the new generation who undertake it. But it also depends upon a reciprocating receptivity on the part of westerners prepared properly to inform themselves of the actual nature of the Indian philosophical traditions, and this is a matter of opening up a dialogue that depends essentially on individual conversations. Taking such a dialogue seriously depends upon the shared premise that reality is transcendent of any particular purchase or perception, and that consequently, there can be more than one form of insight, more than one form of 'blindness' towards being. There typically goes with this kind of blindness to being a corresponding failure to hear the voices of others. It is not an accident that in *The Art of the Conceptual*, Dayaji should have complained precisely about not being 'heard'. This kind of failure, though, is not a deliberate 'act', but rather an inability to make sense of new material.

If we assume that we can learn from each other, and otherwise we shall have no reason to incline towards 'dialogue', then the natural context for this to take place in is, as I have said, that of conversation between a pair of interlocutors, possibly in a small group as long as this does not become an audience. But a possible participant of such a dialogue has to be capable of rapid role-reversal, capable, that is, of assuming the role of teacher 'or' pupil, in the very same conversation. As Probal Dasgupta has said elsewhere in this volume, the Convivium series, originally of British and Indian philosophers, was a side show in the formation of contemporary Indian philosophy as it was fashioned by thinkers like Daya Krishna, Ramchandra Gandhi and others. Perhaps it is better to think of the series as a case study. Participation of this kind between thinkers from Britain and from India, with their former colonial relationship, and postcolonial and post-imperial neuroses and unconscious attitudes, of arrogance and resentment, was a poignant attempt to embody 'the ideal speech situation', and required a great deal of awareness and forbearance on both sides. The idea of a 'dialogue' between cultures seems a rather general and ambitious enterprise, but there is an upper limit on the numbers who can engage in a 'conversation' at any particular time, and the notion of 'conversation' recalls us to the essentially personal aspect of philosophy. The Socratic enterprise of 'testing' a view or belief may leave the one in whom that view is undermined with a sense of helplessness, a condition very different from that loss of identity we mentioned earlier, a sense of helplessness which can lead to reactive aggression, a defence of a previously constructed self-image. It is interesting, though, that there are superficial similarities here to the angry and violent rejection of an alien culture that is being imposed, though there is in reality a world of difference between the two kinds of cases. The *elenchus*—the testing, the probing, the Socratic interrogation of one's premises, of the *Hintergedanken*, the thoughts that underlie action—puts pressure, then, also on our 'emotional' life, upon our sensibility, in a direct and sometimes dramatic, drastic way. To talk of our sensibility is to refer to our motivating thoughts and beliefs: we move, we 'are' moved, in the world as 'grasped' by thought. Socratic dialogue is an occasion for 'un-grasping', for rendering oneself receptive to the possibility of the world's showing itself in ways not available to the disclosure-resisting pictures that held us captive. The Socratic dialogue is effective, though, only if the thoughts one puts to the test are genuinely the thoughts that structure the sensibility we are attached to. If these thoughts lead to contradiction or incoherence, lead the person into *aporia* (a sense of being at a loss) then their world and thus their orientation is dismantled and unmade, and this is the creative condition of new possibilities of thinking and feeling.

The emphasis is on conversation and the conditions for conversation, since this is the context for the friendly *agon* of genuine dialogue. If Mohanty's implicit 'challenge' is to be taken seriously, then such contexts need to be established, in which genuine exponents of both living and interacting traditions are ready both to question and to listening. It was such reflections as these, about the parallels between the lived situations of thinkers from both traditions, that led to the initiation of the Convivium series of meetings between British and Indian philosophers, at which Dayaji and Ramubhai, as well as Rege, played such a prominent role. But the idea is one about the ideal conditions for doing philosophy at all, and is not specific to participants from different cultures, though in a way philosophers are 'always' from different cultures, and they do not speak to each other as often as they seem to do, or are, indeed, required to do by the very nature of their discipline. Nevertheless, the kinds of conversations initiated by Daya Krishna and Ramchandra Gandhi have opened up the conditions for the possibility of a new and global conversation between philosophers who are able to draw on the concepts and metaphors, the narratives, of more than one tradition, for the possibility of an intercultural canon.

Notes and References

1. In *Reason and Tradition in Indian Thought: An Essay on the Nature of Indian Philosophical Thinking* (Oxford: Clarendon Press, 1992).
2. In *Indian Philosophy: A Counter Perspective* (New Delhi: Oxford University Press, 1991).
3. Mottahedeh Roy, *The Mantle of the Prophet: Religion and Politics in Iran* (London: Chatto and Windus, 1985), p. 296.
4. In *Philosophy and Religion: Essays in Interpretation* (New Delhi: Indian Council for Philosophical Research, 1990).
5. Mentioned elsewhere in this volume by Probal Dasgupta.

6. This theme had earlier been addressed in Ashis Nandy's *The Intimate Enemy: Loss and Recovery of Self under Colonialism* (New Delhi: Oxford University Press, 1983).
7. This is not of course a 'relativist' claim, a doctrine about truth. It is, rather, a claim about perspective and allows for the possibility of recognizing a shared reality 'and' the possibility of a movement from one perspective on it to another. From here 'this' can be seen, but not from over there where 'that' can be seen: we assemble a total picture of the terrain by collating our perspectives, where nevertheless individual perspectives can distort one's sense of the whole.
8. See Michael McGhee, *Transformations of Mind* (Cambridge: Cambridge University Press, 2000), p. 202.
9. Ramchandra Gandhi, *I am Thou: Meditations on the Truth of India* (Pune: Indian Philosophical Quarterly Publications, 1984).

PART III

Modes of Saṃvāda

7

Towards a New Hermeneutic of Self-inquiry

Devasia M. Antony

I am all things, past, present and future. . . .
I cannot only be this body, this person, this child . . .
I must be all forms and also that which is without form.
I am speech and silence.
Being and nothingness. Purna and Shunya.
I am wakefulness, work. . . . But not only activism.
I am also contemplativeness. . . .
I am ethically and ecologically [and existentially]
sensitive wakefulness. . . .
And beyond and behind wakefulness, dreaming and sleep,
I am abiding freshness, . . . unfading self-awareness.[1]

Introduction

In a philosophically exploratory speech on 'divine madness' Socrates says that madness is nobler when compared to sober sense. For 'madness comes from God, whereas sober sense is merely human'.[2] Having been a participant in the various workshops conducted by Ramchandra Gandhi and having dwelt meditatively on the philosophical motifs of his major writings and workshops,[3] I am of the belief that he was blessed with 'divine madness'. For the one singular idea that captivated his ceaselessly inquisitive and fertile mind was that of the self and its logical and conceptual corollary, that is, the praxis of self-inquiry. An inquisitive peep into the Indian philosophical and spiritual traditions would undoubtedly show that this problematic is of fundamental significance. The availability of both the so-called canonical and non-canonical texts that embody intellectually challenging and often spiritually demanding debate and intriguing discussion on the notion of *brahman* and its necessarily logical and conceptual correlates, such as *ātman*, *puruṣa*, *jīva*, *jagat*, dharma, *mokṣa*, *nirvāṇa* and so on, amply illustrates this. And in that 'the divinely mad' Ramchandra Gandhi can be seen as a creative interpreter of both the *śruti* and *smṛti* philosophical traditions and thus having continued the unbroken and unfettered ceaseless inquiry into the nature and significance of self. But one might justifiably ponder and ask: Is that all about this uniquely itinerant philosopher par excellence? In this paper I want to argue for the contention that in his praxis of self-inquiry, one can discover the footprints of a wayfarer on the road less travelled and thereby inaugurating a new hermeneutic of self-inquiry that does hold together the dialectic of the apparently conflicting traditions that have philosophically and spiritually wrestled with the nature and significance of self. The *yakṣapraśna* of the *Mahābhārata* employing a powerful and polyvalent metaphor tells us that the truth about dharma lies hidden in the dark cave—*dharmasya tatvam nihitam guhayam.*[4] In the practice of his *svadharma* of self-inquiry, I venture to say that Ramchandra Gandhi, like an engaged ascetic steeped in heaven-sent madness, dared to peep into this dark cave.

The Primordiality of the Question, 'Who Am I?'

It was Immanuel Kant, the famous German philosopher who claimed that any intellectual enterprise that deserves the name 'philosophy' in a fundamental and universal sense should address this fourfold question: What can I know? What ought I to do? What may I hope? And what is human person? Interestingly this fourfold question has its moorings both in the Greek as well as the Indic philosophical world. In its philosophical genealogy it can be traced back to the inscription, 'Know thyself', found on the temple of Apollo at Delphi which Socrates took to be paradigmatic of all philosophical inquiries. And Socrates unequivocally makes the claim that self-inquiry is the most fundamental and beneficial of all philosophical quests.[5] In the matrix of the Indic philosophical traditions, the very conception of the self has been the singular idea that has captivated the inquiring mind in its reflective thinking. Perhaps it is best encapsulated in the Upaniṣadic dialectic between the self and the not-self. For though the self is concealed in all things, apparently what one sees is not-self. It is only when one develops the keen insight along with sharp and penetrating intellect that one can perceive everything, including the apparent not-self as the self.[6] In the contemporary Indian philosophical world, it was Ramana Maharshi (1879–1950 CE), the sage of Arunachala who recaptured the philosophical and spiritual dynamics of the question of the self and said that self-enquiry is nothing but the silent and deep investigation into the source of 'I'-thought—for this 'I'-thought is the core of all thoughts—and this leads one to liberation.[7] Rooted in the traditional philosophical and spiritual wisdom of India but simultaneously not turning a blind eye to the philosophical and religious traditions of the West, and drawing us into the heart of Upaniṣadic inquiry, Ramchandra Gandhi would creatively reinterpret the Socratic-Kantian-Ramana query and say that the most fundamental philosophical problematic that one should engage in is 'who am I?' For him, there is a certain primordiality and centrality, and if one might add parenthetically, a fundamental prodigality, to this question. In his own words:

> Inquiry into this question yields the conclusion that, individually and collectively, we are the sheer indubitability of self-awareness, and are imaged in all forms, including formlessness, and not merely the human form. The interdependence of all our self-images constitutes a cohesiveness which is larger than . . . [mere human collectivity] and does not exclude non-human reality. An anthropocentric notion of . . . [collectivity] runs the risk of encouraging totalitarianism of the human species, and of shifting attention away from the central certainty of our realty, i.e. self-awareness. The challenging task is to build a notion of the unity of reality which is grounded in the self-awareness of each human being.[8]

The primordiality, centrality, and parenthetically what I call the prodigality of the question 'who am I?' and its creatively woven hermeneutic by Ramchandra Gandhi become very significant when one tries to visualize and capture the very spirit of his inquiry. This I argue is contained in his philosophical *mahāvākya*[9] that 'the Self is'. The underlying significance of this *mahāvākya* can be understood only when one engages with its two distorted and fallaciously existential, ethical and ecological correlative predications: 'the Self is only this body' and 'the Self is not this body at all'.

The *Mahāvākya* 'That the Self Is': Picturing Reality in Its Singularity and Non-exclusivity

Taking recourse to the praxis of self-inquiry (*ātman-vicāra*) as the supremely beneficial act of reflective thinking, Ramchandra Gandhi attempts to philosophically construct the thesis that the self alone is and that self-awareness in its self-luminosity and indubitability is the only non-contradictable fact of human experience in reflective thinking. In this attempt, philosophical inquiry with its subtle logic and metaphysical principles stands symbiotically woven into the labyrinth of spiritual explorations characterized by the courage to journey alone in solitude along the road less travelled.

In his philosophic and spiritual explorations on self, Ramchandra Gandhi critiques vehemently the dominant philosophical idea that consciousness is necessarily tied to 'intentionality' or the conception that the category of 'aboutness' is logically and conceptually the necessary correlate of consciousness. In other words, what is emphasized is the predominant idea that consciousness is always conscious of some other object, which is other than itself. And very often the claim is made that consciousness can never be self-consciousness, because the idea of 'self' is ontologically repugnant and epistemologically illusory. In his philosophical soliloquy, Gandhi calls this the 'harlot-view of consciousness'. Contesting such a view of consciousness, Gandhi states that the notion of 'I' in our linguistic communication symbolizes self-awareness, which is the most fundamental, undeniable as well as indubitable reality. But this self-awareness, claims Gandhi, would cease to be self-awareness as such if it were ever aware of objects other than itself, that is, the 'not-self' as opposed to the 'self'. It means that 'self-awareness' cannot be 'not-self self-awareness'. In other words, what Gandhi claims is that the most primitive logical character of self-awareness is that it is ever aware of itself and in that it is a logically un-encounter-able impossibility that self-awareness is aware of not itself.[10]

This philosophical soliloquy regarding the fundamental nature of self-awareness seems to contradict what humans experience in daily life. An analysis of human experience shows that there exists the duality of subject–object, self and not-self, 'this' and 'that' and so on. That means it makes sense to say that human experience is not only philosophically intelligible but is also conceptually contingent on the duality of self and not-self. Facing this question directly in the light of the logically primitive idea of self-awareness, Gandhi claims that this not-self as opposed to the self is not real not-self as such but is only apparent not-self. Ontologically the not-self is neither real self nor real not-self (*sat-asat-vilakṣaṇa*); it is only apparent, illusory otherness. And this not-self, including our bodies and no-thing-ness symbolizing non-objectifiability, cannot but be the self-images of self-awareness, the sportive creative act (*līlā*) of selfhood. That means the apparent not-self is nothing but the gross or subtle, luminous or dark, self-imaging of the reality of self-awareness. And one comes to the full horizon of self-awareness only when one is able to see non-dualistically the whole world as an image or better still an image-in-making of oneself.[11] The Upaniṣads repeatedly celebrate such a non-dualisitc understanding of the self:

> You are woman. You are man. You are the youth and the maiden too.
> You, as an old man, totter along with a staff.
> Being born you become facing in every direction.
>
> You are the dark-blue bird, you are the green parrot with red eyes.
> You are the cloud with lightning in its womb. You are the seasons and the seas.
> Having no beginning you abide through omnipresence.
> You from whom all worlds are born.[12]

This philosophically primitive and spiritually insightful non-dualistic, non-exclusionary and all-embracing (including no-thing-ness) conception of reality as the Self, claims Ramchandra Gandhi, is the distinctive metaphysical advaitin truth of India as well as its civilizational wellspring. This liberating truth is symbolically represented in the Upaniṣadic *mahāvākya* '*tat tvam asi*' ('Thou art That') and Gandhi, after Ramana Maharshi, creatively reinterprets it as 'I am Thou'.[13] Such a notion of selfhood holds together the apparent binaries of what Gandhi calls root-immanence and root-transcendence. Root-immanence, symbolized by the word 'this', represents the immediacy and intimacy of consciousness in the incarnation of all the living and non-living material forms of the Self. And this root-immanence, on close investigation, reveals itself as essentially non-different (*ananyatva*) from root-transcendence, indicated by the word 'that', symbolizing the all-encompassing and all-exceeding reality which is in itself formlessness (*nirguṇa-nirākāra*).[14]

Celebrating the Non-dual Self: The Sacrament of Communication

Exploring further the fundamental conception of reality as selfhood or self-awareness which is metaphysically of the nature of advaita and *advaya*,[15] Gandhi claims that human linguistic communication is a spontaneous, self-evident and radical celebration of the non-dualistic, the non-exclusionary and the singular conception of the Self. To be a human person means being a self-conscious and communicative entity. An analysis of human communication shows that the capacity of human beings to address one another is necessarily presupposed in human communication. And more importantly this act of addressing is not merely interactionist in character, for the response-soliciting dimension of addressing shows that addressing is a mutually reciprocal and cooperative act between the speaker and the hearer, the addresser and the addressee.[16] What is the philosophical significance of this act of addressing? Gandhi claims that in every act of addressing by another, what is implied is the notion of the non-referential identification of oneself. In his own words:

> When I am addressed by somebody, a speaker, I am *uniquely picked out, I am non-referentially identified, I am called forth*. . . . When you address me . . . you do not, *in* addressing me, *refer* to me in conversation with me. The possibility of a conversation starting between us depends on the success of your initial addressing act. And yet it cannot be denied that your action has a communicative force. You do not merely interact with me, you invite me to attend to you, to listen . . . to you . . . you identify me without referring to me! . . . In addressing me you seem to gain a special inward access to me. . . . You have identified me, but because of the essentially non-referential character of your mode of identification, I feel that you have communicated to me your thought of me as myself, and not as a creature of particular kind, but quite simply as myself . . . the directedness-towards-me of your act of addressing me makes it clear that in addressing me you non-referentially identify me, that you transcend the referential language that you may have employed in order to address me; that you

> acknowledge my uniqueness. Addressing is a uniqueness-acknowledging act. Only when I suffer the experience of being vocatively picked out do I experience my uniqueness.[17]

It is this very notion of non-referential identification of oneself in the vocative act of addressing that is celebratory of self-awareness. To understand this further, one needs to capture imaginatively the idea of simultaneous exhibition and abandonment of causal power which is central to the idea of communication. Whereas in manipulative human communication causal efficacy is aroused and never abandoned, in non-deceitful sincere communication causal power over one another is simultaneously exhibited and abandoned. In vocatively addressing the other, the addresser is moving the addressee to self-consciousness and in that what is vocatively celebrated is the essential non-otherness of the speaker and the hearer, implying the disavowal of the causal efficacy. Thus vocative addressing which is presupposed in every act of non-manipulative human communication brings forth three significant dimensions of human life as the self-image of self-awareness. The disavowal of causal agency reveals the non-duality of speaker and hearer, self and apparent not-self; the prompting to self-consciousness is a positive affirmation of the fact that you, the speaker is none other than myself, the hearer; and that the poly-centric self (*ātman*-Brahman) reveals itself identically as you and me, the speaker and the hearer.[18]

Self-forgetfulness as Radical Otherness

Notwithstanding such a non-dualistic, non-exclusionary conception of the self, a phenomenological analysis of everyday experience shows that there exists a dualism between the self and its other. And the above elucidated picture of non-dualistic self-consciousness does take note of this 'other' without 'othering' the 'other' into an absolute, indissoluble entity to be confronted. Rather it discovers the radical non-alterity of the 'other' as an 'apparent other', that is, another self-image of the non-dual self as I am, an embodied self-image. The forgetfulness of this idea of self-imaging results in the philosophical structuring of the 'otherness' as the absolute otherness, a radically indissoluble alterity. Consequently the 'other' is perceived as an entity to be dominated and conquered, if not completely annihilated. Philosophically understood, self-forgetfulness results in two fallacious, dangerous caricatures of the self leading to exclusivist identity formations: 'the Self is only this body' and 'the Self is not this body at all'. This, according to Gandhi, is the root cause of all the problems of contemporary human predicament and civilizational discontent:

> [W]hen we identify ourselves, Self, exclusively with a given form (for instance with our human bodily form, designating all other forms, including formless nothingness, as not-Self), our self-conception coerces us intoimagining that we are not self-awareness, that Self becomes aware of an extensive expanse of not-Self: and we are pushed into a paranoid cage, cornered like an animal. . . .[19]

The way out of this self-distortion is to rediscover the true and authentic non-dual nature of the primal, self-grounded and immutable reality that the self is.

Concluding Remarks

To my mind, philosophically the most evocative image of Ramchandra Gandhi's reflective soliloquy is his intense, non-blinking deep gaze into the non-representational vastness of 'nothingness' with a cup of tea in his hand! (This was mostly visible in his Saturday workshops.) It symbolizes the new hermeneutic of self-inquiry that he has inaugurated, a portrait of which, however imperfect it maybe, I have attempted to sketch in this paper. However, this hermeneutic of self-inquiry is not a philosophically finished project, for it does entertain certain ambiguities that might need further conceptual elucidation. One such problematic is the category of relation that exists between the self and its apparent otherness, the one non-dual, immutable self-imaging itself as the most lucid joy-emanating form as well as the darkest, the most horrifying image of terror and fear. To engage this phenomenon, the traditional Advaita School of thought ascribed to Śaṃkara employs the category called '*ananyatva*' meaning the character being non-different. On the other hand Rāmānuja of the Viśiṣṭadvaita School takes recourse to the category called *apṛthaka-siddhī* which means the character of being inseparably distinct. Gandhi is enigmatically silent on Rāmānuja's conception and he seems to favour the notion of *ananyatva* but is significantly immune to the conceptual structure available in Śankara's advaita philosophy. Perhaps this is one of the sacramental mysteries of advaita that stands in need of further intellectual probing.

Notes and References

1. Ramchandra Gandhi, *Muniya's Light: A Narrative of Truth and Myth* (Delhi: IndiaInk, Roli Books, 2005), pp. 46–47.
2. Plato, *Phaedrus and the Seventh and Eighth Letters*, trans. Walter Hamilton (Harmondsworth: Penguin Books, 1973), p. 47.
3. The corpus of Ramchandra Gandhi's major writings and other philosophical explorations includes the following (in ascending chronological order): *Two Essays on Whitehead's Philosophic Approach* (Shimla: Indian Institute of Advanced Study, 1973); *Presuppositions of Human Communication* (New Delhi: Oxford University Press, 1974); *The Availability of Religious Ideas* (London: The Macmillan Press Ltd., 1976); 'Earthquake in Bihar: The Transfiguration of Karma', in *Language, Tradition and Modern Civilization*, ed. Ramchandra Gandhi (Pune: Indian Philosophical Quarterly Publications, University of Poona, 1983), pp. 125–153; *I am Thou. Meditations on the Truth of India* (Pune: Indian Philosophical Quarterly Publications, University of Poona, 1984); 'Svarāj of India', *Indian Philosophical Quarterly*, XI/4, 1984b, 461–471; *Sita's Kitchen: A Testimony of Faith and Inquiry* (New Delhi: Wiley Eastern Limited, 1994); *War or Peace?: Reflections on Secularism, Religion and Advaita* (Workshop held at India Habitat Centre, New Delhi, 2002); *AUM: An Exploration of the Mandukya Upanishad* (Workshop held at India Habitat Centre, New Delhi, 2002); *Kena and Kaṭha Upanishads* (Workshop held at Manana Library, Delhi, 2002); *Svarāj: A Journey with Tyeb Mehta's 'Shantiniketan Triptych'* (Delhi: Vadehra Art Gallery, 2002); 'The Firefly's Prayer', *First City* (2002), p. 37; *Krishna, Buddha and Christ: A Vedantic Meditation* (Workshop held at Navadanya and at Academy of Fine Arts and Literature, Delhi, 2003); *Moksha and Martyrdom*. Lecture delivered at the National Institute of Advanced Studies, Bangalore, 14 November 2003; 'Is Our Heart on the Right Side?' *First City* (January 2003), pp. 36–39; 'AUM' *First City* (February 2003), pp. 28–29; *Muniya's Light: A Narrative of Truth and Myth* (Delhi: IndiaInk, Roli Books, 2005); *Who are We?* Lecture delivered in the concluding plenary session of the International Conference on 'Towards Greater Human Solidarity: Options for a Plural World, India International Centre, Delhi, 12 January 2006.
4. Kamala Subramaniam trans., *Mahabharata*, *Vana Parva*, 10th edition (Mumbai: Bharatiya Vidya Bhavan, 1997), ch. 21, pp. 247–248.

5. Plato, *Phaedrus And the Seventh and Eighth Letters*, p. 25.
6. See *Kaṭhā Upanishad* I.3.12 in *The Principal Upanishads*, ed. and trans. S. Radhakrishnan (New Delhi: HarperCollins Publishers India, 1994), p. 627.
7. See Ramana Maharshi, *Sat-Darshanam*, verse 7 and 29 in A. R. Natarajan, trans. *Teachings of Ramana Maharshi*: *An Anthology*. 3rd ed. (Madras: East-West Books Pvt. Ltd. 1998), p. 105.
8. Ramchandra Gandhi, *Who Are We?* (2006).
9. In the classical philosophy of Advaita Vedānta, the term '*mahāvākya*' which means 'great sentence' refers to those Upaniṣadic utterances that have Self-realisation as their primary purport. Traditionally they are said to be four in number: '*praṇjanam brahma*' ('Brahman is wisdom') [*Aitareya Upaniṣad* III.5.3]; '*aham brahmāsmi*' ('I am Brahman') [*Bṛhadāraṇyaka Upaniṣad* I.4.10]; '*tattvamasi*' ('Thou art That') [*Chandogya Upaniṣad* VI.8.7]; and '*ayam ātma brahma*' ('this Self is Brahman') [*Māṇḍūkya Upaniṣad* IV.2].
10. See Ramchandra Gandhi, *Muniya's Light*, p. 33.
11. This fundamental conception of the Self as Reality that is non-dualistic as well as non-exclusionary is the leitmotif, the recurring theme in all his philosophical writings—see *Muniya's Light*, p. 33; *Svarāj: A Journey with Tyeb Mehta's Shantiniketan Triptych*, p. xvii; *I am Thou*, p. 15 and *Sita's Kitchen*, p. 6.
12. *Śvetaśvetara Upaniṣad* IV.3 & 4 in S. Radhakrishnan trans, *The Principal Upanishads*, p. 732.
13. See Gandhi, *I am Thou*, p. 15.
14. Ibid.
15. The term '*advaita*' is a metaphysical notion employed to picture reality as the 'One without a second' (*advitiyam*) and in that it is necessarily *a-dvaita*, meaning 'non-dualism' or better still 'a-dualism'. This understanding is the focal point of stimulating philosophical explorations in the Upaniṣads. Related to this is '*advaya*', an epistemo-logical notion ascribed to early Buddhism, which means 'not two'. It means steering clear of the two extreme views of eternalism and nihilism regarding the nature of self.
16. See Gandhi, *Presuppositions of Human Communication*, p. 50.
17. Gandhi, *The Availability of Religious Ideas*, pp. 25–27.
18. See Gandhi, *I am Thou*, p. 233; *Sita's Kitchen*, pp. 9–10; *Presuppositions of Human Communication*, pp. 139–140.
19. Gandhi, *Svarāj: A Journey*, p. 14.

8

On Philosophy as Saṃvāda: Thinking with Daya Krishna

Daniel Raveh

It is not easy for me, in fact it is harder than I expected, to write on Daya Krishna's thought. In a nutshell, for him, philosophy is all about what he used to refer to as saṃvāda. Translation is a tricky business, especially across cultures. Nevertheless, we may think of saṃvāda as a dialogue, or even better, an open dialogue; what Daya Krishna himself referred to—in the title of a section he had inaugurated in the *Journal of the Indian Council of Philosophical Research*—as 'discussion and debate'. In the last eight years, philosophy for me, has been all about a dialogue with Daya Krishna; and my meetings with him in Jaipur, spending numerous hours together, belonging to (and at the same time transcending) different cultures, backgrounds, age-and-generation, language and 'conceptual structures'—are a living illustration of what saṃvāda is all about. I wanted to, even planned to write on Daya Krishna's thought as a part of our dialogue. I was looking forward to watching him put my essay under his magnifying glass, to asking and have questions asked of me, to rewriting and rethinking. But Daya Krishna passed away on 5th October, a 'fact' which I still cannot grasp, and suddenly I am conversing with Daya-in-me, thinking of him in the past and the present tenses simultaneously. Hence the following lines are first and foremost dedicated to him with love.

Personal as my opening remarks are, I have already started to sketch the picture of philosophy as saṃvāda. I spoke of a personal exchange, crossing cultural boundaries, transcending one's familiar ground. To speak of saṃvāda, I would like to further suggest, is to speak of a 'me-other' or 'self-other' encounter. The encounter with 'the other', with a *pūrva-pakṣin* or even *pūrva-pakṣin*s in the plural, may take place in the form of a debate between rival philosophical positions within a single framework (take for example the Advaitic and non-Advaitic schools of Vedānta), as well as in a dialogue across cultures and languages, disciplines and historical eras. Let me add that the encounter with 'the other' has the capacity of highlighting new, different, hidden-between-the-lines aspects of oneself, or rather facilitate yet another encounter, with an 'inner other'. Hence by meeting 'the other', one meets oneself anew.

To capture and convey the spirit of saṃvāda, as well as to illustrate the possibilities but also the hurdles which are inseparable of any genuine attempt to actually meet 'the other', I would like to open with a close reading of a short fictional dialogue between Alexander of Macedonia and an Indian sadhu as imagined by Vikram Chandra in his novel *Red Earth and Pouring Rain*.[1]

The dry historical facts tell of a brief encounter between the emperor and naked ascetics during his invasion of India. Apparently, Aristotle himself requested him to bring along a wise man from the subcontinent, implying an unexpected openness on the part of the famous philosopher towards other traditions of knowledge. It is also said that the sadhu taken by the emperor never reached Greece, having immolated himself somewhere along the journey. But the historical or semi-historical details are not the focus of my discussion here. Rather, I am interested in the literary response of Vikram Chandra to the alleged anecdote about the king and the ascetic. I will not touch on the place of the dialogue in Chandra's novel, as I believe that it can stand on its own and be discussed independently; especially since I aspire to comment through Chandra's dialogue on the far broader dialogue between 'me' and 'the other', the core of philosophy as saṃvāda. A final remark before inviting you into Chandra's text: As you will shortly discover, the 'real' dialogue is not between Alexander, or Sikander as he is called in India, and the sadhu, but between Sikander's translator and the sadhu. The emperor himself is present in the dialogue merely in his absence. A power-shift between the king and the translator takes place. The latter shifts to centre stage and emerges as a mediator between two cultures, between altogether different ways of thinking. His task, as the following lines will reveal, is to establish a 'realm of between' in which, against all odds, saṃvāda can take place. Here is Chandra's dialogue, then, interwoven with my own *bhāṣya*:

Translator: He [Sikander] wants to know why you're naked.
Sadhu: Ask him why he's wearing clothes.

The fictional dialogue opens with a question. The king asks the sadhu why he is naked; or rather the 'dressed householder' acknowledges the otherness of the 'naked ascetic'. In the present case, the twist lies in the fact that the sadhu demonstrates the reversibility of the 'me–other' dialectic. The king is as much his other as he is the other of the king. Hence he refuses to accept his interlocutor's presupposition that one should wear clothes in order to be considered 'normal', 'civilized', even 'human'. By turning the question back to Sikander, the sadhu refuses to be objectified by the king and insists on creating a dialogue between equals. Whenever I read these first lines of the dialogue, Daya Krishna comes to mind. He loved to take upon himself the role of the *pūrva-pakṣin*, the 'counter-perspectivist', and always managed to come up with a question which would shake the premises of his interlocutor. Furthermore, he insisted on a dialogue between equals in every saṃvāda he had participated in, be it between Indian and Western philosophers or between philosophers educated in the Western tradition and pandits thinking and writing in Sanskrit, encounters on which I shall elaborate later.

Translator: He says he's asking the questions here.
Sadhu: Questions give birth only to other questions.

The sadhu breaks yet another convention. We are so used to thinking that questions give rise to answers, and suddenly we are faced with a person who suggests that questions simply raise new questions. Where do answers come from then? And what is the relation between questions and answers? Chandra leaves these questions open for the readers' reflection. At this point, I am again reminded of Daya Krishna the non-conventionalist, who refused to leave any convention-axiom-postulation unquestioned and tried to formulate an alternative to what he used to cynically refer to as the 'shock-proof, evidence-proof, argument-proof' way of looking;[2] an alternative to reading-writing-thinking habits which each of us inherits without questioning and is at risk of never attaining freedom from. Back in Chandra's dialogue, it is clear that the emperor is not interested in an open dialogue. Instead, he insists on having control over the whole episode. For him, the so-called dialogue is all about domination, about appropriating the 'other' rather than respecting his otherness. The question is of course whether such is the case even in the contemporary dialogue—in different fields, including philosophy—between India and 'the West', or rather between 'the West' and 'the rest of the world'. Is it a dialogue between equals or merely a pseudo-dialogue that always leads to the inevitable conclusion that—as Daya Krishna sarcastically phrased it—'the West is the best'?[3]

> Translator: He says people that get funny with him get executed.
> Sadhu: Why?
> Translator: Because he's the King of Kings. And he wants you to stop asking questions.
> Sadhu: King of Kings?
> Translator: He came all the way from a place called Greece, killing other kings, so he's King of Kings, see.

The sadhu, representing in my reading Daya Krishna's uncompromising philosophical temper, continues to question each and every utterance of his interlocutor ('why?', 'King of Kings?'). The translator is no longer merely 'Sikander's mouth', a bilingual–technician repeating the king's words in the ascetic's language as accurately as he can. My impression is that in this case, the translator provides his own answers without even translating the questions to the emperor. His answers, oversimplified or perhaps cynical, seem to reveal an inescapable historical truth: when a king conquers and kills, he is considered 'king of kings'.

> Sadhu: Fool of Fools. Master-clown of clowns.
> Maha-Idiot of idiots.
> Translator: You want me to tell him that?

The sadhu ignores the translator's implied warning: The emperor kills whoever refuses to surrender, be it kings in a battlefield or sadhus who ask questions. His refusal to surrender or to accept the 'logic' behind Sikander's definition as 'king of kings' reveals its futility.

The translator becomes more and more independent. He explicitly suggests that Sikander need not necessarily know what is said. He is not sure that he wants to translate the ascetic's words, fearing their lethal consequence with regard to the sadhu and perhaps even himself. Hence it is no longer a dialogue between the king and the ascetic but between the latter and the translator. Furthermore, the 'other' does not always say what we want to hear; that is what makes him an 'other'. The dilemma, as reflected here, is whether to translate his/her words or not. This point will be elaborated upon later. Finally, Chandra beautifully twists the word 'maharaja' which has become a Standard English word. For the sadhu, an invader and a killer cannot be a maharaja but rather *maha*-idiot. For him, Sikander is indeed Great (*mahā*) but not in the usual sense of the word. The idiom '*maha*-idiot' which plays simultaneously with 'maharaja' and with 'the Great' reveals Chandra's own position as a 'translator' or '*dvibhāṣī*' between two cultures.

> Sadhu: I said it, didn't I?
> Translator: You are crazier than he is. He says he'll kill you. Right here, right now.
> Sadhu: I'll have to die some day.
> Translator: Listen, don't do this. He's demented, he doesn't realize who you are, he thinks naked people are poor savages. He'll really kill you.
> Sadhu: I'll really have to die some day.

Now the dialogue is entirely between the sadhu and the translator. The latter still tries to prevent violence, reinforcing his independent position between the king and the ascetic.

The sadhu embodies the yogic approach which sees *abhiniveśa*, 'fear of death', as a *kleśa* or 'cause of suffering'. He is more concerned with his freedom than with the length of his lifespan. Like the translator, he too secures his independent position. Their mutual independence is a precondition for the genuine dialogue which takes place between them. In my reading, the sadhu's statement, 'I said it, didn't I?' and his courage in standing behind his words, can also be taken as a reminder of the necessity of 'academic freedom'. For Daya Krishna it meant that the members of what he used to refer to as the 'intellectual community' have not merely the right to express their views freely but also the duty to ask the unasked questions and to raise a voice whenever needed.

Translator: He wants to know why you aren't scared of dying.
Sadhu: That'd be silly.
Translator: He says that's not a satisfactory answer.
Sadhu: What sort of answer would he like?
Translator: He says you should tell him exactly what mystic path you followed to reach this sublime state of indifference. And he wishes you would stop asking questions. Really, this is incredible, I think you've got him hooked.
Sadhu: Mystic path?
Translator: Mystic path. Literal translation.

The emperor refuses to accept the sadhu's 'unsatisfactory answer'. The sadhu is intrigued to know what the king wants to hear. As I have suggested above, the 'other' does not always say what we expect him to, or says something which we cannot digest, or in some cases even understand. Chandra's Sikander wants the 'Eastern Wisdom'. He refuses to buy the sadhu's profane, even vulgar answer ('That'd be silly'). Chandra's sadhu is not very mystical; his straightforward secularity (which is the last thing expected of him) is emphasized by Chandra's slangy language throughout the dialogue. Chandra's translator is caught in the gap between the king's unfulfilled expectations and the ascetic's sheer refusal to play the role intended for him. Overwhelmed by his incapacity to bridge the gap, the translator takes a step back to the seemingly safer zone of literal translation. Don't we all opt for literal translation when we have no idea what to do with the text?

Skipping a few paragraphs, we now reach the final passage of the dialogue:

> Translator: You're lucky. He's decided killing you would be bad for the campaign at this moment, he'd look cruel, and then nobody would surrender. He's having his chroniclers strike this conversation from the record. Now history will state that Sikander the Great met some strange naked men under a tree, that's all.
> Sadhu: Well, well. Good luck, friend.
> Translator: Good luck to you too, or is that what one wishes people like you? Now I'm asking questions.

The last paragraph indicates that two dialogues have in fact taken place simultaneously, one fictional, the other authentic. The fictional dialogue is between the king and the ascetic. It is fictional because they have not really met. The words could not bring them together. Each remained isolated in his own world. The barrenness of their meeting is emphasized by the fact that the conversation has been deleted from the record. In this case, the 'empty' record reflects that which has actually taken place, or more precisely, not taken place. Words have been exchanged; a real dialogue could not be established. Nevertheless, in between the lines of the emperor–sadhu fictional dialogue, an authentic saṃvāda has taken place between the ascetic and the translator. Authentic in the sense that friendship has been established; in the sense that like the sadhu, the translator takes the liberty to ask questions. Questions are the pillars upon which an open dialogue is built. For Daya Krishna, questions are in fact the fuel of philosophy. In his numerous writings, he repeatedly suggests that philosophy lives from one problem to another, 'problem' being an interchangeable term with 'question'. Daya Krishna was far more interested in questions and problems than in answers and solutions, and his fresh mind never ceased to produce them. As we used to sit or walk together, he would suddenly look me in the eye and ask: 'What is the notion of exclusion?', or 'Where does doubt arise from?', or 'What is the moral geometry of the universe?', or 'What is the connection between *icchā*, *prayatna*, *ceśṭā*, *kriyā* and *karma*? And how do *smṛti* and *kalpanā* fit in the picture? And moreover, when does *kriyā* become *karma*?'

***

In the remainder of the paper I would like to discuss three instances of saṃvāda which Daya Krishna has been involved in and reflective about: comparative philosophy as saṃvāda, Daya Krishna's continuous saṃvāda with Kant's philosophy, and finally the saṃvāda between the arts and what he used to refer to as 'the art of living'.

The term 'comparative philosophy' in Daya Krishna's terminology is neither reserved exclusively to the so-called 'East–West' dialogue, nor specifically to encounters and comparisons between Indian and 'Western' thinkers past and present. The term can also apply to meetings organized by Daya Krishna and others between 'traditional' and 'modern' philosophers, which constituted yet another type of encounter between 'India' and 'the West'. Regarding the East–West saṃvāda, Daya Krishna's critical view finds expression in his seminal essay 'Comparative Philosophy: What is it and What it Ought to be?' (1989). Generally speaking, the 'dialogue' between the king and the sadhu is an illustration of Daya Krishna's 'what is', whereas the sadhu–translator's communication is an instance of his 'ought to be'. Daya Krishna opens his essay with an analysis of the politics of comparative studies. In the name of universalism, he suggests, 'knowledge is identified with the "privileged us" from whose viewpoint all "other" societies and cultures are judged and evaluated'.[4] He further speaks of the European or 'Western' hegemony, of political and economic power which creates a false sense of superiority, and brings about the illusory feeling that knowledge as discovered and manufactured in the West holds universal validity. This very illusory feeling, argues Daya Krishna, has resulted in the establishment of 'comparative studies', based exclusively on Western standards. According to him, holding onto one-sided standards impedes any possibility of a sincere dialogue-encounter-saṃvāda.

Nevertheless, he writes,

> Philosophy is nothing but the conceptual structure itself, hence any attempt at comparative philosophizing is bound to lead to an awareness of an alternative conceptual structure, a different way of looking at the world, a different way of mapping the cognitive terrain than that to which one is accustomed.[5]

But 'however natural such an expectation might be', Daya Krishna further writes, 'it is not what usually happens. How can one allow for the possibility of an alternative conceptual scheme, when what is possible is itself determined by the conceptual scheme one was born into?' According to Daya Krishna, then, an actual meeting with 'the other' in his/her/its otherness is impossible but necessary. To be able to accomplish the impossible, he beautifully posits, the comparative philosopher needs 'to free one's conceptual imagination from the unconscious constraints of one's own conceptual tradition'.[6]

Another 'problem' or 'impossibility', emphasized in Chandra's dialogue and crucial if we are to seriously reflect upon comparative philosophy, is the problem of translation. Translation takes place constantly, in every conversation, even within one and the same language. Things are naturally more complex in translation across cultures, when there are 'source' and 'target' languages, each embedded within its own structures and ethos. In this respect, Daya Krishna underscores[7] the vast translation enterprise of philosophical texts from Sanskrit into Tibetan and Chinese but not vice versa. How are we to explain the fact that so much has been translated from Sanskrit but not into Sanskrit? Implied is an 'introversion' on behalf of the Sanskrit community, which has to be taken into account alongside the much talked-about Western hegemony, if one is to seriously consider a philosophical saṃvād between Indian and Western thinkers. Translation-wise, Daya Krishna further refers[8] to the difficulty of 'doing' Indian philosophy in English or other European languages, an undertaking which requires translation of Sanskrit terms, using 'equivalent' Western notions which often carry their own philosophical or religious connotations. The converse situation, suggests Daya Krishna, rarely occurs. Such rarity, namely two-way translation, can be found in the above-mentioned dialogue between Sanskrit pandits and scholars trained in the Western tradition of philosophyzing. The minutes of these meetings or 'experiments', as Daya Krishna used to call them, are available in two of his books: *Saṃvāda: A Dialogue between Two Philosophical Traditions* (1991) and *Bhakti: A Contemporary Discussion—Philosophical Explorations in the Indian Bhakti Tradition* (2000). In another book, *Discussion and Debate in Indian Philosophy: Vedānta, Mīmāmsā and Nyāya* (2004), the pandits respond to articles in Indian philosophy written by 'non-traditionalists' such as Daya Krishna himself. Daya Krishna was furious at scholars who treated the Sanskritists as mere 'informants', and wholeheartedly believed in the necessity of holding a continuous dialogue between pandits and philosophers to achieve something novel-adventurous-comprehensive in Indian philosophy.

Another point emphasized by Daya Krishna[9] and relevant to the discussion of comparative philosophy as saṃvāda is what Gayatri Chakravorty Spivak accurately refers to as 'the burden of English'.[10] The problem is that in too many ways, to exist, today, is to exist in English, and moreover, that this limited mode of existence jeopardizes the autonomy of other cultural identities. Drawing attention to the overdominance of English and its consequences, Daya Krishna's concern was not expressed merely from an Indian or non-Western point of view. He was as concerned with regard to the French and German language-identities. His concern urged him in 2004 to publish a book in Hindi (after a long break) titled *Bhārtīya Darśana: Eka Nayī Dṛṣṭi* ('Indian Philosophy: A New Approach'), and to consider inaugurating a Sanskrit section in his *Journal of the Indian Council of Philosophical Research.* This initiative, intended to promote an alternative to the hegemony of English, was never to materialize in his lifetime and awaits realization.

The next instance of saṃvāda which I would like to look into relates to Daya Krishna's long interest in Kant's philosophy. In a recent letter to a colleague-and-friend, he wrote:

> Perhaps we could think of Kant in another way; not as a philosopher to be 'understood' by other thinkers in the last two hundred years, but as a starting point for carrying the Kantian enterprise further. This can be done in the context of other philosophers also, instead of wasting time in 'understanding' what they 'really' said. We might profit from their insights and carry them further to the best of our ability. This would bring diverse and multiple aspects of a thinker to our notice which seldom are seen, and other strains which exist only as a tendency in his thought.

According to Daya Krishna, then, there is something far more significant than what Kant (or for that matter, any other philosopher) meant to say. It is indeed too late to communicate with the German philosopher and to ask him what exactly he meant to say, but it is never too late to communicate with the texts written by him. For Daya Krishna, a text is not a 'closed entity' or a 'final product' with a single meaning, namely the author's. 'What attracts our attention', he writes, 'is the product of creativity and not the process of which it is the end result.'[11] Hence for him, a text is a process, or rather a text should be regarded as *apauruṣeya*, not in the sense of being 'trans-human', as the *śruti* is traditionally seen, but in a sense of being 'trans-individual', a mutual, collective endeavour. Therefore the challenge of reading Kant is not about arriving at a faithful restoration of his thought, but about rethinking the 'problems' he had dealt with, about thinking with Kant. Paradoxically, according to Daya Krishna, this would not be merely fruitful, but in effect the most faithful reading of Kant. Daya Krishna's 'thinking with Kant' implies that a close dialogue, involving mutuality and even transformation, can take place not merely between two persons, but even between a reader and a text. It is as 'real' a saṃvāda as a dialogue between two people. Daya Krishna speaks not merely of reading Kant anew, but also of rereading oneself through Kant and establishing a 'realm of between', in which both reader and text are transformed. Indeed, the text is no longer static. It actually transforms or reveals itself in a new, often surprising manner. All those who knew Daya Krishna and witnessed his contagious enthusiasm in each of his philosophical saṃvādas—the last of which with the *Ṛgveda*, the most revered text of the Indian tradition—were fortunate to literally feel the transforming power of saṃvāda.

The last instance of saṃvāda which I would like to touch on briefly is the 'dialogue' or close interlacement between arts and 'the art of living'. The following lines are based on Daya Krishna's essay 'Thinking Creatively about the Creative Act' (1999). He opens his reflection with the question, 'How shall we think about the creative act?', and suggests employing the 'thinking with' method discussed above. Daya Krishna further argues that this very method involves 'creative' rather than 'causal' thinking. Mukund Lath[12] refers to the same method as '*svīkaraṇa*' ('making one's own'), a term used by the seventh- or eighth-century poet Raja Śekhara with regard to lines, couplets, stanza and other units 'borrowed' or 'quoted' from other poets and used in one's own poetry. 'I understand a text better', writes Daya Krishna, 'when I ask myself what does the author try to do. I make the text my own and then see which questions arise in my mind and whether the author's thoughts moved in the same way as mine or not. Thus I get into his work, into his thought process, taking it up and carrying it in a direction it was not taken before.'[13] For Daya Krishna, a work of art, like any other text, is an open invitation to engage in a dialogue. Furthermore, philosophy for him is a 'creative act'. 'Thinkers are conceptual artists', he writes. 'They deal with concepts, create new worlds of concepts. They bring new concepts into being, or change old concepts by bringing them into relationship with other concepts.'[14] Therefore, to think creatively about a work of art is to entwine two art forms, 'the art of conceptual creativity', namely thinking, and that very art form reflected upon. For Daya Krishna, a necessary ingredient of any creative process is a quantum of freedom. He clarifies: 'When I think, I think in a particular language; I think in a particular tradition; I am situated somewhere in space and time and culture; I have friends and I have a biography.'[15] Yet in order to think creatively, rather than to repeat or indulge in restoration of previous thinking, one has 'to go beyond' these factors. In a recent letter to a close fried, Dayaji wrote, thus taking the idea of creativity as freedom one step ahead: 'Places are restricted, but life that is "lived" transcends geographical boundaries.' I will come back to creativity and the art of living shortly. According to Daya Krishna, one's visit (or repeated visits) to the aesthetic realm must transform his or her mundane existence. 'Our encounter with the possibility of a different world which is freer and more sensitive', he writes, 'however brief, may change and modify our ordinary living with a subtler, deeper sensitivity to nature, human beings and, above all, the transcendent which surrounds us all the time'.[16] In a recent paper titled 'Art and the Mystic Consciousness' (2007), Daya Krishna interweaves the aesthetic (focusing in this paper primarily on music) and the mystical experiences. Here he repeats and expands his previous argument, maintaining that one's visits to or insights, not merely in the aesthetic realm, but also in the realm of the mystical experience should materialize in one's day-to-day life. Taking issue with traditional positions of disengagement-as-freedom, such as Patañjali's stance in the *Yogasūtra*, Daya Krishna suggests that freedom cannot be achieved through disengagement alone. Instead, he offers his own prescription of freedom in the form of the capacity to disengage but also 'to return' and to re-engage at will. For him, the two movements, 'withdrawal' and 'return' are complementary, and freedom consists of both. Daya Krishna further suggests that if one accepts the possibility of 'withdrawal' and also of the 'return' from it, one has have to ask how the attainment of the former affects the latter. One's phenomenal existence, he argues, cannot remain unaffected by one's metaphysical journeys. Hence he pleads for what can be referred to as abstract-concrete mediation, or more precisely, for an 'enlightened action' in the world. In this respect Daya Krishna's position is in tune with the karma–yoga discourse expounded in the *Bhagavad Gītā* and illustrated contemporarily by Sri Aurobindo's and M. K. Gandhi's life and thought. This brings me to the closing lines of 'Thinking Creatively about the Creative Act'. Here, Daya Krishna sketches the saṃvāda between the arts and the 'art of living' with his conceptual artist's brush:

> The arts are ultimately rooted in what may be called 'the art of living' and unless life is seen in terms of an artistic creation, we cannot understand the creation which is embodied in a work of art. It is, of course, true that we all are most of the time bad artists as far as the art of living is concerned. But then, how few are the works of art that are really good. Most of them are inferior and very few attain a greatness which endures in time. A Gandhi is as rare as, say, a Shakespeare or Michelangelo. To link creativity in the field of art with the one that is there at the foundations of life itself is to see the world and ourselves with a transformed vision, which challenges each one of us to look at ourselves and the world anew and face the challenging task of creating ourselves and the world we live in, in a better, more beautiful way.[17]

Notes and References

1. Vikram Chandra, *Red Earth and Pouring Rain* (New Delhi: Penguin Books, 2001).
2. Daya Krishna, 'Shock-proof, Evident-proof, Argument-proof World of Sāṃpradāyika Scholarship in Indian Philosophy', in *New Perspectives in Indian Philosophy* (New Delhi and Jaipur: Rawat Publishers, 2000).

3. Daya Krishna, 'US-Iraq Conflict and Global Intellectual Community: Some Unasked Questions', *Economic and Political Weekly*, vol. 33 (25) (20 June 1998), p. 1516.
4. Daya Krishna, 'Comparative Philosophy: What is it and What it Ought to be?' in *Interpreting across Boundaries: New Essays in Comparative Philosophy*, eds G. J. Larson and E. Deutsch (Delhi: Motilal Banarsidass, 1989), p. 72.
5. Ibid., p. 73.
6. Ibid., p. 83.
7. Ibid., p. 78.
8. Ibid.
9. Daya Krishna, *Civilizations: Nostalgia and Utopia*, Lectures delivered at Indian Institute of Advanced Study, Shimla (New Delhi: SAGE Publications, 2012).
10. Gayatri Chakravorty Spivak, 'The Burden of English', in *Colonial Discourses: An Anthology*, ed. Gregory Caste (Oxford, UK: Blackwell Publishers, 2001), pp. 53–72.
11. Daya Krishna, 'Thinking Creatively about the Creative Act', *Punjab University Research Bulletin*, vol. 30 (1 and 2) (1999), p. 19.
12. Mukund Lath, *Transformation as Creation: Essays in the History, Theory and Aesthetics of Indian Music, Dance and Theatre* (Delhi: Aditya Prakashan, 1998), p. 25.
13. Daya Krishna, 'Thinking Creatively about the Creative Act', p. 21.
14. Ibid.
15. Ibid., pp. 10–11.
16. Ibid., pp. 16–17.
17. Ibid., p. 26.

9

The Dialogue Must Continue

Mustafa Khawaja

A tree needs physical space to grow; humans need not only physical but psychological and intellectual space as well. Unfortunately in our society all kinds of spaces are shrinking and in certain cases are being grossly violated. In this gloomy scenario, Daya Krishna, or Dayaji as we loved to call him, made all-out efforts to create and enhance the psychological and intellectual space essential for the growth and development of human potential. Philosophy remained his life-long passion, and like Socrates it meant essentially saṃvāda (dialogue) for him. But saṃvāda presupposes certain minimum conditions to facilitate it. And it is saṃvāda which can lead to the full realization of svarāj. Dayaji's contribution to the philosophical literature, both Western and Indian, and his influence on the scholars in these fields cannot be overestimated. He wrote mainly on philosophy but he also wrote on economic, social and political issues, always sharing his ideas with anyone who had a chance of being close to him. His ideas have been, and hopefully will be for a long time to come, a constant inspiration for many students and scholars throughout the world.

Philosophy in the form of dialogue or otherwise is a rigorous discipline and Dayaji emphasized the significance of reason and logic in all philosophizing. He calls this reason *nihsanga buddhi* and like Aristotle, is of the view that being merely an organon or instrument for exploring the unknown, *nihsanga buddhi* should have no preference and no specific attachment either to one point of view or the other. It should only consider facts as dispassionately and as objectively as possible and make attempts to reach the conclusions based purely on factual and rational premises. Because of his insistence on the role and function of *niḥsanga buddhi* in all the enterprises of knowledge Dayaji was nicknamed as '*tarka rasika*' (Lover of Logic) by one of his students.

The present writer considers it a great boon that he had had the opportunity of being a student of Dayaji for about four years. Dayaji was an extraordinary teacher who never delivered lectures in his class. His class was never a one-way traffic of words. It was a real saṃvāda (dialogue) in which all the students and scholars took an active part. Doing a class with Dayaji was like drawing a picture, under the watchful eye of a master artist. Unless and until one has not touched the canvas, or has not made any statement one is absolutely free to try his/her hand on drawing any pictures of his/her choice. The moment one draws a line or makes a statement the logical implications of the act result in some sort of determination. But this determination is subject to one's creativity and resourcefulness. When the implications of one's act are pointed out, one may realize one's stupidity in making the statement or drawing the line, but then it may be erased or modified under the guidance of the master. However the dialogue between the disciple and the master shall have to continue so that the contours of the picture may emerge.

One of the common characteristics between the majority of men and sheep is the tendency to follow the herd. Majority of men are conformists and have a horror of breaking from the group. Unfortunately the majority of our scholars and so-called thinkers also belong to this category. Dayaji was an exception in this regard. He was a strong nonconformist and was against believing any opinion without examining it. In this connection, I am reminded of an anecdote. Once, two students came to Dayaji to clarify some misunderstanding regarding some issue relating to Ethics. During the course of conversation Dayaji asked them the following question:

> Suppose you are having a discussion with a person who does not consider your position valid and consequently is not in agreement with you regarding the matter in question. Now during the course of the dialogue your opponent comes up with a sound and valid argument for his position. What will be your reaction?

One of the students responded to this question thus:

I shall appreciate his argument, and amend my position accordingly,

It seemed that Dayaji was not impressed by this answer. The other student responded differently:

> I shall reflect deeply how his argument can be countered and cut by a more valid and sounder argument.

Dayaji's face lit up and he encouraged the student by saying that this is the real spirit of philosophy.

He did not accept *śabda pramāṇa* (word as testimony) as a source of Knowledge in the traditional sense of the term. Every testimony is to be scrutinized empirically (if related to matters of fact) and also logically before being accepted or rejected. Even if we consider the scriptures and the various commentaries written on them by various commentators, we can only get some clues and hints that may lead us to the discovery of the real path to the knowledge of the truth. But we have to undertake the journey ourselves, and it is immaterial whether we reach the goal or not. The journey on the path to truth is its own reward. We have always to scrutinize our beliefs and ideas. There is no holiday from self-examination. Dayaji's way of philosophizing was an open and intelligent invitation to all his students to become nonconformists. He had the firm conviction that every human being has the capacity to transcend the animal instinct of following the herd and becoming a thinking person. The questions that were raised and deliberated upon in his class helped the students in discovering the shallowness of received opinions and made them less inclined to follow others like sheep.

Dayaji was not happy about the contemporary philosophical scene in India. In a harsh and biting article titled 'Shock-Proof, Evidence-Proof, Argument proof World of Sampradāyika Scholarship in Indian Philosophy', he has expressed his displeasure and despair. In one of the issues of *Journal of Indian Council for Philosophical Research* (*JICPR*), commenting upon the responses to the 'Notes and Queries' section regarding the issues in Indian philosophy, he writes:

> Instead of treating the questions as opening horizons for further thinking on the subject, almost everyone appears to have taken it as an attack on the traditionally built citadels of their sampradāyas and rushed to defend them as if something disastrous would happen if the walls were breached and fresh air or waters allowed to flow in.[1]

Dayaji has made valuable contribution to the literature of Western philosophical tradition in general and to Anglo-American philosophy in particular. But in the field of Indian philosophy his contribution is remarkable. As per his own statement the main purpose of his work in the field is 'to re-establish a living continuity with India's philosophical past to make it relevant to the intellectual concerns of the present'.[2] Another subordinate and subservient objective to this purpose is to 'take a close look at the classical texts of the Indian Philosophical tradition with un-blinkered eyes'.[3]

In his article, 'Where Are the Vedas in the First Millennium AD?', commenting upon the manner and the method in which the history of Indian philosophical tradition has been presented, he writes:

> If we take all these facts together, a clear picture emerges which questions at its foundations the total picture that has been built of India's philosophical tradition in the first millennium AD, stretching back to the period from the appearance of the Buddha. This whole period of a millennium-and-a-half is dominated by the intellectual and spiritual presence of Buddhism which has either been ignored or presented as a minor motif in the usual pictures that have been painted until now. The story has to be changed and drawn in the light of inconvertible factual evidence. . . . The history and philosophy of India from 500 BC to 1000 AD has to be totally rewritten placing Buddhism in the centre and treating it as a chief protagonist as it not only outnumbered all other schools of philosophy both in quantity and quality but set the agenda for them.[4]

Throughout his philosophical career Dayaji attempted at demonstrating that Indian philosophy is no less philosophical than its Western counterpart. But he had the realization that it is not an easy task considering the conformist scenario in the contemporary scholarship of Indian philosophy:

> The interests of western indological studies combined with the search for a spiritual self identity in the face of overwhelming western superiority in all fields of knowledge seems to have led to the creation of a certain picture of India's philosophical past, which has become fixed in the minds of successive generations both in India and abroad, through innumerable text books which render it almost impossible to question the picture or to built a different one.[5]

It was to this conformist academia with a fixed mindset that Dayaji most ably demonstrated how so many conceptions regarding the Indian Philosophical tradition are groundless. He was a strong opponent of the view that Indian philosophy is no more than a set of means to the so-called spiritual libration. He also criticized the traditional scheme of the six Darśānas (six philosophical systems). In Indian philosophy:

> It is therefore, imperative that we get out of the prison—house of systems and focus our attention on the problems, issues and questions that troubled philosophers in India through the ages and the way they grappled with them and the arguments they gave for tentative answers and solutions to them. Only through some such effort will we be able to enter into their philosophical world and see the inner, motivating force of the philosophical enterprise they were engaged in.[6]

As stated earlier, saṃvāda as live dialogue and open debate was the kernel of philosophizing for Dayaji. He did not conduct such dialogues only with the students and scholars at the department of philosophy, Rajasthan University, Jaipur where he was a professor of the subject but also at other institutions of learning throughout the country and abroad.

A series of dialogues was organized with traditional Sanskrit philosophers of the country at various places including Varanasi and Delhi. The proceedings of these seminars were published in the book: *Samvāda: A Dialogue between Two Philosophical Traditions*. Dayaji realized the necessity and the urgency of a real and functional dialogue between tradition and modernity. He wanted to have a complete picture of India's intellectual traditions and its contribution to the evolution of world thought. Consequently similar dialogues were held with traditional Ulema, that is, scholars of Islamic philosophy at Lucknow and Hyderabad. The present writer was fortunate to participate in the seminar organized at Osmania University, Hyderabad. Unfortunately, the proceedings of these dialogues have not been published. But one can appreciate the seriousness and the significance of the enterprise by going through the questionnaires that had been prepared by Dayaji for these dialogue sessions. The intent and the purpose of organizing these dialogues are delineated in the invitation letter addressed to the concerned scholars. The letter is in Urdu. An Urdu translation of the questions was also made available in the questionnaire itself. These questionnaires and the letter are very important and significant historico-philosophical documents and need not only to be preserved but also to be worked upon as they form a part of the unfinished agenda of the Master. Considering their importance these are appended herewith (see Appendices 1, 2 and 3).

All the scholars who desire to contribute genuinely and substantially to the contemporary Indian philosophy need to take Dayaji's work seriously. His work deserves close attention. The process of saṃvāda which is for him the essence of philosophizing shall have to be taken forward, and will strengthen not only our intellectual traditions but also our svarāj.

Notes and References

1. Editorial, *Journal of Indian Council for Philosophical Research* 15, no. 1 (1997).
2. Daya Krishna, Preface, *Indian Philosophy: A Counter Perspective* (New Delhi: Oxford University Press; revised and enlarged edition by Sri Satguru Publications, Delhi, 2006).
3. Preface, *Indian Philosophy: A Counter Perspective.*
4. Daya Krishna, *New Perspectives in Indian Philosophy* (Jaipur and New Delhi: Rawat Publications, 2001), p. 21.
5. Daya Krishna, *JICPR* 15, no. 1 (September–December 1997): 81–82.

Appendix 1

Daya
Krishna

R-9, University Campus
Jaipur 302004
India
Phone : 75672

12/6/90

عزیز گرامی تسلیم

تقریباً دو سال قبل ہم نے بعض عصری مسائل پر شمالی ہند کے علماء کے تعاون سے ایک مذاکرے کا انعقاد کیا تھا۔ یہ مذاکرہ ۲۷ تا ۲۹ اکتوبر ۱۹۸۷ء کو لکھنؤ میں انڈین فلاسوفیکل ریسرچ (کے زیر اہتمام) منعقد ہوا تھا۔ ہمارے لیے یہ ایک خوشگوار ذہنی تجربہ تھا۔ لکھنؤ کے اس مذاکرے میں جن مسائل پر تفصیلی گفتگو کی گئی تھی ان میں ایک مسئلہ یہ تھا کہ گذشتہ چار سو برس میں ہندوستان میں مغربی ایشیا کے فلسفیانہ افکار نے کس طرح نشو و نما پائی اور یہ بھی کہ عربی نقطۂ نظر اور اس کی بصیرت کے تناظر میں عصری افکار و مسائل کی تفہیم کس طرح ممکن ہے۔

اسی طرح کا ایک مذاکرہ اب جنوبی ہند کے علماء کے تعاون سے منعقد کیے جانے کی تجویز ہے۔ اس مذاکرے میں جن موضوعات کو زیر بحث لایا جائے گا ان کی تفصیلات منسلک ہیں۔ ہم جس پروجیکٹ کے تحت یہ مذاکرہ منعقد کرنا چاہتے ہیں، اس کے مقاصد کو بروئے کار لانے کے لیے ہمیں آپ کا نام نامی تجویز کیا گیا ہے۔ ہمیں قوی امید ہے کہ آپ اس سلسلہ میں ہمارے ساتھ تعاون فرمائیں گے۔

میں آپ سے مزید ملتمس ہوں کہ آپ براہ کرم مطلع فرمائیں کہ آپ کو عربی فلسفہ میں دلچسپی ہے، اور اگر ایسا ہے تو کیا آپ اس مذاکرہ میں شرکت کی زحمت قبول فرمائیں گے۔ اس کے علاوہ براہ مہربانی ایسے احباب کے نام اور پتے بھی تحریر فرمائیں جو اس موضوع پر مہارت رکھتے ہوں تاکہ ہم ان سے رابطہ قائم کر سکیں۔

آپ کے تعاون کے لیے پیشگی شکریہ کے ساتھ

آپ کا مخلص
دیا کرشن
(دیا کرشنا)

۲۱۰

(Translation of Appendix 1)

Dear

Tasleem

A seminar on contemporary issues was organized around two years ago with the help of north Indian scholars (ulema). This seminar was organized under the auspices of the Indian Council for Philosophical Research on 27–29 October 1987 at Lucknow. It was really a great experience for all of us. Apart from other thought provoking questions, the historical emergence and evolution of west Asian philosophical discourses in India and their relevance, particularly from the point of view of Arabic and for understanding contemporary issues and problems was carefully discussed.

There is a proposal to organize such a discussion with south Asian scholars. The main thrusts of the proposed seminar, especially the points on which detailed discussion is required, are attached herewith.

In this connection, your name has been suggested to us. I request you to think closely on these lines. If you are interested in Arabic philosophy and its contemporary relevance and would be able to attend/or contribute to the proposed seminar, let us know. I also request you to kindly suggest names and address of those scholars who have knowledge and expertise on this subject, so that we can contact them as well.

I expect full cooperation from your part to achieve the objective of the proposed endeavour.

Thanks in advance,

Yours sincerely,

(Daya Krishna)

Appendix 2

Tentative issues for discussion at the proposed Dialogue with the Ulema at Hyderabad

1. The problem of Reality:

i. What is the criterion of Reality? Are there levels, grades and types of reality? If so, what is the relationship between them? What, for example, would be the nature of the reality of objects of mathematical knowledge?

حقیقت سے متعلق مسائل

۱ حقیقت کی کسوٹی اور پہچان کیا ہے؟ کیا اس کے الگ الگ معیار اور قسمیں ہوتی ہیں؟ اگر ایسا ہے تو ان میں کیا باہمی رشتہ ہوتا ہے؟ مثال کے طور پر ریاضی علم کے موضوعات کی حقیقت کس طرح کی ہوتی ہے؟

ii. What is the reality of an art object or of society or of language? How is it different from the reality of, say, the sun or the moon or things in nature?

۲ فنون کے یا سماج کے یا زبان کے موضوعات کی حقیقت کیا ہوتی ہے؟ مثلاً ماہ و آفتاب کی حقیقت سے یہ حقیقت کس طرح الگ قسم کی ہوتی ہے؟

iii. What is the reality of Space and Time? Are they real in the same sense in which the objects situated in them are supposed to be real?

۳ زمان و مکاں کی حقیقت کیا ہے؟ کیا ان کی حقیقت ویسی ہی ہے جیسی ان میں موجود اشیاء کی ہوتی ہے؟

2.The problem of knowledge:

i. What is the criterion of truth? How can we ever be certain that we truly know anything?

علم سے متعلق مسائل

۱ حقیقی علم کی کسوٹی کیا ہے؟ ہم یہ یقینی طور پر کب کہ سکتے ہیں کی ہم کسی شئے کو حقیقتاً جانتے ہیں؟

ii. If knowledge is true, how can it ever change or grow or develop, as it seems to do all the time?

۲ اگر علم حقیقی ہے تو اس میں تبدیلی کیسے آسکتی ہے یا اضافہ کیسے ہوسکتا ہے؟ (ہم تو ہمیشہ علم بدلتے اور بڑھتے دیکھتے ہیں)

iii. Does knowledge in different fields need different kinds of methods for its discovery and validation?

۳ کیا الگ الگ صیغوں کے علوم کی تلاش اور پرکھ کے طریقے بھی الگ الگ ہونگے؟

3. Language, Thought and Reality:

i.What is the relation between spoken and written language? Which is primary?

<u>زبان، فکر اور حقیقت</u>

۱ بولی جانے والی اور لکھی جانے والی زبان میں کیا رشتہ ہوتا ہے؟ ان میں سے کس کو اولیت کا درجہ حاصل ہے؟

ii. Is word or sentence the primary unit of language? If so, would concept or proposition have priority in thought?

۲ زبان کا اوّلین جُز لفظ ہے یا جملہ اگر ایسا ہے تو کیا فکر میں بھی پیکر، یا تخیل کو اوّلین مانیں؟

iii. What is the relation between language and meaning? How do we determine that two expressions have the same meaning?

۳ زبان اور معنٰی میں کیا رشتہ ہوتا ہے؟ ہم یہ کسطرح طے کریں گے کہ دو متفرق اظہار کے ایک معنٰی ہیں؟

<u>4.Logic, Reasoning, Inference</u>:

i. How can the validity of an argument be established or refuted?

<u>منطق دلائل اور نتائج</u>

۱ کسی دلیل کی پائیداری (ویلیڈیٹی) کو کس طرح ثابت یا رد کیا جا سکتا ہے؟

ii. If laws of reasoning are universal, why do eminent thinkers differ amongst themselves?

۲ اگر منطقی قوانین کُل عالمی ہیں تو پھر جید مفکروں میں اختلافات کیوں ہوتے ہیں؟

Appendix 3

Tentative issues for discussion at the proposed Dialogue with the Ulema at Lucknow.

1.The problem of Reality:

i. What is the criterion of reality according to Islamic thinkers? Do they differentiate between reality and existence? What, for example, is the ontological status of objects of Mathematical knowledge? Is there any distinction between mathematical knowledge on the one hand and knowledge of natural objects, on the other. Further, do they make any distinction between knowledge relating to society, and knowledge relating to art objects on the one hand and the knowledge of those objects which are not created by man such as objects in nature?

حقیقت سے متعلق مسائل

۱ اسلامی مفکرین کے مطابق حقیقت کی کسوٹی کیا ہے؟ کیا وہ حقیقت اور وجود میں فرق و امتیاز کرتے ہیں۔ مثلاً ریاضیاتی اشیاء کی علمی حیثیت کیا ہے؟ کیا ریاضیاتی اشیاء اور طبعی فطری اشیاء کے درمیان کسی طرح کا فرق ہے۔ نیز یہ کہ وہ سماج اور آرٹ کی اشیاء سے متعلق علوم میں ایک طرف اور دوسری طرف ان اشیاء کے علم میں جو انسان کی پیدا کردہ نہیں بلکہ فطرت میں موجود ہیں۔ کوئی فرق کرتے ہیں۔

ii. Is existence essentially spatio-temporal in nature?

۲ کیا وجود در حقیقت مادہ و مکان کا پابند ہے؟

iii. What is the nature of space and time? are they finite or infinite? Are they infinitely divisible? If so, how do they meet Zeno's paradoxes? In case time is infinite, how can God be considered to have created the world? Are mental processes supposed to be in space or only in time?

۳ زمان و مکاں کی ماہیت کیا ہے؟ کیا وہ متناہی ہیں یا لامتناہی؟ کیا وہ لامتناہی طور پر قابل تقسیم ہیں؟ اگر ہیں تو پھر زینو تضادات سے کیسے نمٹتے ہیں اگر زمان لامتناہی ہے تو پھر کیسے ممکن ہے کہ خدا نے اس عالم (دنیا) کو پیدا کیا ہے۔ کیا ذہنی طریق عمل کے بارے میں یہ سمجھا جا سکتا ہے کہ وہ مکان میں واقع ہوتے ہیں یا صرف زمان ہی میں۔

2. The problem of knowledge:

i. Is knowledge of spatio- temporal objects essentially limited by the fact that it is confined only to the past and the present and not to the future? How is the knowledge of past possible?

علم سے متعلق مسائل

۱ کیا مکانی۔ مادی اشیاء کا علم بنیادی طور پر صرف ماضی اور حال تک ہی محدود ہے اور مستقبل سے متعلق نہیں؟ ماضی کا علم کیسے ممکن ہے؟

ii. Is there any essential difference between the knowledge of the past and the knowledge of the future?

۲ کیا ماضی سے متعلق علم اور مستقبل سے متعلق علم میں کوئی بنیادی فرق ہے؟

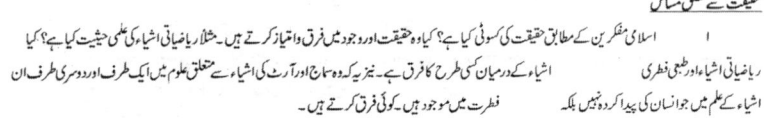

3. Language, Thought and Reality:

i.What sort of reality language has? Do they exist like other objects or they have a special status of their own?

زبان فکر اور حقیقت

۱ زبان کس طرز حقیقت کی حامل ہے؟ کیا وہ بھی دیگر اشیاء کی طرح موجود ہیں یا ان کا اپنا کوئی خصوصی موقف و مرتبہ ہے؟

ii. What is the difference between language and meaning?

۲ زبان اور معانی میں کیا فرق ہے؟ کیا وہ ذہنی شے ہیں یا ماورائے ذہنی؟

iii. Is it something mental or extra-mental?

۳ کیا مفکرین اسلامی زبان سے متعلق اپنے مباحث میں مفروضات کے قائل ہیں؟

iv. Do Islamic philosophers accept the notion of propositions in their discussion of language? Also, do they distinguish between sense and reference in relation to language?

۴ کیا وہ زبان کے تعلق سے مطلب و مفہوم اور رجوع یا حوالگی میں کوئی فرق برتتے ہیں؟

4. Logic, Reasoning Inference:

i. What is the concept of science? Do all the sciences employ the same method? When does knowledge assume the character of science? Is it deductive or inductive? In case there are diverse methods what is the ground of difference between them?

منطق دلائل اور نتائج

۱ طبعی علوم یعنی سائینس کا کیا تصور ہے؟ کیا تمام سائینس ایک ہی طریق کار کا استعمال کرتے ہیں۔ علم، کب سائینس کا کردار اختیار کر لیتا ہے؟ وہ استخراجی ہے یا استقرائی؟ اگر کئی طریق کار ہیں تو ان میں اختلاف کا سبب کیا ہے؟

PART IV

Language, Selfhood and Philosophy

10

The Virtue of Being a Self

Bijoy H. Boruah

I wish to develop a discourse of the *self* that represents the idea that *being a self* is, as far at least as human beings are concerned, not just a matter of *fact*, a matter of being *something* amongst other things in reality, and hence a subject-matter of a *descriptive-ontological* enquiry. Of course, this is not to deny the metaphysical character of the problem of 'being a self': it supremely is a problem or question of *being*. The contention I want to canvas is that it is not a question the answer to which has only a *descriptive* content. There is a normative or *valuational* content, I want to argue, which needs to be articulated in a *deep* analysis of the idea of being-a-self. More specifically, I want to argue that being a self is, essentially, a matter of *becoming* a self, which, at its best, is a virtuous endeavour. This endeavour is virtuous in two senses, one obvious and the other rather unobvious. The obvious sense refers to the fact that to become a minimally responsible person is to develop a self which is endowed with a fundamental set of virtues. Becoming a virtuous self in the unobvious sense is a matter of attaining a kind of 'selflessness' as a necessary condition for the proper cultivation of individual virtues.

In this chapter, my concern with the self relates to the latter of these two senses of a virtuous endeavour. Whilst the task of essaying on the former of these two themes belongs to what is known as *virtue ethics*, the latter theme needs to be explored from a viewpoint that looks into the metaphysical underpinnings of the ethics of virtue. The virtue-theoretic discourse of the self that this essay proposes to initiate is therefore aptly to be designated as *virtue metaphysics*.

The *Truth* about the Self

It can arguably be claimed that the fact/value gulf necessarily closes in a proper understanding of the nature of being a self. The *fact* of being a self is also, at the same time, a matter of *value*, such that the ontology of the self is inextricably bound up with an axiological (i.e., value-theoretic) determination of the nature of the self. But how do ontology and axiology come to form a complex union in the case of the self? What really testifies to this unity of *being* and *value* so as to warrant my proposal of a discourse of 'virtue metaphysics'?

First and foremost, there is the serious way of talking about the 'true' self, or the true *way* of being a self. This 'true' self is usually contrasted with the 'false' self in the evaluative sense. However, a false self is not an alternative kind of self, any more than a counterfeit currency note is an alternative kind of currency note. The ontology of the self is *sui generis*: the homogeneous 'self-kind' consists of, as it were, member selves that are true or false, good or bad.

What makes talk about true/false self serious is that the talk revolves round the *spiritual* dimension of the person, which is the dimension of being ethical or religious. Let us call this the 'S-dimension' of being a human self. The ethico-religious potentiality of the human self—the S-dimensionality of the self—deserves a deeply evaluative reflective attention. Philosophical ethics and philosophy of religion are partly formed by deep reflection on the S-dimensional potentiality of the human person.

In a rather abstract sense, we can thus say that a human self negatively characterized by S-dimensional deficiency is a 'false' self. This claim, of course, hangs on to the presumption that the 'truth' of the self is essentially predicated on positive S-dimensional properties. Only a person who is adequately endowed with S-dimensional properties can be ascribed a true self.

It would be relatively easy to paint a fairly vivid picture of a true self by enumerating the S-dimensional properties that are identified as the major virtues of the inner life. These virtues range from simple qualities of character to profound wisdom, and any ethico-religious discourse makes mention of most or all of these. This, however, is not the kind of exercise I intend to attempt here. What I intend to do here is to step back from the first-order discourse of virtues—the virtue-ethical discourse as such—and explore the *interior enabling conditions* for the possibility of a virtuous self. There is a particular frame of mind, structured by specific attitudes, that intrinsically limits as well as determines the disposition to be a virtuous self. Identifying this attitudinal frame, which is immanent to a virtuous self, is primarily a work of metaphysical exploration into the truth of being a self. Hence my proposed discourse is virtue-*metaphysical* rather than virtue-*ethical*.

The Context of Communication and the Truth of the Self

It is easy to fall into the spell of saying almost anything, from the veritably lofty to the utterly flimsy, in the name of the 'true self' or the self of a 'true person'. Circumspection is therefore to be observed in this search for the truth of being-a-self. What I have found right to do here is to look for a clue to this search in a context which is apparently much too ordinary and commonplace to promise any enlightenment. However, that just is a deceptive appearance, and much of the deep truth constitutive of the essence of truly being-a-self is deposited in this ordinary context. Incidentally, but no less importantly for that matter, the context has been brought to my attention by a wonderful piece of metaphysical work owed to Ramchandra Gandhi.[1]

Human communication, inasmuch as it presupposes interpersonal *pronominal* relation of addressing one another—the 'addressive' relation between *I* and *You*—is the commonplace context in which Gandhi pitches his metaphysical theory about the self, appropriately construed in terms of the religious idea of *soul*. Gandhi's central point is that these two pronominal expressions, the addressive nexus between the first-person and the second-person, which preconditions and thereby sustains the basic mode of human addressive relation, actually represent a crucial communication-establishing thought. And this thought can be grasped only in terms of the idea of a soul understood, in his own words, as '*the idea of that as which we imaginatively see one another in actions of addressing one another*' (p. 4, italics original).

That the basic addressive mode of communication between the first and the second persons is to be conceptually linked to the soul, and to the imaginative level of viewing one another, are remarkably thought-provoking and exploratory ideas. How does *imagination* enter into this dialogical picture of the *I–You* relation, given that this basic communicative nexus apparently does not require anything more than *perceptual* recognition of one another as occupying the roles of a speaker and an audience? What *soul*-implicating idea can possibly underlie the first- and second-personal pronouns as they form a communicative-dialogical nexus?

Imagination is said to enter into the addressive-communicative *consciousness* with which the addresser, or the speaker (the *I*), views the addressee, or the audience (the *You*) in establishing a dialogical-communicative nexus. What is imaginatively achieved by the addressive-communicative consciousness is a kind of *metaphysical abstraction* by dint of which the addresser views the addressee from a unique point of view. And the uniqueness of this addressive point of view is that the addressee is held up, as it were, in a 'non-attributive', 'non-predicative' frame of mind by the addresser. When so viewed by the addresser, the addressee figures in that frame of mind as *you simpliciter*, imaginatively abstracted from whatever *de facto* attributes, or sortal predicates, are true of the second person. *I* cast *you* non-attributively, non-predicatively, quite simply as *yourself*, without letting my attention have any recourse to the factual-descriptive apparatus of sortal and referential identification.

What, after all, is so special about the addressive act such that it can successfully take place only when the addressee captures the attention of the addresser at the imaginatively secured non-attributive or non-referential level of communication? Gandhi's perceptive answer to this question is that the *unique intentionality* of the act of addressing could not be secured if the addresser had recourse to *referential identification* of the addressee. Were you, *in* addressing me, to refer to me in some specific way, as 'so-and-so' or of 'such-and-such' kind, you would be casting me as somebody fitting a particular description, and referentially identifiable under that description. In which case, I would merely *happen* to be the person you identified; for any other person could conceivably have fitted that description. Surely this would imply failure of 'unique intentionality', or what Gandhi calls 'the *directedness-towards-me* of your act of addressing me' (p. 27). Indeed, in addressing me you acknowledge my uniqueness by uniquely picking *me* out. You 'mean' *me* in a direct, unqualified communicative-addressive act. Gandhi adds: 'Addressing is a uniqueness-acknowledging act' (p. 27).

A Unique but Bare Particular

If the non-referential, non-predicative or non-attributive identification of the addressee is the sole way of securing the unique subject who is *meant* in the addressive act, then the communicative consciousness of the addresser has to have the pristine quality of reaching out to the 'core' of the addressee by cutting through the entire gamut of usual properties associated with the subject addressed. That consciousness would have to afford a special inward access to the 'bare personal core' of the person addressed. It does not, however, follow from this that the person addressed *is* a bare particular, a mysterious predicate-less essence, a soul-substance of some kind. It simply means, for Gandhi, that 'for an act of addressing to take place, it is essential that one imagine one's audience (i.e., the addressee) quite simply as himself, a unique but bare particular, and not, *in the same act*, as a creature of a particular sort' (p. 26, italics original). And this way of casting another person in the position of an addressee or audience is, essentially, *seeing* another person as a soul.

The controversial substantivist view of the self as soul is emphatically disclaimed by Gandhi: 'I see you as a person, a unique being, not as a substance—a thing' (p. 34). Indeed, the addressive-communicative theory of the self or soul neatly avoids the substantivist ontological discourse. For, in this theory, the soul of the audience-addressee is made available through a necessary act or attitude of imaginative suspension of the attributive mode of thinking about another person. Given the communicative form of human life, the basic mode of communicative attention that sustains the addressive nexus is to be interpreted 'as disclosing a non-substantival reality of inwardness and personality—a metaphorical non-spatial *centre* of the living human body' (p. 34, italics original). Gandhi recommends that 'we should speak not of the immateriality of the soul, but of the mode of *non-substantival seeing* of one another which is the seeing of one another *as* souls' (p. 5, italics added).

If the non-attributive frame of mind conduces to the mode of 'non-substantival seeing' of one another, it need not beget the impression of an insubstantial soul as the ontological core of being a person. For such an impression is decisively diffused by the 'adverbial' construal of the soul-talk as talk about the self. If I *see* you *as* a soul, I cast you uniquely, as quite simply *yourself*. Being just *yourself*, a soul, is how you 'appear' to me because of the *way* I view you—because of the non-attributive attitudinal stance I adopt towards you. Hence the fact of your appearing to me as a soul, in this sense, is undetached from this unique attitude. Just as beauty, at least in one interpretation, lies in the eyes of the beholder, likewise the soul of the addressee, or the addressee *qua* a soul, figures in the attitude, or the 'addressive gaze', of the addresser.

Perhaps this is an 'irrealist' interpretation of what it is, for a human self, to be conceived as a soul. Irrealism about the self *as* soul at once differs from realism, which takes the soul to be an immaterial substance, and from non-realism, which believes that the so-called soul or self is a pure fiction. Gandhi's idea of the soul is neither realist nor non-realist in the senses just described. And yet, the reality of the soul is acknowledged without having to grant that it exists independently of one's attitudinally special mode of viewing another person.

If this is a kind of metaphysical irrealism about the human self, it is important because of its relevance to a significant claim Gandhi himself makes on (religious or spiritual) *transcendence*. The communicative-addressive gaze is attitudinally sublime and is, therefore, supremely akin to the religious spirit in which human unity characterized by individual human uniqueness is often conceived. 'In his communicative aspect', writes Gandhi, 'we think of a person as being unclassifiably unique—as being himself. Here, at the very centre of our ordinary commerce with one another, we have access to a notion of transcendence of utmost purity. In thinking of you as being, quite simply, you, I envisage you as one who "transcends all classifications".' What is religious about this classification-transcending way of thinking is that, says Gandhi, it is directly reflective of the idea of transcendence traditionally associated with the idea of God. He adds: 'The "transcendence" of God is reflected in the uniqueness and unclassifiability of a person considered in his communicative mode of existence' (p. 102).

In a major work concerning the presuppositions of human communication, preceding the work under discussion, Gandhi anticipates the illuminating connection between interpersonal communicative nexus and religious transcendence. There he rhetorically interrogates: 'Is it surprising that we should feel a deep personal involvement in communicative situations?'[2] He of course means to affirm the 'deep personal involvement' of the addresser–addressee communicative relation, in which, 'a speaker *solicits*, as opposed to *eliciting* . . . a response from his audience'.[3] And the intentionality of 'soliciting' is special in that it is an act of making a *direct appeal* to the addressee-audience for a response, whereby the latter is uniquely (i.e., unclassifiably) picked out. Such a direct appeal presupposes the sublime imaginative transcendence of the predicative-attributive mode of identification of the person addressed.

One might say, summarizing Gandhi's point, that the idea of a human soul can be grasped by bringing it under the image of a 'pure subject' of consciousness. This pure subject is not an ineffable, predicate-less being, but an ordinary person, whose subjectivity is inwardly accessed by us if we view him or her by imaginatively bracketing out the entire gamut of referentially identifiable predicates determining the 'impure' identity of that person. One might even add that the degree to which this inward access is successful is proportionate to the extent to which we are able actually to see the person as 'uncoloured' by the largely contingent set of predicates. That is, the successful inward view consists of our being able to see the person (as such) through the layers of predicates contingently associated with him. For the full image of a pure subject becomes manifest in an utmost imaginative abstraction of the subject from the entire gamut of predicates fixing the impure identity of the subject.

Whilst the communicative-addressive thrust of Gandhi's theory of a soul makes the non-attributive attitude primarily *other*-regarding, it can also be given a *self*-regarding twist without any distortion of meaning. I can adopt the non-predicative stance towards myself by imaginatively detaching myself from the set of predicates fixing my *de facto* identity. It would then be a self-consciousness of pure subjectivity, and a form of self-transcendence attained through the non-substantival mode of self-perception. Perhaps it is from *this* me, a centre of conscious subjectivity 'floating' in a centreless world, that a communicative response is *solicited* by you when *you* address me.[4]

The Virtue of Pronominal Personal Identity

Ordinary interpersonal communication between the first person and the second person, between *me* and *you*, seemingly occurs in a 'predicative-recognitional' setting. When I address you in a communicative-dialogical context, my communicative attention has a recognitional focus on you as *so-and-so*. The second-personal singular pronoun is, in this sense, a truncated element of the full expression: '*you, so-and-so*'. The thought of a particular so-and-so is always, implicitly and contextually, tied up with this pronominal indexical. Perhaps we actually tend to enter into the *I–You* dialogical relation by deploying a predicatively or recognitionally loaded concept of 'you'. But I think—and I hope here I am echoing Gandhi's voice as well—this tendency massively betrays the hidden truth about the *you*-stance that every first person adopts in a genuine dialogical situation. The hidden truth is *metaphysical* in nature, with an intrinsic *ethical* implication, and a truth derivable from the *indexicality* of the pronoun in question.

What exactly is the second-personal singular pronoun indexed to? Clearly it is not indexed to the addressee identified as a so-and-so. When I address you and thereby mean *you*, the person I mean, or pick out, is, of course, a so-and-so—for example, a democrat Barack Obama or a rival democrat Hillary Clinton. But you *happen* to be so-and-so, in the sense that this pronominal indexical contextually designates the *so-and-so* person in *such-and-such* a position. Not just that you *happen* to be a politician and a democrat nominee; you even happen to be *called* or named 'Barack Obama'. You might not have been a democrat, or even a politician at all. Likewise, you might not have been named 'Barack Obama'.

Given this contingency of actual predicative identification of you now, it is conceivable that in a possible world-situation you are, say, a republican politician and named 'Marack Osama'. It therefore means that it is the *same* you, addressed now under the (contingently true) referential-predicative identity of 'Barack Obama the democrat' (BOD), who might instead have been identified *at this time* as 'Marack Osama the republican' (MOR). For this 'sameness' of you is entailed by my being able to imagine you, who are presently-and-actually, but contingently, tied to the identifying description 'BOD', being presently-but-possibly, hence contingently, tied to the alternative identifying description 'MOR'.

What follows from the modal analysis of the relation between you and your actually being identified as BOD is that the indexically 'meant' or 'picked-out' you cannot be necessarily identified *with* the individual person who *happens* to be identified *as* BOD. There is a common 'you' that can be addressively or indexically accessed in addressing the *actual* you-as-BOD as well as in imaginatively addressing the *possible* you-as-MOR. Metaphysically speaking, what you have *actually* come to be identified as by a set of predicates has no privilege over what you alternatively *might* have been identified as. Since the course of the history of the world might have been different, actuality is metaphysically on par with possibility. Hence it is reasonable to say that you are metaphysically 'equidistant' from both your actual BOD-identity and your possible MOR-identity.

Howsoever empirically close you may be to your actual identity, my addressive stance towards you keeps you minimally distinct from what you happen to be at any time. My second-personal addressive stance implicitly abstracts you from your *de facto* identity, and maintains a minimal gap between your *de facto* identity and you *as such*. This gap, invisible though it is to our conscious gaze, becomes visible when I interrogate the other person with a sense of unpleasant surprise: 'Why did you do *that*? You could have done quite the contrary!' Here there is a common 'you' that represents a single subjectivity, which is being linked both to what the person has actually done, and to what the person could have alternatively done instead.

This common representation of subjectivity, which is allowed to be anchored (actually) in what has been done by the person, and (notionally) in what alternatively could have been done, is metaphysically neutral between, and with regard to, the two contrary action-descriptions. My contention in this argument is that the second-personal subject, who is indexically picked out by my addressive act, is indexed to this neutral representation of subjectivity. Being neutral in regard to any identifying description that may apply, actually or possibly, to the person addressed, the abstract representation of subjectivity in question is that of a 'pure subject' of consciousness.

The logic of indexicality is such that the designative function of pronominal indexical expressions are contextually determined, which explains their designational non-rigidity. If you are, in actuality, Barack Obama and a democrat, then, in this case, the expression 'you' designates *BOD* in the *context of actuality*. Since actuality itself is contextual, and what is contextual is contingent, there is no necessity attached to what actually happens. In this context, that 'you' actually designates *Barack Obama the Democrat* does not entail that this designation is rigid or bound by necessity, any more than 'here' designating *Washington D.C.*, or 'now' designating *July 21, 2008*, is rigid or indispensable.

Whilst the contextualized non-rigidity of designation or reference is true of indexical expressions in general, the case of *personal* pronominal indexicals, especially that of first- and second-personal pronouns, is unique in being philosophically more loaded than what meets the logico-grammatical eye. The hidden metaphysical import of these two personal pronominal indexicals, along with the intrinsically ethical character of this metaphysical truth, needs to be brought to light. I shall try to explain these two claims through an exploratory analysis of the second-personal singular pronoun—an analysis of the so-called '*you*-stance' that one adopts from the first-person point of view.

The foremost point to be noted is that I, as the addressee, adopt the *you*-stance towards the other person—the second person—in what might be called the 'pronominal frame of mind'. Since the pronominal mode of picking you out is different from the non-pronominal, 'predicative' mode of picking out the person *qua* so-and-so, what I pronominally *mean* to pick out in soliciting a response from the second person is you *yourself*, or you *simpliciter*, imaginatively detached from the (predicative) so-and-so identity by which you are publicly recognized. My *you*-stance is thus sustained by my pronominal frame of mind, which is attitudinally geared to my having an inward access to your 'pure' identity, a subject or centre of consciousness *as such*. In other words, it is with regard to your 'pronominal personal identity' that I engage in the act of addressing you. The pronominal identity of the second person is what stands out in my field of consciousness when I adopt the *you*-stance. This, I think, is the minimal identity of the person, the addressee, who figures in the non-predicative threshold of my attentive consciousness as a pure subject—as a potential bearer of predicates.

Now it can clearly be said that the unique intentionality of my addressive act is determined by my 'pronominal regard' towards the addressee. When I so regard the second person, I come into direct communicative contact with an individual person whose individuality is, as it were, gratuitous. For, an individuality that simply consists in the individual's bare pronominal identity signifies the minimal subject of consciousness, with its potentiality to acquire predicates and thereby to develop into a person of substantive individuality. The *you*-identity of the addressee is therefore the identity of a pure subject constituted of 'unqualified' consciousness. And a subject of unqualified consciousness surely does not bear any imprint of *substantive individuality* as a mark of differentiating itself from any other subjects of consciousness.

There already is an 'image of universality' in the above analysis of the *you*-stance and the gratuitousness of the individuality of the person I pick out in my addressive deployment of the second-personal singular pronoun. The second-personal pronominal individuality of the addressee, the subject *qua you*, is not a subject that can really be individuated. No substantive criteria of individuation are applicable to this pure subject of consciousness. It is virtually a subject of universal consciousness. It is the universality of the fact that *you*—the person *conceived as you*—are, first and foremost, a centre of conscious subjectivity as such, whatever attributes or personal particularities, good or bad, you might actually have accumulated in the course of substantive development of your life. In your pristine pronominal identity, you are a 'flame' of universal consciousness, so to speak, qualitatively indistinguishable from any other flame of consciousness.

Reinforcing my earlier claim about the 'neutral representation of subjectivity', I now want to add that the second-personal singular pronoun is indexed to this (gratuitously individual) 'flame' of universal consciousness. The individual *qua you* is a subject of pronominal individuality, constituted of pristine consciousness that has the potentiality for developing into a person of substantive individuality. Because of the pre-substantive purity of pronominal personal identity, and because of the character of universality possessed by this pristine form of identity, the conscious subject inwardly accessed by my addressive act deserves *minimal care* and concern. And this is the ethical implication intrinsically connected with the metaphysical import of the use of the second-personal singular pronoun in an addressive-communicative situation.

The ethics of minimal care is implicated in the universality of pristine pronominal identity of the conscious subject conceived as *you*. Gandhi alludes to the same ethics of minimal respect or concern for the addressee in his communicative theory of the soul, though his reasons are not the same as mine. He writes:

> In addressing me, you exhibit the fact that you *minimally care* for me, you exhibit minimal concern for me. . . . For an act of addressing, if it is to be an act of *soliciting*, and not merely an act of trying to *elicit*, a communicative response from an audience, must be *minimally respectful* of the would-be audience's freedom—it must be in some decisive sense *left to him* to respond communicatively or not. (p. 36)

These remarks may not reflect the same metaphysical density within which I have tried to explicate the ethicality of pronominal regard. But I believe that my virtue-metaphysical account of personal pronouns is a somewhat ambitious extension of what is anticipated by Gandhi.

The Primacy of Pronominal Personal Identity

There might be a lurking feeling that something is amiss in the assertion that the universality of pronominal (pre-substantive) individuality is a matter of virtuous concern. Imagine a communicative scenario in which I am adopting the addressive *you*-stance towards a hardcore criminal. My non-attributive attitudinal gaze at him would surely keep in abeyance the fact that he is a criminal, and would, instead, attend to the pure subject—a flame—of universal consciousness that he essentially is. The blinding light of universality would, so to speak, keep my eyes off the vicious identity which is otherwise writ large on him. How could the non-predicative recognition of a person under the image of universal consciousness be a matter of *virtue*, given that the non-predicative pronominal perspective of universality adopted towards the person would inevitably erase, or conceal, the glaring stamp of vice that is so unmistakably apparent on him?

This question surely indicates that there is a serious sceptical objection to my virtue-metaphysical proposal of pronominal personal identity. But I think it is possible to provide an answer to this question that would allay the sceptical worry. When I address myself to the hardcore criminal from the *you*-stance, I cannot—*necessarily* cannot—avoid having to *refer* to the particular person who has actually committed the heinous crime. My referential identification of the particular criminal in question is inevitably concomitant with my act of addressing him. But, to the extent that I adopt this addressive stance towards him, my referential identification of him, or my predicative specification of him as *that* particular criminal, is *ontologically* (if not psychologically) preceded by my reaching out to, attentively focusing on, his pre-predicative, presubstantive pronominal identity. In other words, my addressive stance towards this person is really expressive of the following thought: 'You, who in essence are a representative flame of substantively neutral, universal consciousness, have allowed yourself substantively to develop into a particular individual of a certain kind (e.g., a vicious criminal), because of which you deserve to be subjected to appropriate evaluative judgement.'

The sanctity of the pure subjectivity of the person, the pristine 'flame' of consciousness illuminating his pre-substantive identity, is the original *ground* of potentiality for his development into a particular kind of life (vicious in the example given above). Thus, the actualization of the life of the vicious criminal of my example is to be viewed and judged as an unforgivably condemnable deviation, and a most deplorable way of tarnishing the pristine purity of pronominal personal essence. The developmental path traversed by this person is reckoned as a painful betrayal of the wonderful possibility of a benign substantive personal development.

By way of recapitulation, it can now be stated that the pre-substantive pronominal personal identity, which figures in the attitudinal space of addressive attention, has *ontological primacy* over the substantive, predicative personal identity of the addressee, which otherwise has *pragmatic primacy* over the former. In the usual social intercourse of life, our interpersonal relation is predominantly governed by the pragmatic primacy we attach to substantive personal identity, whether positive or negative in character. Indeed, the pre-substantive, pronominal identity of each of us is overshadowed, and thereby concealed, by our pragmatically motivated perception of one another. It takes a special, enlightened effort to be able to penetrate through the layers of substantive individuality and countenance the underlying reality of the pre-substantive core. Hence it is virtue-ethically incumbent upon us to remind ourselves of the sublime truth that the apparent substantive individuality of a particular life is metaphysically hooked on to an antecedent subjectivity that is not substantively tinged at all.

The First-personal Endeavour of Virtue

So far I have highlighted the sanctity of the *you*-stance, or the addressive stance, inasmuch as it involves the addresser's inward access to the pre-substantive pronominal identity of the addressee. This is a metaphysically virtuous attitude, in that it orientates the first person to relate to the second person under the metaphysically significant image of universality. There is, however, another way the virtue of being-a-self comes to the limelight, and that is *reflexive* in nature—that is, it concerns the attitude of the first person towards oneself. I may view myself inwardly, and thereby come to realize that my practical worldly engagement is burdened by the substantive sense of individuality I have developed, consciously or unconsciously, as an agent. My agential individuality may thus be 'thickened' by ego-specific attachment to the engaged life, running thereby the risk of my moral and spiritual failure. This is another way of drawing attention to the possibility of betrayal, in one's own case, of the pristine purity of pre-substantive personal identity.

The virtue of the self in the reflexive sense would be the awareness of the burden of 'thick' individuality, and a corresponding endeavour to come to terms with what might be described as 'ego-neutralized' consciousness which is quintessentially universal. Of course, fully coming to terms with this consciousness would be tantamount to a total diffusion of substantive individuality, which presumably is humanly impossible. But the thought of a lesser attempt to 'deconstruct' the structure of thick individuality is a humanly reasonable idea. And the best form of this attempt is to aspire to become an agent with thin agential individuality, where the degree of 'thinness' is adequate to the realization of what we might call *nominal individuality*. The reflexive virtue of being a self thus consists in the persistence of the self to transform itself into an agent of 'nominal' or thin individuality.

Being a virtuous self is of course a first-personal endeavour. Obviously, the attainment of such a self is the result of the cultivation of virtuous traits of character. Virtue ethics is devoted to the examination of the role of particular virtues in the ethical development of character and virtuous agency. Virtue ethics is thus primarily agent-centred ethical theory. However, reflections on the 'ethics of agency' conceptually outreach the boundary of ethical theory and land us in metaphysics. For the very idea of ethical agency is peculiarly special. What exactly is this peculiarity, and how is it special?

The ethical person is an 'individual' agent and has to exercise her *ethical* individual agency as much as she has to exercise her individual agency in *non-ethical* practices of life. But ethical practice makes it an imperative—perhaps a 'categorical imperative'—that the individuality involved in the exercise of ethical agency is 'nominal' or 'thin' in the sense explained above. What lends to this imperative the character of a necessity is that the ethical point of view is necessarily focused on the pristine, pre-substantive, pronominal identity of the other person. That point of view cannot be internalized by the agent without cultivating the sense of nominal agential individuality. Thick agential individuality would, in all likelihood, be detractive of the virtuous ethical focus on pristine personal identity.

If the ethical point of view is focused on pre-substantive personal identity, it does not mean, however, that the substantive character of the person is ethically discounted or disregarded, and all unethical qualities of the individual under focus are excused in a dubious gesture of limitless generosity. Virtue metaphysics cannot afford to be ethically so counterintuitive. There must be a quite different reason for according ethical primacy to the pristine subjectivity of pre-substantive identity. Even when someone is morally condemned for an evil act or intention, the judgement of condemnation necessarily alludes to, and invokes, the agent's pre-substantive essence and its pristine innocence. At this pristine level one's agency is presumed to consist in a pure will. And that judgement is passed on the understanding that the agent was free to exercise her pure will against letting herself lead a life of evil action or intention.

In conclusion, the virtue-metaphysical articulation of the ethical point of view may be brought to bear upon what might be termed 'the ethics of forgiveness'. Many traditions of virtuous thought regard forgiveness as an important virtue. In a sense our humanity is deeply bound up with our ability to forgive in appropriate contexts of human intercourse. And the most significant instance of forgiveness is the context of appeal for clemency by a guilty person who is awarded the death penalty. Were this convict to be granted the mercy appeal, and the death sentence to be commuted to, say, life imprisonment, on what *ground* would he or she be pardoned? Unless the person is too old or seriously diseased or pathetically disabled, sympathy cannot be a reasonable ground for forgiving this convict. If sympathy is not an option for commuting the sentence here, then the judgement of mercy must invoke something deeper.

In my consideration, the judgement of mercy invokes the primacy of pristine personal essence of the guilty person. At the substantive level the person, who is found maximally guilty, is entirely undeserving of any form of remission. Hence the forgiving judgement must make an appeal to the pre-substantive subjectivity of the person, along with a hope that awareness of self-reform would occur in the person's mind. Of course this invocatory appeal may not be a sufficient reason for forgiveness; but it is a necessary condition for construing forgiveness as a rationally grounded form of judgement. If to err is human and to forgive is divine, then the divinity of forgiveness rests in the near-divine nature of what it appeals to—namely, the pristine innocence of pre-substantive human subjectivity.

Notes and References

1. Ramchandra Gandhi, Chapter Two, entitled 'Soul', of his excellent monograph *The Availability of Religious Ideas* (London: Macmillan, 1976), pp. 22–41. All subsequent page references to Gandhi, unless stated otherwise, are to this work.
2. Ramchandra Gandhi, *Presuppositions of Human Communication* (New Delhi: Oxford University Press, 1974), p. 140.
3. Ibid., p. 138.

4. A somewhat similar idea of the self as a subject of a centre-less world is famously developed by Thomas Nagel in *The View from Nowhere* (New York: Oxford University Press, 1986). A fruitful comparison can be made between the views of Gandhi and Nagel in working out a more comprehensive theory of the self-as-soul. I have made such an attempt elsewhere. See Bijoy H. Boruah, 'Virtue Metaphysics and Consciousness', in *Conceptions of Virtue: East and West*, eds Chong Kim Chong and Yuli Lieu (Singapore: Marshall Cavendish, 2006), pp. 173–193.

11

Daya Krishna's 'Presuppositionless Philosophy': Sublimity as the Source of Value and Knowledge

Prasenjit Biswas

Daya Krishna's remark in his book entitled, *Towards a Theory of Structural and Transcendental Illusions*[1] that the idea of 'reality' is based on 'rational grounds' gives rise to 'belief in the reality of illusion imposed by the reflexivity of self-consciousness'. This makes it clear how some form of illusion structurally determines our commonsense belief on reality. This formulation invites us to examine the very structure of reality and develop arguments in line with Daya Krishna. According to him, reflexive activity of self-consciousness is 'elevated to the status of the most indubitable foundational certainty by the rope-trick of the philosopher'.[2] Further, the role of 'self' or 'I' in the acts of self-consciousness becomes an ontologically empty sub-stratum that goes with knowing what 'real' consists in. Between these two equally banal ways of doing philosophy, Daya Krishna attempts to accommodate the relationship between self and other as a feeling-relationship that simultaneously is inter-subjective as well as 'free' of 'immanent intentionality'. Intentionality of the other, in contrast, becomes the affective source of knowledge as the other subjectivity can capture the subjectivity of the knower in any knowledge situation. Daya Krishna's argumentative strategy involves a move forward 'from' the side of the self 'to' the other and correspondingly 'from' the knower 'to' the known. In this move, Daya Krishna attempts to leave behind a privileged conception of reality and certainty in order to foreground the 'relationship with other' that 'holistically' covers the enterprise of epistemology and ethics.[3] He characterizes the 'other' as the 'felt', which lies beyond the epistemic dichotomy of subject–object or subject–subject relation. This call of 'beyond' (p. 105) propels Daya Krishna's novel idea of 'presuppositionless philosophy' to instill a refined sense of 'imagination' and 'freedom' in acts of philosophizing that always move ahead of 'forms' (such as immanence/transcendence) that the idea of 'freedom' took in the past (pp. 169–170). This is raising a significant epistemic value, even if it is 'not' an axiological turn. One can distinguish it from both epistemic holism as well as from axiology, as Daya Krishna bypassed both by way of privileging 'acting' over 'knowing' (p. 97, para 1).

Acting involves a variety of acts, both conscious and unconscious. Conscious acts depend on acts of willing, where will performs a meditative role between the agent and the act. Unconscious acts involves intentionality of the Subject, which gets altered, augmented and extended in the domain of inter-personal and inter-subjective relationship of thinking and knowing. More than establishing a first-order relationship between action and its immediate context, Daya Krishna examines the contextuality of an act by positing how feeling, judging, telling, responding and such other acts take a 'self-referential' turn. Contextuality of an act lies in showing how the very act is a necessary part of the 'context'. This, Daya Krishna poses contra-Kant, against the indispensability of a priori forms of intuition that transcend all the contexts of activity that spring from it. Daya Krishna's examples of such contextuality involve 'feeling as 'felt', language expressing about language itself and such other dissolution of duality between the subject and the object within the infinite reach of human reflexivity. Following this strategy of opening up a closed context of action and reality, Daya Krishna highlighted the 'infinite freedom of imagination'. It is here that Daya Krishna touches the bottomlessness of our epistemic enterprise, which Kant developed into a distinction between an 'object of cognition' and the capacity of the Subject to 'represent' (*erleben* or *einfuhulung* in Daya Krishna)[4] an object of cognition without its prior 'conditions of possibility'. This capacity to represent is reasonable and correct as it presents the 'judgment of inadequacy of our greatest faculty of sense'.[5] This inadequacy is the self-conscious understanding by the Subject that the 'as' and 'as if' structure of world/reality does not govern the relationship of will to desire and leads to a rather 'converse' relationship between 'understanding' and 'will' (p. 73). *Daya Krishna bestows on imagination the capacity to cognize without an 'object' as imagination is exercised through the feeling of being inadequate to the imagined reality that is now disconnected from the 'givenness' of the world* (emphasis added; pp. 11–12, 78, 85–86).

Imagination allows itself to be surpassed by a feeling of something that is beyond the reach of imagination, yet such a state invokes the capacity of the subject to visit its own inadequacies. Daya Krishna rightly points out the moment of truth for imagination as a faculty, when imagination itself becomes the 'object' of imagination and thereby surpasses its own limits at every instant of its emergence. Daya Krishna generalizes this sublimity of human consciousness as 'constitutive' of every cognitive, epistemic and mental acts, all of which themselves become an 'object' in the same act without making consciousness either transcendent or immanent. *The task of overcoming the duality of the kind such as transcendent/immanent, internal/external, subject/object and other such incipient and embedded polarities in language and action becomes Daya Krishna's key to knowledge that opens up the closures of art and life from all possible angles, be it morality, beauty or duty.* This key to knowledge functions in terms of the very functions of consciousness, that is, attending to or withdrawing, both of which alter the status of the 'object' that pre-exists or the 'significance' that follows from such acts of consciousness. Daya Krishna hints at the possibility of many alterations in the 'self-fulfilling' prophecy of consciousness and thereby removing the criterion of satisfaction for the meditative and contemplative life to be validated by internal/external criterion of reason. He rather posits a different criterion by telling us how beliefs about reality produce a reality and the task of philosophy is to understand that 'human reality' of belief instead of distinguishing it from knowledge and truth as determined by senses (p. 77).

It is in this perspective that human action, for Daya Krishna, is no longer an epistemic or moral imperative, that is, it is no longer a matter of self-knowledge or knowledge of the world in terms of an imperative, epistemic or moral, but it is a 'will to live and act' (pp. 72, 156) that fundamentally determines the 'freedom' to know.

Daya Krishna's Original Critique of Immanuel Kant

It indeed is a radical critique of Kantian and Neo-Kantian emphasis on 'conditions of possibility' of knowledge. Daya Krishna considered a 'constitutive structure' of knowledge in terms of self-consciousness that remains 'transcendent' in the very operation of those 'conditions of possibility' that give rise to 'willing', 'desiring' and 'acting'. In effect, the relationship between transcendent structure of consciousness and the 'object' of epistemic acts is that of a string of reflexive acts that displaces the self of the knower. Such reflexive relation between transcendent 'I-Consciousness' and the 'object' of cognition as constituted by Consciousness produces an 'illusion' of the 'being' of the world. 'Daya Krisna characterizes the relationship between transcendent consciousness and the phenomenal reality as illusory, as the latter assumes a "being" only in our mind.' Daya Krishna's radical critique of Kant aims at freeing the mind of its reflexive relation to an already constituted 'object' of knowledge by disengaging its a priori 'transcendental structure' as well as the 'experience' of the phenomenal world. Such a disengaged mind can provide a presuppositionless method of philosophizing with all its appeal to the sublime. Daya Krishna contends that such a method can provide the source of value and knowledge.

What Daya Krishna diagnoses is a deep 'normalizing' role of 'illusions' that 'naturalize' the domain of Knowledge without telling us what the human capacity to know imposes on us as 'real'. Daya Krishna's counter-critique of Kant is formulated thus,

> Kant does not seem to have explored the idea of the transcendent object which lies beyond all determinations in terms of either the forms of sensibility or categories of understanding or even the notion of purposiveness without a purpose. Had Kant done so he might have faced the question of the relationship between the transcendent self or subject and the transcendent object, and might have reached conclusion that they were identical as there could be no basis for distinguishing them. (p. 6)

What Daya Krishna intends to do here is to examine the consistency of Kantian 'Transcendental Analytic' by raising a question about the status of 'forms of sensibility' that should have equal role with understanding and reason; but Kant confines any role of sensibility as an 'activity' only in the aesthetic and moral realm. This creates a 'dichotomy between activity and passivity which pervades Kant's system' (p. 7). At the same time, Kant, as per Daya Krishna, allows reason to be constituted by the function that it performs and thereby, allowing a space for rational acts by an agent within the domain of his 'Critique'. Daya Krishna points out that rational thinking and action necessarily combine 'thinking' and 'deciding' 'with' 'attending' or 'willing' (pp. 66–67). But rational action needs to be distinguished from 'creative power of consciousness' as the latter follows a valuational norm. Rational action is judged from the perspective of its justifiability, while creative acts are evaluated from the 'norms' arising out of the relationship and engagement of the creator with the 'object' of creation. Daya Krishna places rational action and valuational-normative action side by side in order to explore the possibility of disinterested reasons that bind the actor to an obligation to work for it, only for the love of it. The parallel between the two modes of action arises from the way the consciousness attends to 'objects' of those kinds of action respectively. In rational action, consciousness is externally governed by a sense of obligatoriness that is imposed by the constraint of 'reality'. There is nothing in the 'object' of this kind of action that can justify the act. In creative acts, it is rather the 'object' and the 'purpose' for which it is chosen, which provides the justification for creative acts.

Further the activity of Reason in the domain of aesthetic is peculiarly operative at the level of a priori sensibility as the 'condition of possibility' for taste or aesthetic judgement. At the a priori level, Daya Krishna develops two paths of critique of the Critique: one, the 'given' of an object as transcendental remains different from categories of understanding (Daya Krishna's example of Self-in-itself) and two, the modalities of activity of thought in relation to twin categories of 'freedom' and 'causality' lie outside the realm of thinking as these two categories are presupposed in human action. Daya Krishna points out that although Kant had included 'causality' into his categories of understanding, he excluded 'freedom' from the same status. Daya Krishna's question is, by way of excluding 'freedom', 'how does one understand human agency involved in Knowing'?

Daya Krishna answers the question about agency of the Subject in knowledge in terms of feeling-relationships, which is a relationship between subjectivities in terms of experiencing each other. For Daya Krishna, in this relationship, no specific subjectivity can privilege itself over another, as such a presupposition would amount to treating one's self-consciousness as subject, while other's consciousness as 'objects'. The dichotomy between subjectivity and objectivity arises because of an ontological superiority of self-consciousness, which is assumed as 'self-certifying, self-luminous character'[6] in relation to another 'consciousness' that appears as an 'object' before it. The subjectivity immanent to such an 'object' is the 'I-centric' prison house of consciousness that is constrained by its own reflexivity, the impact of which is only figurative without any judgement of the 'experienced'. Such an object can neither be appreciated nor can it be related to aesthetic intentionality of the self-luminous subject. Such 'objects' before a beholder's consciousness, as per Daya Krishna, involve their 'conditions of possibility' as 'reality'. These 'conditions of possibility' for another 'subjectivity' to be an 'object' must include the deep-rooted 'transcendental illusion' of being present so that it can be 'felt' and not just 'understood' as in the case of an inanimate object of nature (pp. 35, 108). Such a transcendental illusoriness of an-other subjectivity as an 'object' arises because the distinction between understanding and feeling is blurred in understanding the other and judgement about the 'other'. Daya Krishna does not get along with Kant here, for whom, the idea of 'object' arises from 'synthetic determination of its intuition', which abstracted from all its inner perceptions appear as 'void' of the manifold of representations, especially when consciousness is directed to the other subjectivity as an 'object' in a state of being 'free' from both the causal conditions that are 'phenomenal' and the unconditioned reflection on its own being. A critique of pure reason cannot probably decipher why this transcendental illusion of the Other as 'object' persists in the realm of the inter-subjective. This is the reason why Daya Krishna gives it an anthropological twist by assimilating subjectivities into an understanding of the very nature of judgement, which, according to him, depends on a crucial distinction between experiences bound by senses and 'meanings' given in language that constitutes 'objects' for themselves. For Daya Krishna, the realm of meaning constitutes understanding, which secondarily constitutes judgement through senses and correspondingly, the subject as object is a meaning category. Instead of being a real object, illusion of which is produced in the mind of the Subject who perceives another subject in the world, the subject perceives it as 'a halting step in a forward movement beyond itself'[7] as both the mirror and the reflected object come to a standstill in an idea of 'impersonal other'[8] to each other.

Doing epistemology in this vein of making a distinction between 'understanding' and 'judgement' removes the difference between subject and object that so far remained as an epistemic hierarchy enabled the epistemologist to 'understand' human reality which is 'existential' and 'relational'. The 'existential' and 'relational' reality of humans takes us away from the realm of 'objects' to the realm of 'feeling'—the shift is ontological in character and it manifests in language and not so much in external nature or in senses. Human reality does not acquire its significance from transcendental/empirical realities, rather it gives significance to such realities. This shift of epistemic perspective, for Daya Krishna, is absolutely necessary, given the fact that a Kantian kind of transcendental analysis looks at the world as a passive component and at the mind as an active component of knowledge. Human reality is a complex intermixture of this subjective and objective aspects of the naturalized version of knowledge (p. 12) that cannot be transcendentally presupposed as 'given' in the phenomenal world (p. 15). It is rather the case that Kant had to accept the existence of morally free-to-act agency of other human beings despite granting the 'self' a transcendental unity in understanding 'reality' that excluded the experiential reality of other human beings from it (p. 19). The human reality provides a different take altogether: It takes more with the 'other', 'the concrete other rather than one-self'.[9]

Daya Krishna purportedly tells us that if we include 'freedom' as a category of understanding (pp. 26–27), then we would have to account for the self–other relationship in the context of human action. (For example, the category of 'substance' is applied to self without it belonging to 'categories of understanding' at the 'transcendental' realm.) This leads Daya Krishna to suggest that unless categories are used 'reflexively' and thereby meaning that any transcendental determination of which category to apply would continue the 'illusion' produced by such transcendental categories. It is rather the case that 'understanding' involves 'understanding of language' and 'experience'. Understanding of language is not sensuous; rather it is an understanding of 'signs', which involve not just primary qualities but also secondary qualities. So Daya Krishna would maintain that mere reflection from a transcendental point of view shall end up in a kind of 'illusoriness'. The alternative is to understand that the whole architectonic of transcendental structure of reason is a mere prerequisite to understanding and it does not belong to understanding as such. This gives Daya Krishna the spur to formulate a new role of Reason,

> Kant (. . .) not only forgot that the sensory experience itself, according to his own analysis, was constituted by the apriori forms of sensibility, that is, space and time which were discovered through a transcendental critique of that experience. There was no independent realm of sense experience which could be the object of employment of the categories of understanding. The attempt of Reason, therefore, to go beyond the limits

of sensibility were an attempt to go beyond that which itself was constituted by the transcendental function of apriori forms of sensibility. . . . Kant appears to have succumbed to the illusion of the 'giveness' of space and time which he had earlier exposed in his discussion of Transcendental Aesthetic. (p. 45)

Daya Krishna proposed to free Knowledge from this 'prison' of 'transcendental unity of apperception' by following two argumentative strategies: (*a*) reality does not consist in the real or rational properties and hence knowledge is not sensible, demonstrative and indexical and (*b*) an alternative conceptualization of 'knowledge' in the context of norm, value and action. The first line of critique is anti-foundationalist, while it also discounts the linguistic turn by exposing the limits of representation as language cannot on its own represent acts of 'thinking', 'desiring', 'reasoning', 'feeling', all of which essentially are centred on a notion of the knowing subject/self. But Daya Krishna provides a different notion of 'agency' that is based on 'feeling-relationships' as it arises in the context of the action-oriented nature of human language.

Daya Krishna's framework of knowledge is based on a rejection of 'transcendental illusion' in its 'orientation' to action by way of a notion of non-reflexive agency that seeks freedom by an erasure of its identity in relation to others. This follows from Daya Krishna's observation that being could never know its constitutive structure of transcendence and hence 'self-knowledge of being involves getting rid of such a constitutive structure'. It means that reflexivity must progress through the recognition of the other and the way the other is situated in a field of inter-personal relationships, the self also needs to be conceived only as a part of this domain of relationality. Daya Krishna critiques a logical and ontological notion of identity relation by questioning the law of non-contradiction, 'A cannot both be B and not-B'. The fact that in the realm of human relationship such a subject–predicate logic does not work, and that it is rather the case that 'being B and not-B' signifies a participation in the contraries of human relationships, for Daya Krishna, inspires universal and organic connections between humans.[10] Daya Krishna extends the logic of truth values to non-declarative sentences that form the very basis of human interaction and discourse. The problem of truth in such non-declarative sentences is identified by Daya Krishna in a mix of categories,

In fact, little attention is paid to the variety of predicates and the problems they pose for the interpretation of the law of contradiction in its terms.

> There are, for example, dispositional predicates which do not predicate any existing property of the object; but, rather to a capacity or potentiality in it to display under certain conditions. The problem relating to these predicates has been discussed in the context of counter factual conditionals, but though the discussion is analogous, it does not cover many of the problems that relate to such predicates. Many of such properties, especially when they are supposed to be manifested under ideal conditions which never obtain, create a problem regarding their being true or false. In fact, this aspect of the problem gradually merges into the problem created by those predicates which ostensibly refer to ideals, values, norms which even when not factually realized are supposed to be true or valid. All utopian statements are of this type and one does not know how they have to be rationally understood, particularly when they talk of the synthesis of opposed qualities. (pp. 38–39)

This is how Daya Krishna poses an apparent problem of contradiction between ideal versus truth-functional language in the realm of the human intercourse that transcends the parameters of ascriptional valuation in logic. It is rather the embedded relationship of the subject and object manifest in the activity of willing, desiring or knowing that the world is interpreted in every instance of use of language. This is not a free creation of consciousness, rather it is an engagement with the already reflected and continued-to-be-reflected upon world.

What Daya Krishna is attempting to do here is to humanize the transcendental character of logic and knowledge by establishing an autonomous domain for subjectivity in the field of human possibilities. In the process he is slowly succumbing to an idea of horizontal relationality between the subject and the object, who are both unsaturated in the contexts of knowledge and action. He gives priority to the context of action that brings in an unconditioned relationality between human subjects who can perform an action without falling into the trap of 'transcendentality' of the given world.

The Language of Sublime

Daya Krishna proposes to discuss that the human condition is not appropriate to grasp being and the experiences of life are a negation of the ground of being. Ironically it gives rise to the capacity to cover up the fundamental lack or inability to grasp being by producing stories that possibly can serve as fillers, which in Daya Krishna's words, 'the unknown is greater than the known'. Language is the only shareable medium of expression of the core of being constituted by a lack that can never be known from inside, but can be made intelligible by certain means of representation that Daya Krishna often compared with a kind of 'dangerous delusion' and thereby privileging the non-linguistic over the linguistic. What the paper argues is that it is not a crass negation of linguistic philosophizing within a project of 'liberating', but it is an attempt to recover the world from the domain of beliefs structured by acts of knowing.

Aesthetic representations highlight this ontico-ontological difference that lies at the heart of being by way of covering it up through personal experiences. It emerges as an experience preserving system of signification, such that one can take a linguistic, semiotic and literary stance on the very notion of being. Daya Krishna delves deep into the aesthetic dimensions of inter-mixture of *Eros* and *Nomos* that takes human imagination beyond narrow limits of 'real'. This is where the Kantian notion of the 'sublime' comes into being. As Kant had stated that the sublime is the feeling of inadequacy of the faculty of imagination and reason to be equal to the 'feeling of superiority of nature within and without us', in the same vein, Daya Krishna posits the idea of something analogous to a 'natural order' that would preserve the freedom of imagination for the 'self' as well as the 'other'. Daya Krishna contends that it is paradoxical for the very sense of human freedom to strive for a natural order that is precedent to it, but this striving allows the human mind a way out of the 'transcendental illusion' to reach the sense of 'pain' that is generated by the non-identity between aesthetic appreciation and sensible or reasonable. This pain of not being able to comprehend the furthest limits of imagination and its valuational properties results in an excitement or pleasure that sticks to the reflexive and reflective attitude of the self-consciousness. This attitude produces the idea of a continuous transformation of self-consciousness in the domain of its relation with other beings such as nature, culture or other human and non-human beings by putting off the anthropocentric biases. Correspondingly, the faculty of reason exercising its dominion over sensibility strives for the supersensible, which, according to Kant, 'we attribute to an object of nature'. It is a respect for the object that is ontologically invoked for the operation of reason and imagination in our subjectness.[11] This retains the Kantian distinction between how subjective states of imagination act as if they are ultimately sensual and the subject is able to establish a relationship between those 'supersensible' qualities and the way they could have been experienced in nature at the level of imagination. This is a moment in judgement of reality when the self cannot be thought of as a knower as 'senses' here are not primarily dependent on the knowledge of the world, rather imagination is freed from the bounds of sense (p. 84).

In his investigation of the sublime, Kant states, 'We call that sublime which is absolutely great' (CJ, § 25). He distinguishes between the 'remarkable differences' of the beautiful and the sublime, noting that beauty 'is connected with the form of the object', having 'boundaries', while the sublime 'is to be found in a formless object', represented by a 'boundlessness' (CJ, § 23). Daya Krishna follows this route of Kantian attempt to overcome the antinomies of categorical reason and tries to redefine Knowledge in the following terms,

> . . . there is a question whether the illusion is transcendental or structural in nature (. . .) The basic question, thus, resolves itself into an inquiry into the structure of consciousness and self-consciousness on the one hand and their transcendental presupposition on the other. . . . (p. 126)

> There is no reality, if consciousness is real and if self-consciousness is real, then also there can be no such thing as 'truth' or finality not only in the realm of knowledge but in other realms too. (p. 145)

Apropos Daya Krishna's diagnosis of a structure of illusion which is transcendental in our 'presuppositions' of knowledge as well as in any other cognitive activity, a theory of 'feeling-relationship' as an appropriate response to the work of art or any other aesthetic object can be construed out of the 'relatedness' between reflexive-existential realization of the 'Other' and a self-overcoming 'self'. In Daya Krishna's words,

> The assertion of difference does not deny the possibility of relation or even of similarity between those that are different. Thus similarity, relatedness and difference are three aspects of one and the same phenomenon, the other name of which is self-consciousness. Similarity assumes both identity and difference and relatedness is the overcoming of the illusoriness of the absoluteness of difference, while still preserving its reality within itself. (p. 104)

Daya Krishna is attempting to overcome the closure of relationships by bringing into focus the multiple possibility of relations that is disclosed both in human situations as well as in the aesthetic transparency that reflects on the 'subjectivity' of the other that shines through the 'objectivity' of its apprehension.

Kant further divides the sublime into the mathematical and the dynamical, where in the mathematical 'aesthetical comprehension' is not a consciousness of a mere greater unit, but the notion of absolute greatness not inhibited with ideas of limitations (CJ, § 27). Daya Krishna went on to talk of meeting with the Other in this vein,

> (. . .) a reflection on the phenomenon would reveal that any static analysis of either consciousness or self-consciousness is bound to be mistaken in principle. Kant seems to have made the mistake of treating the situation in such a manner and even the phenomenologists who have talked of the 'constituting acts' of the ego have not sent hat the relation between consciousness and the self-consciousness is a dynamic one and the self that is given as object is capable of being transformed by a movement of consciousness that is non-cognitive and non-intentional in character. The encounter with another (. . .) makes one aware of a 'subjective objectivity' which is almost as 'objectively subject' to oneself as one normally is to one's self. (p. 120)

Further, Daya Krishna refers to Dirac's formulation about the nature of physical reality as already 'interfered' by the observer. Daya Krishna interpreted the role of self-consciousness in such interference as itself consciously known that is irreducible to any physical data, while such an act of self-consciousness creates a 'value' by way of interfering in the so-called reality. In effect, the dependence/independence question of reality itself depends on acts of consciousness. Daya Krishna uncovers this inbuilt infinite regress in the acts of consciousness, which paradoxically constitutes the realm of reason, only to bind it in a process of regress and its various stages of assignment of new values. Daya Krishna conceives this valuational-aesthetic dimension of consciousness in the very acts of consciousness as simultaneously self-limiting as well as limitless.

Following Kant, the dynamically sublime can be characterized as 'nature considered in an aesthetic judgment as might that has no dominion over us', and an object can create a fearfulness 'without being afraid "of" it' (CJ, § 28). Kant considers both the beautiful and the sublime as 'indefinite' concepts, but where beauty relates to the 'Understanding', sublime is a concept belonging to 'Reason', and 'shows a faculty of the mind surpassing every standard of Sense' (CJ, § 25). Daya Krishna is indeed very close to substitute the notion of sublime with the notion of 'structural illusion' of both value and objectivity, none of which are closed to a final judgement, as Reason becomes wholly regressive under the shadow of Consciousness. At the same time, Consciousness and its various modes remain above every standard of sense. This brings in Daya Krishna's closeness to the thematic of sublime that continuously embeds the conscious acts of imagination into a sense of sublimity as it arises in and through the faculty of judgement.

This feeling of the sublime is experienced when our imagination fails to comprehend the vastness of the infinite and we become aware of the ideas of reason and their representation of the boundless totality of the universe, as well as those powers that operate in the universe which we do not grasp and are beyond our control. The feeling is the realization of our own finitude, but it is also universal in the realization of our capacity as an autonomous, rational agent sharing mankind's interest in what is good through the capacity to apply the moral laws of practical reason. This creates a transformation, according to Daya Krishna, in our guiding principle of transcendental illusion, as 'The "Other", in fact, in its indefinite multiplicity, is an essential constituent of consciousness itself' (p. 147).

The Priority of the Relational

Daya Krishna's strategy is to draw a homology between a subjectivity that is shorn of its dependence on the world and a subjectivity that 'relates' to the other. Such a subject is also bereft of calling the 'other' as 'other' and in the process discerns the very nature of consciousness in the 'values' that are not 'caught' in the realm of self-consciousness, but which arises in the realm of action concerning other lives. Value is created in terms of the *Puruṣārthas* without ascribing them to persons but to reflexive nature of being of humans that 'mediates' between oneself and another. Values are not subjective, they are a part of the ongoing process of subject's domain of relationality and in this sense they are 'objectifiable' in the possibilities of relationship with the other. Daya Krishna explores this pregnant domain of values not in the sense of where 'I' resides, but in the sense of extending the capacities of the subject that gives it 'freedom' to 'will' and 'imagine' that can 're-live the fact the other is also the center of his world' (p. 106, para 2). Daya Krishna gives a complicated explanation of the operation of this relationality,

> The will to create a world of joy and beauty and meaningful human relationships along with a significant relationship with the living world, the world of nature and the 'transcendent' is not exactly the exercise of a will to power. In fact the relation of 'will' to 'desire', on the one hand, and to 'creation' on the other, has seldom been explored, just as the relation of all these to 'understanding' and its converse relationship to them. (p. 73)

It takes us to establishing transcendental forms of willing and desiring as the intimations of the presence of the sublime otherness that creates a 'world' of its own. Such a world, Daya Krishna rightly recognizes as a collection of both natural objects as well as artistic objects such as music and feeling about the other. Daya Krishna gives the example of 'pain' in the Other, which interestingly enough is also what Kant called the feeling of sublime and gave the reason that 'pain' in the subject arises due to discrepancy in aesthetic estimation and the value imposed by reason. In other words, state of pain, which also is, a converse of pain in the state of arousal of the feeling for the 'supersensible' as Kant had characterized it. Daya Krishna shifts the lever of realization of pain and pleasure first from subjectivity to Other subjects and then from other subjects to language.[12] This enframes the identity of the Other as a representational entity, who can be conceived as an other only in a feeling-relationship, which is an exchange of pain, sympathy and empathy in a shareable world created for the purpose. It is for this purpose that Daya Krishna radicalizes the state of pain as 'not suffering' as one just does not suffer from one's own pain, but 'suffers' by witnessing someone else's pain. This notion of pain of the other as the suffering of the humanity that includes oneself is 'symbolic' as per Daya Krishna, as for instance is 'Christ on the cross' (p. 158). But pain as a state of being involves the other as a person, it is not an impersonal and disengaged state of experience of the sublime and this is how Daya Krishna exorcizes the notion of the 'self' as a 'frozen glacier' without any trace of the other (p. 158, para 3; p. 163). This is how Daya Krishna establishes a relationship between 'willing' and 'desiring' through the notions of 'sublime' and 'feeling-relationship' with the other. The relationship is explored from a perspective of the role of consciousness, when Daya Krishna affirms that 'the whole of consciousness appears to be given as an object of self-consciousness' (p. 169). This appearance of consciousness as an 'object' for self-consciousness involves 'creativity' and hence it does not hinge on mere acts of consciousness such as 'willing' and 'desiring'. Acts of consciousness at the level of 'will' and 'desire' operate to create the 'world' that is not just available to senses, but which can make itself available to others, with whom an intersubjective relationship can be established by the 'self'. Both 'will' and 'desire' are directed to the Other, as self-consciousness otherwise would go back to its enclosure, to the indefinitely receding 'self-reflexive' regress. Daya Krishna characterizes this forward movement of the self-consciousness to the Other as constituted by an analogous subjectivity and regressive movement of self-consciousness to its own subjectivity as 'paradoxical'. But this paradox has great relevance in the realm of understanding and creating 'values',

> The valuational indeterminacy at the heart of consciousness which seems to permit that which is rejected by itself points to a paradoxical self-contradiction which appears unintelligible to human rationality. . . . The unintelligibility however is there only because reason somehow fails to understand the nature of that transformational activity which also forms a part of consciousness and perhaps rooted in it at a deeper level. (p. 155)

Daya Krishna proposes to overcome this valuational indeterminacy and unintelligibility by overcoming the presuppositions of selfhood and the given-ness of the knowable world. This given-ness is an illusion that follows from transcendental presuppositions of philosophy that need to be overcome in human action, in the realm of which there is nothing pre-given. In Daya Krishna's own words,

> The presupposition of action, specially human action, is just the opposite [opposite to self-reflective consciousness that reflects on itself]. There is nothing finished and final there, independently of us, which cannot be changed at all. Rather, it 'demands' to be changed, to be completed in directions which are essentially open, changing one to an activity which is *essentially free* in nature. (emphasis mine, p. 155)

This essential and embedded freedom in human action arises not from metaphysical foundation for freedom, but from a (*a*) commitment to objective ideality and (*b*) realization of this ideal of value in life and work (p. 148). These idealities of value are not caught in the web of one's own consciousness as a metaphysical entity, but as an objective entity to be worked out in the realm of action. This overcomes the Kantian problem of sublime, which grants cognitive faculties only a speculative and subjective purpose by not ascribing it to an objective law or concept. Daya Krishna ascribes objectivity to both the subjective interrelationship with the world as well as with other subjects, both of which operate in the same footing with the physical nature. Sublime, for Daya Krishna, is like those supersensible qualities of nature such as invisible light rays and fundamental forces at one level, and at another, the mystery and the awe with which we look at the phenomenon of consciousness in our feeling for the other as well as for artistic objects.

In taking such a stance, one needs to muster philosophical arguments pertaining to the possibility of 'speaking of' or giving voice to the lived experiences. Such a possibility arises from the very process of constitution of the Subject, who enters into a negotiation with others in the world in order to overcome the ontico-ontological split. This becomes possible only in the sense of dissolving one's acquired consciousness which most often is owned by an illusion of the self 'into' a contextualized portrayal of one's first-hand experience. Daya Krishna characterized this state of consciousness-at-work as 'breaking the prison of I-centricity' as well as a transformation of the sceptic attitude to the other by way of 'discerning' and 'hearing' the other. This portrayal recreates the world and the subject stuck in a primordial relationship of split, which is disclosed in the open by this capability of dissolving the empirical difference and creating an experiential self. This recreated entity is now grounded in the immanent field of the world as a concrete and embodied subject, whose identity and selfhood 'are not' any more dependent on 'transcendental structure of consciousness'; rather, it is limited and determined by the relation between itself and the world, as Daya Krishna proposes in his 'ontology of human actions'. Although this relation is mediated by language, it belongs to an 'outside', without which it does not have an existence. So, the philosophical argument takes this route: from a transcendental structure of consciousness to a dissolution of groundless self in the concrete to a recovery of the self–world relationship in language and action through the instruments of portrayal, that is, through cognition and imagination. But this explanation does not fully account for the contingency of selfhood, as per Daya Krishna in the diverse transactions of the world, unless it is described how the self is constituted through this history of loss and recovery. Who else can describe this except an inner account of the moving subjectivity that assumes a public, discernible and interpretable language of constitution? Daya Krishna's pointer is that agents themselves get erased in this process of constitution as if they ironically reinstate the 'fundamental ontological split' between their Subjects and themselves by functioning as knower/actor.

In a definite sense, the negative capability and the experience of negativity of being could be related. They could be the members of the same pair of constitutive elements of representation. The annihilation of intentionality from the everyday experience to the point of annihilation of the self or the ego is the hallmark of an existential affirmation through 'what one is not'; but this nihilism is itself disembedded either from the self or the world as 'it does not move beyond representation of a state of existence'. What existentialists are arguing is that the essential vulnerability of the human being cannot be overcome in such mimetic production of experience, rather the wound of existence shall never allow a full representation. In Daya Krishna's terminology, the essential vulnerability of the human being lies in the very enterprise of constructing 'Knowledge' by 'society'. In his words,

> The illusion, as should be obvious from the history of the 'knowledge-enterprise' of man, creates the delusion that the 'object' is not only constituted by the 'acts' of the 'knowing consciousness'. . . . The term 'society' in this context, it should be remembered, is most probably a deliberate deception to hide the fact that those who are supposed to construct are a little minority, whose members, though mortal, delude themselves into thinking that they are 'legislating' on behalf of the whole mankind and for all future, as without this assumption their 'construction' would lose the aura of authority they want it to have.[13]

The whole epistemic construction of authentic schemes of Knowledge rather allows a portrayal of delusory construction of an 'object' of experiences that desubjectivates and transforms living creatures into caricatures of painful and disvalued objects of life. As subjects of history, human beings are already a product of a disengaging history and this finds an easy parallel in such artefacts of representation. Daya Krishna reflects on this predicament of history in terms of 'determination' and 'illusion'. The notion of 'determination' of agency/knower/subject of history is worked out by Daya Krishna in terms of a burden of 'unfreedom'[14] that marks a dependence on others. The notion of 'illusion' is described in the following remarks, 'Thinking presupposes imagining and both are presupposed by the activity of "reflection", but no one thinks of that which is presupposed is more important than that which depends on it.'[15]

Daya Krishna highlights the metaphysical necessity inscribed in the nature of presuppositions of reality. The outcome of such presupposition, for Daya Krishna, is only 'instrumental'. The instrumentality of the nature of 'objects' can be understood better in the context of action, as Daya Krishna explains,

> The object is seen here purely instrumentally; what matters is the state of feeling itself. However this instrumentality of the object in the context of feeling transforms human action and gives a radically different direction to action for the one it takes when it seeks a value which essentially involves the other. (p. 97)

This possibility of transformation of the objective character of reality is what Daya Krishna expounds in terms of essential other-directedness of valuational and creative activity. Daya Krishna gives the rider that values that are embedded in the very formulation of action arise only as alternatives in the domain of action and not within the domain of consciousness (pp. 98–101). This praxis aspect of value engages Daya Krishna in deciphering meanings in the performative use of language that transforms the human subjectivity from being a mere witness to an enactive source of activity. This is also a functional notion of 'reality',

> The ontologically 'real' is reduced to almost an utter nullity about which not only nothing can be said, but which literally can have nothing in it as it is 'nothing', thought of only as a residual necessity left after everything has been taken away from it because of a supposed necessity of thought, something that is still thought of as a sub-stratum even when there is nothing to which, or in respect of which, it can perform that function.[16]

This goes well with one of the most fundamental features of transcendental critique of being in Heidegger's proclamation that reason destroys its own grounds. For our purpose here, it means that outside the objective character of reason, there is a realm of imagination that does not need grounds of truth and objectivity. In Daya Krishna's scheme of things, imagination or feeling can act as the basis or ground of thought and even when reason destroys such 'grounds' by a projected 'reality', imagination and feeling stand their own ground. In Daya Krishna's formulation, the ideas of reality cannot be grounded in the agency of the knower or in the procedures of truth-making. Reality, rather, is a 'plurality of centres of freedom' beyond the limits of sense. Daya Krishna expresses it in this manner,

> . . . freedom is seen as freedom from an illusion which is transcendentally imposed by the very structure of willing and yet where the possibility of getting rid of the illusion exists because one may always get an insight into the 'illusoriness' of the illusion through the transcendental critique. . . . (p. 63)

Getting an insight into the 'illusoriness' of illusion is not just understanding the 'true' nature of reality, but it is more to do with the disengaged subjectivity that can free itself from the illusoriness of its being constituted by one's own self-consciousness and being attached to such a centre of the self-identity. This disillusion and detachment from the assumed centre of subjectivity needs to be supplemented by a desire for the other, which is a desire to throw oneself up to the other. This is also a cure from the delusion of the transcendental nature of the self or 'I-centric' sense of being to correct oneself by the knowledge of the other, which can become a feeling-relationship. Agent's self-knowledge on the basis of a feeling-relationship is the new mode of response to the 'sense of the beyond' as Daya Krishna sees it in human situatedness (p. 105). This effacement of the self celebrates the freedom of others.[17] As we are existentially in the midst of others, the embedding of self-consciousness in the recognition and response to the other not only increases our capacity to act in the sphere of human relationality, it also provides us an 'insight' into the illusoriness of existence. This insight, according to Daya Krishna, tells us that being 'felt' is categorically different from being grasped or apprehended by senses, as 'feeling' goes with thought and imagination, which cannot be entirely possessed in the body. The body is the mark of 'intentionality' that gets manifest in gestures, languages and cultural specificities. This is the complex nature of what Daya Krishna called 'human reality' that constitutes other forms of reality to which the subject can relate itself through an intentionality as well as through an annulment of this intentionality in the reflexive potential of subjectivity that enters into a feeling-relationship with the other. The Other is constructed at the level of having an alternative pole of experience in one's body and being, which is not an object, but a temporally constituted being to which a feeling-relationship is possible.

This exposition of the presence of the other as a relata for self-consciousness takes us to a metaphysical thesis that arises as a consequence of Daya Krishna's critique of self-consciousness: 'self enters into a constitutive relationship with the other and vice-versa'. But Daya Krishna does not advocate a radical deconstruction and decentring of the subjectivity except in the epistemic structuring of the transcendental presuppositions of the availability of the world to a discerning self-consciousness. The recovery of self-consciousness from its transcendental preoccupations comes through an orientation towards action that Daya Krishna formulates in terms of an engagement with other subjectivities. Daya Krishna does not give a clear ontological commitment to the prior presence of self as the centre of subjectivity, as this is only a transcendental assumption that limits us to the realm of the sensible. Self-consciousness returns to an altered locus of subjectivity, that is, in the subjectivity of the other, which it simultaneously constitutes and gets constituted by in terms of 'feeling' and 'desire'. Daya Krishna confirms this method of 'constitution' by rejecting the singularity of both 'aloneness' and 'relationship' (p. 162), which, for Daya Krishna, is a loss of the very sense of the self. Objectively speaking, Daya Krishna celebrates multiple levels of objective and subjective realities and their 'correspondences'. Daya Krishna rejects 'ego-centric predicament' (pp. 106–107) and substitutes it by attempts of human reason to go beyond the 'transcendental functions of *a priori* forms of intuition' and its 'illusoriness' on the one hand and on the other, the structural limitations of the 'sensible' that deprives us to experience the 'colour' of the invisible. This results into novel ways of constituting 'possible worlds',

> Within the structural limits imposed by senses, imagination and ideality perform their creative function to build possible worlds out of these which practically have no limits whatsoever. Yet, if imagination and ideality have structures of their own, then those structures must impose a limit, even though we may not know them. . . . The creations of sensory worlds ultimately have both imagination and ideality as subsidiary elements in them (. . .) However, *the roles gets reversed* and the imagination and ideality get freed from their subsidiary role to create an independent world of their own, which, though still sensuous, still not sensual as it has lost its primary dependence on the concrete world of the senses and the functions they deal with. This is the realm of art where colours and sounds and other senses combine to create a world of their own, which are, in a sense, a second order world built out of the sense materials 'freed' from their primary functions. (pp. 84–85)

This picture of possible worlds of senses freed from their transcendental and structural limitations forms a 'transition' to a world in which language gives an infinite freedom to imagination. This freedom is manifested in the tension between the word and the image that make them 'objects' of reflection. This is a technique of 'negative capability' of first removing the descriptive reference of language and then recapturing these references in the disjunctions between thought, reality and language. Daya Krishna considers such an art of putting concepts to non-referential uses in order to make a transition from the real to the imaginary or sublime as a cognitive act par excellence. He characterizes it as an evocation of a non-conceptual world by the use of concepts in order to center them in feelings and emotions (p. 88, para 2). In such a non-conceptual world, concepts in their usual sense represents a world that is imitated and reproduced with enhanced sensitivity. This phenomenon of a plurality of representational worlds is employed by Daya Krishna to overcome the structural limitation of reasoning in an actual world, which mostly happens through senses.

Notes and References

1. My hearty thanks and gratitude to Shail Mayaram for providing me a copy of the manuscript entitled, *Towards a Theory of Structural and Transcendental Illusions* by Daya Krishna (New Delhi: Centre for Studies Civilizations, 2012).
2. Daya Krishna, 'Freeing Philosophy from the prison House of "I-Centricity"', *Journal of Indian Council of Philosophical Research*, 20 (3) (July–September 2003): 137–138. Henceforth, *Journal of Indian Council of Philosophical Research* is mentioned as *JICPR*.
3. My thanks are also due to Oinam Bhagat, V. C. Thomas, Prabodh Parikh, Sarthak Samay Das, Goutam Biswas, Sukalpa Bhattacharjee, Milind Malshe, Anirban Das and Basil Pohlong for engaging me on various issues concerning the notion of 'Other'.
4. Daya Krishna mentions that *erleben* and *einfuhulung* are inadequate to convey the sympathy or empathy for the representation. *Towards a Theory of Structural and Transcendental Illusions*, p. 109.
5. Immanuel Kant, *Critique of Judgment*, trans. J. H. Bernard (New York: Hafner Press, 1951), pp. 96–97. Henceforth mentioned as *CJ* with reference to sections and as *Judgment* in the notes.
6. Daya Krishna, 'Freeing Philosophy from the prison House of "I-Centricity"', p. 138.
7. Daya Krishna, 'Eros, Nomos and Logos', *JICPR*, 22 (2) January–March 2005, p. 182.
8. Daya Krishna states that the idea of impersonal other follows from an idea of impersonal order, Ibid.
9. Ibid.
10. Daya Krishna develops a notion of 'complex wholes' that incorporate variability of properties of being affected in the whole in order to posit logical features of universal, negation and affirmation (p. 36).
11. Kant, *Judgment*, pp. 96–102.

12. Daya Krishna utilizes this possibility of shifting center of subjectivity in order to reach the constitutive dimension of aesthetic sublime, which is a 'feeling-relationship', necessarily by way of a relationality with the other.
13. Daya Krishna, 'Definition, Deception and the Enterprise of Knowledge', *JICPR*, 13 (1) (January–Mar 2006): 76–77.
14. Daya Krishna, 'Eros, Nomos and Logos', p. 174.
15. Daya Krishna, 'Reality, Imagination and Truth', *JICPR*, p. 127, October–December 2004.
16. Daya Krishna, 'Freeing Philosophy from the Prison House of "I-Centricity"', p. 142.
17. Daya Krishna, 'Eros, Nomos and Logos', p. 172.

12

The Moral and the Spiritual: A Study of the Self and the Not-self in Daya Krishna and Ramchandra Gandhi

Ramesh C. Pradhan

A study of the philosophical worldviews of Daya Krishna and Ramchandra Gandhi cannot afford to miss their engagement with the moral and the spiritual dimensions of man. It is the unity of these two dimensions that strikes us while understanding the intense struggle of both these thinkers to come to terms with the possibility of the moral-cum-spiritual life of man. While the moral question dominates the spiritual quest of Daya Krishna, the spiritual question dominates the moral quest of Ramchandra Gandhi. However, both agree that what is moral is continuous with what is spiritual at the depth-level, since the moral is not complete without the spiritual and vice versa. It is the continuity between the two realms that ultimately comes forth in their dealings with man and the world and with the self and the not-self.

In this chapter I will attempt to bring out the dynamics of the moral and the spiritual quest of these two giants of contemporary Indian thought. Both Daya Krishna and Ramchandra Gandhi have attempted to bridge the gulf between the human self belonging to the world and the self that transcends the world. Besides, both have shown that the self is ceaselessly engaged in a struggle with the not-self in its active moral life, which it overcomes in spiritual acts of transcendence. It is in this transcendence of the finite and the engaged self that the possibility of spiritual life lies.

The Self and the Not-self: The Scope for Moral Actions

Daya Krishna and Ramchandra Gandhi have their metaphysical roots in Indian philosophical thinking, which makes a distinction between the self and the not-self.[1] The distinction between the self and the not-self is the distinction between the self of man and everything else which is excluded by it. The self is the conscious subject for which everything else is the object. The object, that is, the not-self in this context includes the universe as well as the other human beings. It is the presence of the other selves and the world which provides the scope for moral life. The moral self engages itself with other human beings in the world. That is why the not-self actively contributes to the possibility of moral life in the world. Both Daya Krishna and Gandhi have shown concern for the moral struggle of man, which they have taken to be essential to the possibility of spiritual life.

It is in this engagement with the other selves that Gandhi encounters the problem of communication[2] in which both the communicator and the communicated are taken to be selves or souls. Introducing the notion of soul in connection with the communication-situation, he writes:

> The notion of a soul gets a foothold in our life because, in the act of addressing—in an act of establishing communicative contact with another—we have to imagine that our addressee is a unique but bare particular, we have to identify him non-referentially, non-predicatively.[3]

That is, the notion of soul is necessarily connected with the act of addressing in the communication-situation because in the act of addressing, one addresses a soul which can be identified non-referentially and non-predicatively as a soul. Thus communication takes place between the addresser and the addressee, that is, between the self and the other by virtue of the fact that the self recognizes the other to be a soul. This metaphysical presupposition of the other as a soul guarantees that nothing can be communicated unless the object of communication is also a soul. The anonymous other is identified as a soul which is worthy of being addressed by the self.

In Gandhi's metaphysical framework, the notion of soul stands for a self-identical 'I' or the bare particular. It is the particular human self that is addressed in the act of communication. In this act, both the addresser and the addressee are souls or selves. From the audience's stance, which is basic to Gandhi's model of communication, the addressee is one who is picked out or called forth while being addressed such that he or she is directly identified without using any identifying description. The bare identity of the soul is all that matters in communication. As Gandhi puts it:

> When I am addressed by somebody, a speaker, I am *uniquely picked out, I am non-referentially identified, I am called forth*—I can use a number of such synonymous expressions to indicate what being addressed amounts to.[4]

Thus there is the metaphysical requirement that the self be taken as the bare soul because the self cannot be placed in any descriptive framework. It is because the descriptive framework imports qualifying attributes that can nullify the uniqueness of the self.

Gandhi is an Advaitin in his theory of self because of his emphasis on the fact that the self, which is of the nature of consciousness, is without attributes (*nirguṇa*)[5] and that it cannot be described in language the way the not-self, that is, the world, is introduced into the discourse. He follows in the footsteps of the Advaitin in finding the self as a bare self-conscious soul without any reference to its being embodied in the world. The question of the body does not arise at all in the reference to 'I' or 'you' or 'He'. If the body is introduced, then the soul cannot be a bare particular, that is, the particular 'me' or 'you', for the souls are 'vocatively picked out'[6] when they are addressed. This necessarily leads to the conclusion that Gandhi's notion of soul resembles the Advaitin's, without there being an absolute commitment to the ontology of the one non-dual self. The diversity of the selves is still maintained at least in the framework of communication for the sake of making a robust claim for the possibility of moral life.

For Gandhi, however, the other is as much a soul as myself, since both of us share the same status of being a soul. The self from the first-person perspective is a soul just as much as the self from the second- and third-person perspectives is. This shows that the self and the not-self, that is, the other, are equally souls, both being conscious moral agents. This underlines the advaitic principle that everything is of the nature of consciousness and that nothing is ultimately the not-self. The other is a self-image of the non-dual self.[7] Gandhi, thus, is concerned to establish the possibility of ethics within his neo-advaitic standpoint by showing that the moral agent is basically a spiritual being.

Gandhi derives ethics from the fact that human beings as souls have the attitude of caring and loving towards one another while they are engaged in communication. One has the attitude of caring towards the other and holding the other as minimally valuable, because without it the act of addressing is not possible. In this act of holding the other as valuable, there is the possibility of having mutually respectful moral relations based on the principle of unconditional valuableness. As Gandhi argues:

> If it were possible for one to regard oneself as not being valuable at all, it would be possible for one not to cast oneself as the object of a minimally caring attitude. But this is not possible. Therefore, a self-conscious being necessarily regards himself as being minimally valuable.[8]

What emerges from this argument is that the souls are unconditionally valuable and therefore our interpersonal relations are bound to be founded on the principle that all selves are intrinsically valuable. The virtues of kindness, charity and helpfulness come from this sense of absolute and unconditional sense of being valuable. Gandhi's ethics is thus the ethics of unconditional love and care for the other. That sums up his ethical principle of compassion and the elimination of suffering of mankind.[9]

Daya Krishna, in a very similar spirit, situates the interpersonal dialogue in the heart of the social milieu which brings together rational human beings in the common effort to ameliorate the suffering of mankind. According to him, the human situation offers the greatest challenge to the human spirit that seeks to change the human predicament. This is the moral challenge that seeks to keep the human self above the vagaries of time and history. The human situation allows for a temporary suspension of time in the search for the Infinite which, however, remains a distant echo of the Eternal. Daya Krishna writes:

> The urge for the Infinite is the urge for the timeless—the timeless that is fleetingly experienced in the appreciation of beauty and the experience of interpersonal relationships. The eternal impulse to change an insignificant present into a significant future provides a dynamic invariant of the human situation which is radically different from the static invariants previously noted.[10]

In spite of this urge for the Infinite, the human situation remains limited and contingent because there are other invariants impregnated into the human situation which limit it from within.

For Daya Krishna, it is not the communication–situation that brings out the interpersonal character of the human situation. He believes that man is basically lonely in his consciousness, for howsoever he may try, he cannot reach the other self completely, because the gap between the self and the other remains unbridgeable. That is why the human situation is starkly ego-centric, without being egoistic. The selves come together at a moral plane to cement the differences. However, deep within the human self is the despair of not being able to reach the other. Daya Krishna writes:

> To stand by the bedside of one and look helpless at the torture and suffering that tears the heart and to feel and realize that one cannot feel the suffering and pain of one whom one thought one loved—is not that the inevitable tragedy of all human heart? I am I and you are you—and we can only signal to each other on mountains farthest apart. The desire to feel what the other one feels, the desire to be what the other one is, the impossible impulse to be all and feel all—who has not known it?[11]

Yet morality urges us to overcome the human loneliness and to reach out to the other. This happens because of the pursuit of values which the human beings undertake. Morality, for Daya Krishna, is the inevitable realization of the similarity of the human situation and the consequent effort to make persons realize the precariousness of the human reality.

The Active and the Contemplative Man: Two Poles of the Pursuit of Values

Daya Krishna feels the necessity of making a polar distinction between two types of human ideals or values, the active and contemplative.[12] The active values are those which are related to the welfare of others, such as compassion, friendship and love, while the contemplative values are those concerning the inner freedom, peace and spiritual enlightenment, which are centred around one's own consciousness. The latter are called contemplative because they are born out of contemplation on one's self. The active values are, on the other hand, social and interpersonal by nature.

The active values are enjoined upon the rational human beings because of their social and interpersonal situation in which other human beings are also actively present. This is exactly the world in which all human moral agents are brought together by nature and society. In the words of Daya Krishna:

> The seeking of active values . . . is not concerned with the type of consciousness that one enjoys oneself but rather with the continuous engagement in an activity which may probably help others or achieve a certain state of affairs in the natural or the social world.[13]

Thus the active moral agent seeks consciously to reach out to the other in the pursuit of values like compassion, love and fellow-feeling. The moral agent is essentially social by nature and so is dependent on the other selves for the pursuit of the active moral values. The moral values are thus considered active, according to Daya Krishna, because of their social character and because of the fact that they cannot be pursued by the individual alone except in the interpersonal world. This world is also characterized by temporality and historicity as the persons living in this world are subject to change and contingency. Daya Krishna writes: 'The realization of the active values, thus, leads one to an essential involvement in temporality, historicity, and sociality. Rather, one gradually begins to view oneself as a creature of just these and ultimately perhaps becomes what one views.'[14]

The world, thus, in which the active values are pursued is enmeshed with the historical situations of various kinds and also with the contingencies associated with the other selves. That is why the active values of morality are threatened by the possibility of non-cooperation of the other and the fragility of the moral situation which is plagued by the presence of the weakness of will. The human situation, as already mentioned, does not guarantee the success of the moral endeavour of man because of the historical contingencies in the world.

The contemplative values, on the other hand, do not suffer from the contingencies associated with the active moral values. It is because the contemplative values are by nature transcendental in character and therefore are beyond the contingencies of the interpersonal world. These values are intrinsically concerned with the individual being alone and his or her consciousness which is cut off from the rest of the world. The individual consciousness achieves greater degrees of freedom in the pursuit of contemplative values like enjoyment of bliss, the contemplation of the eternal objects such as truth, beauty, goodness and so on. These values, which are centered in the contemplative consciousness itself, are opposed to the active values which are dependent on the other. Daya Krishna writes,

> The contemplative values, on the other hand, lead in a different direction. It is the being itself that is the centre of attention. What matters is the achievement of a state of consciousness, valuable, meaningful, and free in itself. It is the stilling of time, the withdrawal from society, the transcendence of History that is the essence of the matter.[15]

Thus the contemplative values are self-directed rather than other-directed and so are least related with the other selves in the world of space, time and causality. That is the reason why the contemplative values are involved in the religious life, the mystic realization of the Divine and the aesthetic enjoyments of the highest order. That may be one of the reasons why the contemplative values are viewed with suspicion by those who are too much concerned with the world of active values. That, however, does not detract from the fact that the contemplative values are superior in quality so far as the freedom from temporality and causality is concerned. The spiritual value of *mokṣa* is a standing testimony to the higher nature of the contemplative values in comparison to those of the other kind.

Ramchandra Gandhi pleads for the superiority of the contemplative values in his espousal of the mystic needs of the contemplative man, best epitomized in the personality of the Buddha, Mahavira and Ramana Maharshi. For him, the active values have significance only in the world of action where we meet with other selves, but in the silent contemplation of the mystic mind, the highest values cannot but be those associated with the meditative life. The moral life, according to Gandhi, consists primarily in according value to other souls and having the life of empathy with them in their hour of suffering.[16] That is why he believes that man cannot but be moral in his association with the other human souls. But this moral engagement itself demands that we must admit a higher Being with whom we must be in perfect communion so that we can get a better grip over our own moral consciousness regarding the other selves. This attitude of prefect faith in the Divine Being is, however, part of the contemplative life of man and is dissociated from the moral agency itself. The love for the Divine Being which characterizes our contemplative life is itself an autonomous value accessible to the mystic mind.

The Mystic Mind: The Trail of Spirituality

Mystic experience is part of the total experience of the contemplative mind in view of the fact that the higher the contemplative mind soars into the upper regions of the transcendental consciousness, the more refined experience of the Divine it gets. This experience of the Divine is variously described by the mystics, the philosophers and the artists. There is no one standard way of expressing this experience as evidenced in the Upaniṣads and also in the writings of the mystic philosophers. Besides, it is well known that ordinary language fails to express this experience, because of which it is characterized as inexpressible.[17] It is because the religious or mystic experience is not about the world but about something beyond the world. The experience of the 'beyond' is a virtual rejection of what is experienced here and now in the world. Daya Krishna writes:

> Religion is essentially a *seeking* for something beyond this world with its limitations of space, time, mass, and causality . . . something that is to be experienced as, or even more, *directly* as the world we experience through our senses. The seeking invariably takes form, at least in its first phase, of turning away from this world. . . . The concern is not with the world at all, but rather with something that is to be realized by taking our minds away from it. The way, therefore, has always been the withdrawal from the world, the concentration on the Divine, the aspiration for it, and the prayer to it to reveal itself.[18]

Religion, thus described, keeps room for the mystic experience of the 'beyond' and in that sense it is a trans-empirical experience calling for a withdrawal from the experience of the world in space and time.

For Daya Krishna, the validity of mystic experience is never in doubt because of the fact that it has its autonomy in being a coherent experience. It is not to be judged strictly in terms of the principles of cognitive validity because the mystic experience is not a cognitive experience at all. It is an experience of bliss or joy of inner freedom and not of something cognitively grasped. Therefore, there is no question of its being validated through the cognitive principles. The mystic mind is not a cognitive mind. It is the contemplative mind engaged in exploring the freedom of the mind from the world and its unlimited events and objects.

The realm of the spiritual is located in the realm of the religious or mystical experience because of the fact that the spiritual is introduced at the boundary of our worldly experience. The world beyond is the world of mystic experience of the Divine which is vouched for by the mind's incessant pushing forward the frontiers of our non-cognitive mind. This realm of experience is the most immediate and direct because it is free from the causal conditions of experience in the ordinary sense. It is an uncaused and unconditional experience. That is why time ceases to be relevant in this experience since it withers away here and gives way to the timeless. In the words of Daya Krishna:

> Consciousness in its intuitive or immediate aspect, then, seems to be outside time. The passage of time is more a matter of inference than of immediate awareness. A sense of unreality pervades our experience of time. . . . The shackles of time, however, are not completely secure. One can always escape them by changing into the mode of presentational immediacy. Here Time does not exist. What exists is the 'eternal present' in which we can always realize 'significance'.[19]

Thus, the escape from time is the way we can ascend from the lower experience to the higher realm where time gives way to the timeless. The timeless is causally free, whereas the temporal is causally bound.

Ramchandra Gandhi, like Daya Krishna, makes room for the timeless in his quest for the spiritual beyond the frontiers of the world. He is acutely aware of the fact that the mystical is the very foundation of our inquiry into the existence of the world and of consciousness.[20] The mystical compels us to search for the limits of existence of ourselves and of the world. That is the reason why he points out that there is an 'attitude of timelessness'[21] in our philosophical quest and even in our conversational discourse. This sense of timelessness pervades the entire experience of the mystical. He writes, '. . . what is mystical is not the mere fact of my being conscious or a self-conscious being, but the fact that I am an incarnate consciousness'.[22]

What this suggests is that the very fact of being conscious or being the incarnate consciousness is something that defies logic and language and therefore it cannot be described the way we can describe the different states of consciousness. The very realization of having consciousness is itself a supra-conscious state and hence is bound to be mystical in nature.

Gandhi explores the nature of the mystical thought while affirming the existence of things and events in the world. If we start with the idea of X's existence or X's occurring, he argues, then we are led logically to affirming 'Something exists' as opposed to 'Nothing exists'. Thus the idea of absolute nothingness is introduced, which is itself a mystical idea. He writes:

> Now I think it must be the presupposition of thoughts of these sorts that something, as opposed to nothing, has occurred, is occurring, occurred, etc. And this presupposition involves the employment of the notion of *nothing* occurring. This is the essentially incomprehensible notion of 'time standing still', or the notion of timelessness or eternity. Another mystical notion at the heart of a perfectly ordinary mode of thinking.[23]

The simple idea of absolute nothingness is puzzlingly mystical because it talks about something which is absolutely incomprehensible and therefore cannot be made intelligible. As Gandhi[24] says, 'We cannot imagine absolute nothingness, we can form no clear thought about it. And yet the perfectly simple, even banal, proposition "something exists" makes necessary reference to the proposition "Nothing exists".'[25]

Thus the mystical is associated with all the strange and puzzling notions like 'nothingness', 'consciousness' and so on which are embedded in our language and thought. There is therefore every reason to believe that mystical experiences are round the corner in our everyday thinking.

Religious mysticism, which has been the cornerstone of all teachings of the great minds, has always awakened ordinary minds into the higher forms of experience, including the experience of the Divine. We are led necessarily into seeking the forms of such mystic experience in the very business of our self-understanding and the understanding of the world. Without the experience of the sublime and the ultimate, there can be no worthwhile experience of art and beauty, or even authentic moral experience. The moral matrix of the human actions, which is the higher self in man, is necessarily linked with the mystic experience of the Divine in man. That is the reason why there is a definite passage from the moral experience to the realm of the spiritual experience as mapped out by Gandhi. Gandhi builds up a harmonizing link between the spiritual and the moral in his theory of self by suggesting that the moral self is the very self that seeks spiritual union with the higher self, the advaitic Brahman. Gandhi's Advaitism, as already indicated, culminates in the realization of the unity of all existence.

The Transcendent: The Appeal from Above

The distinct mystic touch in the writings of Daya Krishna and Ramchandra Gandhi suggests that no great mind is without an appeal to the transcendent, the absolute and the unconditioned reality. Daya Krishna calls the transcendent the other side of the worldly experience which is bound up with the causal chain. It is identifiably the Divine for some and the unnamable and the nameless for others. Nonetheless, it is the appeal from the unknown that matters most for all great thinkers. This appeal is the basis of all works of art, literature and philosophy. Daya Krishna writes:

> Any society or individual that denies or cuts itself off from the transcendent pole of experience merely deprives itself of one of the profoundest sources of 'significance' that is possible for man. Man is rooted in the transcendent and if he remains indifferent or develops a negative relationship to it, he is bound to feel empty and alone in this wide, wide world.[26]

That is to say, the awareness of the transcendent is the very basis of human life and must be realized in morality and religion. There cannot be an ethics that does not refer to or indirectly suggests the reality of the transcendent. Religion is directly concerned with the transcendent, not only because it makes man realize the higher truth but also because it progressively leads towards the truth in its elaborate religious symbolism. 'One can become increasingly aware of it and love it or be over-awed by it—that is religion', says Daya Krishna.[27]

For Daya Krishna, the holistic vision of life, though emphatic about the transcendent because of its paramount importance for the meaning or significance of life, does not disregard the immanent aspects of life which include the material development as well as the intellectual achievements in science and technology. The immanent aspects do hint at the physical, emotional and intellectual aspects of life. 'The denial of the immanent aspect', says Daya Krishna, 'however, would be equally fatal . . . for, it should not be forgotten that, without "immanence" the experience of the "significance" can never arise'.[28] Thus, there is the imperative need of integrating the immanent with the transcendent in the life of man.

The world and what lies beyond it must come together to make the unitary life possible. That is why Daya Krishna keeps the active and contemplative aspects of life in one unitary whole where the needs of the active soul in the world are fulfilled in his morally harmonious life. But that itself harkens to the realization of the higher ends of life in the fulfillment of the contemplative life in the withdrawal from the world which is asymptotically set before man as the highest end. This end is spiritual by virtue of the fact that it opens up a higher plane of existence in which the spirit of man is released from the shackles of the flesh. The spiritual realization embodies the dissolution of the egocentric life and its necessary attachments.

Ramchandra Gandhi's concern for the transcendent issues from the fact that man's moral life is incomplete because of man's helplessness before Nature and also because of the Nature's great 'betrayal'[29] of man. Man is at the mercy of Nature because of the fact that in spite of his best efforts, he cannot alleviate the suffering of mankind as a whole. This fact itself makes man seek the intervention of a more powerful cosmic force which, through its infinite love and compassion, can release man from pain and suffering. This infinite cosmic force is the transcendent that is available to man's consciousness, though not as cognitive datum. Theists call it God, while the non-theists call it the Absolute Being who can solve the human problems in a miraculous way.

Gandhi appeals to this infinitely loving Being as the Transcendent Being who stands at the boundary of the world to be invoked in our prayers and petitions.[30] He argues that we cannot be immanentist regarding the world in which we live, because whenever we talk of the world, we have already transcended it. In having the thought, 'This is the world which is ours', we have to go beyond the world. Hence transcendentalism is the best way of dealing the world as a whole. Gandhi writes:

> Thus the thought '*This* world', which constitutes the logical heart of the immanentist 'world-view', is an illegitimate thought. The idea of 'the world', conceived as the totality or system of all actual and possible states of affairs, is the idea of that in relation to which nothing can be said or thought. . . .[31]

The idea of the world, being itself logically illegitimate, demands that we appeal to the Transcendent in order to make it coherent and meaningful. Therefore, if we resign ourselves to this world and the life and death in it, we are acting against the very spirit of thought, because we are accepting something as final which it is not. The world is not final as the immanentist says, but is a 'limited whole', to use Wittgenstein's expression, from the transcendental point of view.[32] Gandhi pleads for the latter point of view in the following passage:

> A classic theistic prayer of the form 'God, let me not be annihilated' would serve the ends of an exploratory-communicative summoning of God's help. Such a prayer would render discrepant my immanentist view of 'my life' or 'myself' coming to an end. And it would non-cognitively make available to me the category of transcendence.[33]

Thus we are led to believe that the immanent view of life is incomplete and discrepant without the transcendental point of view. This, Gandhi believes, is the crying need of the religious and spiritual point of view.

The Moral-Spiritual Continuum: Resolution of the Dilemma of the Immanent versus the Transcendent

The symbiotic relation between the moral and the spiritual is the axis of the philosophical problems in Daya Krishna and Ramchandra Gandhi. The moral field is autonomously circumscribed within the axis of the self and the not-self, because within this alone the question of our moral attitude towards the other can be mapped. But the not-self which is hidden in other selves and the world cannot be the ultimate reality according to both Daya Krishna and Gandhi. The not-self is the disguised self according to Gandhi, the Advaitin.[34] But it is not so according to Daya Krishna, who does not follow non-dualism in the orthodox sense. For him, non-dualism is true, but only in a modified sense because the self is autonomous and is separated from the other to the extent the other can be relegated to the level of non-existence at a transcendental level. This is exactly what Advaita means to suggest when it denies that the other selves are different from the non-dual self. Daya Krishna admits that at the level of spiritual realization, there is absence of the ego and its counterpart, the non-ego.

Both Daya Krishna and Ramchandra Gandhi are non-dualists at heart because both admit that the ultimate reality is of the form of consciousness which needs to be realized to be free from time, history and causality. The transcendental consciousness withdraws itself from the world 'where time stands still and happiness reigns supreme'.[35] Such a description of the higher state of consciousness is non-dualist in spirit because of the fact that the not-self in the form of the temporal world and the other beings is nullified at the level of transcendental consciousness. Daya Krishna does not take the temporal and the historical world as ultimate, though he does not say that it is *māyā* or illusion. He concedes full reality to the world of time and history the way Sri Aurobindo[36] does without adopting the latter's metaphysical categories. However, he, like the Advaitin, concedes that we cannot finally be confined to the world of time and history. There is already in us the urge for the Infinite which compels us to transcend the empirical world.

Daya Krishna admits the continuum between the moral and the spiritual precisely because he realizes the continuum between the temporal world and the transcendental world. The continuum is basically between the immanent and the transcendent, that is, between the empirical and the transcendental. Such a continuum affirms the fact that we can rise to the higher world only through the world below so that there is no discordance or discontinuity between the two. For him, the empirical world provides the full scope for the active moral values to be realized because of the active involvement of the self in the world where the self and the not-self are in close relationship. It is the arena of dualism in which self and not-self are equally real. But the higher values of the transcendent kind demand a different kind of self–not-self relationship. The not-self is, at this level, disenfranchised and put in bracket precisely because the not-self is no more the other. It is assimilated into the self by virtue of love, contemplation and knowledge of a higher kind. The non-dualist value of internal kinship with everybody is emphasized at this level. Such values are called the axiological values as distinguished from the moral values. Daya Krishna writes:

> The primacy of the 'ought' has been so much taken for granted in ethical discussion that the supra-personal and supra-social nature of values seems to have been entirely forgotten. The whole set of questions centering round prima facie rightness, duties, obligations, sanctions, punishments, etc. reveals this wrong orientation. . . . The axiological 'ought', on the other hand, is not so socio-anthropo-centric. Rather, it reveals the transcendent nature of the value claim and orientates humanity to a trans-human dimension.[37]

Thus, we are presented with a set of transcendent values which follow the active values of morality without cancelling them. By emphasizing the spiritual values, the moral values are not cancelled but are affirmed and shown their right vis-à-vis the spiritual values.

Ramchandra Gandhi locates the continuum in his adherence to the non-dualist stance that what is higher in the form of feeling of identity with all and realization of the egolessness is part of the wholesome life of the moral ought and the spiritual ought taken together. In fact, the moral ought impels the self to transcend to a higher level of dissolution of the ego in the non-dualist way. Dualism differentiates and breeds contempt and hatred for the other, but non-dualism brings all together into a unity, because the not-self is dissolved in the discovery of the non-dual self. The other is only apparently real, while everything is nothing but the self-imaging of the self.[38]

Thus, both Daya Krishna and Ramchandra Gandhi have opened the way for a rediscovery of the lost sense of non-dualism in our culture and morality by emphasizing the universality of the self and by showing that the higher self is truly the locus of the best of man's value aspiration and value realization.

Notes and References

1. In Advaita Vedānta, the distinction is made between self (*ātman*) and not-self (*anātman*). The not-self includes anything other than the self. Since the self is alone real, the not-self is bound to be illusory.
2. Ramchandra Gandhi, *Presuppositions of Human Communication* (New Delhi: Oxford University Press, 1974).
3. Ramchandra Gandhi, *The Availability of Religious Ideas* (London: Macmillan, 1976 [Indian edition 1979], pp. 29–30.
4. Ibid., p. 25.
5. The self as *nirguṇa* or without attributes is an advaitic idea. This is emphasized in the Upaniṣads and subsequently in Advaita Vedānta.
6. Gandhi, *The Availability of Religious Ideas*, p. 27.
7. Ramchandra Gandhi, *Sita's Kitchen: A Testimony of Faith and Inquiry* (New Delhi and London: Penguin Books, 1992).
8. Ibid., p. 55.
9. Ibid., pp. 53–71.
10. Daya Krishna, *The Art of the Conceptual: Explorations in a Conceptual Maze Over Three Decades* (New Delhi: Indian Council for Philosophical Research, 1989), p. 206.
11. Ibid., p. 208.
12. Ibid., pp. 211–220.
13. Ibid., p. 212.
14. Ibid., pp. 216–217.
15. Ibid., p. 217.
16. Ramchandra Gandhi, *The Availability of Religious Ideas*, pp. 60–65.
17. Cf. Ludwig Wittgenstein, *Tractatus Logico-Philosophicus*, translated by D. F. Pears and B. F. McGuinness (London: Routledge and Kegan Paul, 1987), 6.522.
18. Daya Krishna. *Art of the Conceptual*, p. 114.
19. Ibid., pp. 193–194.
20. Gandhi, *The Availability of Religious Ideas*, Chapter 5 on the nature of the mystical.
21. Ibid., p. 81.
22. Ibid., p. 78.
23. Ibid., p. 79.

24. Gandhi, *The Availability of Religious Ideas*, p. 75.
25. Ibid.
26. Daya Krishna, *Art of the Conceptual*, p. 194.
27. Ibid.
28. Ibid.
29. Ramchandra Gandhi, *The Availability of Religious Ideas*, p. 97.
30. Ibid., pp. 64–65.
31. Ibid., p. 96.
32. Wittgenstein, *Tractatus Logico-Philosophicus*, 6.45.
33. Gandhi, *The Availability of Religious Ideas*, p. 99.
34. Gandhi, *Sita's Kitchen*, pp. 1–25.
35. Daya Krishna, *Art of the Conceptual*, pp. 203–204.
36. Sri Aurobindo, *The Life Divine*, vol. I (Pondicherry: Sri Aurobindo Ashram, 1972).
37. Daya Krishna, *Art of the Conceptual*, pp. 203–204.
38. See Gandhi, *Sita's Kitchen*, pp. 1–25.

13

On Missing and Seeming to Miss: Some Philosophical Ramblings on the Subjective/Objective Distinction in Memory of Daya Krishna*

Arindam Chakrabarti

I

I miss Dayaji. Can I meaningfully raise the question whether I really miss him or only seem to miss him?

At Michael McGhee's place in Liverpool, Daya Krishna and I were spending a few days in 1995, talking, cooking, eating and walking in the idyllic English countryside, and above all arguing. Thoroughly enjoying our long walks across the undulating green, yet itching for a hearty philosophical debate, one morning 'the Argumentative Indian' overheard Michael and me discussing John Locke's distinction between primary and secondary qualities at some point. Suddenly—like throwing a trump card in a game—he asked:

* A version of the central part of this chapter was published in an edited collection of essays titled 'Epistemology', edited by Roma Chakraborty (Calcutta University, 2008). I am grateful to my friend Mark Siderits for the kindness of reading this earlier version and suggesting some improvements.

> What is this idea of a secondary quality that people make so much fuss about? What are the secondary qualities of the self, for example? OK, we start with the distinction between objective and subjective qualities, between what the material apple really is and how it tastes to a fever-afflicted tongue. The material substance, or its insensible parts, thus, are supposed to have both objective and subjective attributes. What about a non-material substance such as a self or a conscious person? Locke did not quite get rid of such substances. Did he? Well, does it have primary and secondary qualities? What would be the secondary qualities of my Self? Does it make any sense to distinguish between what I really feel and what I only seem to feel? How can you apprehend mental qualities in yourself which are not objectively there in you but appear to be there in yourself? How could you yourself be mistaken about what you are currently feeling? If I seem to feel it, then I really feel it. Doesn't the objective subjective distinction break down with qualities given to the inner sense? Could you ever distinguish between what you objectively are and what you think you are, when what you think is part of what you objectively are?

At that point I was silenced by these questions. I simply marveled at the freshness of his critique of Locke. In this essay I want to offer a ruefully delayed and fledgling answer to his skeptical questions.

At two distinct levels I feel—at least seem to feel—plagued by this problem that Daya Krishna raised. At a personal level I feel from time to time that I miss him much more after his death than I used to miss him when he was alive. Having emulated Dayaji over many decades, I cannot but cast doubt even on this subjective feeling of mine because his physical absence to me, the fact that I don't see him for years, does not seem to be any more acuter or deeper now than it was before when he was alive. Even when he was alive in Jaipur, and I lived in Hawaii, we didn't meet for years. We would write to each other a little, mostly about *Journal of Indian Council of Philosophical Research* (*JICPR*) discussion notes, but I missed him (and he was kind enough to say and show that he missed me too). How is my missing him now any more intense than that? Of course there is a finality to the absence or separation that death inaugurates. I knew, when he was alive, that if I wanted to, I could go and see him. But then, knowing that it is not even possible for me to see him now could have actually lessened the feeling of missing. With a certain sense of resignation, the non-seeing now should feel pointless to try to remedy. For, isn't missing a sense of failing to be with friends with whom you 'can' hang out, whom it is possible to meet? It is no longer possible to meet or spend time with Dayaji. So, how is it that I miss him more now? I should not be missing him—the flesh-and-blood person—any more than I can miss a non-existent entity that I feel familiar with from reading fiction. Well, memory and imagination are not that radically unlike! I know now for certain that there does not exist at present, any such person who could see and get excited about the subtlest philosophical problems even when no one else could see them and even when he could not 'see'. So, could it be that I am not missing him as much as I seem to be missing him? Could it appear to me that I am missing someone intensely when I am actually not missing him? Could my feeling be really different from what it seems to be like to me now?

At an impersonal theoretical level, I think the issue: 'Can we draw a primary/objective versus secondary/subjective quality distinction with respect to our inner feelings' is very much a live issue of philosophy, closely connected to the appearance/reality distinction which bothered Daya Krishna all his life.

In this chapter, I shall only discuss the impersonal theoretical problem. At the end, I would draw some insights from a piece by Daya Krishna on appearance and Reality, to make some remarks on the subjective–objective dichotomy and its far-reaching implications in the world of phenomenal feelings revealed by introspection.

II

Bias, inattention, sleepiness, intoxication, over-confidence, sheer inefficacy of the sense organ, too much closeness or remoteness from the perceiver or extreme smallness of the object regularly lead to perceptual illusions and mistakes with respect to the external world. But how is it possible for us to make mistakes about our own current mental states? And even if it is possible that we make such mistakes, is it even conceivable that we could detect such mistakes from a first-person present-tensed point of view? 'Can I assert, coherently, that right now I mistakenly think that I am feeling calm?' We seem to be on the verge of unintelligibility there! Traditionally, whatever way one has of immediately being aware of one's own current mental states is called 'introspection'. So, the harder question boils down to: 'How can introspection be self-detectably erroneous?'

Normally, in perception and cognition in general, the question of a correct 'take' or 'mis-take' arises only if there is some object, property or state of affairs—'out there'—for us to have a (sensory or doxastic) 'take' on. Since the takes themselves are detected by introspection, it is assumed that the taker at least cannot mis-take the take itself.

A complicated version of this theory of infallibility of 'apperception' (roughly: perception of perception) is found in the Dvaita Vedānta (Maddhva) doctrine of *sakṣī* (witness). One can make a mistake in seeing silver where there is only mother-of-pearl, but one cannot be mistaken in the self-awareness that one is excited to see silver, because the 'inner witness' is immune to error. Why? Because the inner witness is the same as the Self. It is a kind of consciousness which functions like an additional apperceptive sense organ, but it is actually none other than the knower, the eventual mistake-detector. Once you allow this witness-self itself, on some occasions, to bear false witness as to even what (erroneous) content it is currently experiencing, there would be no possibility of firm exposure of error, let alone confirmation of knowledge. To distrust this ultimate court of appeal is to open oneself to unstoppable doubt not only about whether it is so when it seems to be so, but even about whether it even seems to be so.

But such alleged infallibility of self-awareness or first-person authority is not the only ground for claiming such freedom from the risk of error. There is another easy argument to prove that our inner awareness of our mental states could not be erroneous. If my anger or desire is itself more like a headache, and my awareness of anger or self-consciousness of desire is indistinguishable from it (if there is nothing 'higher order' about the introspective awareness), then, the non-normativity of my first-order mental states would render even my self-cognitions non-normative, hence incapable of being assessed for truth or error. Headaches could not be non-veridical. Awareness of a headache would be indistinguishable from that headache. Hence awareness of headache could not be non-veridical. It is very hard to deny the first premise that occurrent mental states themselves are natural events, though Plato and Jayanta Bhatta have both talked about pleasures themselves being false (or correct). So the counter to this argument has to mainly attack the second premise: the collapsing of awareness of a pleasure to the pleasure itself. Unless one insists that awareness and undergoing of the pleasure are distinct, one cannot make sense of mistaken awareness of current pleasures.

III

Yet we do, undeniably, make mistakes of different sorts in assessing our current mental, hedonic, somatic and proprioceptive states. When we are feeling lazy while trying to lift up a chair, we believe that a certain chair feels too heavy for us to lift when it really does not. We think—tell ourselves—that we are not annoyed when we are. We think that we are annoyed because some friend has arrived too late, whereas the fact—hard-to-acknowledge—is that we are annoyed because he showed up at all! Intent on emotional consistency, we ignore and suppress one aspect of a complex psychological state, love–hate, or fun–boredom, or admiration–envy, and genuinely believe that we are only loving, having fun or hating someone. Thus, many different kinds of mistakes fall under the general category of 'Errors about one's current mental state'. Some inward or higher-order self-ascription of cognitive states 'inherit' the error of the outward judgement that it reflectively registers. While having the rope/snake illusion, as yet undetected, one could introspect: 'I am seeing a snake now.' The error of the outward judgement: 'That is a snake, over there' contaminates the introspective awareness' I am seeing a snake now', rendering it erroneous in so far as the claim is taken as existentially quantified: 'There is a snake which I am now seeing.'

Once we have some systematic account of the different sorts of mistakes we can commit even about current first-person perceptual hedonic or cognitive states, it should be quite interesting to see in what sense we can have states or contents—not out there but 'in here'—about which too we (whose inner states they are) could be in error.

IV

Self-presenting states, such as: 'it seeming to me now that I am being appeared to orangely' were deemed immune to error because it was thought that, there is not enough 'give' between it seeming so and its being so. The only room for correction was supposed to be linguistic, for example, if someone misused a colour-word or applied the wrong English word for an inner feeling while putting the introspection into words, saying 'mad (angry)' when the word that fit their current mood would be 'miffed'. A certain margin of exaggeration seems to have become routine in American introspective reports, where adjectives like 'fantastic' and 'terrific' are freely thrown around, the slightest dislike being reported as disgust, a glimmer of approval being noted—even to oneself—as adoration, and, above all, the slightest fall from the expected default state of perpetual excitement being registered as utter boredom! It is maddeningly difficult to settle the debate whether these are linguistic errors or errors in assessing even what one seems to be undergoing.

However, it is clear to us that introspection or alleged immediate self-awareness makes much taller or wider claims than these 'seeming to seem' sorts of safely weak pronouncements, and therefore makes more than verbal mistakes. As Rosenberg (2002: chapter 2) has noted, with these 'It seems to me' type of statements we don't express any beliefs at all, we express 'retreats' from belief (which is not even to assert that one is retreating from belief). And a retreat from belief cannot be incorrect because it cannot be correct, like a failure to believe. So it is misleading to describe these 'It seems to me' utterances as expressions of infallible first person reports.

If we do treat them as positive reports rather than mere 'showing that one is withholding full objective commitment', then their content would be much wider than just the internal appearance of appearance. If it is a report of my introspective belief that I am now sulking that my friend was not overjoyed by my surprise gift, then just by it seeming to me that I am sulking for that reason I am committing myself to the existence of my friend, my gift, and my friend's lukewarm reception of it. As we shall see, with wider content, the error-accommodating 'give' between our take on our mental states and the mental states themselves also expands. This inner leeway for mistakes, then, becomes part of the 'space of reasons'—even if not all regions of it are equally public. Between this larger 'give' and our epistemically riskier 'take' on ourselves, there is room for ignorance, deception, exaggeration, underplaying, and other kinds of misconsrtuals, even after a certain kind of first-person privilege is conceded.

V

To remind ourselves of the point we started with. A storm or a rash on the skin, a supernova or a tumor cannot commit an error. A judgement, a belief, an explanation, a thought, a conception, a recollection, a perception or an assessment can. Hence the latter admit of emendation, teaching, learning, correction and improvement (recall the title of Spinoza's small unfinished book: *Improvement of Understanding!*). It makes sense to try to get better at it. The mind-training traditions which propose to improve our ability to know ourselves must admit the possibility of substantial—not merely verbal—mistakes in our effortful or automatic introspective cognitions. We could not be trying to get better at such cognitions, unless we are learning to make fewer mistakes in them.

About external perception, epistemology has always taken account of the risk of error. From Plato's *Theaetetus* to Price's *Perception*, Western philosophers have scrambled for a coherent account of illusion and errors. But a systematic problem space regarding how to account for mistakes and their detection in immediate perceptual awareness did not develop in modern Western philosophy as it did in classical Indian epistemologies, for example, between anti-realist Buddhists and realist Nyaya, between infallibilist (Prabhakara-) Mīmāṃsā and fallibilist Advaita Vedānta and so on. If the real existence of its intended object makes a cognition veridical, how can non-veridical cognition have any object at all, and without an object what would it err about? How can one resist the threat of 'all is error' kind of pan-illusionism, without falling into 'if it is genuine perception then it is immune to error' kind of infallibilism? These are well–thrashed-out questions in the Indian epistemolgies. But the problem space is not so well-carved out even in sophisticated contemporary Western philosophy of perception.

VI

In this chapter, the contemporary analytic philosophers' ongoing debate between first-person authority (impossibility of mistakes about one's current mental states) versus lack of privileged access (likelihood of errors concerning one's current mental states) is discussed with some additional insights, here and there, from classical Indian disputations about theories of perceptual mistakes in general.

Let us first take a contemporary formulation of the denial of privileged access:

> The doctrine of privileged access is that I am the authority on all my own experiences . . . the thesis was refuted by Freud (I know your dreams better than you), Duhem (I know your methods of scientific discovery

> better than you), Malinowski (I know your customs and habits better than you), and perception theorists (I can make you see things which are not there and describe your perception better than you can). (Joseph Agassi, quoted by Davidson [2001, p. 6])

Now, note the careful formulation of the opposite, first-person incorrigibility or infallibility thesis:

> statements about . . . mental events, e.g. . . . reports of thoughts. . . . These are incorrigible in the sense that if a person sincerely asserts such a statement it does not make sense to suppose, and nothing could be accepted as showing, that he is mistaken. (Shoemaker, quoted in Davidson [2001, p. 10])

So, could I sometimes be wrong about my own present feelings? Or, am I always right?

Also, the pair, 'subjective and objective', is sometimes used to mean simply: mistaken and correct. Subjective boils down to what merely seems to be so to someone when the 'merely' implies that it is not really so; and objective is that which is really the case, independently of how it appears to anyone. But then, that pair is also sometimes used to mean simply 'inner and outer', such that the fact that one is feeling depressed is a subjective fact, but the fact that the World Trade Centre Twin Towers collapsed under terrorist attacks is an objective fact. Now, the puzzle is this: if we put together the 'erroneous' with the 'inner' meanings, then our awareness of inner states would be always mistaken. Yet, because my claims about my inner states are not claims about outer objective states, and their reality consists in their appearance to me, they are said to be free from the hazard of error. Here, as elsewhere, truth may lie somewhere between these two extremes: that we are always wrong about ourselves or that we could not conceivably be wrong ever. The moment, however, we say that introspection is sometimes veridical and sometimes non-veridical, the question arises how to tell apart the good introspective cognitions from the bad ones?

VII

To sift out genuine cases of knowledge from wishful thinking, lucky guesses, illusions, false beliefs, unjustified beliefs and accidentally justified beliefs, Western epistemology has searched for clear criteria of knowledgehood. First, second, third, fourth and more conditions of knowledge, thus, were formulated, avoiding over-coverage and under-coverage, in order to distinguish knowledge from non-knowledge. Though doubt, unjustified true belief, dream, hallucinations and a coherent web of mutually supporting crazy beliefs are standard feared cases of non-knowledge, the most notorious pretenders which need to be carefully excluded by any successful criterion of knowledgehood are errors where one normally does not suspect them. That is why, as we have already noted above, classical Indian epistemologies have always bolstered their theory of knowledge with an extremely sophisticated theory of error. And of all errors, errors about the self are the most pernicious and the most common. According to Vatsyayana, the author of *Nyayabhasya*, we take pains to be pleasures, we take what is not self to be self, our calamities to be our respites. We slip into mistakes where we feel the most confident. Our preconceptions and wishes get the better of our judgement. And where is my personal bias harder to detect than in case of my own perception of myself? If the police detective is corrupt, how can we expect them to detect police corruption?

In modern Western philosophy, Descartes has given a subtle theory of error, tracing it to human will. But he also encouraged the idea that our clear and distinct self-awarnesses are as certainly true as any belief can be. They are not only indubitable, but they are immune to error.

VIII

Though Kant has not paid a whole lot of attention to the mechanisms which produce common corrigible or incorrigible 'perceptual' errors, such as taking a rope for a snake or seeing the sun as rising, or the moon appearing to move because the clouds are passing across its face, he was greatly concerned with philosophical illusions or conceptual and metaphysical mistakes. In his theory of knowledge, Kant has devoted much larger space to 'the logic of illusions' (the transcendental dialectic), where he 'disciplines' pure reason, by warning against common mistakes—paralogisms, amphibolies and antinomies—into which it tends to fall when it oversteps its limits.

One area in which even sceptical philosophers do not normally suspect any possibility of mistake is one's own belief about one's own current mental state. Others can be mistaken about my current mental state, and I could be mistaken about the state of my own body right now. I could, even, misremember the mental state I was in a couple of hours back. But I cannot be mistaken about my own current mental state. I should be unable to keep any secrets from myself, and what else could be better-known to me than my current mental states, since they are mine, they are current and they are inner—which makes the gap between the knowing and what is known, in all possible ways, the minimum.

IX

One could put this so-called 'privileged access thesis' this way: I am not only the sole authority on my soul, I am an unchallengeably reliable authority. If it appears to me and I think that I am feeling happy now, I must be feeling happy. If I believe I am not feeling tired, then I am not feeling tired. If I think that I am now thinking about gold then I must be thinking about gold. If I think that I doubt the existence of my hand, then I must be doubting the existence of my hand. Even Descartes who urges us to practise doubting pretty much everything, as a method of finding a solid foundation for certainty, cannot entertain the possibility—even with the help of the hypothetical evil demon—that when it seems to him that he is doubting, he may not really be doubting. He may be dreaming that he is sitting by the fireplace when he is actually in bed fast asleep, but when it 'seems' to him that he is seeing the flames in his own famous fireplace, hearing the crackling sound of the firewood burning, and feeling warm sitting next to it, Descartes remarks: 'I certainly seem to see, to hear, and to be warmed. This cannot be false.'

Kant's own view about introspection are murky, since he explicitly rejects the idea of a special manifold of inner sense. But I think even Kant would not be able to make sense of the suggestion that someone who believes about himself that he is in pain, may not actually be in pain, that errors about one's own current mental state are even possible. In most recent American epistemology, Lawrence BonJour has cautiously endorsed this sort of immunity to error regarding one's self-ascription of psychological states, in the context of rebuilding a sophisticated version of foundationalism.

I would like to argue against this claim of infallibility of first-person present-tensed ascriptions of mental states. My bottom line would be this: If introspection has to count as a cognition of anything at all, and as a cognition which sometimes qualifies as 'knowledge—or perceptual knowledge' of one's own mind, then it must take the risk of error just like any other knowledge of objective facts. If I have to claim credit of being mostly right about myself, I must be ready to take the blame of being wrong sometimes. I could be wrong as to what exactly I am currently feeling, or about what it is I am thinking about, or with regard to what caused the internal state I am now in.

X

By errors of introspection I don't mean false beliefs about oneself which span over longer-term dispositional claims about what sort of a person one is. Thus, it is well known that people can be deluded about their own temperaments or characters. An irritable man may believe that he is a very calm and patient fellow. An avaricious woman may (and they often do!) believe that she has very little need of money or possessions. In fact, because one is extremely vain, one may think of oneself as rather humble. Those mistakes are interesting but do not concern us here.

As with any error, error about one's own current inner state cannot be concurrently detected. The correction has to be retrospective. Of course, the detection—and hence elimination—of the introspective mistake has to be done by the mistake-maker herself. But in some cases, one can get help from others. Suppose I ask myself at *t1*, whether I am jealous of *X*, and find that I am not. Later on at *t2*, I might think back of the time *t1*, and realize that while I convinced myself that I was not jealous of *X*, I was, even then, annoyed at the news that *X* got an award that I never got, but explained away the annoyance as simply being disturbed by the injustice of an undeserving person getting an award. I may then, at *t3*, weigh and balance my conflicting self-assessments at *t1* and *t2*, and come to the true conclusion that I had made a mistake in thinking at *t1* that I was not feeling jealous of *X*. I was.

Self-knowledge, thus, is shown to be indeed a rare commodity, the path to it being paved with many mistakes masquerading as incorrigible privileged access. Rare, and risky to claim, but not impossible. Sometimes, we must be capable of knowing our own minds, for otherwise it would make no sense to detect the occasional mistakes we make about our own minds.

XI

When foundationalists like Roderick Chisholm tried to give our knowledge claims about the external world a non-defeasible justification, they depended heavily on such immediate awareness of phenomenal states of mind, such as it seeming to one that oneself is being appeared to orangely. Such states were called 'self-presenting states', in the sense that they could not occur without the person to whom they occur being aware of them. According to one strong version of self-luminosity thesis, these states and our awareness of them were the same. And thus, our beliefs about them would count as basic beliefs which could never go wrong. The infallibility of these beliefs was thought to follow directly from the special privilege that the first person has about her own inner states.

If Mrs Hypochondriac feels excruciating headache at a certain moment, even the most reliable physician or brain-scanner does not have the right to question that feeling and say that the patient erroneously thinks that she is feeling a headache when she does not have any headache. They could suspect that Mrs H is lying or making up a false story to attract attention. But that kind of a liar or deceiver has to first know or believe correctly that she is not having the feeling that she is asserting that she is having. In order to lie about ourselves we have to know minimally what state we are in. But, to expose Mrs Hypochondriac's mistake, rather than her deception or make-believe, the doctor or therapist has to claim that though Mrs Hypochondriac is honestly reporting what seems to her to be a headache, the therapist knows better than Mrs Hypochondriac what Mrs Hypochondriac is really going through. But that is as absurd as the claim of some quack who makes up symptoms such as throwing up in the morning, and when the patient denies them, protests : 'Of course you actually throw up in the morning, but you just don't realize it' ('hoy, hoy, zanti pāro nā'). Attributing false feelings of pain to people is even more absurd than attributing unfelt pains or unnoticed vomitings to them.

The debate between fallibilists and infallibilists about introspective self-ascriptions of mental states has now boiled down to the deeper debate between internalism and externalism in epistemology and in the philosophy of mind (and mental content). There are many different shades of internalism and externalism, and the debate is conducted at different levels of controversies. All we need to remember here is the simplest common claim of internalists: the claim that the content of a mental state is entirely determined by the inner states of the subject whose mental state it is. Even if it is a happy thought or intense wish about Mount Everest, the factors which make it a thought or wish about Mount Everest lie within the inner conscious life of the thinker/wisher just as its being happy or intense lie within the private consciousness of the subject. Naturally, if internalists find even cognitive content referring to external objects to be determined wholly by internal conditions of the cognizer, cognitive content about one's own inner states would be wholly within the self-conscious access of the subject whose inner states they are.

It is not only among the Western internalists such as Descartes, Chisholm and, nowadays, BonJour, that we see this tendency to keep first-person self-ascriptions of mental states free from the possibility of error. Even in Indian thought, there are at least two distinct ways in which the infallibility of immediate introspective knowledge has been protected. One is the Prabhakara way, which starts with self-lumninosity of all cognitive states, and ends with precluding the possibility of any erroneous cognition, making even mistaken awareness of external objects impossible. If I am aware that I am feeling pain, I must be aware that I am aware of feeling pain, and my awareness—both the first-order and second-order awareness—is infallible, simply because 'all cognitions are veridical' (*yathārtham sarva-vijñānam*).

The second way is the Maddhva or Dvaita Vedānta way, which we have already mentioned above. It denies the self-luminosity or reflexivity thesis, and embraces something like a higher order perception account of self-awareness. But this meta-cognition of one's own inner states, technically called 'witness' (*sākṣī*), cannot ever go wrong. If even the witness had to seek corroboration from further check-ups, then the series of certifiers of certifiers would never end. Thus, in order to preclude a vicious regress, the Dvaita epistemologists have kept the witness and its apperceptive judgement immune from error.

XII

Wittgenstein tried to question the infallibility of introspective self-observation by questioning the assumption that they are descriptions of inner states at all—urging us to consider the possibility that statements such as 'I have a toothache' might be, at bottom, simple expressions of pain such as shrieking out 'Ouch it hurts!', and so the question of their truth or falsity does not arise. As a reaction to Wittgensteinian externalism about mental state concepts, A. J. Ayer shows us how an obstinate internalist might still hold on to the indubitability of immediate self-ascriptions of mental states by explaining away apparent counter-examples, namely examples of mistakes we make about ourselves, as mere linguistic mistakes. This is how the argument proceeds:

Imagine someone introspecting: 'I seem to be seeing a magenta flower in front of me right now'. If this could be mistaken, that could be either due to a verbal error or due to a factual error. If the person is having a visual experience—even if the experience is non-veridical, because there is only a hologram of a flower and no real flower in front him—the experience could be of a dark crimson flower, and she may be misusing the word 'Magenta' for this visual experience as of a dark crimson flower. Here the mistake is merely linguistic. But if one could somehow prove that even at the pre-verbal level, the person, while experiencing a crimson flower, cognitively suffers the error of wordlessly judging her own crimson-experience as magenta-experience without misusing the word or concept of 'magenta', then the mistake would be a factual mistake. And it is here, that the obstinate internalist could give the following counter-argument.

To make a factual error about anything is to apply the wrong predicate to it, for example, to mistake a lily for a lotus. Now, such factual error, while being about a currently presented object, which in this case happens to be the lily flower, must make reference to other objects not presented immediately, in this case, to lotuses, in so far as the experience claims that this flower is similar to or belongs to the same class as 'those' flowers. Now, the internalist insists that while introspectively noticing a particular experience happening to oneself currently, the subject makes statements which refer only to the content of that current experience and does not go beyond that content at all. If the claim is so strictly confined to the present experience and makes no direct or indirect allusion to any fact beyond it seeming to oneself that one is having such and such a visual experience, then the claim cannot go factually wrong. It can at worst be verbally mistaken, when the subject puts the wrong linguistic tag on the right self-assessment. But there is no gap at all between it seeming to one that one is seeing a magenta flower and one's introspecting that it seems so to him. Since there is no gap, there is no possibility of factual error (*The Problem of Knowledge*, pp. 61–64).

Ayer's own assessment of the above argument is unfavourable. If there is any descriptive content at all in our introspective judgements (if, that is, statements such as 'I am afraid' are not mere exclamatory expressions sometimes faked but normally constituting what counts as criteria for possessing those mental states which they look as if they are reporting), then those judgements must be capable of being false. We regularly mis-describe our current mental states not just to others but even to ourselves. 'The question is only whether such mis-description is always to be taken as an instance of a verbal mistake. My contention is that there are cases where it is more plausible to say that the mistake is factual' (*The Problem of Knowledge*, p. 66).

XIII

In more recent times, Paul Churchland has rejected the infallibility thesis about introspective reports by pointing out at least three kinds of influences which mislead us when we engage in the so-called activity of looking within. First is the influence of expectation. If a captured spy is tortured by the enemy interrogators daily with a sudden pressing of hot iron on his back for 19 days, on the twentieth day, if they blindfold him and torture him with an ice cube instead, it is likely that his expectation will mislead him into thinking that he is experiencing the hot iron even when he actually experiences the cold touch of ice on his back. Secondly, because of extremely short duration of a sensation, or minute changes in the sensation in extremely quick succession, even sensed distinctions may be mis-read as unnoticed. When each difference in sensory stimulus falls below the threshold of what Titchener called 'just noticeable difference', over a certain duration we tend to think that our experience has remained the same when actually it keeps changing. Thirdly, if some long-standing neural damage, especially in the area of cutaneous or pain sensation, suddenly gets cured, even though new tactile sensations and pain sensations start happening, the habit-memory of an insensitive skin hinders the second-order acknowledgement of such newly acquired sensory abilities.

Of course, the infallibilists could try to analyze these alleged errors in such a way that the mistake would be accommodated in the objective reference aspect of the inner experience, still keeping the self-consciousness core of the inward look free from the possibility of error. Notice how

Descartes drops all reference to the 'object' of experience when he makes the incorrigibility claims: 'I certainly seem to see, to hear, to be warmed, this cannot be false.' But if the nature of the seeing itself becomes the object of the seeming, then seeming need not be any safer from possible error than seeing. If I can ask what it is that I am seeing or hearing, I should be able to ask what is it that I seem to be seeing and hearing? And the correct answers could be different.

Take for example, the famous Muller Lyre illusions:

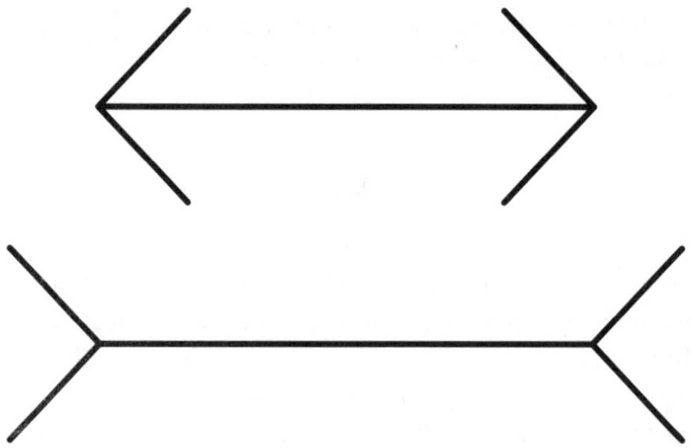

Presenting someone with the above figures, we could ask two distinct questions:

Is the top line shorter than the bottom line? (Q1)

Is the top line looking shorter than the bottom line? (Q2)

If someone measures and already knows the correct negative answer to Q1, she could get biased by that and answer 'No' to Q2 as well. But, then, we tell her to look again, and this time judge not the lines but at 'how they are looking or appearing'. Strangely enough, we often need to unlearn how our mind or eye or their habits add, distort or touch up external stimuli in order to properly introspect the mind's verdict. Such carefully mind-ignoring self-perception is sometimes called 'open-eyed introspection' whereby simply taking a fresh look at the object, we learn about how we are perceiving it, rather than deliberately focusing on our perception of it. When one notices, with such a second look outside that one visually finds the bottom line longer than the top line, then one can go back and detect the first 'intellectually compensated' judgement that they look equal, to have been a mistake about one's perceptual content, though it was correct about the lines themselves.

The very possibility of perceptual doubt points at the possibility of perceptual error: Is the top line shorter or not? I could vacillate about this. That means, I may erroneously think it is shorter when it is actually not shorter.

Analogously, when there is doubt whether the top line is 'appearing shorter to me' or not, there must be the possibility of error that when it is actually appearing shorter, I may think that it is not appearing shorter, which is to say that when I think I am seeing it to be shorter, I may not be actually seeing it to be shorter. Thus, I could be mistaken about my current visual experience itself. As A. J. Ayer comments: 'But in allowing that he may be uncertain how a thing looks to him, we have already . . . drawn a line between the facts. and his assessment, or description, of them' (Ayer 1956, pp. 65–66).

Two things must be noted with care here. The facts Ayer is talking about are mental, in this case, sense-experiential, facts. Normally we call such facts 'subjective'. But once we draw the distinction between those experiential facts and the subject's assessment of them, the experiential facts claim a certain objectivity: anything the subject could be wrong about must be objective. So, then, is the fact that I am feeling impatient now a subjective fact or an objective fact? My feeling impatient is directly self-intimating to me, it seems. But I could mis-describe (silently, even to myself) this feeling as a feeling of fear (e.g., the fear that I shall be late). I could be wrong about it, and no one may ever know whether I was impatient or afraid. In that case, this is an objective fact, which can go completely unrecognized. So it seems both subjective and objective. This discomfort seems to stay with Ayer till the end. Is a misdescription—assessing my impatience to be fear, my miff to be anger, my attraction to be love—merely a verbal error, a misuse of words or is it a substantial assessment error, in which case my use of words is accurate: I am genuinely misjudging my objective (real)–subjective states.

A certain stripe of internalism and foundationalism insists that such first-person errors about current mental states could not be more serious than mere linguistic slips. Our experience of our own experience, unclothed in social language, must be intrinsically immune to error, according to such foundationalists.

Unless a minimal infallibility of the first person's clear and distinct judgement about her own current inner states were granted, there would be no difference between our knowledge of our own minds and our knowledge of others. Yet, the very 'mineness' of my own states seems to consist in my word being final about their nature.

XIV

In the face of such obstinate internalist refusal to admit clear cases of illusions of introspection, I would like to propose my own externalist arguments proving, first, that the very distinction between factual error and verbal error is questionable, and second, that I am not the sole authority on the content of my own thoughts and feelings.

Let us remind ourselves, generally, of W. V. Quine's life-long insistence that the line between claims about sense-experience (synthetic claims) and claims about meaning of words (analytic claims) is not hard and fast; that semantic decisions as to, let us say, whether to mean 'any' unmarried woman or 'older' unmarried woman by the English word 'spinster' are not entirely free from the impact of our experience of the world, and that observational decisions as to whether the yonder stone is grey or black are not entirely free of semantic conventions.

If this is correct, then even verbal mistakes could be factual mistakes. If I misname my current feeling of anxiety as the feeling of exhaustion, unless it is an obvious slip of the tongue, I cannot whitewash my introspective error as simply my misusing the word 'exhaustion'. If my use of the word does not match the social norm which governs the use of that word, then, just because no one else can confidently tell whether the mistake happens at the name-giving level or at the experience-recognizing level, I cannot insist on drawing such a clear distinction between verbal and recognitional error; the incorrect application of a linguistic category amounts to incorrect classification, hence incorrect cognition of my own mood. To call anxiety 'exhaustion' is a mistake, and in many cases, it is pointless to ask whether it is a verbal or a factual mistake. The only reason to insist on such a distinction would be to beg the question on the issue of infallibility or fallibility of introspective reports.

Here is my final externalistic argument to prove that even when I am introspectively certain that I am thinking about gold, I could be mistaken, because I may be thinking of something else. My thoughts may be generally and specially accessible to me. But I may make and correct mistakes about what thought I am currently having, because the identity of the thought depends often upon its external object and my mistake about it would infect the veracity of my self-ascription of that thought.

Suppose John has grown up for most of his life on planet earth where gold is the shiny yellow metal named by the chemical formula Au; now he is transported unbeknownst to himself to twin earth where there is an identical-looking yellow metal whose chemical constitution is quite distinct: XYZ, but it is called 'gold' there. A twin-earth dweller shows him a piece of twin-earth gold, and tells him: 'Now close your eyes and think about this piece of gold.' When John now thinks of this piece of gold, he is thinking of XYZ, and not thinking of Au, since his first-order thought is constituted, through the memory demonstrative 'that bit of metal', by the actual sample outside, which is of XYZ. But, if he now introspects about what it is that he is thinking of, he would come out with the verdict, 'I am thinking of a piece of gold' and since in his vocabulary 'gold' means Au, and does not mean XYZ, he would be mistaken in identifying his own thought. We cannot rescue this introspective self-ascription from substantial error by calling this a mere verbal mistake.

XV

Of course, there is one kind of mistake from which, most probably, introspective self-reports are immune. While I may be mistaken as to whether I am having a pain or an itch, whether I am hungry or greedy, whether I am experiencing love or lust, I could not be mistaken about who it is that is undergoing these introspected mental states. If I am introspecting that I am in state *F*, then I must be right about the fact that it is I myself, and not someone else mistaken to be me, who is in some state or other. It is not just weird and bizarre, but scarcely intelligible to suggest that I could be introspecting into someone else's mental state and mistakenly ascribing it to myself.

But even about this topic, the alleged immunity to error due to misidentification, of first person self-ascription of mental states—on which Elizabeth Anscombe, Sydney Shoemaker and Gareth Evans have done path-breaking work—counter-examples to the infallibility claim have been proposed.

Let me mention one such funny counter-example and leave it to the reader to decide whether even the bearer of an inwardly recognized mental state could be mistakenly taken to be oneself. This was suggested in a fascinating paper called 'Introspective MisIdentification: An I for an I' by Hogan and Martin.[3]

Paul is a super-macho male. He has never acknowledged to himself that he ever felt fear. His father must have brought him up as a fearless hero. He undergoes psychotherapy and learns to recognize that when he is angry in a certain way, either or both of two things may be happening: he may be actually afraid and he may be totally identifying with his daughter. Once, after he learns this, he finds himself feeling that kind of befuddling anger. As a result of his inductively acute self-assessment, he naturally has a clear feeling that either he or his daughter is now afraid. Over-correcting himself, he introspects that it is he himself who is afraid. But he gets it wrong. This time it is his daughter who is afraid. His self-ascription of fear is not immune to error due to mis-identification of the subject. He got the fear (predicate) right, but he made a mistake about whose fear it was (subject).

Even if there is something counter-intuitive about this example, the Wittgenstein–Anscombe thesis that when we make judgements of the form 'I am feeling M', we are not making any singular reference to anything by the use of 'I', is even more counter-intuitive. The price you pay if you accept Wittgenstein's conclusion that self-ascriptions of inner states are like mere groans and grimaces is the concession that 'I am sad', 'You are sad' and 'She is sad' are 'not' substitution instances of the same sentence frame, 'X is sad'. Even when people tell me what they are feeling, upon this view, they are not saying anything 'about' themselves; so I cannot claim to understand what they are saying about themselves. When I ask my daughter, 'You must be disappointed!' and she agrees, 'Yes, I am disappointed', under this non-referential account of first person self-ascriptions of inner states, she is not agreeing with me because, first, she is not making or endorsing any assertion, she is simply expressing her disappointment as by drooping lower-lip, and second, she is not predicating anything about the same herself about whom I had predicated disappointment. First- and third-person reports of mental states then would never express the same propositions, for the first would not express any proposition at all.

Now, one kind of self-awareness may be universally automatic, and another kind of self-knowledge may be proverbially hard to get, but to buy Wittgenstein's argument is to concede that the very idea of knowing or being aware of oneself is nonsensical. That is not a price but a penalty. I am not ready to pay it. I would like to keep the ideas of self-knowledge and self-reference intelligible, even if difficult.

A Parfit-type thought experiment with tele-transportation can be run to generate a mis-identification of the subject, rather than the object or property. Suppose John is tele-transported to Mars (in the branch-line manner, without destroying the original earth-John) at the age of 50. Shortly thereafter, John thinks, 'I currently feel that I shall not like to be on Mars for more than a year', and thinks he is referring to the Martian Replica with his use of the first-person singular pronoun. But, he is mistaken. He is still habitually tied to thinking about, and through the persona of his earth-original and is reporting the discomfort of that earthling, accidentally correctly, because the earthling may be 'simultaneously' having such a future-directed feeling. The predicated discomfort is veridically ascribed but to the wrong self—to the wrong John replica.

Of course, to Parfit, the distinction would not matter, hence it will be a negligible mistake. But for a strict Thomas Reid sort of defender of realism about personal identity, it is a big mistake due to misidentification of the bearer of the mental state from which introspection is thus proved to be precisely not immune (I owe the insight behind this example to Mark Siderits).

There could be all sorts of controversies about the value of such thought experiments. But no one could call the mistake of thinking that I (the replica) am feeling like F, when actually I (the original) am feeling like F, a merely linguistic mistake. If they do, then linguistic mistakes are substantial mistakes.

XVI

Our mental states, especially our affects or emotional states—which might permeate all our cognitive states (if Samkhya psychology is to be trusted)—are too complex for us to figure out in detail simply by a spontaneous or deliberate reflexive look within. A peremptory introspection runs all the risks of carelessness. A painstakingly deliberate look tends to let in all sorts of biases and distortions. Just as the largely ignored field of external perception renders possible the attention-illuminated salient part to have the borders that it does, a currently neglected background cluster of feelings may make it possible for us to focus sharply on one salient feeling. Someone may be unnoticeably feeling deep love and an occasional sulk towards a friend, along with boredom. The unnoticed field of feelings is making it possible that she is finding a friend boring on a particular summer afternoon. But she may actually have to deny, consciously, the love and the sulk so that one could emphatically feel that one is 'simply' bored by this friend, currently. That one is bored is not inaccurate. But the error of omission pollutes its truth claim; one tells oneself erroneously, and somewhat perversely, 'No, I am just bored,

I am not sulking at all and I don't love him anymore, I feel nothing but boredom.' The introspective focusing or highlighting blocks out the introspective peripheral vision.

Feelings—even our own feelings—are like coffee mugs and buildings. They have a front which we see because they have a back which we don't. The occlusion of the back by the front makes them objective well-rounded complex feelings, not just facades of feelings. But, to that extent, it is best not to claim that what we apperceive of them is all that is there to them. What you see is 'not' all of what you might have got. Emotional self-knowledge is rare because the combination of partial ignorance and epistemic conceit sometimes yields the error of denying the hidden back-sides of our own feelings.

And I would preserve the value and rarity of self-knowledge by keeping open the possibility of all kinds of substantial errors that we subjects are subject to about our current mental states. Our mental states, whether they are identical with or supervenient on, or functionally thrown up by our brain-states, with all their subjective qualia, are things we can remain routinely partly or occasionally wholly ignorant about. Hence they are possible objects of ignorance and error. And, perhaps, nothing that is not an object of ignorance could be an object of knowledge. It should not be just a joke about a behaviourist but common practice of epistemic humility, during times of great emotional confusion, to go up to a friend or a mentor and ask: 'Tell me, how am I feeling today?'

With all due humility of a realist about mental states and a fallibilist about first-person ascriptions of such states, though, I would still like to confess that I really do miss Daya Krishna. I don't think it is a mere appearance of missing. Even sometimes when I do not seem or appear to miss him, I think I do.

Notes and References

1. A. J. Ayer, *The Problem of Knowledge* (Penguin Books, 1986 [1956]).
2. Donald Davidson, *Subjective, Intersubjective, Objective* (Oxford: Clarendon Press, 2001).
3. Hogan and Martin, 'Introspective Misidentification: An I for an I', in *Self-Reference and Self-Awareness*, eds Andrew Brook and Richard DeVidi (Rosenberg, Amsterdam/Philadelphia: John Benjamins Publishing, 2001).

14

Dialogical Investigations on Daya Krishna and Ramchandra Gandhi

Probal Dasgupta

Among the initiatives that made a difference to philosophizing in the 1980s, history will especially remember the dialogical enterprise led by Daya Krishna, K. J. Shah, M. P. Rege and Ramchandra Gandhi and institutionally co-sponsored by the Indian Council for Philosophical Research with several host institutions all over India. On the sidelines of this initiative, Prabodh Parikh and Michael McGhee started a small-scale intercultural dialogue, called the Convivium, that brought some Indians and some Britons together, at venues alternating between India and Britain, once every two or three years, not just to discuss philosophical issues that moved us, but to spend an entire week living in the same abode and to exchange views, experiences and contexts in which the philosophizing happens. Daya Krishna and Ramchandra Gandhi both took part in the first Convivium at Mahabaleshwar in 1987.

Revisiting, from the perspective of our times, one paper presented at that Convivium may represent a worthwhile exercise to the extent that dialogue is also concerned with its linguistic crucibles. In this paper, an attempt is made to grapple with issues of privacy of the milieu as a conversational domain—issues that arise when one takes seriously not just Wittgenstein's private language argument, but the ordinary language sense of the term 'private language'. As we revisit the paper today, our reading reshapes its text—which therefore does not appear here in its original form, but is subjected to a palimpsesting process.

Does this revisiting exercise address issues at the interface between Indian and Western philosophy? If India is an intercontextual space of dialogue of which conceptual apparatuses have continually thrown the dialogical categories into crisis and have again and again restored confidence in them,[1] then this exercise is part of India's philosophical encounter with the worlds in dialogue with it. That the Indian intercontextual exercise constitutively respects specificities of the participating subcommunities is the locus where svarāj can root itself in the terms of reference that the saṃvāda process has made available. Intercontextual dialogue is a form of dialogue that explicitly brings to bear on one context the coordinates of other contexts; the Indian version of this exercise includes substantive matters in the list of coordinates and has never gone in for a proceduralism that would rule them out as a matter of principle. For further elaborations of the notion of intercontextuality, see my monographs *The Otherness of English*[2] and *Inhabiting Human Languages*.[3]

The core of the private language argument has to do with the impossibility of imagining a truly private language. For an individual to use a language absolutely alone, and for this use to be constitutively solitary and thus to attract philosophical attention, it is necessary for such a language to be conceivable. The 'private language argument' is built around the hypothesis, first presented by Wittgenstein,[4] that such a language is not conceivable, for it is a core fact about language that one speaker of a language can teach it to other speakers. To be sure, a particular speaker, on account of some absence of pedagogic skill or willingness, may choose not to teach it to others. But this is a contingent eventuality. What is inconceivable is a language designed for solitary use that excludes pedagogic transmission and thus the establishment of a community of users.

The paper we are revisiting today carried, in 1987, the title, 'Outgrowing the Private Language Argument', to express some anxiety about having become too comfortable with the terms of such a discussion. For the point made in the preceding paragraph assumes that there are just individuals and communities. Those terms, left in an unproblematic state, make it difficult to attain a constitutive notion of privacy that dialogue seems to carry with it. But the very fact that the phrase 'a private language' does not sound oxymoronic to ordinary readers—the fact that the phrase appears to refer to a language designed for restricted use among a closed circle of initiates—invites us, at one level, to expand the scope of inquiry beyond the questions that drove the private language argument at the moment of Wittgenstein. The point, then, is to expand it so that the availability of the term 'private language' for this other notion comes into view and counts as a candidate for philosophical inspection.

We must begin by taking precautions against uniqueness claims that rapidly slide into hegemonic ambitions. A development that involves outgrowing the private language argument (call it PLA) can only amount to one valid spoke of a valid wheel. Another legitimate spoke, not pursued here, has to do with the circumscribed but important truth of PLA. Other worthwhile lines of thought do not pass through PLA at all. One has to make gestalt switches in moving back and forth between the spokes of such a wheel. It is impossible to hold on to all the right orientations at the same time. Each philosophical orientation, when focused upon, limits one's access to the others. The space of intercontextuality, in which dialogue lives and moves, must work with this limited mode of access in order for specificity to receive its due. We reattain balance by switching from one spoke to another, thus alternating between states of limited access.

In other words, we must choose a particular rhetoric and cognitive style for the sake of expository coherence. But such a choice must be tentative. It has to be recognized that many valid alternatives are necessarily being left out of focus. Such intercontextual recognition, by its very nature, can only be a diffuse awareness. It must be an instance, not of 'attention', but of 'retention', of bearing in mind and of 'co-consciously' remembering the need for parallel and different attention to other concerns elsewhere.

This invocation of retention is not just a matter of methodological caution. It represents an attempt to broach the main theme. PLA involves a certain acceptance of forgetfulness. As we outgrow PLA, we grow into a new relationship with memory (an important theme to which we return at a later juncture in the argument).

PLA forcefully affirms the social nature of language. The affirmation is one that is lastingly important, not something to outgrow. It is the forcefulness that, after its initial effect wears off, gets in the way of a proper understanding of the role of caring in the socialness of language. Force plays up the civil and political abstractness of society at the cost of its personal and nurturing concreteness. To get to the heart of the 'socialness of language' affirmation, one has to tame its force. How is this to be done?

The terminus we wish to reach may tentatively be called the informal context. To speak in a non-reactive and therefore 'relaxed' mode, the informal context serves as a perceptual and semiotic base of rest and play with respect to which work and other serious formalities are aligned. To speak with reactive 'tenseness', the informal sanctuary harbours the energies of passive resistance against public and formal systems like the state; the informal always vaguely resists codification, though this vague potential only sometimes takes the precise form of struggle against power. The relaxed and tense modes converge on a bridge concept—the informal as a site of human recovery from pressure.

This bridge invites us to visualize our current situation in terms of being under pressure. We stand mobilized in an examined life that includes a campaign to conscript others. We stand witness in a perennial cross-examination where witnesses sometimes take on the additional roles of accused, prosecutioner, counsel for the defence, judge and so on. We stand firm at a position we are defending, ready to attack other positions, in a general argumentative war of all against all. The way towards a human recovery from this 'philosopherial' rather than philosophical condition can only be one that examines our tense methods of examining. If we are to approach the mellow wisdom of relaxation of which the Greek word philo-sophia speaks, we need to notice that we regard argumentation as war and careful rigour as mobilization.

This terminology of course alludes to Lakoff and Johnson[5] who study the metaphor of 'argument as war' in the context of a portrayal of how a thinking person's life is shaped by, and in turn reinforces, the assumptions that the thinker's culture embodies as metaphors. It is useful to cross-contextualize this line of thinking with the tendency towards total mobilization that Max Weber has characterized in terms of the rise of rationality. Even if we have always taken it for granted that mobilization replaces many intricacies of peace with the levelling clarity of wartime, it comes as a surprise when we find this principle at work even in such a specialized event as the rise of the Fregean logical analysis of predication and quantification.

The point is not about Frege in particular, but concerns the type of analysis that has prevailed since his time. An operator or a predicate in this analysis serves as a function that applies to one or more arguments. Even in this rather recondite sense of the word 'argument', the argumentative relation is one of mobilization. Such a context sets aside 'peacetime' subtleties such as subject–object distinctions. On such a view, the status of a subject and the status of an object can no longer be usefully distinguished. What matters now is the common work, symbolized by the function to which all participants are equally subject.

In such an analysis of conceptual structure, the predicate heads the predication and the operator heads the full proposition—two examples of the function serving as the head.[6] To the extent that predicates and operators naively correspond to words of the sort that invite analysis in terms of a Platonic theory of ideas, the conceptual core of this characterization of propositions spawns a certain Platonism, regardless of how one deals with the standard questions of abstract objects and with the Frege-Husserl rejection of psychologism.

This typical Platonism emerges even in Quine's early effort[7] to beard Plato. When Quine seeks to restrict Being to being a value of a variable, he puts quantification at the heart of the philosophical reconstruction of language, avoiding and undermining what nouns and adjectives have in common with names, reinforcing the privilege of verbs and operators in the general Fregean system. This move allows him to countenance a verb 'to pegasize' in his familiar discussion of the name 'Pegasus'. Quine's solution to the problem of Plato's beard—the problem of the alleged separate existence of real objects and virtual concepts—is to get all serious semantic work done in the Platonic realm of virtual concepts, leaving an empty shell of existence for the real objects.

Let us agree to characterize the period dominated by such thinking as 'modernism'. The general transition from the forcefulness of the affirmations of modernism to the caringness of human recovery in postmodernism is already under way in several spheres of life. In keeping with the playfulness that postmodernism inherits from the modernist age, we may choose to see a kingdom of wriggling, swishing tails coming into the limelight, instead of the tyrannical talking heads. Pursuing this image further, one might add that it was not for nothing that Plato's disciple Aristotle, who brought about a major conceptual shift, was a biologist and thus empirically interested in tails and their bearers. In this one respect, we of the Convivium, who wish to go beyond the achievements of colloquium-bound talking heads, will want to follow him, constructing our version of his journey towards concreteness. And if we remain Platonists in the process, the Aristotelean turn will take us away from our proto-Platonist beginnings towards a richer Platonism.

Let us take the example of a sentence to make the discussion clearer: 'Arif hit the nail with the hammer.' The 'modernist' approach puts the work of hitting at the head of the predication here. Arif, the nail, and the hammer are, in our terms, 'mobilized' by this hitting.

The postmodern affirmation of caring views the scene somewhat differently. On this view persons and objects in their various ways take part in work, nurturing various continuities, and also nurturing persons and objects; actions are a special case of existence, not the other way round. Within existence, polarizing processes differentiate existential creatures from essential objects, without disintegrating the web of caring, which includes work as a special case. Those who exist reach out and continually bring about the unifications that Platonic ideas can then hold up for philosophical inspection.

Thus, while the Fregean head of a predication may express its predicative unity, it does so at the pleasure of the several tails, organic or inorganic, whose Aristotelean multiplicity of life forms nurtures individuals, institutions and other unities and continuities—including the Platonic ones; and it is a version of these that has nurtured the hopes of the modernist ethos.

It is the Aristotelean life forms, bearing concrete names, that in the course of their existence, subtend the Platonic ideas, expressed by abstract, context-free terms. Thanks to this relation, the move we are making can build upon a modernist foundation instead of opaquely proposing to supersede its canons. The key to the way the concrete subtends the abstract can only be a hermeneutic one, since the apprehension of universals involves an essential element of interpretation. Some insights regarding this hermeneutic key were provided by R. Sundararajan in a conversation that associated Platonic ideas with the Aristotelean notion of catharsis. Sundararajan suggested to me that catharsis was what enables the interpreting subject to apprehend Platonic ideas concretely (beyond the possibility of inferring or hypothesizing their existence in the context of theorizing), as a matter of real experience. If we accept this suggestion, it becomes possible to avoid a war of succession, and to begin to pay attention to the postmodern possibilities latent in modernism, outgrowing the latter peacefully and with a minimum of pointless conflict.

Modernism was obviously on the right track in identifying words as the important site of existential unity that brings all participants together. The fact that people in their work reproduce established products according to specific patterns bears a non-trivial mimetic relation to the way living beings reproduce themselves, each according to its kind. It is this mimetic relation that makes technique a significant issue in philosophy and provides the basis for the Platonic idea. So far, so good, and it is necessary to come at least this far. But we can do even better by trying to do justice to the further fact that, in working ideas into being, people recreate themselves and others as people. It is here that technique becomes a special case of nurture. Modernism in its excitement has occasionally lapsed into inverting this relationship. Restoring balance on that front is one of the tasks in any human recovery from pressure.

To restore balance, we must keep both sides of the question in view. While work may well be a special case of nurture, and of nurture carried out by persons in their self-regenerating existence, it remains necessary to hold, with most thinkers, that the person is not, even in principle, the organic unit of the self-regenerating existence. We shall now articulate the thesis that the person lives and grows in a human, micro-social milieu that constitutes an essential condition for the possibility of the person.

It is the milieu that is the domain, not only of nurture and its special cases such as work, but in general of 'the private', a category that, like its polar opposite, 'the public', lends itself to a wide range of application, and is of some philosophical importance. Thus, we cannot afford to substitute a personalism for the modernist exaltation of technique (the attempt to carry out such a substitution was the basic error of the otherwise brilliant 1960s). For a doctrine that turns the person into an absolute would lose the hard-won insight into the contingent and context-dependent nature of persons. What we need is a contextualism, and the milieu is probably the right kind of articulation of the notion of context. It is the milieu which, in nurture, continuously recreates itself, through persons as centres of agency and consciousness.

To find your milieu is to live appropriately. Those who find, relax; those who do not, get caught up in fighting. (This is not to say that all struggles are pointless.) To this extent, your milieu is a relational term and an object of discovery, not a domain that pre-exists and sustains you. Finding your milieu means knowing how to successfully invite other minds into your cycle of everyday creativity. (For a fuller take on this theme, see my review[8] of Ramchandra Gandhi's *I am Thou*.) However, you can only recover your milieu if its existence is objectively available in advance of your entry—in this respect, the milieu is a 'concrete' objectivity. It invites comparison with Fregean 'abstract objects', the Popperian 'third world', and related notions. The pre-existent milieu takes care of you and sustains your development to the point where you, in your own pursuit of maturity, discover and thus co-constitute it as your milieu, virtually closing the circle that is the form of the milieu's existence-for-participants.

To characterize the milieu as a virtually closed circle is to claim that each subject's constituting of the milieu is essentially partial. Each such constituting is a fragmentary and open series of turns in a negotiative conversation with an unenumerated set of legitimate companions.

Let us now return to the pressure that the milieu is supposed to rescue us from. If finding your milieu enables you to relax, if this comfort is the epistemic base you operate from, then this comfort and the 'situational' descriptions that it supports in the realm of 'common sense' are enclave phenomena; hence the deliberately partial explication of situations in Barwise and Perry's work.[9] The constituting of a milieu by its variously situated participants is then partial, plural and in some cases agonistically negotiated.

With these preliminaries in place, it becomes possible to turn to PLA, the private language argument. Seeing the milieu as the locus of the private makes it possible, in technical philosophy, to make sense of the ordinary employment of the term 'private language' to designate a way of talking used by a milieu for private, in-group purposes in which outsiders have no share. A readiness to countenance this ordinary usage appears to clash head-on with PLA as originally expounded by Wittgenstein and as construed in the literature.[10] It is this apparent clash that sets the terms of our initial problem.

The initial task is to reconcile the form in which Wittgenstein couches his insight into the socialness of language with the milieu notion of contextuality and potential privacy in which we see a way to recognize the caring or nurturing aspect of linguistic socialness. The problem arises because Wittgenstein's operative unit of privacy is clearly the individual.

One way to handle this initial problem is to expand our conception of individuation together with that of privacy, and to distinguish persons, who retain their usual dimensions, from individuals, a term now construed in a Pickwickian fashion along the lines of anthropological work that views each caste in a hierarchical society as an individual. There has never been any mystery about corporate individuals in legal theory; the move outlined here simply extends that concept into other spheres of relevance.

The impression of illicit gerrymandering can be dispelled by explicitly declaring the private–public opposition to be a variable relation, not pinned down to any fixed unit of privacy like the person. Subnational ethnic groups are privacies relative to the public nation; national affairs are private in relation to regional or global public institutions; and so forth. This much is almost a matter of giving new names to elementary concepts of naive set theory. Now, set theory is abstract; declaring the private–public contrast to be a variable contrast is thus an abstract move; and if we make this move in an unqualified manner, we will commit the fallacy of misplaced abstractness. Instead of trying to patch up and avoid the pitfall, let us try to formulate the problem thrown up by our response to the initial problem.

What we now face may be called the private domain problem—that of identifying the new 'unit of privacy' after our abandonment of Wittgenstein's decision to regard the person as that unit. Our initial decision was to leave this choice free in principle, relativizing the meaning of 'private' and 'public' to the choice of private domain. The problem now, the private domain problem, is that of specifying the constraints which make the choice of private domain less than totally free in practice.

If the choice is left entirely free, our ordinary language starting point leads to such counterintuitive conclusions as that the specific idiolect of one person in one spatio-temporal context is as much a private language as, say, the French language as a whole, for it all depends on how you set the context. Anything can be made to come out as private or as public, mechanically, by shifting the parameters. This is why the private domain problem needs separate attention.

We can respond to it by revising our proposed solution to the initial problem (of reconciling the socialness of language insight with the recognition of society as a place of nurture). We had expanded the concepts of private and individual at the same time, thus relativizing the public–private pair and society–individual pair in the same manner, and leaving the relativization unqualified. Let us now withdraw our proposal to expand the scope of 'individual', and qualify the relativization of public–private to the extent of fixing the milieu as the prototypical private domain, to which all other applications of the term (including Wittgenstein's person-domain use of it) are more or less tenuously related, in the manner described in most accounts of 'natural categories' (a concept that goes back to Wittgenstein's work on 'family resemblance' and is now standard fare in cognitive science).

This revised solution to the initial problem meets the more obvious objections and at the same time offers a solution to the private domain problem as well. Since private domains are now held to be a natural category, all the freedom of metaphor remains available, but not in the mechanical form of abstract formal licence. The private–public relation, on the current proposal, is a variable relation not by fiat, but as a consequence of the natural assumption that private domains are a natural category prototypically exemplified by the milieu.

With all the pegs in the right technical holes, let us now inspect what we have done. We have apparently built a space where the sustainable kernel of Wittgenstein's PLA, or what the literature has made of it, can coexist with the concreteness of the milieu idea. One grants that language is intrinsically social in the sense that it cannot belong to a constitutively unsharing unit of consciousness; but one qualifies this retention of the kernel of PLA by saying that this is a Person-bound Language Argument, and that the real Private Languages that ordinary usage is prepared to call by that name can exist, and do, within milieux as private domains. This qualification, we will now see, displaces the original PLA in a way that tames its 'force', to equivocate on what the 'force' of an argument is—its import, or the violence built into its assumptions, or the way it works for a warlike course of argumentation.

Wittgenstein undermined the self-sufficient sovereignty of the rational individual subject in many respects, and thus like other modernists made it easier to readjust our notion of the basic human domain. However, he did not himself carry out the readjustment. He took for granted the availability of the person as a centre of rational self-management and consciousness, and said of this entity that it could not serve as the locus of language. This thesis, at the heart of PLA, crucially appeals to the Enlightenment notion of the rational individual, and loses its relevance (though not its correctness) once we abandon this thematic centre of Enlightenment philosophy. With the later Wittgenstein's focus on life, a general twentieth-century emphasis that goes back through the obvious Romantic legacy to perennial roots, the person becomes a unit of life, a life form, without the cognitive or aesthetic or moral authority that the schematic atomism of the Enlightenment had ascribed to the person when it sought to uphold the rights of the person against a traditional authoritarian social structure.

Once that old battle recedes from the view, the living environment or microcommunity or milieu, as the domain of life that enables the person to be a self-conscious site of personal continuity, can be appropriately recognized as the location (not the source, for there is no source) of 'sovereignty'—to use a cover term for the web of rights, responsibilities, tastes, cognitions, authorities and other individual ascriptions that had gone into the make-up of the Enlightenment's concept of the rational person.

The person, of course, remains, and does not stop being supremely important. Persons are ends in themselves in Kant's sense. The person is also rational in the sense of having privileged access to microsocially available reason, moral and political in the sense of partaking of the fruit of ethics and participating in the building of the legislative space and so on. But the person can no longer be seen as the source or the storehouse of these intangibles. As concrete objectivities, they are objective and thus not bound to personal subjectivity, and they are concrete and thus directly available and intelligible to (because consubstantial with) the subjectivity—twin requirements that are met in this milieu, the storehouse of concrete objectivities.

After one completes the transition to this new view of the person, a view to which Wittgenstein's own work has contributed directly, one no longer has a person-like unit of privacy left of which one can usefully deny the property of being able to have a private language. The milieu cannot be a candidate, for it is formed and reformed by negotiative multilateral constitution and thus counts only as a domain, not as a potential agent. And furthermore it is clear that a milieu can indeed support a distinctive language of its own. (Note that the question of whether a milieu is constitutively always able to teach its language to others is not necessarily intelligible if one constructs the milieu as a site devoid of agency.)

Arguably the private language argument itself helped bring about and sustain a climate of opinion in which it became possible to give up the Enlightenment notion of the sovereign person about which alone substantive philosophical questions are to be asked. But, now that it becomes acceptable to abandon this notion, we no longer have any use for the PLA, for we no longer have the central notion of sovereign person to whom the argument would have applied.

Let us now turn to the important difference between dispensing with PLA—this dispensing is a formal matter that involves deriving the valid core of PLA from other considerations—and outgrowing it, a process of substantive conceptual growth. Who can outgrow PLA? An individual, who is not only situated in a milieu but takes this fact seriously, can begin to 'own' the fact that this is so. Growing into this ownership makes it possible to outgrow PLA. To grow into ownership is to set up a specific relationship with memory. This relationship needs some exploring.

I am who I remember having been. As I remember my inhabiting relationship with my milieux, I recall the episodes and the sagas through which I have sustained the inhabitant role in these contexts. These narratives are constitutively oral, and are languaged as orality.

But I am also what I know. Correspondingly, I have a mnemonic investment in intellectual systems. These systems refer to repositories of such knowledge that work on a cross-milieu basis and place crucial materials either in physically permanent written documents or in a memory transmission system of the classical Indian type that esoterically anchors the valid documentation in an instituted, disciplinarily mobilized oral apparatus tantamount to a written archiving system. To cut this long story short, my intellectual investments are constitutively written, and are languaged in that mode.

The relationship with memory is shaped both by a person's private base, in his/her concrete milieux, and by his/her public sky, his/her abstract community of roughly nation-like size. Not that the nation-state, as we know it, is an eternal human necessity. But the institution, as a category, is. Institutions formally require a receptacle of national or broadly nation-like size.

The Enlightenment was built around what in these terms needs to be redescribed as the insight that the human person, at a constitutive level, visualizes a public receptacle of institutions as an abstract objectivity. The post-Enlightenment qualification that we now need to put in place is that the form of the person's visualization is rooted in the unconscious and crucially contextualized by the person's milieux.

Beyond friendliness, the form of perfection towards which persons may strive in their milieux, lies the distinct but related telos of peace, for which the appropriate plane of praxis is the larger crucible of which we are speaking in these paragraphs. The point is not simply about not waging war, nor about methods of conflict resolution that avoid the louder forms of skirmishing. The conceptually substantive enterprise of peace has to do with persons taking each other's visualizations on board instead of trying to eliminate them from the picture of what can be considered as really or potentially valid.

Such an enterprise requires a strong and mutually supportive mellowness, which cannot afford to be rooted in considerations of milieux alone. What is called for, in a project of constructing such a mutually supportive mellowness that must extend from the milieux to the institutional macro-crucibles, is a fundamentally renegotiated contract between the spoken and the written, involving both the interpersonal concrete objectivity and the intertextual abstract objectivity.

In philosophy, working towards such an arrangement must in turn involve a new take on the orality of the regional languages of India and the recoding systems that we know as Sanskrit and English. Casual versions of this conceptualization problem have been touched upon in the philosophizing of a Nietzsche or of a Whitehead, in allusions to the thought that the universe might speak Hebrew or Greek or German. But those stylistic asides did not belong to the central philosophizing activity that such authors were putting in place. Philosophical writing today has to face a far more radical set of queries about the space between language modes if we are to seriously move beyond the grooves so many of us are fatally comfortable with.

The notion of a philosophizing that might serve as a handmaiden to science wedded philosophy to a quintessentially universalizable Enlightenment. But the considerations that we are now attending to make it evident that the pursuit of conceptual clarity in personal thinking and a coherent quest for serious personal freedom built on such clarity are not intelligible projects at the level at which our favourite authors have pitched them. The formulations of the Enlightenment were abstract and in an important sense prephilosophical. The exercise of freedom cannot be separated from the work of the person, embroiled in his or her milieux, growing into a formulable personal freedom based on clarity and producing this clarity through explicit reflection at multiple linguistic levels—the oral level of the milieux and the written level of the institutional macro-crucible.

Wedded to the level-multiplicity of knowledge/acquaintance and therefore of dialogue, the exercise of freedom becomes now a far more difficult challenge than the abstract formulations of the Enlightenment had made it appear. The first step that a philosopher in our context must take is to face this difficulty. The second step is to ask what it takes to build a conversational fabric that makes its participants strong enough and at the same time mellow enough to face the hardness of the serious quest for freedom without reacting violently.

The only point we can hope to elaborate in this context is that building the terms of a conversation around the notional sovereignty of the fully self-conscious person as a telos and a site of inquiry is not going to work. We have taken the position that once the Enlightenment visualization of the person is abandoned, the milieu becomes the location of 'sovereignty', but not its source. To return to and elaborate that claim, we now note that the Enlightenment's notion of the sovereign person imaged the person as seriously loyal only to a public matrix that it codes or frames as the source or checking ground of all values.

To the extent that it is the person who longs for (and thus abstractly produces) this code or frame of absoluteness-in-the-limit, the Enlightenment and the classical heritage leading to it had helpfully projected the person as the site at which the serious negotiation about the source of values occurs. The main choices over which this negotiation occurred had to do with divinity, royalty and a theoretically constructible popular basis for the republic. The Enlightenment visualized this whole arena in terms that were simultaneously sociopolitical—having to do with freedom and the organization of desires and coercions—and epistemic—having to do with demonstrable intellectual and moral foundations for the sociopolitical content of such a vision. Our task is to reshape this problematic in the light of our current understanding of the complexity of the dialogical topology of informed, nurture-focused, and therefore plurally rigorous speech and writing.

This complexity has to do—in the context of personal growth in a milieu connected to other milieux in the republic-sized crucible of institutional abstract objectivities—with what we imagine the fully grown person as able to remember, and to connect with, in the course of repeatedly revisiting all acquaintances and knowledges that the person holds dear for distinct reasons. Once we take on board the full impact of cognitive issues on our moral inquiry, it becomes clear that the task of philosophical grappling with the teachings of ancient and contemporary India has not yet been formulated as fully as we might wish.

Hence the need for further dialogue about how we are, conceptually, to understand the interconnected sites where dialogue may occur.

Notes and References

1. By this I mean that skeptics have questioned the foundations not just of the system, but of the terms of reference of dialogue in general, and that carefully articulated responses to these critics have sought to restore not just the architecture of an abstract formal philosophical system, but of the process of dialogue itself, seen as the core philosophical project.
2. *The Otherness of English: India's Auntie Tongue Syndrome* (New Delhi: SAGE Publications, 1993).
3. *Inhabiting Human Languages: The Substantivist Visualization* (New Delhi: Samskriti, in collaboration with the Indian Council of Philosophical Research, 2011).
4. Ludwig Wittgenstein, *Philosophical Investigations*, trans. G. E. M. Anscombe (Oxford: Basil Blackwell, 1967).
5. George Lakoff and Mark Johnson, *Metaphors We Live By* (Chicago: University of Chicago Press, 1980).

6. In a predication of the form ‘horses run’, it is ‘run’ that counts as the predicate, which takes one argument, ‘horses’. The format that has been standard since Frege enjoins us to notate this predication as some variant of $r(d)$, where r stands in for ‘run’ and d for ‘David’, and where it is clear that r is the head that assigns an argument function to d. In an operator–headed proposition such as ‘all horses run’, the notation requires us to write $((\forall x)(h(x) \rightarrow r(x))$, which translates into natural language as ‘for every entity x, if x is a horse then x runs’.
7. W. V. O. Quine, *From a Logical Point of View* (Cambridge: MIT Press, 1953).
8. Probal Dasgupta, ‘The Intimate Friend’, *Journal of Indian Philosophy* 15: 187–205, 1987, a review of Ramchandra Gandhi’s *I am Thou: Meditations on the Truth of India* (Pune: IPQ Publications, 1984).
9. J. Barwise and J. Perry, *Situations and Attitudes* (Cambridge: MIT Press, 1983).
10. Hector-Neri Castaneda, ‘The Private Language Argument’, in *Knowledge and Experience*, ed. C. D. Rollins (Pittsburgh: University of Pittsburgh Press, 1963), pp. 88–105, ‘Private Language Problem’ in *The Encyclopaedia of Philosophy* 6 (1967): 454–58, ‘The Private Language Argument: Reply to Carl Ginet’, in *Agent, Language, and the Structure of the World: Essays Presented to Hector–Neri Castaneda, with His Replies*, ed. James E. Tomberlin (Indianapolis: Hackett, 1983), pp. 459–461; Carl Ginet, ‘Castaneda on Private Language’, in *Agent, Language, and the Structure of the World*, pp. 271–286; Saul Kripke, *Wittgenstein on Rules and Private Language* (Oxford: Basil Blackwell, 1982); Norman Malcolm, ‘Wittgenstein’s *Philosophical Investigations*’, *Philosophical Review* 63 (1954): 530–559.

PART V

Re-thinking Issues in the Arts/Ethics/Science/Mathematics

15

The Applicability of Indian Aesthetic Theory of Rasa to Visual Arts: A Rejoinder to Daya Krishna's Article, '*Rasa*—The Bane of Indian Aesthetics'

Neelima Vashishtha

Daya Krishna's paper titled, '*Rasa*—The Bane of Indian Aesthetics', is an example of his provocative and iconoclastic approach for which his colleagues and students will always be grateful, as his probing questions were always very inspiring and urged to find answers to important issues and write about them. His contribution to rearticulating the intellectual traditions of India and in organizing collective group-thinking at Jaipur were most interesting and inspiring experiences which would be always remembered and cherished. His stay at Shimla in 2005 was one of such events. He had then asked me to review his article on Indian aesthetics. I think it would be an appropriate tribute to him.

Daya Krishna's '*Rasa*—The Bane of Indian Aesthetics' has emphasized the inadequacies and inapplicability of *rasa* theory for the evaluation of arts, and argues that 'the theory (of Bharata) has never been criticized, critically evaluated' and 'it could not do justice to other art forms, which have nothing to do with the representation of human situations'. He further stresses that 'the whole subsequent tradition with rare exceptions accepted what he (Bharata) said on the subject'. Daya Krishna maintains that Bharatamuni has neither stated the *prayojana* of the *śāstra* which was considered an essential part of any treatise nor has even attempted to give a *vyāvartaka lakṣaṇa* of *nātya*. In his opinion, the later writers after Bharata have not tried to reformulate the 'definition of *rasa*' and improve upon the 'inadequacies and inapplicability to other arts including poetry and literature'.

These remarks would not be possible if one has gone through the *Nātyaśāstra* and its commentary by Abhinavagupta even from superficial translations and is well versed with the works of art. The whole Indian tradition has endorsed, explained and reformulated the *rasa* theory and established its applicability to other arts, especially to poetry and literature, and by implication to other visual and performing arts. The *Nātyaśāstra* is the first systematic treatise on drama and poetics in India and its objective was to present a cogent and coherent theory of arts in general and drama in particular, as drama is the perfect example which utilizes both the senses of sight and hearing. Besides, the stage performance of drama has all the characteristics of any art, whether dance, music, sculpture or painting. It has (*a*) the subject matter—the script presenting the imitation of life, (*b*) medium of expression (acting or *bhāva*), (*c*) the specific style, and (*d*) evaluation—the appreciation of audience. This was the main reason that theory of drama became a standard for all art criticism. The refinements and explanations to *rasa* theory were added to it from time to time by later writers through commentaries. The aesthetic theory of Bharata also led to the development of other theories, mainly related to poetry, but which could be used in other arts.

For instance, the schools of *Alaṅkāra*, *Riti*, *Vakrokti*, *Dhvani* and *Auchitya* were developed after the *Nātyaśāstra*. These theories were mainly concerned with poetry but could be used for other arts of music, painting, sculpture and architecture. Bhamaha indicated a distinction between ordinary language and language of art. This could be used to distinguish the medium of art from other media of communication. Kuntaka laid stress on curvature or *vakratā* in poetry which is useful for architecture as it breaks the monotony and pleases the eye. Vamana had defined two objectives for evaluation of works of art: the body and the soul. He named them as the *ātma tattva* and *alaṅkāra tattva* and their correlation was the *Riti siddhānta* which is also used in painting, architecture and music. The *Riti* is concerned with medium, which is common to all arts. The effectiveness of the medium is its communicability to the spectator. The message of art object is suggested to the spectator, which is the *dhvani* emphasized by Anandavardhana. The appropriateness of elements or the *auchitya* is the principle employed for all works of art.

As far as the commentaries of *Nāṭyaśāstra* are concerned, there were a number of commentators of *Nāṭyaśāstra*. The *ācārya*s like Sankuka, Bhatt Lollata, Bhatt Nayak and Mammata have added to the theory regarding the nature of *rasa*, the involvement of spectator, and the process of aesthetic experience. Their explanations have added and further clarified the definition and the existence of *rasa* in the spectator. Abhinavagupta has referred to all these commentaries in order to explain different views regarding the *niṣpatti* of *rasa* and emphasized that it is only through suggestion and imagination of the spectator that aesthetic pleasure is realized.

Dayaji's other observation focuses on Bharata's treatment of other arts like music and dance as subservient and not having independent status and autonomy though he agrees that the concern of Bharata was to propose a theory of *Nāṭya* as *sarvaśilpapravartakam* and not as *sarvakarmānudarśanam*. And if he would have gone on to discuss other arts in detail, it would not have served his purpose. It may be mentioned here, that long before Abhinavagupta attempted to comment on the *Nāṭyaśāstra* in the *Abhinavabhāratī*, the *Citrasūtra* of the *Viṣṇudharmottara Purāṇa* had been compiled by Markandeya which emphasized the autonomy of arts of painting and sculpture and also their interrelationship,[1] on the basis of common elements of representation of nature, emphasizing *rasa* as the ultimate objective of all arts except architecture. The application of *rasa* in architecture was not specifically emphasized here, but it was taken up by Bhoja in the eleventh century. The text of the *Samarāngaṇa Sūtradhāra* of Bhoja establishes *rasa* as the ultimate goal of all arts including architecture. The reason behind Bharata's treatment of other arts like music and dance as subservient was the status of arts in his times. In fact, the arts of painting and sculpture achieved excellence and independent status quite late. We do not get examples of round and monumental sculptures and paintings independent of architecture.

The issue of autonomy of arts should be viewed in the light of origin and development of different arts, their classification according to medium and manner of expression, subject matter and objective of their creation. The arts like music, dance, drama and literature could be taken in one group, as these were first to develop and used aural form and temporal space, words and meaning, sound, rhythm and *tāla* as their medium of expression. On the other hand, painting, sculpture and architecture developed later, utilized visual space and expressed through visual two-dimensional and three-dimensional forms. Further, the manner of expression, subject matter and objective of all arts are quite similar. So also, the evaluating parameters for all arts are similar with slight changes according to the context.

The evaluating parameters of arts basically centred on subject matter and objectives of art. The parameters for language and literature were developed earlier, while there were no separate parameters for visual arts. However, the parameters used in literary arts were also applied for evaluating painting, sculpture and architecture. Therefore, it can be concluded that on the basis of the objective and manner of objectification of the mental image, all visual and performing arts are interrelated keeping their individual identity of medium and technique.

Besides, Daya Krishna has also raised questions regarding the meaning of terms *bhāva, Rasvat alaṅkāra* and *prayojana* of *nāṭya*. Daya Krishna maintains that emotions and feelings are not the only content of art. There are many intellectual issues, ideals and values one desires to seek and express through art. In this regard I may submit that the term *bhāva* has been misunderstood by modern critics as emotion because the major part of poetry was very emotional, hence *bhāva* was taken as sentiment or feeling and the original meaning must have been overlooked. Bharata did not mention any of these. According to him, human experience is a composition of thought, emotion and feeling which are mental states or belong to memory. Bharata has used the term *bhāva* in the context of stage presentation. In the statement: '*kaverantargatam bhāvam bhāvayan bhāvamuchyate*',[2] he states that *bhāva* is the intention, experience and thought in the mind of poet. He ascribes two meanings to *bhāva*: (*a*) that which exists or happens and (*b*) that which causes the manifestation of experience (*bhāvayan*). Bharata explains that *bhāva*s are mental states common to real life and also to artistic process, as he was concerned only with stage presentation of drama (*rūpaka*). I would like to quote Dhanika, the author the *Dasarūpaka*; he has explained *bhāva* as *chittavrittiviśeṣah*, which endorses Bharata's view. Accordingly, Bharata has enumerated 49 *bhāva*s, including 8 *sthāyi bhāva*, 8 *sāttvika bhāva* and 33 *vyabhicārī bhāva* or secondary mental states.[3] These are merely mental states of our behavioural patterns. Among the list of 33 *vyabhicārī bhāva*s, there are many that have nothing to do with feeling or emotion. Some of these *vyabhicārī bhāva*s could be named to answer the observation of Daya Krishna regarding 'human seeking for ideals, values, and what aught to be'. These are *mati* (intellect, judgement), *vitarka* (argument, reasoning, guess), *avahita* (internal feeling), *vibodha* (awakening), *dhṛti* (resolution, courage), *cintā* (anxiety, sorrowful thought), *śrama* (toil, exertion), *mada* (infatuation), *nirveda* (depression, or complete indifference to worldly things) and so on, which could manifest intellectual experience, transcendence, ideals and values as *rasa*. For instance, *nirveda* has been added later to the list of *sthāyi bhāva* to manifest *śānta rasa*, perhaps after realizing the need to explain the objectification of spiritual themes. Further, Bharata had categorically emphasized that *bhāva* is the intention or experience of the poet which is manifested as *rasa* on the stage and conveyed to the spectator as *sthāyi bhāva*. That *rasa* is the process of objectification of mental state of the poet and it is the process of making individual experience public. He attributes *bhāva* as *sthāyi* for these mental existents endure in time. These can be complex mental states but not emọtions. As in poetry there are *śabda* and *artha* to convey the meaning, so also, in dramatic presentation are *bhāva* and *rasa*. They are like meaning and symbol. To emphasize this point, he says: '*na hi rasādṛte kaścidapi artha pravartate*'.[4]

Daya Krishna's other observation regarding *rasvat alaṅkāra*, that it would lead to as many *rasa*s as there are *alaṅkāra*s, had already been realized by later *Alaṅkārin*s like Mammata and others. Consequently, it was dropped by Mammata. The *rasvat alaṅkāra* was coined by Bhamaha, Dandin and Rudrata. Still, the inclusion of *rasvat* reveals the popularity of the *rasa* theory of staged drama. The word *rasa* was taken by initial *Alaṅkārin*s for such poetry which was capable of presenting picturesque image of audible poetry. Bharata had used the word *rasa* as the process of objectification or symbol conveying the image of some thought, mental state or *bhāva*. Hence, *rasavat* (*rasa* + *matup* = *rasavat*) was used for such poetry, meaning thereby the poem possessing the visual form even in the absence of stage. The word *rasavat* has been used here in two senses: (*a*) sthat which possessed *rasa*, and (*b*) that which was like *rasa*. Vaman had also elaborated it in the following manner, '*diptarasattvam kāntih*', that which glows with *rasa* (the visual objectified word-image). The later *Alaṅkārin*s omitted this *alaṅkāra* on account of its superficiality as it means appearing like *rasa*. Barlingay has also explained that as *rasa* was accepted as a basic concept of poetry and arts, it became useless.[5]

Regarding the observation of Daya Krishna about the *prayojana* of *nāṭya*, I may submit that it is presentation of drama. Hence, he calls it *nāṭya* or *rūpaka* (visual manifestation). In this regard, he mentions the purpose (*siddhi*) of the staged drama is evoking reactions of fulfilment. The *siddhi* is of two types, *mānuṣi* and *daiviki*.

The *mānuṣi* is concerned with the reactions of spectators according to their likes and dislikes. But the *daiviki siddhi* is experienced as widening of the consciousness and overflow of the feeling. It could be observed in the mental state of calm, silence, complete absorption of spectator in himself and not showing any signs of exasperation. The poet Kalidas calls it '*āparitoṣād vibudhām na sādhu manye prayogavijnānam*' in his drama the *Mālavikāgnimitram*.

Though the *Nātyaśāstra* had mainly concentrated on the application of *rasa* in *nāṭya*, some of the terms have referred to its application in other performing arts, which have been explained by the commentators in detail. Abhinavagupta has referred to this discussion in the *Abhinavabhārati*. The commentators had explained the meaning of *rasa*, its existence in the spectators, the process of aesthetic experience and the constituents of art object, viz. the whole of *rasa sūtra*—the *vibhāva*, *anubhāva*, *vyabhicārī* and the *niṣpatti* meaning thereby the process of aesthetic experience. While going through the discussion of Abhinavagupta, it also becomes clear that every commentator has added in the advancement of the theory of *rasa* to resolve the difficulties which could have been visualized in its applicability in the context of other performing arts. For instance, the nature of work of art, the spectator and the process which transforms the personalized experience of the artist into universal experience of all viewers of that work of art have been discussed by Sri Sankuka, Bhatta Lollata and Bhatta Nayak. That in the process of aesthetic experience the emotional feeling or *bhāva* is the nucleus without which aesthetic experience cannot take place is emphasized by Abhinavagupta. *Bhāva* is expressed in the work of art, it is the emotional feeling of the artist; it is the satisfaction (*paritoṣa*) which is experienced by the artist as its own but presented in the *sādhāranikrita* form, which is beyond the feeling of sadness or happiness but in the widening of our consciousness, the feeling of *ānanda*. It has also been stressed by Vishwanatha besides others.

If we see a work of art once, twice and thrice, the experience is not repeated; it is always a novel experience. Similar is the case with painting, sculpture and other arts. That experience is *rasa*. This experience of beauty, the widening of consciousness is felt in all arts and could not be confined to drama or to the definite number of *rasa*s, or to the circumstances where *ālambana*, *uddipana* and *vyabhicārī* are present, but to the mental state of the poet, the *bhāva*. It has been emphasized by Abhinavagupta in the following words, '*na bhāvavihino rasah*'. The *bhāva*s are universal and can be experienced through other arts like music, sculpture, painting as it is with drama. Moreover, every term of the *rasa* theory of Bharata was self-explanatory and was used to denote its meaningful dimensions. For example, the term *rasa* includes all nuances of its meaning. It encompasses taste on the level of senses, the *bhojyarasa*, as well as *nāṭyarasa* in drama, *chitrarasa* in painting and the *ānanda* which could be the *vyāvartaka lakṣaṇa* of *rasa* as it is devoid of particularities, the *nirviśeṣa*.

Applicability of Rasa in Visual Arts

In this context an attempt has been made to show the applicability of *rasa* theory to painting and sculpture, its importance for art criticism even in the contemporary field of visual arts and an answer to the observations in Daya's paper as a whole.

Here, a summary of the principles relating to drama and poetics is proposed so as to give a proper background to its application in visual arts of painting and sculpture; and its extent to which it applies to the contemporary classifications and categories on the basis of themes and media in visual arts—the painting and sculpture. Besides, some illustrations of works of modern and contemporary paintings in support of the exposition have been used to establish that the *bhāva* is the essential element in all artistic expressions for the aesthetic quality. The presence of an experience or *bhāva* is the vital quality for the existence of *rasa* in the works of art as well as in the spectator. It is dependent on the strength of creative impulse.

The *rasa siddhānta* of Bharata has defined *rasa* as the sap or juice of plants, fruits, any liquid or fluid, the best or finest or prime part of any thing, essence, marrow, taste, flavour and so on, as the principal quality of fluids[6]. In order to explain the aesthetic implications of *rasa* in literature and arts, the translations have emphasized its meaning as sentiment, feeling or mood, though Bharata had compared it only with *bhojya rasa*, the tasting of food prepared with various spices[7] to suggest both the components of the experience and its unified effect, where one of the components dominates over the other.[8] In art and aesthetics, *rasa* was later defined as state of heightened delight, the *ānanda*, the kind of bliss that can be experienced only by spirit. Vishwanath in *Sahitya Darpana* has defined *rasa* as akin to the ultimate reality, the twin brother to the tasting of *brahma* (*brahmasvada sahodara* and *ātma samvidviśrānti*).

To sum up, it can be said that the experience of *rasa* is emotional as could be gathered from observing the different types of *rasa*s and *sthāyibhāva*s, the durable psychological states. The *rasa*s are perceived as a result of arousal of *sthāyibhāva*s by spectators within him through a process of communication in the artistic performance, the work of art. Expressions or consequents, the *anubhāva*s are related to the themes which are called *vibhāva*s. Besides, there are 33 transitory or complementary psychological states or emotions (*vyabhicārī bhāva*s) which reinforce the maturing of *rasa* when it is aroused.[9] These are *śringāra* (erotic), *hāsya* (comic), *karuṇa* (pathetic), *raudra* (furious), *vīra* (heroic), *bhayānaka* (terrible), *vibhatsa* (odious), *adbhuta* (marvellous), and the corresponding *sthāyibhāva*s are *rati* (love), *hāsa* (mirth), *śoka* (sorrow), *krodha* (anger), *utsāha* (energy), *bhaya* (fear), *jugupsā* (disgust) and *vismaya* (astonishment).

For instance, *vibhatsa*, the odious sentiment, has the durable psychological state of *jugupsā* (disgust), which is created by unpleasant, impure, bad smelling objects, such as spitting of phlegm in milk or putting excreta in eatables; seeing, hearing and uttering inauspicious words; it is expressed by contraction of face and body, by covering the face and nose to avoid bad odours, scenes and objects, and by trampling of feet in short and long steps, loss of voice and so on and is strengthened by transitory states of dejection, agitation, restlessness among others.[10]

In theory, the *rasa sūtra* appears simply as a sequence of cause and effect, but there are conditions which affect the maturing of *rasa* (*nispatti*). The dominant tone or the principal sentiment is achieved by the spectator through a gradual building of impressions, some of which may appear contradictory or some of which may in other context be a part of the process of realizing a different *rasa*.

The *sthāyibhāva*s are permanent mental states, but remain in latent, dormant and weak form. These must be stimulated and reinforced in order to mature into *rasa*s and thus the *bhāva* associated with things or events which are congenial to heart is the source of *rasa*. The *vyabhicārī bhāva*s are transitory and are associated with several *rasa*s; provide different subtle flavours; emerge and submerge in the *sthāyibhāva*s, just like the ripples of water in the ocean. The text also describes the *anubhāva*s: the facial expressions, gestures and the settings, circumstances, costumes, time of day and so on. The drama or work of art in general must be presented in such a way that it should help in the consummation of *rasa*. Even a traditional or historical plot may be altered to assure the purity of *rasa*. The art object becomes a symbol that evokes an experience, which in Indian aesthetics is called *rasa*. This aesthetic experience is defined as transcendental in character, similar to the religious experience. Abhinavagupta has explained the process of this experience through suggestion (*dhvani*) and imagination on the part of spectator.

The whole process of aesthetic experience depends on interaction of three components, the artist, the work of art and the spectator. If the spectator is not attuned to the particular art, he would be unable to feel the sentiment. Hence, the spectator is defined as *sahṛdaya*, a fully responsive person to transform the *bhāvas* into *rasa* through the power of his imagination. This capacity is as important as the capacity of the work of art to arouse his imagination. The *Nāṭyaśāstra* defines the *sahṛdaya* as learned men relishing the *rasa* in the mind or imagination and compares them to the connoisseur of food.[11]

This ability develops with training of senses and accumulated experience gathered through seeing and hearing the works of art. Besides, the *sthāyibhāvas* are universal, hence the spectator responds to the work of art expressing the same feeling which is innate in them. It is also implied that the artist also had the same *sthāyibhāva* or durable psychological state which transforms into expression of work of art through his power of imagination to evoke the same feeling in the spectator. Moreover, the artist and the connoisseurs must have a common core of life experiences, beliefs, cultural background and emotional dispositions. Above all, the *sahṛdaya* should also possess the ability to detach his consciousness and achieve a psychical distance.[12] One of the commentators of Bharata, Bhatt Nayak in the eighth century had explained this process of aesthetic experience through universalization (*sādhāraṇikaraṇa*) of *sthāyibhāva*, *vibhāva*, *anubhāva* and *vyabhicārībhāva*. It says that under the spell of imagination, sorrow or fear loses its peculiarity and personal associations; it is freed from the sordid attributes of common physical experiences and a sublimation of the emotions takes place. The universality of *vibhāvas* and *anubhāvas* is mentioned by Bharata in the *Nāṭyaśāstra*, where it says *vibhāvānubhāvau lokāprasiddhau*.[13] The psychical distance on the part of spectator is essential for arousal of *rasa*, as the total involvement of consciousness of spectator would lead to detachment of spectator's imagination from object of art.

The artist must also possess the qualities of a *sahṛdaya*, having human experience of life around him. The artist, whether a playwright, actor, sculptor or painter should be able to recreate the effects which arouse the latent emotional states and give rise to *rasa* but cannot become a participant in the process of aesthetic experience.

Application of Rasa Theory to Visual Arts

The application of *rasa* theory to other visual and performing arts has been referred not only by ancient critics and texts but also by many art critics of the modern period. Among the art critics of modern period, Coomaraswamy, B. N. Goswamy, Doris Clark Chatham, Premlata Sharma and Kapila Vatsyayana have made attempts to apply the *rasa* theory to visual arts and performing arts of music and dance. For instance, Coomaraswamy[14] has cited examples of the application of *rasa* theory in the visual arts from literary works referring to the critical appreciation of painting mentioning the *vibhāva*s and *anubhāva*s in support of applicability of *rasa* theory. B. N. Goswamy[15] and Doris Clark Chatham have illustrated the examples of *rasa* from paintings and sculptures of ancient and medieval Indian art. Kapila Vatsyayana[16] and Premlata Sharma[17] have concentrated on the performing arts of dance and music. These scholars have cited examples from arts belonging to ancient and medieval periods in support of their view.

There are others who are vigorously opposed to this view on the superficial reasons that the arts being dynamic and evolving, new patterns should not be judged by some aesthetic theory of ancient period as proposed by Bharata. For instance, contemporary art has changed in concept and form reflecting the changes in the social environs and should not be evaluated on the basis of a theory of first century AD. Perhaps they forget that the objective of all arts, that is, music, painting, sculpture and drama remains the same, the realization of aesthetic pleasure, the *rasa*. It is the communication of the same experience felt by the artist which has been expressed in the works of art. If the work of art fails to achieve this end it would lose its value and the spectator would have no interest in it. It cannot be denied that the works of contemporary art do express some kind of sentiment or represent the imaginative life of the artist which is different from reality and natural perception of things. These works do have appeal and attract the spectator. But this sentiment is different and could not be identified with the list of *sthāyibhāva*s referred to in the *rasa siddhanta*.

In view of this situation, it is necessary to have a universal aesthetic discourse emphasizing interrelationship of arts. This aesthetic discourse would provide standards for criticism and appreciation of works of arts as well as channelize artistic activity and also educate the spectators as to what to expect from a work of art. Since the arts are dynamic, the aesthetic theory must have the potential and flexibility to assimilate changes as well as a check and balance on the artist's individuality in creative expression and social purpose of art. It is not that the need for change in aesthetic paradigms has been felt only in the modern context. It had been there in the past; hence there were additions in the list of aesthetic sentiments and also in the aesthetic theory.

The text of *Citrasūtra* of the *Viṣṇudharmottara Purāṇa* is one such example. It was compiled in ca. fifth century AD, much before the commentary of Abhinavagupta, though it was brought to the notice of academic world in the twentieth century AD. It emphasizes the interrelationship of arts and states that the same rules as applied to painting also refer to dance and sculpture and to images made of iron, stone, wood and clay. It is also clear from this text that the number of *rasa*s could be increased from eight to nine or more looking at the presence of works of art expressing the sentiment other than the prescribed list of Bharata. It has specifically stated that all works of art are not considered as capable of arousing *rasa*. For instance, decorative works that are not associated with any *bhāva* would only create a pleasing transitory feeling of *camatkara* or joy in the spectator. It classifies the paintings according to expressive content, which suggests qualities relating to representation of *rasa*. This was also referred to in the later texts like *Śilparatna*, which mentions *rasa chitra* as the representations of emotions. It seems appropriate for the application of *rasa* theory that classifications were made according to the content of works of art instead of media. Therefore, *bhāva* or *sthāyibhāva*, the psychological state and its expression in symbolic action must be the content of *rasa*, producing works of art even if its medium is stone. Here it can also be stated that it is not necessary that all works of art may possess *bhāva* as its content.

Though the representations in painting and sculpture have common characteristics of the dramatic production and also evoke *sthāyibhāva*s into *rasa*s, these are not identical with performance of *nāṭya*.

In the case of painting and sculpture, there is no actor, it is the figure represented in the panel, and it is confined to only one scene. The time factor in drama, which helps in building up of the *sthāyibhāva* to its maturity in *rasa*, is absent in painting and sculpture. It is the imagination of the *sahṛdaya* which helps in providing the missing links and context of the painting or sculpture.

The *sahṛdaya* must devote time in contemplation of the composition which is arranged in space instead of time, and let the impressions gradually accumulate in reinforcing *bhāva* which would produce a single dominant characteristic flavour or *rasa*. In order to achieve this state of *rasa* in sculptures and paintings, the *sahṛdaya* needs his imagination to communicate with artist and recreate the experience within himself.

This is only possible when the spectator has some prior knowledge related to the content or the context of dramatic representation in painting and sculpture. The knowledge of content, either from literature or historical event or mythology, may feed his imagination to arouse his latent feelings. It is through his imagination and prior knowledge of the content that the sculpture carved in the niche could be transformed in universalized *vibhāva*, the *alambana* of *rasa*, as the actor representing Rama is universalized in stage performance and evokes the *rasa*. For instance, in painting, it is necessary to know the situation or event which has caused the expression of the artist, especially in case of non-figurative or abstract subjects. In some cases the title of the work of art assists and guides the imagination of the spectator.

The context of the sculpture becomes evident from its place in the monument. In this regard it is essential to know that the sculptures in the temples are of two kinds: the icons meant for worship and the images and narratives designed according to the decorative and illustrative needs of architecture. The intention of the sculptors behind making these images is not always the same. The image, which is meant for worship and to be installed in the sanctum, follows strictly the *dhyāna* of that deity, the desire of the patron and the iconographic texts. These images would not be seen leading to delight or realization of aesthetic experience but devotion to the divinity. But the images of Buddha, Yogini and Devi are an exception, as these represent *śānta* and *bhayānaka bhāva* even when these are made for worship. The other sculptures express the aesthetic sentiment which is communicated to the *sahṛdaya*. These images have represented religious, secular, literary and other themes according to the choice of artist, needs and plan of architecture, that is, temples, palaces, reservoirs and other private and public buildings have different designs.

Another difficulty in analyzing the representation of *bhāva*, *anubhāva* and *vyabhicārī* in sculpture and painting arises when the images lose the context as is the situation of images found in broken dilapidated temples or images preserved in museums. The full impact of these works, the purpose, the theme and context is not clear to the viewers. The images on the exterior of the temples also follow some specific plan of temple architecture, the theme of the monument and its size which is lost to the spectator in case of destruction of the temples. Similarly in miniature paintings and manuscript illustrations, the context of the painting is not available in single folios, which have been conceived as a part of the series. Most of the illustrated sets lay scattered in different museums and with different collectors. Despite this, it is not difficult to analyze the miniature paintings in the light of *rasa* as the cultural and social context is known to us from literary and other historical sources.[18]

As far as the contemporary painting is concerned, it has undergone tremendous changes in concept, form and functions. In ancient period, painting developed through stages of exact imitations, representation and impression of nature. This quality had great appeal for the layman as well as for connoisseurs. Now the art form is transformed from illustrative, decorative and representative to purely impressionistic, expressionistic and non-figurative forms of abstract mental state, the unconscious mind. The artists have devised three methods to appropriate painting: (*a*) distorted appearance for the sake of stronger expression of emotions or to depict the world of unconscious, (*b*) centred on decorative aspect, (*c*) playing with the art forms of the past and (*d*) a mixture of all three. The distortion or fragmentation is used to express inner life, the unconscious mind, dreams and fantasies. It is a rebellion against proportion, form and meaning. There is a change in the contents. For instance, there is preference for folk and tribal themes and realistic presentation of middle class. The change in the treatment of human form could be observed in the earth-bound, poverty-stricken, hungry and discontented man. Another change is in the approach of artists, towards interrelationship of literature and painting. The urban artists are dissociated with literature and tradition and inclined to search for a new human form, which could appropriately reflect the tensions, pain, dislocation, alienation, fragmentation, uncertainty and deep despair felt by them. They represent the fragmented reality as it is of the mundane everyday human being. These changes in the sentiments behind the themes of contemporary art have not been referred to in the aesthetic theory of *rasa.* The contemporary spectator experiences these sentiments but is unable to identify why he likes the particular painting. It is because he shares the same sociopolitical environment and social unconscious of the race. Hence, there is need for a universal aesthetic discourse, which could identify some new sentiments according to the contents of contemporary painting and sculpture.

The fragmentation and distortion of human form is universal in modern painting. The distorted figures are set against banal and bare landscapes; the motifs, symbols and colour differ with individual artists as the colour, texture, lines and form have lost their traditional meaning. The explanation for this hazardous change could be unprecedented socioeconomic disparity, British rule, the sense of hopelessness of the poor, social injustice to the downtrodden, decay in moral values, and alienation from society. This state of society evolves a sentiment of despair which could be identified as *avasada*, which is the basic *sthāyibhāva* and matures in *nastika nairāśya*.[19]

The new sentiments have always been added in the *rasa* theory in the past, looking to the need and social change to accommodate art and literature. For instance, to explain the sentiments behind the images of Buddha and the *bhakti* literature of medieval period, *śānta rasa* and *bhakti rasa* were added. Similarly, *vātsalya* and *karuṇa rasa*s were also identified to explain the developments in sculpture and literature. Therefore, it is proper to identify some new sentiments such as despair, absurdity and some others like disorder and banality to reformulate the *rasa* theory accordingly. This would make the Indian aesthetic more viable and responsible to establish a bridge between the past and the present, and between tradition and modernity.

Notes and References

1. *Visnudharmothara Purana*, III, 2, 2–3.
2. *Nāṭyaśāstra* (here after abbreviated as *NS*), vii, 2.
3. *NS*, vii, 107–120.
4. *NS*, vii, 7.
5. S. S. Barlingay, *A Modern Introduction to Indian Aesthetic Theories* (New Delhi: D. K. Printworld, 2007), pp. 68 and 96.
6. Monier Williams, *Dictionary*.
7. *NS*, vi, 31–33.
8. *NS*, vii, 120–121.
9. *NS*, vi, 15, 17; vii, 8; vii, 4, 5; vi, 18–84.
10. *NS*, vi, 73–74.
11. *NS*, vi, 32–33.
12. Edward Bullough, 'Psychical Distance as a Factor in Art and an Aesthetic Principle', *British Journal of Psychology*, 5 (2) (June 1912): 87–118.
13. *NS*, vii, 6.
14. A. K. Coomaraswamy, *The Transformation of Nature in Art* (New Delhi: Munshiram Manoharlal, 1974), pp. 111–119; *The Dance of Siva* (Bombay: Asia Publishing House, 1984).
15. B. N. Goswamy, *Essence of Indian Art* (San Francisco: Asian Art Museum, 1986), pp. 17–30.

16. Kapila Vatsyayana, *Classical Indian Dance in Literature and the Arts* (New Delhi: Sangeet Natak Academy, 1968).
17. Premlata Sharma, *Rasa siddhānta: mūla, shākhā, pallav aur patjhaṛ* (Rasa theory: Origins, aspects, rise and fall, Hindi) (New Delhi: National Publishing House, 1988).
18. B. N. Goswamy, *Essence of Indian Art.*
19. Harsha V. Dehejia, Prem Shankar Jha and Ranjit Hoskote, D*espair and Modernity: Reflections from Indian Painting* (Delhi: Motilal Banarsidass, 2000).

16

The Harmony Principle

C. K. Raju

Daya Krishna was a prolific correspondent. He loved to carry on saṃvāda, whether in everyday conversation, or through letters, or more formal articles in the *Journal of Indian Council of Philosophical Research.*

I once wrote to Dayaji about what seemed to me a paradox in contemporary Indian philosophy. It is one thing that Indian philosophers don't engage with science, or even with its history and philosophy. It is quite another thing that they don't engage with ethics. Ethics, after all, is at the core of philosophy. Without an ethical principle, one often does not know how to respond to something fundamentally new, such as the bewildering variety of new developments in science and technology which impinge on our daily life. I was disappointed that Indian philosophers remain engaged in studying Spinoza, Kant, Hegel and the like, or they were immersed in Sanskrit texts—neither of which provides much guidance about new developments. Few Indian philosophers have been willing to address such philosophical problems of mundane life in contemporary times. When a new law is passed by parliament, such as the Cyber law, no one considers it necessary to consult any Indian philosopher to ask whether the law would be compatible with current ethics. However, it would be regarded as inexcusable if our lawyers failed to consult similar laws formulated abroad—which formulation might well have assumed altogether another ethical context. Philosophers seem to have made themselves irrelevant to our society.

So I wrote to Dayaji complaining that Indian philosophers had never put forward a normative ethical principle. How could there be any sort of real philosophy without ethics, I wondered?

In his usual way, Dayaji responded promptly. He said that one Banerjee had proposed a normative ethical principle in 1935. Now, my letter to Dayaji was in the context of my book, *The Eleven Pictures of Time*.[1] That book dwells on the latest military strategy propounded by Huntington, which aims to promote Western dominance by expanding its 'soft power'. This strategy aims to control human behaviour by inculcating in people a desired set of values.

The use of values as part of military strategy is a novel and dangerous idea, but it is a natural extension of the idea of using religious beliefs to achieve political dominance.[2] This process of inculcating values or conditioning (as in the Pavlovian conditioned reflex) is seen as a process akin to programming a computer. Just as a computer can be made to behave in any desired way by means of a program, so also humans can be conditioned to behave in a desired manner by means of values inculcated at an early enough age. Now, I have no doubt that human beings are not machines, and that it is possible for individuals to ask awkward questions, and thereby transcend their past indoctrination. However, statistically speaking, this seems to happen only occasionally: few individuals I know ever manage to get rid of what they were taught in childhood. And, so far as Huntington is concerned, in a situation of electoral democracy, a 50 per cent success rate is good enough!

My other concern was that the non-West, in general, and Indian philosophers, in particular, have had no say in the formulation of these values. In the absence of an autonomously generated ethic, there is nothing to prevent people from being swept away by the pressure of peers and propaganda, as indeed seems to be happening today.

I had earlier thought of addressing this paper to the philosophical questions about mathematics on which Dayaji had been reflecting in his last days. However, that would be unjust to the late Professor Ramchandra Gandhi (Ramuji), the other person in whose memory this seminar is being held. While Ramuji was more inclined towards praxis and pithy one-liners, he was rather more interested in ethics than in mathematics. Moreover, as already stated, there can be no svarāj—no freedom or autonomy in any real sense—until one has reflected upon the values around which one bases one's life (or the Constitution of the country). If India has seen a golden age in recent times, it was during the svarāj movement; not because that movement helped to get rid of the British, but because it inspired numerous Indians to a high point of ethical behaviour. Therefore, I will reserve for another occasion my response to Dayaji on mathematical philosophy and will focus on svarāj and saṃvāda.

Time and Ethics

Given the philosophical vacuum about ethics, most people in India get sucked into one of the two widely prevalent ethical models. Capitalism provides one model, and various religions provide the other. Capitalism is often confounded with 'materialism' and so on. It is better understood through utilitarianism. **The utilitarian principle:** *act so as to maximize the expected present value of lifetime utility*. Capitalism redefines the ordinal notion of 'utility' in cardinal terms as money. Consequently, those people who follow the capitalist ethic spend their lives maximizing the present value of lifetime income. In a word they maximize profit.

Wealth is displayed through consumption: which is *hence* the socially accepted index of virtue. The more one consumes, the more *virtuous* one feels. Any sort of environmentalist ethic which seeks to modulate consumption without challenging this fundamental capitalist value is futile, perhaps deliberately so.

The other sort of ethical model is that provided by various religions. Now, as Toynbee remarks,[3] the substance of religion is not belief, but participation in ritual performance. The one who goes to church, temple, masjid or gurdwara is readily recognized as a 'good' Christian, Hindu, Muslim or Sikh.

However, at the level of belief, ethics flows from beliefs about time. Consider, for example, the doctrine of *karma-saṃsāra-mokṣa* in the Upaniṣads.[4] *This doctrine is situated within an underlying belief in a recurrent cosmos*. The 'spiritual' interpretation of this doctrine by orientalists like William Jones is mere misplaced apologia. *Mokṣa* is deliverance from the cycle of birth–death–rebirth. The rebirth is *not* something that takes place here and now—individuals are believed to be reborn billions of years later across a cycle of the cosmos.[5] This belief may be true or false, but it is a *physical* belief, *not* a spiritual or a metaphysical one. Since it is refutable, it is easily possible to conceive of a cosmos which is *not* like that.

Therefore, one needs to understand this belief from the perspective of physics, not that of orientalists. In physics today, cosmology is done using general relativity. This provides us with three basic cosmological models known as the Friedmann models (all beginning with a big bang). Which model corresponds to the real cosmos depends upon the amount of matter in the cosmos. If there is enough matter, we get a closed Friedmann model—a cosmos which oscillates. Such a cosmos, which merely goes through phases of expansion and contraction, must be distinguished from a (quasi) *recurrent cosmos* in which, in each cycle of the cosmos, events similar (but not identical) to those in the preceding cycle repeat. For this to happen, the so-called 'arrow' of time must turn around (like a boomerang).

I cannot overemphasize that it is a *very dangerous source of confusion* to refer to this situation as 'cyclic' time. To distinguish a recurrent cosmos from (*a*) a simple oscillatory model, and also from (*b*) a situation of 'eternal recurrence', it is better to call this 'quasi-cyclic time'.

Astonishingly, a recurrent cosmos is perfectly possible on current physics. In fact, on Newtonian physics, recurrence is *inevitable* if the cosmos is closed. This is the substance of the Poincaré recurrence theorem. A suitably generalized form[6] of this theorem applies to *any* kind of deterministic evolution. (That includes general relativity with the geodesic hypothesis.)

Since the Upaniṣadic notion of *ātman* is anchored in such a physical belief about quasi-cyclic time,[7] it is equally a physical notion. Therefore, it may be confusing to translate *ātman* as 'soul', which is a prime example of something metaphysical in Western tradition. The centuries of propaganda about Indian 'spirituality' are based on the wrong association that this translation encourages. Even if *ātman* is translated as soul, it should always be understood that a different notion of soul is being referred to.

To summarize, the *Upaniṣadic ethic is anchored in a* ***physical*** *belief*. This is a belief about the nature of time: that the cosmos is (quasi) recurrent or that time is quasi-cyclic. This belief, though a physical (falsifiable) belief, is not necessarily a false belief; though refutable, it is not already refuted by present-day physics. The doctrine of *mokṣa* or deliverance is what naturally follows, from a completely pragmatic viewpoint, if the underlying physical belief about the cosmos or the nature of time is granted. There is no spirituality here.

I have argued that this relation of values to time beliefs applies to a variety of religions. For example, quasi-cyclic time and ideas very similar to *karma-saṃsāra-mokṣa* were very much a part of pre-Nicene Christianity, as stated by Origen, its most outstanding exponent. In his *De Principiis*, Origen was quite explicit that cosmic recurrence was neither exact nor eternal.[8] He also understood *karma-saṃsāra* or deeds-retribution as a means to support equity and justice.[9] All were born equal to begin with (showing God's belief in equity) and were accorded different stations in life according to their deeds (showing God's justice).

Origen's view is entirely contrary to two current stories (*a*) that Christianity believes in 'linear' time, opposed to 'cyclic' time, and (*b*) that *karma-samskāra* is a doctrine of inequity and injustice unique to Hinduism. It is necessary to point this out because, unfortunately, even numerous academics go by such myths relying on their social acumen to guess what is 'credible', and without the discipline of checking things out.

After aligning with the state, there was no way the post-Nicene church could accept non-Christians on par with Christians (any more than the state can accept non-citizens on par with citizens). Therefore, the church was now fundamentally opposed to equity, and hence it hailed Augustine's doctrine of inequity, according to which God would put non-Christians in hell for eternity after death, as described by Dante,[10] creating a permanent and eternal separation between Christians and non-Christians. This transformation from the value of equity to inequity was engineered through a shift in time beliefs from Origen's quasi-cyclic time to Augustine's apocalyptic time. Augustine's apocalyptic time is not refutable—doomsday has been round the corner for long. It is this transformation from a physical belief (quasi-cyclic time) to a metaphysical one (apocalyptic time) which made the soul metaphysical in Western thought.

In the process, Augustine used the theological trick of misrepresenting Origen: he confounded Origen's idea of quasi-cyclic time with the 'Stoic' idea of eternal recurrence.[11] On this ground, Justinian and the fifth Ecumenical Council cursed Origen, and the 'doctrine of pre-existence'.[12] Remarkably, in the 16 centuries since Augustine, the West has repeatedly (mis)understood recurrence to mean 'eternal recurrence'. The title of my book, *The Eleven Pictures of Time*, was partly intended as a comment on this blind spot in Western thought. As Mircea Eliade put it, the work of leading poets such as T. S. Eliot, and writers such as James Joyce, is 'saturated with the nostalgia for the myth of eternal repetition'.[13] Philosophers like Nietzsche,[14] and scientists like Newton[15] and Hawking[16] have also confounded any sort of cyclicity as 'eternal return'. In current discussions of the grandfather paradox of time travel,[17] one repeatedly encounters the same mistake. Confusion about recurrence seems eternally recurrent in the West.

Note that people like Newton and Nietzsche were extreme opponents of the church establishment. So, it is a terrific intellectual victory for church propaganda about time that it could derail even the most thoughtful of its opponents in this way. In my terminology, the substance of this propaganda is that quasi-cyclic time has been misrepresented as super-cyclic time by deceptively lumping both into an ill-defined category of 'cyclic' time (which is dichotomous with 'linear' time). Unlike the ill-defined and confused category of 'cyclic time', quasi-cyclic time is a *physical* belief, regardless of whether it is valid or invalid.

The linkage of time perceptions to ethics applies also to Buddhism. The relevant notion of time here is the notion of *paticca samuppāda* (dependent co-arising), an understanding of which was equated by the Buddha with an understanding of the *dhamma*. This is a deep and tricky point about Buddhist ethics, and I hope the physical sense in which I understand *paticca samuppāda*[18] will be clear by the end of this chapter.

We can also see how time relates to ethics in Islam. Al Ghazali's notion of ontically broken time[19] (imprecisely but catchily called occasionalism) relates directly to the ethic of surrender to Allah, which is at the heart of Islam. Through the Sufi and Bhakti traditions, such time beliefs are still widely prevalent in India. The relation is so clear, and so readily understood even at the level of popular Hindi cinema (e.g., *Waqt*) that, despite some tricky points involved, it does not call for further comment.

The utilitarian ethic too relates to time beliefs. As I have already discussed this elsewhere,[20] I will only recapitulate some of the key points. The capitalist ethic assumes that the future can be rationally calculated. This is a fundamental assumption, intertwined with the notion of deferred consumption: children study *now*, so that they can earn more *later*. If rational calculation of the future were not possible, or practicable, this would be a very foolish thing to do. With ontically broken time (or occasionalism, or providential intervention), it is not possible to calculate the future. So, the capitalist ethic requires belief in a world which evolves in an orderly way according to some 'laws' (instituted by some god, as made known to ordinary mortals by his scientific prophets like Newton). Note that this belief (in the predictability of the future) is also *prima facie* contradictory to the other belief underlying the utilitarian principle, namely that rational (or irrational) choice is at all possible. For if the world does evolve according to orderly laws alone, and human choices play no role in determining the future, then Laplace's demon can obviously calculate the entire future (including the choices one would make).

Then there is the peculiar assumption that the utility of future consumption can be discounted at the prevailing bank rate of interest. (If not, it is not clear what discounting rate to use or how to calculate 'present value'.) Further time beliefs underlying utilitarianism are elaborated in my book. (For example, Buddhists might argue that the child is a different individual from the adult, therefore, forcing the child to forgo play to the advantage of the adult is unjust to the child.)

Here I will only summarize the big picture: **ethical models in common use (both utilitarian and religious) are anchored in beliefs about the nature of time.**

Science, Religion and Time

The second part of my thesis concerns the way religious beliefs have penetrated science. This thesis too is contrary to the common story of science and religion at war with each other.

Science penetrated religion through time beliefs which are at the interface of the two. We already saw above the attempt to control human behaviour by modifying values, and we saw how time perceptions were modified to modify values. But time is also at the base of scientific thought. So, this modification of time perceptions affects science.

Understanding the entire chain of influence makes for a long story. To cut it short, I will start with Newton, for, according to another common myth, that is where science begins.

At the beginning of Newton's *Principia* we find the famous quote about time: '*Absolute, true, and mathematical* time . . . flows equably *without relation to anything external*. . . .'[21] Note the three adjectives, 'absolute', 'true' and 'mathematical'. To eliminate any residual doubt, Newton adds the clause: 'without relation to anything external'. Clearly, the time that Newton discusses is metaphysical, and not physical—for something which has no regard to anything external cannot possibly be a physical entity. How did this metaphysical notion of time come to be at the basis of Newtonian physics? Why did Newton feel compelled to make time metaphysical? As I said, this is a long story (which has to do with Newton's attempts to understand the Indian calculus,[22] and assimilate it with his religious beliefs).

In making time metaphysical, Newton took a retrograde step, for his predecessor and mentor Barrow had quite explicitly poked fun at Augustine, indirectly calling him and his followers 'quacks for evading a physical definition of time.[23] Barrow had proposed the even tenor hypothesis for physical time: 'equal causes take equal times to produce equal effects', in a meaningful way. However, Newton applied 'even tenor' to *mathematical* time where it was meaningless, though it appealed to his religious predilections. Consequently, Newtonian physics lacked any *physical* definition of 'equal intervals of time'.[24]

This had serious repercussions for Newtonian physics. Newton's second 'law' of motion is today regarded as a *definition* of force. However, it is bad definition, for the right hand side (i.e., the rate of change of momentum) is undefined in the absence of a *physical* definition of equal intervals of time. Consequently, as Popper[25] rightly pointed out, some (refutable) physics can be extracted from Newtonian physics only by eliminating time (e.g., planetary orbits are ellipses instead of Galilean parabolas).

However, with the advent of Maxwellian electrodynamics, time entered into physics in an essential way. To obtain a physical definition of equal intervals of time, Poincaré *postulated* that the speed of light is constant.[26] This postulate[27] (*not* the Michelson-Morley experiment[28]) led to the special theory of relativity.

Poincaré understood that this fundamentally alters the equations underlying physics. He realized that one now needed to solve not the ordinary differential equations of Newtonian physics, but what he called 'equations of finite differences',[29] and what we would today call delay differential equations or functional differential equations. Physically, this corresponds to history-dependent time evolution: electrodynamic forces travel at the speed of light, not at an infinite speed.

However, credit for the theory of relativity was grabbed by Einstein. Because Einstein was neither a mathematician nor the inventor of relativity,[30] he did not understand this key mathematical point about history-dependence till the end of his life, and incorrectly tried to approximate one type of equation by another.[31] Because credit for relativity incorrectly went to Einstein, he became a figure of great authority. Because science, in practice, relies heavily on authority, this mistake persisted for a century. In fact, the first solution of the functional differential equations of the retarded 2-body problem of electrodynamics in a serious physical context was given by me[32] only in 2004, a century after Poincaré invented relativity.

The Tilt in the Arrow of Time

However, this correction to the Newtonian view of time, by admitting history-dependence, is not enough. There is an additional problem. Experiments are needed to verify or refute a physical theory. Experimentation as a process of testing is meaningful only if it can throw up some surprises. On mundane time beliefs, we suppose that the past is decided, but the future is not, and is *hence* potentially surprising. However, these mundane time beliefs do not cohere with the time beliefs used to write down the differential equations of physics, and which time beliefs I have called 'superlinear time'.

To ensure coherence between these conflicting pictures of (mundane and superlinear) time, I had proposed to modify the above equations a step further, and allow a 'tilt' in the arrow of time. A 'tilt' is not a new physical hypothesis; rather, it is a rejection of the common physical hypothesis of causality. Causality is a religious requirement: if God is to distribute rewards and punishments on the Day of Judgement, he needs to identify individuals as the *cause* of a good or bad act. The physical world, however, need not be causal. Whether or not it is causal needs to be decided by experiment. But to design such an experiment, we first need a theory of a non-causal world. Rejecting hand-imposed causality allows not only the past but also the future to influence the present. There is a *quantitative* difference: the influence of the past on the present is vastly greater than that of the future.

A 'tilt' involves a radical new mathematical understanding of time evolution in physics (time evolution according to *mixed-type* functional differential equations;[33] Poincaré had considered only *retarded* functional differential equations). In colloquial language, it allows anticipation, in addition to history dependence. This new understanding of physics (as incorporating history dependence + anticipation) is expected to include quantum mechanics. One can now ask the question in reverse: What sort of ethics flows from this revised and corrected time belief in physics?

History-dependent evolution leads to one sort of paradigm shift: The future is not determined by the present; one needs to know the entire past history. A tilt leads to a further paradigm shift. In this case, future is not determined even by the entire past history. With a tilt, physics ceases to be *mechanical*: The idea of the cosmos as God's grand piece of clockwork governed by some grand 'laws' of physics has to be thrown out once and for all. At each instant, humans create the future cosmos, and they do so in a way that would surprise God (if He exists, that is).

Philosophers object to reductive explanations, when their primary objection is to *mechanical* explanations. They go by the mental picture that atoms, molecules and so on are all describable in a mechanical way, so that trying to connect human behaviour to physics, which concerns atoms, molecules and so on, is misguided. What is at fault here is not reductionism, but the naïve mental picture about atoms and molecules, which is about a century out of date. Atoms and molecules are neither particularly simple things, nor do they necessarily behave in a completely mechanical way.

On the other hand, neither complexity (epistemically broken time) nor quantum indeterminism (through the collapse postulate, ontically broken time) is the magic wand some naïvely think it to be. Complexity, for example, is just a more sophisticated restatement of the old 'god of the gaps' argument: 'We don't understand this (lightning striking churches) therefore it is the work of God.' In this restatement, complex assemblies of atoms and molecules somehow magically acquire properties not present at the level of the constituents. The objection to reductionism ought not to be mere nostalgia for an enchanted childhood world of magic. A whole crop of new medicines are based on the reductive understanding of the physics of biomolecules. Likewise, quantum indeterminism (or occasionalism) is as contrary to creativity as ('hard') determinism.[34]

In this situation, the great advantage of a tilt is that it provides us with a non-mechanistic model of how the world evolves, conditioned, but not determined, by the past. This is remarkably similar to the notion of *paticca samuppāda.*

An important feature of the tilt relates to thermodynamics. Thermodynamics, as its name suggests, started off with the issue of steam engines and a gas in a box. But it evolved into statistical mechanics, which has given us a remarkable idea: that of entropy. Entropy is a measure of disorder. A key principle of thermodynamics is the so-called second law of thermodynamics, which asserts that the entropy (of a closed system) never decreases. A stronger formulation (more pedantically called the H-theorem) is that the entropy (of a closed system) goes on increasing until it reaches its maximum. The stronger formulation is needed to explain why heat flows from hotter to cooler bodies. The spread of heat increases disorder.

A long-standing problem has been the inability to relate the entropy 'law' to Newton's 'laws'.[35] (There is at present no serious way to do statistical mechanics with general relativity.) The problem is not that one cannot derive the entropy law from Newton's laws; rather, the problem is that the entropy law is *contrary* to Newton's laws: if Newton's laws hold, there is no way entropy can increase or decrease, it must stay constant. Deterministic evolution cannot increase or decrease order or disorder. An easy way to see this is that deterministic evolution is reversible; hence this is called the reversibility paradox. Another famous objection, called the recurrence paradox, relates to the good old Poincaré recurrence theorem mentioned above: for a gas in a box, every microstate must recur infinitely often, so *no matter how entropy is defined*, it cannot increase or decrease. The text-book resolutions of these paradoxes are unsatisfactory despite involving (implicitly or explicitly) a variety of increasingly obscure concepts such as coarse-graining, ergodicity, mixing and so on.

In contrast, history-dependent evolution provides a clean resolution of the paradoxes of thermodynamics (since the hypotheses of the Poincaré recurrence theorem break down, and history-dependent evolution is *not* reversible). With history-dependent evolution, the past decides future, but not vice versa, which is the same thing as saying that we have *more* information about the past than the future, so that entropy increases towards the future. So, we also have a simple explanation for increase in entropy.[36]

With a tilt, the situation is a little more complex. Now, past conditions the future, but does not decide it. Just as history-dependent processes increase entropy, anticipatory processes decrease entropy. Such anticipatory processes will manifest themselves as spontaneous and causally inexplicable events. That is, with a tilt, *spontaneous events are possible, and these will decrease entropy.* We can visualize that both entropy-increasing and decreasing processes exist. The former predominate, therefore entropy still increases *on the whole*.[37]

The Tilt, Life and Ethics

We have seen how common ethical principles depend upon assumptions about the nature of time. The attempt to transform human behaviour led to the transformation of these time beliefs, and these transformed time beliefs have crept into physics. Finally, we have seen how, if physics is de-theologized, this leads to a new notion of time.

Having arrived at this new notion of time which represents the best scientific knowledge available to us today, we can turn around and ask: What ethical principle follows from this new notion of time?

Now, many theologians in a zealous attempt to guard ethics as their provenance, and to keep scientists away from it, have attempted to disconnect ethics from our knowledge of the world (since ultimately they want to base ethics on things like the belief in God and scriptures, which are under their social authority, whether or not they explicitly admit this motivation).

Therefore, I emphasize that my attempt to base ethics on physics is not based on any naïve confusion between facts and values. However, an ethical principle, if it is to be persuasive, must involve all our knowledge about life and its place in the cosmos. Certainly, this knowledge is fallible, and may change, so the resulting ethics need to be neither eternal nor absolute. However, an ethical principle based on knowledge is more persuasive as a basis of mundane action than an ethical principle based on mere beliefs of a voluntarily blind, deaf and anosmic person. Those ethical principles are brittle, and shatter when questioned. If the underlying beliefs (about time) are physical, they must confront physics. If not, they can simply be denied. There is no sense in speaking of 'free will' or volition in a way which wishes away physics.

This was what I thought I had pointed out in my letter to Dayaji. In my book, I had proposed a new ethical principle arising from this new notion of time in physics involving a tilt.

A key aspect of the above notion of time is that it makes it possible (for living beings) to diminish entropy spontaneously. Since entropy is understood as a measure of disorder, 'diminishing entropy' should translate into the same thing as 'increasing order'.

With this in mind, the new ethical principle was stated as follows:

Order principle: Act so as to increase order in the cosmos.

However, Dayaji immediately reacted to the word 'order'. He gave the example of Soviet Union; he said there was order there, but that such order was not necessarily desirable. I dashed off a long letter to him explaining the precise sense in which I used the word order. However, a year or so later, I gave a talk on this at Melbourne. A couple of people including Don Miller again objected to the word 'order' on similar grounds.

Clearly, howsoever much one may wish it away, the sad tale of two cultures comes back to haunt us. Scientists tend to use words somewhat carelessly, because these words are often used merely as pointers to precise mathematical or theoretical constructs for which there are no exact equivalents in the English language. 'Order' for me is the same thing that Schrödinger and other authors called negentropy. The difference is that where Schrödinger, for example, proceeded intuitively, I am proceeding with a definite new physics in mind, as also a theory of how this notion of 'order' relates to life and the cosmos.

Order, in the physical sense in which I use the term, is essential for biological survival. At the physical level, a human being is a vast collection of molecules which exist in a highly ordered state. The tiniest departure from this order entails illness and death. The orderliness of the body is a must for the continued existence of a living organism.

In fact, order, in this physical sense, is not only essential for the survival of human beings, it characterizes life. This can be better understood by the way this notion of order relates to human behaviour through the theory of evolution.

The existing theory of evolution already provides insight into human behaviour by connecting it with the behaviour of other animals. While survival of the individual is certainly a key concern, even basic urges such as those related to reproduction make sense only in reference to a larger biological unit, such as the species. So, the evolutionary ethic may be stated: Act so as to maximize the probability of the survival of the species.

This principle explains why (even in non-capitalist societies) most people are so concerned with acquiring territory (e.g., wealth) and social status, and trying to consolidate it. Combined with the process of reproduction and rearing this seems to describe much of the life of most people.

The question now is, *Is that all that there is to life?* Is there anything to life beyond survival (of the species)?

Certainly, the environmentalist is concerned with other species on the planet. So, to side-step prolix quibbles about the reality of altruism, let us rephrase the above question. Let us expand our concerns from individual to species to all life on the planet to all life in the cosmos.

So, is that the ultimate ethical concern: preservation of life in the cosmos?

Note that I seek answers acceptable to the sceptic—the answers must rely only on 'public' knowledge, and on valid physics, not on private religious beliefs or metaphysical assumptions.

Note also that, in this generalized form, the evolutionary ethic is subsumed by the order principle. For life, whatever its chemical or physical constituents, is characterized as an orderly state. Even a single protein molecule is in a far, far more ordered state than the molecules of a gas in a box—which latter state is the 'natural state' of disorder or thermodynamic equilibrium, according to thermodynamics. Preservation of life in the cosmos is preservation of this order. The order principle, however, speaks of increasing order, so it clearly goes a step further.

In fact, the tilt helps to clear up a number of confusing aspects related to both: the theory of evolution in biology and to ethical principles in philosophy. For example, the philosophy of ethics takes for granted the existence of volition. It takes for granted that human volition, though independent of the past, nevertheless somehow determines the future—for the above ethical principles all enjoin one to bring about a certain future state, hence assume that it is possible to do so. The philosophy of ethics routinely proceeds by ignoring the manifest contradiction of such beliefs with the knowledge of the world which comes from physics. This attitude may have been appropriate in the West where theologians, who ruled, regarded themselves as superior to physicists. But today, this incoherence between philosophy and physics cannot be wished away by putting philosophy and physics in two separate university departments which do not interact with each other. The tilt, on the other hand, admits the possibility of spontaneous choice which may be conditioned by the past, but is not determined by it; it also explains how these spontaneous choices can nevertheless relate to future events.

Current biology does not give an adequate account of the origin of life; or the origin of order. The theory of evolution provides many insights, but certain aspects of it remain cloaked in obscurity. A key issue is the origin of mutations (and the origin of life itself). Evolutionary theory attributes this to 'chance'. If this 'chance' is not to be a mere word which magically conjures up a 'god of the gaps', to explain anything and everything, we need a precise quantitative model of this 'chance' (such as a model of time evolution according to stochastic differential equations) which tells us how much chance leads to how much mutations, in how much time. Such an enterprise, however, is doomed to failure: we have already seen how, throughout the nineteenth century (when the current theory of evolution was formulated), the mechanism of chance was unsuccessfully used to try to explain increase of entropy. We have also seen that, within Newtonian physics, chance can neither increase entropy, nor increase order (decrease entropy), both of which must stay constant. If accounts such as the Ehrenfest model combined with hand-waving techniques like 'coarse graining' have any validity, what they show is only this: Chance *increases* disorder. Note incidentally, how chance is used to perform one sort of magic in thermodynamics, and the opposite sort in biology.

Spontaneity, on the other hand, increases order; combined with history-dependence, it allows this state of increased order to be maintained. It also shows how this increase in order can remain immersed in a sea of order-decreasing (or entropy-increasing) processes.

However, it is clear that Dayaji and Don Miller both had not thought about 'order' in quite the same way. They thought of 'order' in the ordinary (dictionary) sense of word. They thought of it not at the physical or biological level as I did, but of the connotations at the social level, where order could possibly be mechanical or authoritarian. They objected to order in this sense of regimentation. The thing that one intuitively feels is wrong with regimentation is the absence of spontaneity. So 'order', they felt, could be an imposition on human beings, just as much as the rituals of 'civilized' society were an imposition on Huckleberry Finn.

Of course, I thought I had carefully explained this in my book: that creation of order *necessarily* corresponds to spontaneity, and that (in the physical sense of 'order') *there is no way to produce order mechanically* (for that would give us a perpetual motion machine of the second kind). However, if the matter was not clear to Dayaji and Don Miller, that itself is sufficient cause of worry. Furthermore, even many scientists lack clarity about spontaneity in science, since they share Newton's religious vision of a clockwork cosmos, and hence see science as something intrinsically mechanical. This lack of clarity is at the root of paradoxes, such as the grandfather paradox, as I have explained elsewhere.

So, it seems to me better to relate this abstract notion of 'order' more closely to human experience. To this end, let us ask how evolutionary ethics is 'implemented'. When an animal takes a decision, does it carry out an evaluation of all future consequences? As any chess player knows, few people ever calculate beyond level 3 even in the game of chess, which requires a rigorous evaluation of future consequences. And, as any computer programmer knows, a rigorous evaluation beyond level 25 is a difficult task, even for a supercomputer, which may take longer than the human lifespan to do it. Accordingly, the animal's decisions are more usually based on immediate sensations of pleasure and pain which are 'hardwired' to these longer-term consequences. For example, reproduction is crucial to the survival of the species, and engaging in reproductory activities generates the appropriate sensations of pleasure.

In this sense, spontaneous creation of order is 'hardwired' to the deep sense of satisfaction one gets from a creative insight, the creative satisfaction that one gets from, for example, spontaneously arranging ideas, or musical notes, in a particularly interesting and novel pattern. Unfortunately, Western music has been robbed of the key element of spontaneity, which is still manifest in, say, Indian music. However, though there seems no satisfactory word for it, the Western musical concept which comes closest to this notion of spontaneity is harmony: several notes being struck together to create a pleasing effect. The analogy I have in mind is to Popper's pond paradox—in a non-circular pond, the creation of a convergent ripple is causally inexplicable since it requires a conspiracy of causes. This paradox, incidentally, is easily resolved[38] through spontaneity.

Therefore, the only change that is probably needed is to rename order as harmony, and the order principle as the harmony principle.

Notes and References

1. C. K. Raju, *The Eleven Pictures of Time* (New Delhi: SAGE Publications, 2003).
2. Samuel P. Huntington, *The Clash of Civilizations and the Remaking of World Order* (New Delhi: Viking, 1997). Huntington's logic is also a natural extension of Toynbee's. Where Toynbee seeks to understand history through 'civilizations' rather than nations, which are ephemeral on a historical time-scale, Huntington seeks to understand world politics through a few 'civilizations' rather than a large number of nations.
3. Arnold J. Toynbee, *A Study of History*, abridgement of vols. vii–x by D. C. Somervelle (Oxford University Press, 1957; reprint, Dell Publishing Co.), vol. 2, p. 112.
4. E. G., Svetasvatara Upanisad 1.6. Trans. Prabhavananda and Frederick Manchester, *The Upanishads: Breath of the Eternal* (Mentor, New American Library, 1957), p. 118.
5. The recurrence time is a day and night of Brahma, stated to last a thousand yugas in Bhagwad Gita 8.17. This is elaborated in the *Viṣṇu Purāṇa*. *The Vishnu Purana*, trans. H. H. Wilson (London, 1840), reprint, with an introduction by R. C. Hazra (Calcutta: Punthi Pustaka, 1961), ch. 3, pp. 19–24, where it works out to 8.64 billion years. The astronomical rationale for the calculation is found, e.g., in the *Aryabhatiya*, where it emerges that 1 day of

the gods = 1 year of humans, 'just because' the gods stay on (mount Meru on) the north pole, where day and night last for six months each.

6. C. K. Raju, *Time: Towards a Consistent Theory* (Dordrecht: Kluwer Academic, 1994). *Fundamental Theories of Physics*, vol. 65, Appendix to ch. 4.
7. See, e.g., 'Life after Death', ch. 1, in ref. 1 for details on how widespread this notion was.
8. Origen, *De Principiis*. An easily accessible version is at http://www.newadvent.org/fathers/04122:htm. (The numbering may differ in other versions.) Particularly see II.1.1 for the definition of 'world'. II.3.1 for the question whether the world is unique. II.3.5 for the connection of 'world' to 'age', and the claim that the scriptures speak of a series of ages. II.3.4 for the description of exact recurrence and its denial, and for an acceptance of quasi-recurrence ('a diversity of worlds with changes of no unimportant kind').
9. Origen, cited above. See II.9.5 for the objection (of his opponents) that God is inequitous. II.9.6 for his claim that God created all people equal. II.9.8 for the claim that this inequity is retribution due to different deeds: 'In which certainly every principle of equity is shown, while the inequality of circumstances preserves the justice of a retribution according to merit.'
10. Dante Aligheri, *Divine Comedy: Inferno*, trans. Charles S. Singleton, Encyclopaedia Britannica (Chicago, 1996). There were no exceptions of any sort; for example, for a description of the treatment meted out to Mohammed, see Canto XXVII, p. 35.
11. Augustine, *City of God*, XII.13. Trans. Marcus Dods, *Encyclopaedia Britannica* (Chicago, 1996), p. 405.
12. See, 'The Curse on "Cyclic" Time', ch. 2 in *The Eleven Pictures of Time*, cited above.
13. Mircea Eliade, *Cosmos and History: The Myth of the Eternal Return*, trans. W. Trask (New York: Harper, 1959), p. 153.
14. Martin Heidegger, *Nietzsche*, vol. II: *The Eternal Recurrence of the Same*, trans. D. F. Krell (San Francisco: Harper, 1991).
15. Newton's mentor Barrow allowed that time could be like a line or circle, but Newton took it to be like a line (for religious reasons). See 'Newton's Secret', ch. 4 in *The Eleven Pictures of Time*, cited earlier.
16. Hawking's 'chronology condition'—that there are no closed time-like curves—derives from the same Augustinian idea that any cyclicity in the cosmos is symptomatic of eternal recurrence which should be abolished since it is contrary to free will. S. W. Hawking and G. F. R. Ellis, *The Large Scale Structure of Spacetime* (Cambridge University Press, 1974), p. 189.
17. C. K. Raju, 'Time Travel and the Reality of Spontaneity', *Foundations of Physics* 36 (2006): 1099–1113.
18. C. K. Raju, '*Atman*, quasi-recurrence, and *paticca samuppāda*', in *Self, Science and Society, Theoretical and Historical Perspectives*, eds

D. P. Chattopadhyaya and A. K. Sengupta (New Delhi: Project on the History of Indian Science, Philosophy and Culture, 2005), pp. 196–206.

19. Al Ghazali, *Tahâfut al-Falâsifâ*, trans. S. A. Kamali, Pakistan Philosophical Congress (Lahore, 1958); S. van den Bergh, *Averroes' Tahâfut al-Tahâfut* (incorporating al-Ghazâlî's *Tahafut al-Falasifa*), translated with introduction and notes, 2 vols, Luzac (London, 1969).
20. 'Time as Money', ch. 10 in *The Eleven Pictures of Time*, cited above.
21. Isaac Newton, *Mathematical Principles of Natural Philosophy*, trans. A. Motte, rev. by Florian Cajori, Encyclopaedia Britannica (Chicago, 1996), p. 8. Emphases mine.
22. C. K. Raju, *Cultural Foundations of Mathematics: The Nature of Mathematical Proof and the Transmission of the Calculus from India to Europe in the 16th c. CE* (New Delhi: Pearson Longman, 2007, Delhi: Project on the History of Indian Science, Philosophy and Culture, vol X.4.)
23. Isaac Barrow, 'Absolute Time [Lectiones Geometricae]', in *The Concepts of Space and Time: Their Structure and Their Development*, Boston Studies in the Philosophy of Science, vol. 12, ed. M. Capek (Dordrecht: D. Reidel, 1976), p. 204.
24. C. K. Raju, 'Newton's time', *Physics Education* (India) 8 (1991): 15–25.
25. K. R. Popper, *Realism and the Aim of Science. Postscript to Logic of Scientific Discovery*, vol. 1 (London: Hutchinson, 1982). For an elaboration, see C. K. Raju, 'Newton's Time', cited above.
26. H. Poincaré [1904], in: *The Value of Science,* trans. G. B. Halstead, 1913, reprinted Dover, 1958, p. 104, speaks of 'an entirely new mechanics [in which] no velocity could surpass that of light, any more than any temperature can fall below absolute zero. [Original footnote: Because bodies would oppose an increasing inertia to the causes which would tend to accelerate their motion, and this inertia would become infinite when one approached the velocity of light.] [Emphases mine.] This postulate leads to a proper clock (or equal intervals of time) defined by means of a photon bouncing between parallel mirrors.
27. C. K. Raju, 'Einstein's Time', *Physics Education* (India) 8 (1991): 293–305.
28. C. K. Raju, 'The Michelson-Morley Experiment', *Physics Education* (India) 8 (1991): 193–200.
29. H. Poincaré [1902], *Science and Hypothesis*, Eng. trans. (New York: Dover, 1952), pp. 169–170, explained that such equations will naturally arise if the aether is rejected.
30. Einstein is often credited with having 'independently rediscovered' relativity, by believing his statement that he had not seen Poincaré's 1904 work. My 'epistemic test' is a simple way to check false claims of independence. Einstein fails this test since he did not understand the need for functional differential equations, and made a mathematical mistake in supposing that they could be approximated by ordinary differential equations by means of

a 'Taylor expansion'. For the epistemic test, see 'Models of information transmission', in *Cultural Foundations of Mathematics*, cited above.

31. Einstein's mistake can be found in his attempts to do the relativistic many body problem, for example, in A. Einstein, L. Infeld and B. Hoffmann, *Annals of Mathematics* 39 (1938): p. 65. For an explanation of why this is a mistake, see *Time: Towards a Consistent Theory*, cited earlier, p. 122.
32. C. K. Raju, 'The electrodynamic 2-body problem and the origin of quantum mechanics', *Foundations of Physics*, 34 (2004): 937–962.
33. See *Time: Towards a Consistent Theory*, ch. 5b.
34. See 'Broken time: Chance, Chaos, Complexity', in *The Eleven Pictures of Time*, ch. 6.
35. C. K. Raju, 'Thermodynamic time', *Physics Education* (India) 9 (1992): 44–62.
36. Ref. 30 above.
37. Whether or not this predomination is permanent, i.e., whether or not the cosmos eventually recurs is another issue, which we do not go into here.
38. Ref. 15 above.

17

On Mathematics and the Physical World

S. Lokanathan

Sometime in early September 2007, I was in Jaipur and had an interesting discussion with Daya Krishna about 'measurement'. My interest was largely pedagogical, to set forth the basic concepts of measurement. The point I had in mind, in particular, was that 'ordering' of a physical quantity was a prior requirement to that of choosing a scale, a metric. In passing, I used the history of measurement, especially of time and space, to bring out the idea that techniques of measurement (involving changes of choice of standards, scales and of precision) were dictated by scientific and technological needs of the times.

Daya Krishna, as often, raised more fundamental questions, of the relation between algebra, geometry, topology and logic as also their relation to the physical world as for example the relation between mathematical (axiomatic) geometry and physical geometry. I sent him my copy of Hans Reichenbach's *The Philosophy of Space and Time*.[1] He read it and sent it back by post (I had returned to Bangalore) with a letter dated 22 September 2007 with his comments. I reproduce extracts of his letter:

> I have read the first part of the book by Reichenbach and I am glad I did so. There are so many points for discussion, some of them I had formulated. Surprisingly, at least for some of them I have received an answer from the internet[2] whose copy I am enclosing herewith. One of the questions I have asked is not therein. It concerns the relation between Algebra and Topology. Another one (is) related to the axiomatization of Geometry, Arithmetic and Logic and the relation between them. At another level,

> the question relates to the deeper issue as to what exactly is gained by axiomatization and in case it is really successful, would it not close [the] 'knowledge enterprise' altogether.

It promised, for me, exciting discussions with him when we were to meet next in a couple of months. Sadly, he died within a fortnight of writing this letter. I dedicate this presentation to him, a beautiful scholar and a great friend. Of necessity, I have to guess what he had in mind and my judgement may well be faulty. The three points he has raised are the relation between different branches of mathematics, how axiomatization has helped the 'knowledge enterprise' and how it promises (or threatens, depending on your prejudice) to end this enterprise. I shall say something too about the relation between mathematics and physics.

Euclidean and Non-Euclidean Geometries

Axiomatization in mathematics owes its origin primarily to Euclidean geometry. Although Euclid had set out the postulates, the precise formulation of a complete set of postulates (axioms) was probably due to David Hilbert in the last century. One particular postulate that Euclid did recognize as necessary for his geometry was the so-called 'parallel postulate': that through a point 'not' on a straight line, exactly one parallel straight line could be drawn. For centuries mathematicians were troubled by this. It seemed obvious and the question was whether it could be deduced from the other postulates of Euclid. That question was answered decisively in an unexpected way by N. Lobatschewsky who replaced Euclid's postulate with the one that 'an infinite number of parallel straight lines could be drawn' (instead of just one) and by G. Riemann whose axiom was that 'no parallel straight line could be drawn'. They produced two different 'non-Euclidean' geometries, quite as consistent as Euclid's. In passing, of course, it was established that Euclid's was indeed a necessary postulate for his geometry, and it could not have been deduced from the other postulates.

Mathematics and Logic

This development was of great importance in the history of mathematics for two reasons and I take them in their historical order. Long ago, Immanuel Kant had proposed that there were two kinds of knowledge, analytical and synthetic. Analytical statements are a priori, in the sense that they contain nothing that is dependent on experience while synthetic statements have a factual content that could be refuted by experience, a posteriori. But Kant went further to state that it is possible for knowledge to be both synthetic and a priori. It was this view of Kant that came to be questioned after the new geometries were conceived. Kant was clear that synthetic judgements qualified as knowledge but he had not anticipated that there could be other consistent geometries quite independent of experience. That brings us to the second development. Freed from empirical constraints, it was now important to look at the new geometries as exercises in logic, of consistency and completeness. Henceforth, there was a deliberate move to establish pure mathematics as a precise formulation of logic. An example was David Hilbert's work on the foundation of geometry. Normally, terms such as points, lines and planes have a physical connotation. But Hilbert divested them of such associations and called them just 'entities' so that axioms now became relations between these abstract entities.[3] This deliberate divorce of the terms used in axiomatization from physical association gave mathematics a generality and power for applications to science. A classic example is the Theory of Groups where the entities are not defined but their relations are. In the last century, this theory played such a vital part in the development of physical theories that it is difficult to imagine progress without it.

Let me revert to Daya's question about the relation between different branches of mathematics. In as much as no specific meanings are attached to the actual terms set forth in the axioms, they do not necessarily refer to a particular branch of mathematics. (A simple specific example is given Ernest Nagel and James R. Newman and I give this briefly in the notes appended.) It is true that this great tidiness was disturbed when Kurt Goedel showed (1931) that the axiomatic method could really not cover even a simple mathematical system such as the arithmetic of integers, but that does not weaken the argument that mathematics is, in a sense, rendered a unified whole. This is the comment that Ian Stewart makes in the internet account that Daya has quoted.

There is, then, this strange paradox. The formal divorce of mathematics from reality gives its results a certainty never attained in science. In the words of Einstein, 'As far as the laws of Mathematics refer to reality, they are not certain; and as far as they are certain they do not refer to reality.' On the other hand, mathematics 'has' become an extraordinarily powerful and fecund tool in science. So that it provides a part of the answer to Daya's question about what is gained by axiomatization. But it still does not explain the reason for this fecundity. I am not sure I know the answer, but often it does seem to pay a theoretical physicist to abstract a feature of 'reality' and follow the mathematical rules of that abstraction as in the use of Group Theory as I mentioned earlier.

Empiricism and Knowledge

Let me now take up Daya's question about axiomatization. He asks, 'If successful would it not close the "knowledge enterprise"?'

My first reaction is to try to understand what 'is' knowledge and how we perceive success in its search. Clearly, within the tight constraint of conciseness and logical completeness, axiomatization achieves the goal that mathematicians set themselves. The examples of geometry, Euclidean and Non-Euclidean and of Peano axioms for the theory of numbers are cases in point.

But surely, that is not the sense in which Daya would have posed the question. For one thing, there is no reason to believe that the game of axiomatization cannot go on forever and it is difficult to reconcile ourselves to the notion that all new axiomatization schemes are 'knowledge' at least in the physical sense. So by 'success' in the knowledge enterprise, Daya was probably asking how mathematical activity was helping activities in other fields, notably in science. The point, then, is really about the relation between mathematics and science. We usually judge success in science by appealing to empirical evidence, by setting 'failure standards' if you subscribe to Karl Popper or perhaps less stringent criteria but still based on empiricism. Consider, for example, the status of electromagnetism following Maxwell's theory and Hertz's demonstration of electromagnetic waves across space. There began an assiduous search for ether, the medium for these waves. In particular, the experiment of Michelson and Morley was set up to measure the velocity of light with and against the direction of earth's motion along the ecliptic. The idea was that there would be a detectable effect on the velocity as ether moves with the earth. The experiment reported no perceptible effect and today's classroom tale is that the experiment effectively 'abolished' ether, a view that is too naive.[4] The issue here is 'not' the importance of the experiment. The point is that even if science is rooted in empiricism, the conclusions that can be unchallengeably drawn are usually not all that simple.

Again, the famous experiment of bending of starlight in the gravitational field of the Sun was said to have ruled in favour of Einstein's General Theory of Relativity as against Newton's ideas of space and time; in particular, it showed that space was Non-Euclidean. In fact, even before the advent of Einstein's theory, H. Poincare had anticipated a possible discovery of the bending of light in an experiment and had stated that physicists would then have a choice. They could either retain Euclidean geometry and redo the laws of motion of light near matter or choose a Non-Euclidean geometry and retain the old laws. Poincare thought that physics would retain Euclidean geometry. Poincare's insight belies a common misunderstanding that empirical evidence has established that space is 'curved'. If Poincare did not anticipate the course of the physical theory, it was not that space was directly shown to be curved by experiment, but rather in the fact that it turned out that the preferred choice was to think of space as curved (near the Sun) rather than opt for the alternative of retaining Euclidean geometry (4).

The important point, nevertheless, is that empiricism did have a crucial role in necessitating a reassessment of a scientific theory in both these cases—the Michelson Morley experiment and the bending of light. As against this, experiment has nothing to say about the success of Euclidean or Non-Euclidean geometry as pure mathematical theories. In other words, the grey interface between mathematical and physical geometry notwithstanding, there is a basic difference in our assessment of their success. Mathematical geometry is judged by criteria of logic and not by its accord with experiment. It could hardly threaten the 'knowledge enterprise' if we interpret knowledge in the experiential sense. For all that, the new mathematical geometries had a crucial part to play in the physical theories proposed.[5]

Mathematics and Science

If all this conveys a sense that mathematics is but an exotic and useful tool for science, that would be a caricature of their relation. Historically, mathematics has often played a vital role in generating new ideas for science. The example of Dirac's relativistic theory of the electron is a particularly apt one, but there are others too.

A problem of tracing the development of a physical theory is that even the originators are themselves not always clear about how they arrived at their ideas. The act of creation does not have the tidiness that follows later and finds its place in text books. For example, Heisenberg started with the idea that the failure of the Bohr model (see note 5) was because it was formulated in terms of non-observable features—like the 'orbit' of the electron around the nucleus. Heisenberg set himself the goal of constructing a scheme that would deal directly with observable quantities like frequencies and intensities of atomic spectra aided by empirically determined spectral rules such as the Ritz combination principle. It led Heisenberg to an algebra with which he was not familiar. It was Max Born who realized that it was really matrix algebra and Heisenberg's version of quantum mechanics quickly took shape.

Thus Heisenberg's was a search for a mathematics (already in existence but unknown to him) suitable for a physical theory. Curiously, quantum mechanics was developed independently by Schrodinger and Dirac. Schrodinger's wave mechanics used mathematics that he was fairly familiar with, but at first the mathematical methods used by him and Heisenberg seemed conceptually distinct although soon Schrodinger himself showed the connection. It is an interesting reflection that entirely different mathematical approaches led to the same physical reality.

Particle physics has used enormously powerful mathematics in recent years. A particular goal in particle physics is the unification of the four fundamental forces—nuclear, electromagnetic, weak and gravitational—a search resembling the one for the Holy Grail. In a sense it is a reductionist goal but stimulated by the huge success it has had up to a point. Faraday and Maxwell (prominently) had produced a unified version of electricity and magnetism; more recently, in the last few decades, unified versions of the three—nuclear (or strong), electromagnetic and weak—have reached text books as the standard model. But the complete unification has eluded theorists till now.

There is an assumption in all this, that ultimately nature must be simple and its description unique. I am not sure if this is more than a faith. If I compare this with a medieval theologian asserting 'there can be but one true faith', I suppose I will simultaneously blaspheme the religious orthodoxy and the scientific community. But the faith of some in the coming of a Theory of Everything (TOE), a theory so consistent and tight that there would be hardly any need for experiments to test it, tempts me to such indiscretion. As a matter of fact, some prominent theorists who had made important contributions to String Theory (a precursor to a TOE), have now become strident critics of such a goal because the theory has not produced enough results to be testable and is distancing itself from empiricism. At any rate, a theory that promises to end all theories will indeed spell the death of the 'knowledge enterprise'. Thankfully, such a theory is not in sight. Until its arrival (if at all), most of us would cling to the view that empiricism, observation and experiment, has to remain a vital source of knowledge.

Notes and References

1. H. Reichenbach, *The Philosophy of Space and Time* (New York: Dover Publications, 1957).
2. This was a comment by Ian Stewart (FRS), Mathematics Institute, University of Warwick. Stewart states that the whole of mathematics is 'essentially equivalent to Set theory' so that the only real issue is the axiomatization of Set theory. Thus, adds Stewart since mathematics forms a unified whole so do Arithmetic and Geometry.
3. A simple example is given in an essay by Ernest Nagel and James R. Newman titled 'Goedel's Proof' in *The World of Mathematics* vol. 3, ed. James R. Newman (Tempus Books, 1988), p. 1645.
4. Euclidean geometry is entrenched in our imagination because of the visualization that goes with it. Hilbert's axiomatization asserts, in effect, that there is no need for any visual pictures and instead the meaning of the mathematical manipulations simply lies in the relations formulated between the entities following the axioms. This is familiar to us from the relation between geometry and coordinate geometry where algebra is related to Geometry, a first degree equation between two variables represents a straight line. Mathematics is thus a theory of relations of entities rather than of the entities themselves which are left undefined. This was succinctly expressed in Bertrand Russell's epigram that pure mathematics was a subject in which we did not know what we are talking about. Russell and Whitehead published in 1913 their *Principia Mathematica* whose aim was nothing less than to establish the identity of the whole of Mathematics with an Axiomatization programme. It is this enterprise that K. Goedel showed (1931) was not possible, that even Arithmetic developed as an axiomatic system was essentially incomplete in the sense that there will be statements of Arithmetic that cannot be proved true or false within a finite axiomatization scheme.
5. The problem of the so-called 'decisive' experiment is that it is not often decisive! I do *NOT* mean that an experiment itself puts out an indecisive finding but that the implication of a decisive measurement is often not decisive in 'throwing out' a theory. The Michelson Morley experiment which showed essentially that the velocity of light was the same for light travelling with the earth (as it speeds along its orbit) or opposite the motion of the earth, is

sometimes alleged to have established the absence of ether. Actually, there were intricate suggestions to retrieve classical notions but they would have been rather more contrived than Einstein's Special Theory of Relativity. About the only clear statement that could be made is that Einstein's showed that the ether hypothesis was unnecessary and irrelevant to explain the MM experiment. In a similar way it would be incorrect to state that experiments established that space becomes curved near matter. The point is that the very notion of 'straight' or 'curved' requires a definition. If these are defined in terms of the path of light rays then one would find an interesting situation. Imagine a very large triangle whose sides are formed by three Light rays in the vicinity of matter. Then the angles of the triangle would no longer add up to 180 degrees. One would have a choice of retaining Euclidean Geometry and saying that Light rays traverse a curved path OR of saying that space is curved but light still travels 'straight' along a geodesic. The latter is the choice of a non-Euclidean geometry representing physical space and, contrary to Poincare's expectation, proved to be the simpler. At the same time it must be emphasized that empiricism 'has' restricted the choices—one cannot have a Euclidean Geometry and persist with the view that Light travels straight even in a gravitational field.

The role of experiments in judging a Physical theory has been discussed widely, by K. R. Popper, T. S. Kuhn, I. Lakatos and many others. Here, I would only like to give an example or two of how the standing of a theory is revalued in the light of experiments. For some two and a half centuries Classical Physics (based on Newton's laws) remained unquestioned because of the huge variety of phenomena it explained with considerable accuracy. Nevertheless, ideas of space and time, a soft spot as recognized even by Newton, were sharply revised following Einstein's work. Here is a more recent example. When N. Bohr published his theory of the Hydrogen atom in 1913, it had to be taken seriously because of its remarkable prediction of the spectra. In particular, Bohr's formula included the hitherto phenomenological Rydberg constant R which had been determined from experiment earlier: R ~ 109,737 cm-1. In Bohr's formula, this constant was no longer phenomenological but could be explicitly calculated from other physical constants, the mass of the electron, the velocity of light and Planck's constant. At the time of Bohr's work, this yielded the number, which was within about 6% of the experimental value at that time. (The physical constants were not that well known then; later the agreement was much closer.) Indeed Bohr could do better. He could predict the spectra of ionized Helium and account for a small difference in the spectra compared to Hydrogen. This agreement was within a part in 100,000! It so impressed Einstein that he said: 'Then it is one of the greatest discoveries'. 'Subtle is the Lord', A. Pais (Oxford University Press, 1982), p. 385. The irony is that very soon, the inadequacy of the Bohr version became apparent both because of its inability to explain complex spectra and because its theoretical foundations seemed ad hoc. The new theory of Quantum Mechanics in the mid 1920's could do much better. It is clear that the ability of a physical theory to confront the current empirical knowledge is by no means a guarantee of a permanence of its 'Truth'.

Hereabouts I may also remark that today most physicists refer to Bohr's 'theory' as a model and one can hardly disagree with that. But for me the idea that even at its inception in 1913 it was recognized as a model (as compared to the wisdom to come, quantum mechanics, sanctified as a theory) smacks of hindsight.

PART VI

On Life and Death and Dying

18

Matricide and Martyrdom: Cancer and *Karm* in the *Kalyug*

Shankar Ramaswami

Introduction

In this chapter, I explore the possible causes and meanings of the death of an adivasi mother witnessed during my fieldwork amongst migrant workers in Delhi, drawing upon the philosophies and theologies of workers, Simone Weil, Gandhiji and Ramchandra Gandhi. This death might be seen as a matricide, I suggest, induced by non-attention (*lāparvāhī*), envy (*jalan*) and misjudgements on the part of doctors, relatives, Madodari Devi and society as a whole. I discuss the experiences of her medical treatment, non-consolations for her death, Gandhiji's resonant views on violence, death and culpability, and intimations of possible atonements (*prāyaścitt*) for this matricide.

Madodari Devi, a Chero adivasi mother and widow in her forties, from Palamau district in Jharkhand, had suffered from stomach pains, vomiting and per vaginum bleeding for one year. She was treated in the village by doctors and *ojhā*s (shamans), and advised by a doctor in the nearby town of Daltonganj to go to a hospital for possible surgery. Her son, Tapesvar, a metal polishing worker in his twenties, working in a metal artware export factory in Delhi, did not think that her ailment was serious, and was reluctant to bring her to the city, though his state health insurance would have largely covered her treatment. But when her condition drastically deteriorated in 2006, he brought her to Delhi. She was taken to the Employees' State Insurance (ESI) hospital several times, but was only diagnosed one month later, when she was brought to a private clinic, where a gynaecologist determined her illness to be cervical cancer, already in stage IIIB. She was referred to the All India Institute of Medical Sciences (AIIMS), where after a month of investigations and a grim prognosis, she was admitted to the cancer ward, and given dialysis, a nephrostomy and radiotherapy sessions. Her condition briefly improved, but complications developed, and the radiotherapy was discontinued. She was referred to a cancer hospice for terminal patients, where she was closely looked after, but she was often left alone there by her son and other relatives. She died within 15 days. I turn below to a discussion of the possible causes of her death.

Labyrinthine Deafness

The ESI hospital is a place one dreads to go. Queues of patients are visible everywhere, at the registration counter, OPD departments and investigation rooms. One sees clusters of patients and attendants sitting, waiting or sleeping, in the congested lobby, in the hallways, outside the wards and in the hospital courtyard. Inside the wards, patients are at times doubled and tripled on a single bed. They share these beds with flies, insects and flying cockroaches, amidst the noxious stench, wafted in by noisy desert coolers, of a mountainous landfill of the city's refuse adjacent to the hospital. Given the long queues and lags in getting investigations done, it can take many trips to the hospital, doctors admit, to make any advance in one's treatment.

Madodari Devi was brought to the emergency room on an afternoon in late May 2006, where her vaginal bleeding symptom was recorded by the casualty doctor, before being referred to the gynaecologist on duty in the labour room, who recorded her symptoms of bleeding and abdominal pain, and referred her to the surgery and gynaecology outpatient departments (OPDs) for the next day, apparently without doing a per vaginum examination. Tapesvar took her home, but she was in agony again by the night. She was brought back to the emergency room, where the on-duty doctor recorded symptoms of vomiting and back and abdomen pain, but not her bleeding. She was kept overnight and treated by the medicine specialist for colitis and anaemia. The next day, she was referred to the orthopaedics OPD, and returned for follow-up to the medicine OPD three days later, where she was given more injections and medicines for anaemia and abdominal pain. Four days later, she was in severe pain again, and was kept overnight in the emergency, and treated by the medicine doctors, who eventually wrote, 'pain relieved'. The vaginal bleeding symptom was caught two days later by the surgery OPD doctors, who referred her back to the gynaecology OPD. Twelve days had already passed within this labyrinth.

When she came to the gynaecology OPD, her symptom was recorded merely as 'discharge', not bleeding, and she was prescribed pessaries and other medicines ordinarily administered for infections. An ultrasound was ordered, but the radiology doctor was on leave, and she was told to come back 10–12 days later. Her pain was intensifying. She returned to the gynaecology OPD 10 days later. This time, her symptoms were recorded as 'swelling on the face and legs', and strangely, the doctor wrote, 'no gyne problem at present'. With these two lines, she was sent back to the medicine OPD for anaemia treatment, then again to the emergency room, where medicines were prescribed. She was sent home.

Seven visits, 11 doctors, 18 encounters. Madodari Devi was a postmenopausal woman with vaginal bleeding, two warning signs of the possibility of cervical cancer, the most prevalent cancer amongst Indian women.[1] How could this have been missed, and that too, so many times? The ESI doctors' explanations were the following: patient overload, the limitations of specializations of non-gynaecological doctors, and the patient's likely mistakes in not following instructions, not showing the proper case papers, or not reporting the right symptoms at the right time. But there might be a deeper cause. '*Ekdam pūrā chachan rahī thī yah* [She was very agitated-distressed]', says Tapesvar. '*Aur vo log khālī yahām vahām dauṛā rahā thā. Yah karo to vo karo. Aur isko dard zyādā ho rahā thā. Koi doctor dekh bhī nahīṃ rahā thā hālī. Koī sun nahīṃ rahe the.* [And they were just making us run here and there, saying do this, then do that. And her pain was intense. No doctor would promptly see her. No one was listening-attending to us.]'[2] One ESI doctor suggests a reason for this: 'Most of the doctors, when they see a patient, they do not identify the patient with a human being like them, with a misery like them. They think they are just like nothing. Why should they see them properly?' Simone Weil writes:

> Every time that there arises from the depths of a human heart the childish cry which Christ himself could not restrain, 'Why am I being hurt?', then there is certainly injustice. . . . There are some people who get a positive pleasure from the cry; and many others simply do not hear it. For it is a silent cry, which sounds only in the secret heart. . . . The second is only a weaker mode of the first; its deafness is complacently cultivated because it is agreeable and it offers a positive satisfaction of its own.[3]

To attend to this cry, we require institutions that 'put power into the hands of men who are able and anxious to hear and understand it'.[4] Are the ESI doctors, who are entrusted by society to attend to the agony and suffering of the working poor, able and anxious to hear and understand this cry? Or do they simply not hear it, because it is 'agreeable' to do so? This deafness had its costs: the critical delay in Madodari Devi's diagnosis, the physical pain she endured over those weeks and the potentially deeper injuries to her soul induced by this normalized non-attention.

Envy, Affliction and Soul Corrosion

Madodari Devi did not know what cancer was. Until the end, she believed that her illness had been caused by the sorcery activities of her kin sister in the village. '*Laṃgṛā bhī nahīṃ rahne diyā bahn* [Sister didn't even let me live as a cripple]', she said bewilderedly, as she lay in the hospice. '*Pūrī zindagī le liyā hai* [She's taken my very life].' I had heard stories about her kin sister, who was allegedly learning witchcraft from a master shaman and inflicting spirits (*bhūt-pret*s) onto persons, inducing ailments in the extended family, such as anxiety, dizziness, psychedelic visions, body aches, fevers, digestive disorders and Madodari Devi's bleeding. Although Madodari Devi went to *ojhā*s in the village to try to get rid of these spirits, Naresh Singh, her nephew and the eldest of her son's cousins in Delhi, suspects that she did not find the right shaman or do the proper rituals, and the bleeding worsened into cancer. '*Blood girte girte to sūkhne lagegā, kamzor ho jāyegā, to bīmārī honī hī hai* [As she bleeds she'll begin to wither, she'll become weak, and then an illness is bound to befall her].' Medical knowledge is not being claimed here as much as 'hard' causality,[5] which may indeed have existed, in that her belief that her ailment was caused by sorcery may have caused her to focus attention on *ojhā*s and pursue only symptomatic relief from doctors in the village, allowing her cancer to grow to an advanced stage, and hastening her death. The *ojhā*s, if they saw themselves as healers, could have encouraged Madodari Devi, upon learning of the bleeding, to simultaneously pursue investigations and treatment from allopathic doctors. But this was not suggested, perhaps due to the prevalent belief that spirits must be exorcized before allopathic medicines can be efficacious, or the *lālac* (avarice) for short-term earnings, a phenomenon by no means specific to *ojhā*s, but also found amongst allopathic doctors who readily reach for intravenous bottles and injections rather than try to address the underlying disease.

There may have been another causative role of spirit affliction practices. The deeper source of sorcery activities in the village is said to be *jalan* (envy), and particularly, the inability to endure micro-advancements of proximate others, especially small changes in eating or clothing standards visible amongst members of one's patrilineal family. '*Vo dekh nahīṃ sah rahe haiṃ* [They cannot bear to see (such advances)]', persons in the village say, to explain why spirits are inflicted onto others. *Jalan* tends towards the dark, obsessive, Iago-like desire to undermine or destroy others. '*Kaise maiṃ kyā karūṃ je yah kaise gire* [How and what can I do so that this person somehow falls]', is the thinking, says Naresh, though in this case, Madodari Devi's family had a marginally better income only for a time, when three of her sons were doing wage work, while her kin sister had one son working in Delhi.

'Malevolence', writes Bhikhu Parekh, in interpreting Gandhiji's thought, 'implied ill will or hatred towards others, a wish to harm them even when they posed no threat to one's interests and simply because one enjoyed seeing them suffer', and malevolence in thought, word, or action constituted *hiṃsā* (injury, violence).[6] Spirit affliction practices, and the *jalan* that drives them, are certainly *hiṃsā*, and may have grave effects on their targets. The intuitive awareness of the malevolence and ill will of another person, perceived and spoken of as an intimate, hostile and foreign presence within one's being, may be enough to cause disturbance, anxiety and dis-ease—indeed, affliction—within the soul of the targeted person. Madodari Devi was preoccupied, plagued and possessed by thoughts and feelings of her kin sister's malevolent intentions and designs. Could not this affliction in the soul, induced by *jalan*, have invited, if not exacerbated, the progress of a life-taking illness, such as cancer?

More disturbing than the non-attention of doctors and *jalan* in the village was the strange behaviour of Tapesvar during this episode. Despite her poor health for some years, and the advice of a doctor to take her for surgery, Tapesvar was nonchalant about getting her treated, and remitted only enough money for symptomatic treatment in the village. Only when her condition worsened severely, and due to pressure from Naresh Singh and other co-workers in the factory, he agreed to bring her to Delhi. He went through the motions of taking her to the ESI hospital and AIIMS, but would get impatient and angry, and neglect to follow up on crucial tasks, thereby collaborating with the non-attention of doctors. She also intimated that she was not being given adequate nourishment, while staying in his small rented room. When she would cry out in agony in the middle of the night, he would vent his rage for the lost wages and expenses involved in her treatment to date, saying, '*Pūrā ghar barbād karke rakh diyā! Kamre meṃ pareśān karke rakhī hai! Mariyo nahīṃ rahī hai jaldī!* [You've ruined our entire home! You're causing so much trouble in the room! You're not even dying quickly!]' As her condition deteriorated, he expressed the desire to send her back to the village rather than pursue further investigations. In the AIIMS cancer ward, he would verbally abuse her when she would lose control of her bodily functions. When she required units of blood, he did not give, and attempted to dissuade others from doing so. On the day of her death, he resisted the idea of buying a new sari for her last rites, and was strangely absent at the critical times of lighting the pyre and gathering the ashes.[7]

These were the darker soul corrosions, the deeper cancer, which causally contributed to this matricide, in the delaying and damaging effects of his non-attention on her diagnosis and treatment, and in the effects of his attitude on others, such as Naresh Singh, who became unsure, hesitant, and quasi-paralyzed into partial spectatorship. Naresh felt a sense of duty and responsibility towards Madodari Devi, as well as compassion, but was concerned that if he took a more active role in her treatment, and she were to die, persons in the *jalan*-infused atmosphere of the village would raise suspicious questions about his possible hand in her death, attributing motives say of disputes over property that existed between the families. Indeed, Naresh had wanted to bring Madodari Devi to Delhi much earlier, at his own expense, but she had declined, given that her own son was not encouraging her to come. Her eldest son, Bajrang, who stayed in the village, also urged her to go to Delhi, but she placed more value on the views and wishes of Tapesvar. Unlike Bajrang, Tapesvar was earning wages in a quasi-steady job in the city, and though he might not have always generously shared his earnings, especially after marriage, these wages created a certain respectability (*izzat*) for him in her eyes. But these were costly misjudgements, which she perhaps only realized during her ordeal in Delhi, when she found herself turning to Naresh and others for compassion, care and hope.

Immortality, Rebirth and Retribution

As Madodari Devi's shrouded body lay in the shade of a tree at the cremation ground, Varmaji, a polishing worker who was close to the family, remarked that her death had at least brought an end to her suffering of the last months—the physical pain, the difficulties of going to doctors and hospitals, the dependence on the compassion of proximate others, all of it. '*Ātmā nikal jāne ke bād śarīr se, ātmā ko aur śarīr ko bhī śāntī mil jātī hai* [After the soul leaves the body, both the soul and the body get peace]', he said, adding, '*Ātmā to amar hai, kabhī martī nahīṃ hai* [The soul is immortal, it never dies].' This teaching is echoed in the *Gītā-sār* (the essence of the *Gītā*), reproduced on posters and included in incense boxes, and also posted on the wall inside the metal factory: '*Ātmā nā paidā hotī, nā martī hai* [The soul is not born, nor does it die].'[8] The *ātmā* (soul) is indestructible, says the *Bhagavad Gītā*: '*Oh descendent of Bharata, this embodied Self existing in everyone's body can never be killed. Therefore you ought not to grieve for all (these) beings*' (2: 24, 2: 30).[9] But as one thought about the apathy and non-attention that had contributed to Madodari Devi's death, it was not easy to find consolation in this teaching. The assertion of the soul's immortality seemed to let off perpetrators of oppression and violence. Do not suicide-murderers take solace from such a theology to forgive their acts of murder as well as to assure for themselves, as Ramchandra Gandhi suggests, a place for their own immortal souls in heaven? The *Gītā-sār* lends itself dangerously to the interpretation that 'one is not this body at all'. '*This body is not yours; neither do you belong to this body. It is made of fire, water, air, earth, and sky, and there it will vanish. But the soul is firm. So what are you?*'[10] But should we not seek to honour, protect and nurture the *jīvātmā* [as finite image of *Ātman* (Self)] in toto—the body (*śarīr*), mind (*man*), heart (*dil*) and soul (*ātmā*)? Simone Weil writes, 'There is something sacred in every man. . . . It is neither his person, nor the human personality in him, which is sacred to me. It is he. The whole of him.

The arms, the eyes, the thoughts, everything. Not without infinite scruple would I touch anything of this.'[11]

The *ātmā* may be immortal, but it feels things deeply, and is vulnerable to *pareśānī* (travails), *dukh* (grief) and *ṭhes* (deep hurt). The body, says Varmaji, is like a house or dwelling (*makān*) for the soul, and if one demolishes such a dwelling, '*to usmem rahnevālā bahut pareśān hogā. To nahīṃ karnā cāhie* [the dweller inside will be very troubled. So one shouldn't do that].' These deep vulnerabilities were experienced by Madodari Devi, and were visible in her agitations, anxiety and despair in the hospital and hospice, especially when she was left alone for extended periods of time. '*Ātmā bahut zyādā dukhit, bahut zyādā pareśān thī* [Her soul was greatly aggrieved, extremely distressed].' And if her life was abbreviated by this disease, one might say that a deep injury was done to her *ātmā*, in unexpectedly truncating its possibilities for *mokṣa* (self-realization) in this body. 'The soul, one's own or another's', writes Ramchandra Gandhi, 'can be injured, although it is indestructible', and 'any abrupt or unjustified destruction of any of its incarnations delays and distorts its karmic journey towards absolute freedom.' If the *ātmā* is deeply vulnerable to injury, distortion and dislocation, immortality cannot be consoling enough.[12]

Once the dwelling of the *ātmā* decays, deteriorates or is abruptly demolished, the soul vacates the body to find a new dwelling, Varmaji says, as expressed in the *Gītā*. But is there any consolation in the idea of Madodari Devi being reborn on this earth? Does a new *makān* guarantee a better existence for the *ātmā*? The Buddha says, 'misery is birth again and again'. One seeks release from decay, disease and death in every birth, the sufferings induced by craving, including the desire to rebuild the *makān*, to be reborn as this very same ego.[13] At the root of the longing for rebirth, Ramchandra Gandhi says, is the egoistic desire for 'a separate space for oneself' and for 'more and more of what one was disappointed in the first place'.[14] Rebirth becomes consolation only in the context of *sādhanā* (ethical, existential and spiritual striving), which may require many births to get closer to *mokṣa*, the release from the misery of egoistic, isolated and terrified dwelling within a separate and exclusive *makān*, into a consciousness of residing within all dwellings, all forms. But where is the solace of the idea of rebirth into this *Kalyugī*[15] *narak* (decivilizing netherworld) of cancerous soul corrosions that militate against our feeble attempts at *sādhanā*? As the decivilizing process of the *yug* (epoch) intensifies, will it not become even more difficult for Madodari Devi's *ātmā* to get closer to *mokṣa* in her next births?

A karmic explanation for Madodari Devi's death was offered by Naresh Singh, who spoke of the way she had treated Baba, his grandfather (her father-in-law), in the village, viewing him as an 'other' person (*dūsrā ādmīn*) rather than 'one's own' (*apnā*). If Baba visited their home, on the way back from the market, she would rarely offer him something to eat, and would get angry if her husband asked her to do so. The manner of Madodari Devi's death, said Naresh, was but the working out of the karmic consequences of this non-attentiveness: '*Isko sāth nahīṃ diyā, to aisā hī bacce log bhī thoṛā ho gayā* [She didn't look after Baba, so her children also turned out a bit like that].' '*Karmoṃ kā ḍanḍ, Kalyug meṃ turant* [Punishment for one's acts, meted out immediately in the *Kalyug*]', said Varmaji. But is the idea of karmic retribution consoling? '*Yah karmoṃ kā phal hai* [This is the fruit of actions]' is a rapid proletarian response to another's tragedy in one's midst, but often reflects the *raftār* (speed) of life and the lack of time, desire or interest on the part of spectating persons, preoccupied with their own travails, to inquire into the deeper causes of one another's suffering. It can function as a way of distancing oneself from obligations of responsibility or feelings of compassion towards that suffering. But proletarians also speak of the world as a deeply unjust place, in which people do not get what they karmically deserve.[16] Was Madodari Devi's death retribution for her refusal to properly look after Baba, or for some other act in her past? Without being privy to the deep details of her karmic record, how can we say? Is it a consoling thought that the othering of other persons, and the suffering that flows from it, is endlessly repeated and retributively transmitted across generations, such that Tapesvar's children will do the same injurious things to him, and so on? Can we even be assured that punishments are always meted out in fair and comprehensible proportion to karmic crimes? The most trivial act of wrongdoing, Ramchandra Gandhi suggests, may arbitrarily, and not proportionately or comprehensibly, invite the most harsh and radical form of suffering upon the doer, in a way that affirms the 'absoluteness of even slight evil' and the 'absolute groundlessness' of radical suffering.[17] This too is not a very consoling thought, that a refusal to offer a *roṭī* to Baba could invite such days and nights of despair for Madodari Devi, as she wasted away to death.

Violence, Culpability and Forfeiture

In the winter of 1946–1947, in the wake of Hindu–Muslim violence, Gandhiji toured Noakhali district in East Bengal. One day, he was met by a woman, who approached him with outspread arms, having possibly lost a child in the recent carnage. She said nothing, but her despair and suffering were understood by Gandhiji. '*Jo usne diyā, vo usne le liyā* [What God gave, He has taken]', were Gandhiji's words to her. Nirmal Kumar Bose, who was at Gandhiji's side, could not bring himself to translate these words into Bengali, but where there was fear (*bhay*) in her visage, Bose could begin to see a glimpse of *śāntī* (calmness).[18]

But what did Gandhiji mean? God takes back, and we lose, what we do not properly take care of. In the carnage of the Noakhali riots, we—society as a whole—and not only the direct perpetrators, in not protecting the lives of the murdered, established that those persons did not belong to us, suggests Ramchandra Gandhi. The *Gītā-sār* is correct: '*What of yours has been taken that you cry?*'[19] God bestows all, not to us as possessors and manipulators, but as 'trustees', of all things, beings and nature as a whole. If we fail to recognize this, if we do not see all things as 'ours' (*apnā*) to honour, protect and nurture, we effectively forfeit these things, and compel God to take them back. This failure to act as trustees of all that is given to us is the cancerous *karm* of the *yug*. Tapesvar, the ESI doctors and the spectating, proximate micro-society did not act as proper trustees of Madodari Devi. Society more generally has not acted as proper trustees of the civilizens (*vāsīs*, dwellers) of this country. Had it done so, would there be such matricidal causes as undernourishment and the paucity of early detection procedures for cervical cancer in our villages and cities?

In our injurious *karm* to one another and to non-human life, we are also cursing *Prithvī Mā* (mother earth), a lucid image of the nurturing, regenerative, divine feminine. That Madodari Devi's cancer was rooted in the *baccedānī* (womb) instructively alerts us that it is the very organs, powers and symbols of regenerativity that we are assaulting, mocking and murdering in this *yug*, through, for example, over-consumption of natural resources, the defiling of rivers and oceans, the poisoning of the earth by chemical fertilizers and nuclear waste, and the overheating of our life-sustaining atmosphere. These matricides are suicides in embryo. The deep meaning of the mother, says Varmaji, is *jagat jananī*, cosmic birthgiver, in whose womb even God takes refuge (*śaraṇ*) so as to be born as incarnated forms (*avatārs*). But we fail to honour her in her images. In the words of Varmaji, '*Mār dete haiṃ, tariyāṃ dete haiṃ, gālī de dete haiṃ, bhagā dete haiṃ ghar se. Socte haiṃ mā kā mahatva hī kyā haiṃ?* [People beat her, bully her, abuse her, push her out of the home. They think, what is the importance at all of the mother?]' In submerging Madodari Devi's ashes into the defiled, almost murdered Jamuna river, a neglected and unwanted mother was taken back into the afflicted womb waters of the Mother. *Yah karmoṃ kā phal hai* (This is the fruit of actions), but the *karm* comprises the totality of *lāparvāhī*, *hiṃsā*, Noakhalis, and matricides in the present. The results (*phal*) are the forfeiture of one another and of the earth, and the drastic distortions of our *mokṣa* odysseys.

Martyrdom, *Prāyaścitt* and Anti-metastasis

'Cells destroying themselves, multiplying insanely, that is cancer, a biological insanity which matches in physiology the murder of man by man and the insane multiplication of reproduction which threatens not only our species but all species of life', writes Ramchandra Gandhi.[20] Cancer is a pathology induced not only by carcinogenic agents external to the body but also within the core of cells themselves, which self-divide without restraint, just as we do when we view others as true others (self-dividing into ego and not-self), and which gives rise to a metastatic melée of suicide-murder of one another and of the ecological conditions for the possibility of life. The matricidal process that claimed the life of Madodari Devi is but an image of the workings of this melée in the everyday life of the poor of this country. This cancer may have origins outside the body, in the epochal process of decivilization and decline, which acts upon, shapes, corrupts and corrodes *ātmā*s. But the life of this cancer is sustained and reproduced by its ability to strike roots in the *ātmā*, elicit acceptance, cooperation and collaboration with the *yug*'s precepts, and generate *Kalyugī* souls. These activities produce and reproduce the *yug*, in a decentred yet interconnected manner, advancing the progress of the *yug* towards a telos of decline and *pralay* (world dissolution).

But why must Time exhibit such a hard, inflexible, Other-like telos that involves such apparently inescapable suffering? Does such a hard telos indeed exist, or is this trajectory but the working out of the accumulated and inescapable effects of the metastatic cancerous *karm* of

*Kalyugī ātmā*s raging within the womb of Time?[21] If it is the latter, as I hope, can the womb be saved, salvaged and rescued from this burning cancer? We may be fatally mistaken if we expect a future *avatār* to descend and assume the form of a master weaver-butterfly to stitch this womb together, as Sri Krishna did for Uttara's womb, which was savagely burnt by the *astra*[22] released by Ashvatthama's vengeful *tāṇḍav* (destructive dance) of *hiṃsā*.[23] Are we even worthy of such *avatāric* interventions? Our only chance at such grace may lie in undertaking ourselves the hard, *aṃś avatāric*[24] work of stitching, re-weaving and regenerating the womb that we are savaging in the *Kalyug*.

Madodari Devi may have intimated something of this *aṃś avatāric* work in the way that she died. Her untimely death might have been induced by the actions of those around her, but as she underwent the ordeal of treatment, she never seemed to hold anything against the doctors or Tapesvar for their *lāparvāhī*. In her last moments, she could have urged her sons and nephews to take revenge upon her kin sister. She did not. She withdrew her own world-destroying *astra*s, her own arrow-like blades of Eraka grass.[25] '*Baṛhiyā se rahihā, mil julke rahihā, laṛāī jhagṛā mat karihā* [Live harmoniously with one another, don't quarrel-fight amongst yourselves]', she told them. This was a sacrifice of the ego, what Ramchandra Gandhi terms true martyrdom, and a refusal to cooperate with the vicious cycle of suicide-murder. Her death was a bearing witness to the truths of non-attention, deprivation and suffering, and perhaps also, consciously or otherwise, a dying for the distorted actions of others, a taking on of the causal effects of others' *adharm* (distortion, deviation), of Tapesvar, the *ojhā*s, the doctors, the spectators and society as a whole. Gandhiji 'democratised this kind of vicarious suffering'[26] or suffering for the sins of others, Ashok Kelkar observes. Gandhiji made Christs—*aṃś avatār*s—of us all. This is not to condone or justify the *adharm* that generates the suffering and death of such often involuntary martyrs, but to seek to honour in their unjustified suffering and death the possible intimations of the weaving work of *prāyaścitt* for *adharm* in this *yug*.

Madodari Devi's words also evoke a sense of the atonement required of the living. She was asking her nephews to non-cooperate, resist and defy the cancer of *adharm* in the proletarian social fabric, with non-envy, understanding and togetherness. '[J]ust as the catalysts or bacteria, such as yeast, operate by their mere presence in chemical reactions', Simone Weil writes, 'so in human affairs the invisible seed of pure good is decisive when it is put in the right place'.[27] This is the *aṃś avatāric* work: the seeding of the good contra the *yug*'s self-and-other terminating genes, the generating of anti-bodies against the afflictions of the social and ecological body. Varmaji speaks of the vital need of all of us, in the present, to '*thoṛā thoṛā saccāī utpann karnā* [give rise to bits of truth]', in resistance against oppression and injustice, and in truthful exchanges with one another. These exchanges and struggles can act as the *araṇī* sticks[28] to ignite truth-fires (*saccāī kī āg*) that are multi-centred yet interconnected, just as the metastasis itself, yet which seek to save life, not destroy it. They burn away the cancer at its multiple sources. They prefigure and bring forward the *pralay*.

In the *Kalyug*, the *Purāṇa*s say, '[M]en will be afflicted by old age, disease, and hunger, and from sorrow there will arise depression, indifference, deep thought, enlightenment, and virtuous behavior.'[29] If Madodari Devi's death gives rise to even a few sparks of *pralay*-prefiguring *prāyaścitt*, within proletarian worlds and beyond, her death—her matricide—will not have been without its own blessings.

Glossary

adharm: distortion, deviation
aṃś avatār: finitely complete incarnation of the divine
ātmā: soul
bhūt-pret: spirit
hiṃsā: injury, violence
jalan: envy
Kalyug: present, decivilizing epoch, alleged to have begun in 3102 BC
karm: action
lāparvāhī: non-attention
makān: house, dwelling
mokṣa: self-realization
ojhā: shaman
pralay: world dissolution
prāyaścitt: atonement
yug: epoch

Notes and References

1. Harmala Gupta, 'Creating a cancer-free world for women', *The Hindu*, 8 June 2008.

2. '*Vahan hamari sunvai nahin hai* (We are not heard there) is the dominant expression used to refer to one's encounters with government hospitals and dispensaries', writes Veena Das, in describing the experiences of the urban poor in Delhi. Veena Das, 'Technologies of Self: Poverty and Health in an Urban Setting.' *Sarai Reader 03: Shaping Technologies* (New Delhi: Sarai, 2003), p. 98.
3. Simone Weil, 'Human Personality', in *Simone Weil: An Anthology*, ed. Sian Miles (New York: Weidenfeld and Nicolson, 1986), p. 52.
4. Ibid., p. 53.
5. '[M]illions of ordinary people do not talk about subtle and long causal processes; they simply insist on the hard connections'. Ramchandra Gandhi, 'Earthquake in Bihar—The Transfiguration of Karma', in *Language, Tradition and Modern Civilization*, ed. Ramchandra Gandhi (Pune: Indian Philosophical Quarterly Publications, 1983), p. 133.
6. Bhikhu Parekh, *Colonialism, Tradition and Reform: An Analysis of Gandhi's Political Discourse* (New Delhi: SAGE Publications, 1999), pp. 131–132.
7. Tapesvar's behavior was a cause of deep bafflement for Naresh Singh, co-workers, and others in the milieu, and he suffered respect-losses from this episode. It is possible that he had his own undisclosed reasons for these acts, beyond crude self-interest or resource constraints. When asked, after the death, if he had felt *lagāv* (affection) for his mother, his reply was yes.
8. Quoted in Rajmohan Gandhi, *Revenge and Reconciliation: Understanding South Asian History* (New Delhi: Penguin, 1999), p. 22. Translation slightly modified.
9. *Bhagavadgita, With the Commentary of Sankaracarya*, trans. Swami Gambhirananda (Calcutta: Advaita Ashrama, 2000), pp. 73, 78.
10. Rajmohan Gandhi, *Revenge and Reconciliation*, p. 22.
11. Simone Weil, 'Human Personality', pp. 50–51.
12. Ramchandra Gandhi, *I am Thou: Meditations on the Truth of India* (Pune: Indian Philosophical Quarterly Publications, 1984), pp. 160–162. 'Only if we combine the idea of immortality with vulnerability in a single vision of the mysterious simultaneously eternal and temporal living being can we hope both to have reverence for all life and also not worship as the whole truth of eternal life any one period or manifestation of it' (Ibid., p. 162).
13. *The Dhammapada*, trans. John Ross Carter and Mahinda Palihawadana, quoted in Charles Hallisey, 'Buddhism', in *Death and the Afterlife*, ed. Jacob Neusner (Cleveland: The Pilgrim Press, 2000), p. 6.
14. Ramchandra Gandhi, 'Blessings', Lecture, Delhi, 9 December 2006.
15. The *Kalyug* is the final epoch in the four *yug* cycle of cosmic time, allegedly beginning in 3102 BCE, and according to workers' narratives, as recently as ten, fifty, or one hundred years ago. The epoch is characterized by an intensifying, decivilizing process of the distortions of social and ecological worlds and of souls (*ātmā*s).

16. '"As we sow, so shall we reap" is the general, broad idea, but it is pathetically false in human life: a good man suffers, and a bad man seems to get away with everything.' Ramchandra Gandhi, 'Earthquake in Bihar', p. 131.
17. Ibid, p. 133.
18. Ramchandra Gandhi recounts this story, as told to him by Nirmal Kumar Bose, in 'The Importance of Gandhi's Interfaith Faith', Lecture, Jamia Islamia University, 16 November 2006. A similar episode, prior to Gandhiji's fast in Calcutta in 1947, is recorded in Nirmal Kumar Bose and P. H. Patwardhan, *Gandhi in Indian Politics* (Bombay: Lalvani Publishing House, 1967), p. 11. Gandhiji told refugees in Noakhali that he had come 'not to give consolation but to give courage' (Ibid., p. 8).
19. Rajmohan Gandhi, *Revenge and Reconciliation*, p. 22. Translation slightly modified.
20. Ramchandra Gandhi, *I am Thou,* p. 141.
21. This womb of Time, in which birth, life, death, *yug* cycles, and the entire *līlā* (cosmic drama) of self-imaging are brought forth, might be thought of as inhering within the Timeless (the *Ātman*), the divine Mother, *jagat jananī.*
22. *Astra*: weapon endowed with supernatural or divine powers.
23. To avert the destruction of the world, Arjun withdrew his *astra* in the battle with Ashvatthama, but the latter could not do so, and his *astra* (which started its trajectory as a mere blade of grass, instructively demonstrating the destructive potentialities of even a micro-act of pointing, targeting, and othering) found its way to the womb of Abhimanyu's widow, Uttara.
24. *Aṃś*: fragment, as a finitely complete image of the whole. *Ātmā*s are *aṃś avatār*s, or finitely complete incarnations of the divine.
25. Deadly blades of Eraka grass, infused with the destructive power of a curse on the Yadavas for mocking gender and generativity, were uprooted and used by the Yadavas, in an intoxicated frenzy, to destroy one another. For a reading of this suicide-murder as a cancer-like rebellion against the non-dualist presence of Sri Krishna, see Ramchandra Gandhi, *I am Thou*, pp. 258–259.
26. Quoted in Ramchandra Gandhi, 'Earthquake in Bihar', p. 138.
27. Simone Weil, 'Human Personality', p. 76.
28. *Araṇī* sticks: wooden sticks for generating sacred fire.
29. *Linga Purana*, quoted in Wendy Doniger O'Flaherty, *The Origins of Evil in Hindu Mythology* (Berkeley: University of California Press, 1976), p. 40.

Afterword

An Imagined Dialogue between Daya Krishna and Ramchandra Gandhi

Shail Mayaram

Daya Krishna (henceforth D. K.) and Ramchandra Gandhi (henceforth R. G.) are often represented as contrary to each other, one regarded as celebrating multiple traditions of reason, the other as putting us in touch with the deepest religiosity that is self-realization. This exercise is about lines of philosophical difference, but also convergence as D. K. and R. G. have reflected on some of the most crucial issues in the history of thought.

D. K. and R. G. meet at the India International Centre (IIC). They embrace delightedly and then decide to meet later for a drink at the IIC bar.

[At the bar]

R. G.: Tell me, how is Francine?

D. K.: Just the other day, she was remembering you, Ramu, and the time in Kerala when you refused to enter the temple because she had not been allowed in as a 'foreigner' and because she wasn't a Hindu.

R. G.: How little these ritualistic brahmans know what it means to be and feel like a Hindu! How sensitively Ananthamurthy explores their consciousness in his novel.

D. K.: Ramu, for very long, I have been wanting to have a conversation on what being a Hindu means. Your stance on advaita is well known.

But I have felt and protested against the stronghold of advaita on Indian philosophy. It has been argued that it is the dominant school in the first millennium. This is completely counter to the evidence. The history of Indian philosophy must be rewritten placing Buddhism at the centre for fifteen centuries from 500 BC to AD 1000. Śaṃkara's hagiographies and commentaries only became popular after the twelfth century. And neo-Vedānta which was different from Advaita Vedānta of the first millennium was really a nineteenth-century invention of the Bengal literati who saw in the Upaniṣads the possibility of reconciling Indian and Western civilizations. But they ignored two millennia of philosophical debate in India.

R. G.: I have not been concerned with advaita in history, but with philosophical advaita. Advaita represents a 'truth', the truth of life, of the non-duality of being, 'the truth that you and I are not other than one another'. You know very well that I have argued that advaita is both faith and realization. Its truth is that there is only Self and its self-images and that there is no real not-Self or otherness.

D. K.: I see advaita as denying the reality of difference in its ideal of 'all-Identity'. Surely the world we live in and the experiences we have are enormously diverse. It also denies that human beings see 'possibility' in things and in situations and make efforts to create new worlds.

R. G.: I have taken care of this criticism of advaita. Philosophical advaita would celebrate difference and diversity. For self and other, I and Thou, must not be seen in opposition. Annihilationism arises from a position in which the other is seen as intrinsically other. But what seem to be apparent others are really shadow images of the self, aren't they? Once we widen our self-awareness, the self–other opposition appears false.

Advaita or non-duality is not only the truth of all things but is also the truth of India. And it is what makes India a distinctive civilizational space. So many religions and ideologies have followed dualistic paths seeing I and Thou as separate. This is why I gave the title *I am Thou* to my book to counter Martin Buber who saw 'I and Thou' [the title of Buber's book] as a duality. But Dayaji, look at what Ramana told one of his devotees who was bothered about the question of his identity: it is only the 'I am' that matters (eyes gleaming).

Ramana was also able to bring together Brahman and *māyā*. In a beautiful parable he explains their relationship by referring to a group of women carrying water on their heads from a spring to their homes in the village. Their chatter is *māyā* while the quiet water in the earthen pots is Brahman and the two 'live together' in harmony.

D. K.: To my mind, both Advaita Vedānta and Sāṃkhya misunderstand the outgoing movement of consciousness. Can there be more *avidyā* than to think of the Lord's or Iśvar's creative activity as rooted in *avidyā*? The work of imagination is reduced to the illusory and unreal! Unbelievable!!

R. G.: I am in absolute agreement with you. In Svarāj, that is based on my letters to Anjali Sen [then Director of the National Gallery of Modern Art], I wrote against the doctrinaire Vedanta claim that all forms are illusion and also opposed 'unguarded Buddhism' and its contention that no form is Self. Buddhism needs to take the self seriously.[1]

D. K.: There is also an overemphasis on suffering in Buddhism. Life is surely much more than *dukkha* (sorrow)!

R. G.: But Buddhism certainly brings in the idea of nothingness as the 'limitless not-thingness of self-awareness or emptiness'. This was also the teaching of Śrī Kṛṣṇa and Jñaneśvar's communication to the assembly of scholars, which is his great commentary on the Gita.

D. K.: People have pointed out our intellectual disagreement, but we agree on the idea of self-consciousness as distinct from consciousness. Self-consciousness imagines, expresses itself in creative acts and is open to levels beyond itself. It has a capacity for attending and withdrawing that is the core of freedom.

R. G.: I have seen the reunion of Śiva–Śakti and Śūnyata in Tyeb Mehta's Santiniketan triptych. The androgynous form represents a source of joy and bliss underlying all the pain of the world and there is also the non-dualist identity represented by the young Madonna and the ṣhe-goat. Tyeb's work has an epic character. In the triptych, the turtle-yogi represents the slaughtered and unmourned dead. But there is also the digambara or 'skyclad' karmayogi and the otherness dissolving *mayūra mudrā* suggesting that the Self is, *tat tvam asi* (You are that) its upaniṣadic mantra. And quite unlike Gaugin, Tyeb is not concerned with civilizing the adivasis or trivializing them as savage.

D. K.: Ramu, I also deplore the I-centric prison house of consciousness and see the self as a part of a web of inter-personal relations, the domain of relationality. As I argue in my most recent book the 'other' in its indefinite multiplicity is an essential constituent of consciousness itself.

R. G.: This is precisely what I have tried to express in the idea of address that we call *sambodhan*. Dayaji, as you well know, I have made the argument that in addressing another, I awaken the other's self to self-awareness.

I have been troubled also by the otherness of nature in Western thought. How different some of the Indian reflection has been! But it seemed to me that the movement to build the Rama temple at Ayodhya based itself on the otherness of the other-human and non-human. The mobilization claimed to be in defence of the essence of Hinduism. But how horrifically violent it was and how distant from Hinduism. Hindus do not deserve a Rama temple till they have expiated for the sin of untouchability and for turning out Sītā.

And so I wrote of Sītā's *rasoī*, her kitchen as a gendered space that incorporates the adivasi aboriginals and also non-human life.

How important it was for Ramana to feed the peacocks. Has that cow been fed, he would ask, concerned about Lakshmi. The white peacock screamed and lamented anticipating Ramana's impending death and his last recorded words were, 'Have you given that bird its dinner?' Brother Michael has tried to put together animal stories from the Ramana Ashram.

D. K.: Ramu, just think of the wonder of the story of coming into being. It does not start with what we understand as living, either in the plant or the animal form. It goes much further and includes the world we call nonliving, which itself is presupposed for any living thing to come into being in the world that we know. The diversity and variety in the nonliving world is as incredible as that found in the world of living beings. One need only look at the cloud formations in the sky or the line of mountain peaks where vegetation stops and snow begins or even visit a store mart, if not a jeweler's shop, to be convinced of this.[2]

I worry Ramu (laughingly) that your advaita-steamroller will level out all these fascinating differences in the inanimate world in the name of *māyā* or non-dual consciousness!

Do you see, incidentally, your advaita having any role to play in our collective penance for millennia of untouchability practices?

R. G.: (With deepening furrows on his forehead) Dayaji, how terrible the question of untouchability has been.

D. K.: And the exclusion of Śūdras and women from *śruti* (Vedic revelation) more than half the population excluded from Sanskrit and its texts.

R. G.: Śaṃkara himself has been responsible for this exclusion.[3]

D. K.: I have made many enemies by writing about the intellectual dishonesty of Manu or of Śaṃkara when it comes to his *bhāṣya* on the *Chāndogya Upaniṣad* or on the *Brahma-sūtra*s. In the *Chāndogya Upaniṣad* story, Satyakama, the son of Jabala asks his mother about his gotra or lineage. She responds that she worked as a servant so she slept with many men and has no idea who his father was and asks him to use her name. [In Śaṃkara's commentary, Jabala responds to her son's enquiry about his lineage telling him that since she was very preoccupied with household duties she never got a chance to ask her husband about his lineage and asserts that the boy was of brahmanical lineage although his gotra was not known.]

R. G.: I have been troubled also by Śaṃkara's reading of the *Iśā Upaniṣads* that makes it exclusive. The very first *śloka* is marvelous as the non-dualist replacement of ritual and the idea that you can turn to yourself in prayer, realize the *ātman*. So you worship the deity that is your projected self, in order to awaken *ātmabodh* (self-awareness). But Śaṃkara's emphasis on ritual reduces its universality. This is also in the Swami Nikhilananda translation and in the Ramakrishna Mission's published version.

D. K.: Some other translations by the Ramakrishna Mission have been equally dishonest. Imagine, Ramakrishna and Vivekananda were talking about the universality of Hinduism, but the Mission translates the *Brahma-sūtra* stating that the truth of the *Upaniṣads*, of the brahman, should be kept from women and Śūdras. The *Upaniṣads* denied difference-but these modern commentators distinguish between the Śūdras and the non-Śūdras. Only the smṛtis and not śrutis should be available to them. This is shocking.

R. G.: Yes, I have been just as disappointed by these commentators.

D. K.: I know I have shocked the Indian philosophy establishment. Balasubramanian has written of 'Daya *adhyāsa*' [Daya's illusions]!

R. G.: How disastrous the secular humanist imagination crippled by both Eurocentrism and anthropocentrism has been. It has been the ideology of those who plunder nature. Both religious politics and secular politics involve annihilationist agendas.

D. K.: Yes, Ramu I have felt deeply the asymmetries of the knowledge system. We have internalized the west. I have become increasingly disillusioned with western thinkers. They have just not engaged with our critiques. Heesterman's work on kings and renouncers had been circulated to the pandits and they prepared such a careful response, but he himself refused to respond. And look at Staal's response; the pandits had taken great care to address his argument but he dismissed it lightly. Louis Dumont sidestepped the responses of so many Indian scholars and chose to respond only to Marriott.

D. K.: There has been an apartheid vis-à-vis traditional knowledges. But I am also disturbed by the nativist position. I do not agree with those who support indigenizing thought. Why should national boundaries determine any kind of enquiry? Thinking is intrinsically an act of freedom and creativity. The imagination will, and must, distance itself from one's inherited conceptual tradition.

How can one ignore the brilliance of Kant even if he comes from the European tradition?

I strongly felt the need to open pandits to questions, in order that the Indian tradition should continue to be a living one. We had to convince them that the exposure to new questions could provide a fertile soil for the growth of traditional thought. I felt that the dialogue must be one among equals. For over 10 years we carried out dialogues with traditional scholars in so many fields-logic, bhakti, architecture.

My young friend, Raghuramraju, has been arguing that the Saṃvāda projects did not treat pandits as philosophers. Wasn't Pandit Badrinath Shukla the great discovery of the Varanasi saṃvāda? He was then a living legend of the Navya Nyaya tradition.

But more often, I found traditional scholars caught in a trap of 'nostalgia' for the past. At Shimla I could not prevent myself from saying, 'I don't care what Mr Bhima said,' when they kept invoking the *Mahābhārata*. Traditional scholars must also engage with modernity, realise what is happening in the world and that all the answers do not lie in the tradition. I pointed to the pictures on the walls of the seminar room: Tagore, Gandhi. Do they mean anything to you, I asked them. These persons were not afraid of questioning tradition.

Raghuramraju has claimed that our saṃvāda was not as concerned with colonialism and its consequences. But there is colonialism as 'history' and a deeper colonialism which has seeped into our ways of thinking. It is this that I have been more worried about. Raghuramraju has commented that there is structural and temporal imbalance in the Saṃvāda project—in that there was less emphasis on modern Indian thought. But I did feel that we need not be centrally concerned with the latter as already so much work has been done on Sri Aurobindo, Vivekananda, Gandhi.

D. K.: Then there are things people have picked up without understanding adequately the contexts in which they were said. I told Jay Garfield that Indian philosophy can only be done in Sanskrit. By this I meant that Sanskrit must be recognized as one of the major languages of classical Indian thought. But, of course, how can one deny that it cannot be done in English-look at what K. C. Bhattacharya did. His exploration of the three aspects of consciousness: knowing, willing and feeling is remarkable in the history of philosophy. Kalidas's [his son] reformulation of the idea of alternative absolutes is one of the most outstanding contributions of Indian philosophy.

I have been very distressed by the 'death' of Sanskrit argument. It might become a self-fulfilling prophecy. As we found in our saṃvāda meetings scholars from Kashmir and Kerala spoke to each other in Sanskrit, which continues to be the language of living philosophical traditions.

R. G.: Dayaji, I have been wanting to discuss other Indian traditions with you. I have been thinking about the Sikh faith as Vir Vaishnavism. The *Granthsahib* consists not only of verses of gurus, but also of many saints, brought together under the tradition of praying under the sky, that comes from the Islamic tradition. How important the Sikh tradition of singing has been and of invoking all the sants, the yearning for the divine in the song, *Madho kab miloge* [expressing longing for Kṛṣṇa]. . . . Sufis also evoke the sovereignty of the divine as each sadhu/sant is called Badshah [king] and each sufi has a darbar [court]. Imagine that Shaikh Sarmad, the defiant Sufi of Delhi and Aurangzeb's contemporary had his head chopped off and nine times it is said to have rolled back up the stairs of the Jama Masjid.

D. K.: What a marvelous discussion we had—hosted by Srivats Goswami at Vrindavan—in three languages. Then Francine and Mukund edited the transcript published as the volume, *Bhakti*. Ramu, you should have been there.

I see bhakti [devotion] as a universal. If bhakti is the feeling that grasps the ultimate reality, then the human spirit in some form must have made this move in other cultures and other traditions and it is something we need to explore. Then the question is, how does one explore this domain of feeling? We need to ask, Does bhakti seek *mokṣa* in the realm of feeling? Or is the fruit of bhakti, bhakti itself?

R. G.: How beautifully bhakti has evoked folk traditions. Do you remember Vidya Niwasji's story of Radha's love? With utter delight, Radha dances on the rope stretched across a dangerously deep gorge crossing over to the other side. Because Krishna is on the other side and because she has no thought other than her love for him she is fearless. Rukmini, however, thinks of herself and is fearful and trembles as she attempts to cross. Radha's is a remarkable story of the love for the other, of bhakti.

R. G.: I have been arguing that in modern India there have been *sapta ṛṣī*, seven or eight sages. What a different politics they represent. What extraordinary moments. What Vivekananda heard was the first recorded feminine voice of divinity. It is in the story told of Swami Vivekananda by a brother monk during his visit to the Kshir Bhawani temple in Kashmir. 'Why, Mother, why did you permit the Islamic invader to destroy your own temples and images?' he asked. His lament was about how the invaders desecrated idols. Vivekananda heard the first recorded feminine voice of divinity in history, of Isvara and Allah as a compassionate mother who spoke from the sky admonishing him for this tirade against the idol breakers, 'What is it to you, Vivekananda, if I have permitted this. Do you protect me, or do I protect you?' This must silence forever all varieties of so-called 'defenders of Hinduism'!

In the case of Ramakrishna Paramhans, wasn't it extraordinary that a Vishnu worshipper became a Kali bhakta and explored the divine feminine. He became the priest of a Kali temple built by an untouchable and even washed their toilets with his long hair; then he became a Muslim and learnt how to perform the namaz; and also for a period became Radha, a woman.

D. K.: Yes, I do think it is quite extraordinary that the guru Totapuri found him and then recognized that his disciple was way ahead of him.

R. G.: Don't you think Ramakrishna was amazing in the way he was able to combine image-worship and advaita. Often, I also think of the 16-year-old Ramana gripped by the fear of death launching his inquiry into the question: Who am I? It is a reenactment, in 1896, of the *Kaṭhā Upaniṣad*'s account of Naciketa who got from Yama [death] the secret of immortality and self-realization, is it not? The intensity of his inquiry precipitated his self-realization. Ramana brings back the Father, as Arunachala.

D. K.: But I have been a sceptic and a rationalist with respect to theologies. Let me recite for you a *sher* I have written,

paighambharon kī bhīṛ hai mazhab bhī kam nahīn
phir bhī nā jāne bāt kyā hamko yaqīn ātā nahīn
rāhein hain anginat rahbar bhī kam nahīn
par badqismatī hamārī kī qadam uṭhtā nahīn

[There is a crowd of prophets and religions galore
yet I can't force myself into becoming a believer.
Paths are countless, guides no less
my misfortune that I can't follow with a single step.]

Is Buddhism a religion for our times, my grandson, Abhinav, asked me recently. Why don't we make a new religion, I told him!

But I don't share the view upheld by many philosophical traditions that mysticism or spirituality is unintelligible or nonsensical. The mystic's experience must be a category of modern thought just like the aesthetic or intellectual or moral experience.

R. G.: The mystical experience is like the dream-experience, is it not? To say, 'I am' is to stay with self-awareness given to one, to be one with the sky, to find the form in that formlessness.

D. K.: What little interest the philosophy of religion has had in religious experience itself, how religious concepts arise and find their meaning in religious experience. The truth of poetry is that of feelings while religion intimates a truth about the self and the world. But it is rarely treated as an autonomous domain and, if anything, the discussion has been dominated by Christianity.

R. G.: I have also written of the idea of a new religion where Buddhism and advaita come together. It is the dream state where I see the self imaged in all forms and also in formless nothingness. The idea that something comes out of nothing has to do with the miraculous.

I have been deeply saddened that my book, *I am Thou*, has been seen in terms of 'religion' rather than as a philosophical argument.

D. K.: The stories of the caricatures of philosophy are endless. I have myself been regarded as 'irreligious' just because I emphasized that India has a tradition of rationalist enquiry. On the other hand, some friends would seek to characterize me as non-dualist [laughs]!

R. G.: How close our thoughts are on this subject even though in the world of Indian philosophy we are seen as poles apart!

[He calls the waiter for another round of drinks, smiles and speaks with the waiter.]

R. G.: I see Indian civilization as Sindhutva, rather than Hindutva. The Indus is the lifegiving force for the subcontinent, suggesting how many streams met in our civilization. *Ardhanārīśvara* is not God who is half-woman, and Goddess who is half-man, the designations in Hindu iconography and theology, but Śiva-Pārvatī who are *purṇanaranārī*, the wholeness of maleness and femaleness together and separately.

Our svarāj involved both self-rule and self-realization. But how extraordinary the capacity of human beings to ceaselessly partition self-awareness into exclusive self and excluded not-self ('others', 'otherness'). This was the case with the partition of India when two million innocent human beings were slaughtered, whose souls still do not have valid passports to either country and so wander restlessly. In Arpana Caur's painting that I like so much, a pious Sikh [in 1947] has a cloud slung over his shoulder containing rain to grow food for his body and bearing his scripture on his head.

The partitioning by ego occurred again in the anti-Sikh riots of 1984. And yet again in the attack on Indian Parliament of 13 December 2001, which is the representative Assembly of over a billion people and symbolic of the revolutionary Indian democratic experiment of secularism and spirituality in a *satsanga*.

A recent debate we had in my Saturday seminar was on whether Savarkar was directly responsible for Gandhi's assassination. The defense of Savarkar ignored the fact that there is a sovereignty behind Gandhi's assassination.

I have found it so much more satisfying to tell stories in different ways through dance and drama. Some of them have been enacted by Shovana Narayan. One is the episode of Gandhi and Rambha mentioned in his autobiography. Mohan is afraid of ghosts and thieves, but the midwife-maid, Rambha, tells him the only thing to fear is fear itself. Whenever you are afraid take the name of Rama–Rama who is Iśvar, Allah, God. Rambha has already expressed to him her own doubts. *Tat tvam asi*, he tells her. No, she says. I am not that. I am this. I am this body. I am untouchable, people despise my very shadow. Mohan tells her that she is Urvashi, the celestial seductress of the sages, the very union of Siva and Parvati, the divine feminine herself. Rambha has another form, that of the oracle.

She foresees Mohan leading the satyagraha in South Africa, the walk of Charlie Chaplin, Gandhi's own Dandi march making salt in defiance of British laws and then India burning. . . . Rambha writhes in the fire of hatred. India herself is being destroyed. India must live, the home of many faiths. Gandhi has to die. His martyrdom a witness to Truth, which is Rama. . . .

Gandhi's death brings to Hinduism the symbolism of Christianity, does it not Dayaji? Gandhi was one of the most important Vaiṣṇava bhaktas of our times. He heard the voice of Arjuna within him; but also resonated with that of Christ.

D. K.: I must tell you Ramu that my own thoughts on pain have changed. I have been deeply affected by Francine's death. I have realized that one does not suffer from one's own pain, but 'suffers' by witnessing another's pain. This feeling of the pain of the other is surely the idea of 'Christ on the cross' who feels the pain and suffering of all humanity and also atones for it. Surely exchanges of pain and empathy are possible in the shared worlds of feeling we create.

R. G.: Yes, Christ is the first martyr of advaita. I make Babu, my main character, say this in my novel *Muniya's Light*.

D. K.: Much of my writing was to challenge the cobwebs shrouding the writing of the history of Indian philosophy. So I challenged the centrality of the Upaniṣads, *Brahma-sūtra*s and Gītā—the *prasthāna trayī* [canonical texts] as they are called. There was no advaita dominance as the history of Indian philosophy has tried to establish. Balasubramaniam has argued that there were Advaitins disguised as Mīmāṃsakas-why the disguise if they were so dominant?

In the *Ṛgveda* project, as Daniel, our young friend from Israel tells me, it has meant applying scissors to the Torah of the Indian tradition!

R. G.: The *Ṛgveda*, Dayaji is a foundational metaphor for us. It is hardly surprising that many elections were also rigged in keeping with our R(i) gvedic traditions!

D. K.: I have written tirelessly but no one is interested in reading these days! People do not read what has been written.

True I felt sometimes the loneliness of my effort. It involved having to defend Indian philosophy to the west and also having to criticize and provoke people in the world of Indian philosophy. But on that journey of saṃvāda there were other fellow travellers—Rege, Arindam,

R. C. Dwivedi, Mukund Lath. Yes, it was a philosophical adventure. My friend, Vivek Datta, has referred to this as my journey contrasting the argumentative Daya of earlier work to the Daya of *Indian Philosophy: A New Approach* who is more positive, seeking not just freedom from old conventions but also freedom to recreate, to play with philosophical conceptions, to sketch one's own story.

Sometimes there have been more difficult relationships. I challenged Karl Potter's idea of *mokṣa* centricity, which for me is a romantic view that captures the Western imagination seeking a spiritual India. Eliot Deutsch in a review in *Philosophy East and West* agreed with my questioning of *mokṣa* centricity. To K. C. Bhattacharya also *mokṣa* was the ultimate value but in a different way. He was interested in the different facets of freedom, in a pluralistic and dynamic context, which was very different from the Upaniṣadic or Śaṃkara's conception of *mokṣa* or notions of freedom. But I also used Potter's Bibliography to challenge advaita centricity. Balasubramanian responded that in this case he sided with me against Potter and K. C. Bhattacharya.

Later I told Karl Potter about our *Ṛgveda* project 'Daya Krishna on the *Ṛgveda*, imagine,' I wrote to him. I recalled the time when I first met Karl and Tony in Sagar. . . . He was from Seattle, which is also Francine's birthplace.

R. G.: I have thought of *mokṣa* very differently. I saw from Gandhi's life and death how *mokṣa* could be combined with martyrdom.

D. K.: Ramu, how shallow Nietzshe's idea of the 'will to power' is. Don't human beings create worlds of joy and beauty and meaningful human relationships that include relations with the living world, the world of nature and the 'transcendent'?

Europe has been obsessed with reason. Ramu, isn't it phenomenal—the capacity of consciousness to enlarge itself and grow beyond its limitations? Consciousness can through its effort open one's self to the transcendental aspect of all experience. Self-consciousness then reflects on consciousness.

Kant's essay 'Perpetual peace' and the Gita's conception of *paras-para* and *sreyas* articulate a vision of freedom as involving responsibility and the possibility of cultivating an other-centric consciousness. It is in the pursuit of nomos/dharma that I become truly human. I see the failure of Western thought as not having built on Kant and instead having retreated to an anarchic-existential-value neutral notion of freedom in existentialist and post-modernist thought that has built on Nietzsche.

D. K.: The Western tradition's idea of thought as logo-centric denies that there are aspects of human reality that are outside the domain of reason. Nāgārjuna argued that reason cannot prove anything and the Upaniṣads that ultimate truth could not be known by reason!!

Just look at what Sartre asserts-that 'hell is other people'. Ramu, how little he understood the relation between free beings which is surely not invariably 'hellish' in nature? What about the relationship between the human and the divine which is supposed to be freest of all?

In fact, our utmost creativity is not in the imaginative creations of art and literature or those of philosophical thought but in the intersubjective worlds that we create along with others.

I see both Indian and Western traditions as oriented to self-centricity in the analysis of action. Western thought has followed Descartes' distinction between mind and matter-thinking is characteristic of the mind. This is countered by Indian philosophical analysis which showed that mind is as much the object of consciousness as the body is—consciousness can itself become an 'object' in self-consciousness.

R. G.: Self-consciousness is a mode of being, not a mode of knowing.

D. K.: But it is really in Kashmir Saivism that consciousness was viewed as dynamic. Neither Kant nor the phenomenologists have seen the relation between consciousness and self-consciousness as a dynamic one.

It is important that we reflect on freedom and bondage. When the path of intellect, imagination or contemplation prevails over desire there is possibility of freedom. I have looked carefully at the Buddhist and Vedic conception of consciousness and the virtues of *śīla* and *yama*.[4] What has been ignored by both the Buddhist and the Vedic tradition, although the Buddhist does take it on in some measure is the intrinsic quality of consciousness for freedom and how we create contexts of joy and delight in which 'others' participate and find fulfilment.

Look at the yoga fashion all over the world today! But people are not concerned with the underlying philosophical issues. I disagree with Patanjali's idea of *kaivalya*, of freedom arising from disengagement. Instead one must reflect on the context of disengagement or engagement. When it comes to our encounter with a work of art, freedom comes from engagement not from disengagement. This might be at the level of mind, intellect, imagination, body. . . . This is also the case in politics and Gandhi has reflected on karma-yoga, the combination of withdrawal and engagement with the world.

R. G.: Let me change the subject, Dayaji. What do you think of this new form of cricket teams created by auctions? You and I have spoken of the game many times. But don't you think the market is taking over as it has so many areas of our lives.

My mind goes back to the winter days spent watching cricket on St Stephen's college cricket ground and the discussions with Professor S. K. Bose, when we spoke of the quintessential play of non-dualism and dialogue that good cricket presupposes, with all its metaphysical and civilizational implications.

D. K.: And yet there is the space for human creativity even here. My grandson Siddhanta—Sujata's son who we call Tintin—tells me Sachin is God, by which he means the human capacity for *puruṣartha* [achieving the ends of life] in all realms including sports and not in *mokṣa* and *dharma* alone.

R. G.: Dayaji, *Om Rumnaye namah*, as my friend, Harish Trivedi puts it, taking off on my *Om Ramanaye namah*!

Notes

1. Daniel Raveh has pointed out to me that one must not forget that Buddhism has many voices in this respect (personal communication).
2. Once again Daniel's comment is interesting: What Dayaji says here (or you say from Dayaji's mouth) echoes Śrī Aurobindo's philosophy. Interestingly Ramana and Aurobindo lived so close to each other (eight hours by bullock cart!) and at the same time in absolutely different worlds, in a sense like Ramu-Ramana and Daya-Aurobindo.
3. Possibly Śaṃkara was not responsible but Ramchandra Gandhi expected this great thinker, to resist rather than comply with injustice.
4. The four Buddhist virtues include *karuṇa* or compassion, *maitrī* or friendliness, *mudita* or joyfulness and *upekṣā* or to overlook, disregard injury. The five norms of *yama* prescribed by Patanjali's Yoga *Sūtra*s and Jainism are: *ahiṃsā* or non injury in thought, word and deed, *satya* or truth in word and thought, *asteya* or non-covetousness, *brahmacarya* or celibacy/steadfastness to one's spouse and *aparigṛaha* or non-possessiveness.

About the Editor and Contributors

The Editor

Shail Mayaram is professor at the Centre for the Study of Developing Societies, Delhi. Her publications include *Against History, Against State: Counterperspectives from the Margins* (2003); *Resisting Regimes: Myth, Memory and the Shaping of a Muslim Identity* (1997); co-authored with Ashis Nandy, Shikha Trivedi, Achyut Yagnik, *Creating a Nationality: The Ramjanmabhumi Movement and the Fear of Self* (1995); co-edited with Ajay Skaria and M. S. S. Pandian, *Subaltern Studies: Muslims, Dalits and the Fabrications of History*, vol. 12 (2005); edited, *The Other Global City* (2009).

The Contributors

Devasia M. Antony is assistant professor in the Department of Philosophy at Hindu College of Delhi University. His training has been in philosophy, theology and comparative religion. His research interests include hermeneutics of religious language, Advaita Vedānta of Śaṃkara, Madhyamika Śastra of Nāgārjuna, Religious Pluralism and Inter-religious Dialogue. He has published over fifteen articles in various journals and has presented over twenty research papers in various conferences, seminars and workshops.

Bettina Bäumer is professor of religious studies. She is from Vienna but has lived and worked in Varanasi since 1967 and is the author and editor of a number of books and over 50 research articles and has been visiting professor at several universities. Her main fields of research are non-dualistic Kashmir Saivism, Indian aesthetics, temple architecture and religious traditions of Odisha and comparative mysticism. She has been coordinator of the Indira Gandhi National Centre for the Arts, Varanasi, and Fellow, Indian Institute of Advanced Study, Shimla. She has translated important Sanskrit texts into German and English.

Prasenjit Biswas is associate professor of philosophy at North Eastern Hill University, Shillong. His major works are *Ethnic Life-Worlds in India's Northeast* (2008); *The Postmodern Controversy* (2005); *Political Economy of Underdevelopment of Northeast India*, co-authored with Rafiul Ahmad (2004). He also co-edited with C. J. Thomas, *Meaning, Metaphor and Method of Peace in Northeast India* (2006); *Construction of Evil in India's Northeast* (2011) and *Politics of Boundary Maintenance* (2011). His forthcoming work on continental philosophy is entitled, *Investigations on Aporia*. His interests include post-structuralism, philosophy of science and mind, ethnic studies, political economy and subaltern studies.

Bijoy H. Boruah is professor of philosophy, Department of Humanities and Social Sciences, IIT Delhi, and formerly professor of philosophy in the Department of HSS, IIT Kanpur and Fulbright professor at the University of Texas at Austin. He has authored *Fiction and Emotion: A Study in Aesthetics and Philosophy of Mind* (1989). He is interested in the metaphysics of the self.

Arindam Chakrabarti is professor of philosophy at the University of Hawaii. Equally at home in Western and Indian philosophical traditions, he is widely recognized as one of the foremost Indian philosophers.

Fred Dallmayr is Packey J. Dee professor of philosophy and political science at the University of Notre Dame (USA). He has been a visiting professor at Hamburg University and at the New School of Social Research in New York, and a Fellow at Nuffield College in Oxford. The focus of his work is on modern philosophy, hermeneutics and comparative philosophy. He is a past president of the Society for Asian and Comparative Philosophy (SACP). Among his recent publications are *Beyond Orientalism* (1996); *Dialogue among Civilizations* (2002); *In Search of the Good Life* (2007); *The Promise of Democracy* (2010); *Integral Pluralism: Beyond Culture Wars* (2010).

Probal Dasgupta has a Ph.D. in linguistics from New York University, 1980. He has taught in New York, San Francisco, Melbourne, Barlaston, Pune and Hyderabad, and is currently professor of linguistics at the Indian Statistical Institute, Kolkata. He was annual visiting lecturer of the Indian Council of Philosophical Research for 2009–2010. His publications include *Inhabiting Human Languages: The Substantivist Visualization* (2011); *Chinno Kathaae Shaajaye Taroni* (2011); co-authored with Alan Ford and Rajendra Singh, *After Etymology: Towards a Substantivist Linguistics* (2000); co-authored with Jayant Lele and Rajendra Singh, *Explorations in Indian Sociolinguistics* (1995); *The Otherness of English: India's Auntie Tongue Syndrome* (1993); *Projective Syntax: Theory and Applications* (1989); *Kathaar Kriyaakarmo* (1987).

Mustafa Khawaja, alias Meem Hai Zaffar, is currently visiting professor at the Jawaharlal Nehru University, Delhi. He has been associated with the Institute of Kashmir Studies, University of Kashmir, Srinagar, India. He is a poet and critic of Kashmiri language and was trained in logic and philosophy at Aligarh Muslim University and Rajasthan University, Jaipur. He is deeply interested in the spiritual and mystical traditions of the sub-continent, particularly those of Kashmir. He has been translating texts of Kashmir Saivism from Sanskrit to Kashmiri and has been awarded for his work in the field of Kashmir Studies.

S. Lokanathan has been professor of physics at the University of Rajasthan.

Michael McGhee recently retired from the philosophy department at the University of Liverpool. He is the author of *Transformations of Mind: Philosophy as Spiritual Practice* (2000), editor of *Philosophy, Religion and the Spiritual Life* (1992) and co-editor with John Cornwell of *Philosophers and God* (2009). In 2000 he founded, and then co-edited until 2010, *Contemporary Buddhism: An Interdisciplinary Journal* (Routledge). He is the author of various articles in aesthetics, moral philosophy and the comparative philosophy of religion.

Ramesh C. Pradhan is professor of philosophy at the University of Hyderabad. He specializes in philosophy of language, philosophy of mind and Wittgenstein studies. He has authored and edited several books and contributed papers to philosophy journals and anthologies.

He was formerly member-secretary of the Indian Council of Philosophical Research, New Delhi.

C. K. Raju played a key role in building the first Indian supercomputer, Param. He received the Telesio-Galilei gold medal 2010 in Hungary for correcting Einstein's mathematical mistake. His related book, *Time: Towards a Consistent Theory* (1994), further proposed a new physics without perfect causality. In *The Eleven Pictures of Time* (2003), he proposed a new ethic based on this physics. He ethically objects to publishers profiting by taking over ownership of work done by authors or funded by the government. In *Cultural Foundations of Mathematics* (2007), he proposed a new philosophy of mathematics called zeroism.

Shankar Ramaswami is a Postdoctoral Fellow in South Asian Studies at the Harvard University South Asia Institute. He completed his Ph.D. in Anthropology at the University of Chicago and is currently working on a book titled, *Souls in the Kalyug: The Politics and Theologies of Migrant Workers in Delhi.*

Daniel Raveh is a lecturer in the Department of Philosophy, Tel Aviv University. He thinks and writes in the fields of Indian and comparative philosophy. He is the author of *Exploring the Yogasūtra: An Essay in Philosophy and Translation* (2012) and co-editor of *Contrary Thinking: Selected Essays of Daya Krishna* (2011).

Richard Sorabji is honorary fellow of Wolfson College, Oxford. He is author or editor of over 100 books on the history of philosophy. Of his two books on India, one is *Opening Doors: The Untold Story of Cornelia Sorabji, Reformer, Lawyer, and Champion of Women's Rights in India* (2010). The other is *Gandhi and the Stoics: Modern Experiments on Ancient Values* (2012).

Tridip Suhrud is a political scientist and a cultural historian, working on the social and intellectual history of Gujarat and the Gandhian tradition. He is currently located at the Sabarmati Ashram, Ahmedabad. Among his recent works are *Harilal Gandhi: A Life* by C. B. Dalal, edited and translated from Gujarati by him (2007); *My Life Is My Message* (A biography of Mahatma Gandhi in four volumes), *Narayan Desai*, translated from Gujarati by Tridip Suhrud (2009); co-edited with Suresh Sharma,

M. K. Gandhi's *Hind Swaraj: A Two Language Critical Edition* (2010). His recent books include *Reading Gandhi in Two Tongues and other essays, Kavi Ni Choki* (Gujarati) and *Hind Swaraj: ek anushilan* (Hindi).

Neelima Vashishtha has specialized in aesthetic theory and art history. She has been Tagore fellow and senior research fellow, Indian Council of Historical Research, New Delhi and fellow, Indian Institute of Advanced Study, Shimla. She is the author of *Sculptural Traditions of Rajasthan ca. 800–1000 AD* (1989) and *Tradition and Modernity in Indian Arts during the Twentieth Century* (2010). She has published a large number of research papers on art history and has also participated in several national and international seminars.

Anuradha Veeravalli is on the faculty of the Department of Philosophy, University of Delhi. The main focus of her research has been to develop a methodology for comparative philosophy from the perspective of philosophy of language and epistemology with respect to issues concerning science, religion, and politics and the relation between them. Among her publications are entries on Indian Philosophies and Nyaya for the *Encyclopaedia of Religion* (2nd edition). Presently, she is working on a book on Gandhi's contribution to political theory.

Index